CHICOREL INDEX TO LITERARY CRITICISM IN BOOKS

VOLUME 23

Chicorel Index Series
VOLUME 23
First Edition

CHICOREL INDEX TO LITERARY CRITICISM IN BOOKS

U.S.A.
Canada

Edited by

MARIETTA CHICOREL

CHICOREL LIBRARY PUBLISHING CORP.
NEW YORK

Copyright © 1978 by Marietta Chicorel

Published and Distributed by
CHICOREL LIBRARY PUBLISHING CORP.
275 Central Park West
New York, N.Y. 10024

Library of Congress Catalog Card Number 78-58455

International Standard Book Number 87729-914-5

International Standard Serial Number 0163-8955

Printed and bound in U.S.A.

All rights reserved. Except for brief passages quoted in a newspaper, magazine, radio, or television review, no part of this book may be reproduced in any form or by any means, electronic or mechanical, including photocopying and recording, or by any information storage and retrieval systems, without permission in writing from the Publisher. This work is defended by special marks against prohibited copying.

Chicorel, Marietta
    Chicorel index to literary criticism in books

    (Chicorel index series; v.23) v.1 U.S.A., Canada
    1. Literature--indexes. I. Title. II. Literary
    criticism in books: U.S.A., Canada
ISBN 0-87729-914-5   LC 78-58455
ISSN 0163-8955

FOREWORD

The CHICOREL INDEX TO LITERARY CRITICISM: U.S.A., CANADA, is designed to bring together in one place the critical literature that deals with the creative writers of our heritage. This book may be accessed by the name of an author writing as creator, and by the name of the critic. When an anthology of criticism concerns more than one work, each author and each work is cross-referenced. Works by European critics about American or Canadian authors are included, as is comparative criticism where U.S. or Canadian authors are involved. In this manner, the user will find that some authors about whom criticism is available in books are also the critics in other instances. The various points of view represented by the critics no less than by the authors of the original works bring us closer to the true appreciation of the spirit behind the work.

Teachers will find this index a valuable reference tool in locating source materials when preparing their lesson plans, and students looking for materials in a subject area in which they have limited knowledge will find that most of their primary research has been done for them and is organized to give access to a maximum number of sources in one look-up. No other source exists today that presents the user with this range of current books of literary criticism, analyzed by contents. We have analyzed 2,448 volumes describing the work of 335 authors, and 1,656 critics. There are 8,463 separate listings under 114 subject headings.

The CHICOREL INDEX TO LITERARY CRITICISM is the first in a planned series of indexes to criticism which are indexed in a comprehensive manner which allows access to criticism of individual works on a specific author, as well as to authors appearing in anthologies of criticism. Our task of indexing has been to analyze and organize the information available into a comprehensive, yet manageable format. To aid in this, the data base has been arranged into several sections.

The first section is arranged by author of criticism or editor/compiler of an anthology of criticism into an authority-file list. This listing includes sufficient bibliographic information with each entry in order to facilitate work in areas of reference, acquisition and interlibrary loan. The entries are filed by author/editor of work of criticism, and then title of work. This is followed by publisher, address, copyright year and last printing, pages, price, hardbound or paperbound edition, ISBN and LC numbers. In this manner the user is presented with sufficient information to locate the materials needed in local facilities.

The second section consists of listings arranged by author of work being criticized. The third contains geographic divisions, with time sub-divisions, and the fourth section is by subject categories, such as literary influences, literary schools and others.

Section Two, the Author Section, has been structured so that in looking up the name of an author one will find listed under it: Biographies; criticism written by the author; criticism about the author; major works by the author followed by a listing of books which contain specific criticism about that work, and a listing of bibliographies and reference books pertaining to the author. Books of criticism have also been cross-referenced under the schools of literature criticized and those elements which have had an influence on literature.

For example: Alfred Kazin's book On Native Grounds will be found listed in the authority section under "Kazin" as well as in the author section under the authors he criticized in his book: (Wharton, Dreiser, Cather, Glasgow, Anderson and Lewis) and also under the categories of Satire, Realism, Naturalism, Women Authors, and the geographic indicators, U.S. 19th and U.S. 20th.

The third section, the Geographical Index, gives the U.S. listings arranged by region and by century, followed by authors' names. The books in the Canadian listings are not broken down by era as they tend to encompass a greater time span. The reason for this might be found in George Woodcock's critical essay "Possessing the Land" in The Canadian Imagination; Dimensions of a Literary Culture, edited by David Staines (Harvard U. Press, 1977). In it he finds "One of the most striking facts I encountered in preparing this essay was that...[the average number of novels published yearly by Canadians remained almost exactly the same, namely 35 since 1880.]Yet, despite the fact that no greater numbers of novels are being published by Canadians now than in 1890 or 1930 or 1940... the novel and the short story both occupy positions of prestige in the 1970s, among both critics and scholars."

Because of the number of brief mentions of authors who were and are part and parcel of Canadian literary history but have not yet become the subjects of individual study, we have listed their names and dates at the end of the Geographical Section.

The selection of indexing descriptors was employed with the user in mind, as well as the need to comprehensively index the material. For instance, the user can find criticism about the works of Isaac Asimov under the author listing as well as under Sci-Fi, and U.S. 20th. This first volume contains 8,463 entries. In preparation at this time is the material for the CHICOREL INDEX TO LITERARY CRITICISM: GREAT BRITAIN; and further countries are planned.

Titles were selected on the basis of current availability and our thanks go to the publishers who cooperated in supplying the necessary information. A great number of titles were already held by libraries and this index should facilitate their use.

Information which appears in the CHICOREL INDEX SERIES is based on primary sources, impeccably researched and verified with publisher, producers, distributors, librarians, and by personal examination of the media. Each volume has been designed to promote legibility and to be aesthetically pleasing. Despite our greatest care and vigilance, errors will creep in. We are not legally responsible for errors, but would appreciate your advice in correcting them.

I acknowledge the help and cooperation of the publishers whose titles are listed, and of the librarians whose advice was utilized in establishing the most useful subject indicators. I especially want to thank Robert J. Sweeney of our staff whose untiring efforts on behalf of this book overcame the severest obstacles.

I appreciate the continuing enthusiastic encouragement we have received from the users of the Series. I especially want to thank those librarians whose suggestions have led to improvements. Your continued suggestions are warmly appreciated.

New York City
January, 1979

Marietta Chicorel
Editor-in-Chief

INTRODUCTION

Literary criticism has itself developed into a literary form which is susceptible to analysis and criticism. Within this vast body of work are discernible trends, fashions and schools. Critical writing may concern one creative work, the work of one author, of a whole school; it may concern itself with underlying themes or may take the approach of subject analysis. Given this variety it is scarcely surprising that indexes and bibliographies are also numerous, since they are essential for the student requiring to find a way through the maze.

Such a student must have recourse to many works since few can manage to be comprehensive anymore. The compilers of indexes must, in order to keep within manageable limits, set bounds to what they will cover. Many confine themselves to one literature, to one kind of literary genre, or to one period and for depth of coverage such publications are essential. More numerous are the bibliographies devoted to individual writers. These, too, may vary from the multi-volume works devoted to authors such as Shakespeare, or even the surprisingly solid volume on James Cook, to fugitive pamphlets in danger of being lost on library shelves.

Each such publication is the result of countless hours of work, yet even when published the task is not complete. New items come to light or fashion unearths a forgotten author and adds to the critical overload. That this should be so is easily understood in the case of a world-renowned author or a literature with a rich and long tradition. Publishing is not a neat and orderly process. Although we pride ourselves today on our omnivorous bibliographic systems, local publications, works from small presses and variant editions frequently slip through the net. Moreover, the great catalogs tend to be so large and so structured that alternative means of access are impossible or at best laborious to achieve. While we might think that in smaller countries the process would be easier, quicker and more manageable, it is not necessarily so. Comprehensive coverage may be difficult to attain since publishing is frequently extra-territorial or fugitive in nature and the necessary bibliographic apparatus may not exist. Nor is it any easier to provide all the desired cross-references or multiple indexing just because the volume is smaller.

In the face of this complexity there is a great need for cross-cultural and multi-purpose bibliographical tools and services. World Literatures in English offer such an opportunity. Thirty years ago the comparative study of such literatures had barely begun. In fact the first course on Commonwealth Literature introduced in U.S. universities was offered at The Pennsylvania State University as recently as 1948. Since then the study has become the subject of conferences and merits its own section within the Modern Languages Association. Later editions, it is hoped, will expand both the geographic and the bibliographic coverage.

The coverage is confined to recent criticism published in book form but includes indexes and bibliographies, the latter covering both individuals and schools of writing. While the absence of periodical articles is to be regretted, their inclusion would have extended the work to unmanageable proportions, thereby reducing its utility.

The work begins with a conventional listing by author of criticism where fuller bibliographical information is provided, including the LC card number and ISBN where available. The second section is arranged by literary author, using, under each, such entries as Biographies, Reference works, Bibliographies as well as Criticism. The geographical index covers approximately forty pages and in the case of the United States is subdivided by century. This is, in itself, a kind of subject index, but the special feature of this publication is the actual subject index. While, at first sight, it is strange to see a topic like "Armed Forces" alongside the more traditional "Allegory", such headings have long been applied to literature, particularly to fiction. It is interesting to contemplate these subject-headings alongside those used in Book Review Digest and the Fiction Index, and to see what has happened over the years. It would appear that criticism has gradually adapted itself to the subject matter of the medium criticized, even while that medium itself has been changing.

Thirty years ago it would, for example, have been difficult to collect any substantial body of Marxist literary criticism, while homosexuality was still taboo, usually disguised in indexes under such terms as Sex Problems and seldom the overt subject of critical analysis. These two examples are cited to indicate the major changes that have occurred in both literature and criticism in the areas of politics and sex. From this it also follows that criticism is no longer confined to the consideration of form or theme, nor devoted to style and influences, but examines literature as a reflection of society. Hence the intrusion into the list of terms like anthropology, culture and psychology. In this way the literary critic has moved from absolutism to relativism, perhaps without realizing the implications. The days when an Arnold might set the course of a generation of critics, or a Dowden suspend the interpretation of Shakespeare, are past and for good or ill critics battle in the marketplace of ideas each one shouting the appropriate catch-cry.

It is, therefore, very useful for a student to have access to a subject index. Even though any classification is arbitrary and open to question, to abdicate the task in favor of providing nothing would be to deny the student any assistance at all. When used in combination with the geographic index and the author index, the subject index makes it possible to produce combinations and methods of access no compiler could ever provide. This is, after all, the true goal of any bibliographical work--to lead and guide the user into developing sound search strategies. No book in itself can do the task, only the book in the hands of a knowledgeable and understanding reader.

University Park, Pennsylvania
January, 1979

Murray S. Martin
Associate Dean
The University Libraries
The Pennsylvania State University

CONTENTS

FOREWORD

INTRODUCTION by Murray S. Martin

MAIN LISTING SECTION 15

AUTHOR CRITICISM ARRANGED BY
   AUTHOR OF WORK CRITICIZED 153

GEOGRAPHICAL INDEX 255
   U.S.A. General 255
   U.S.A. 17th Century 259
   U.S.A. 18th Century 261
   U.S.A. 19th Century 261
   U.S.A. 20th Century 268
   Canada 282

SUBJECT INDEX 289
   Absurdism see Comedy/Humor 289
   Adultery 289
   Allegory 289
   Anthropology 289
   Archetypes 289
   Armed Forces 289
   Authors In Exile 289
   Autobiography and Biography 289
   Behaviorism see Psychology 290
   Bible see Religion 290
   Biography see Autobiography 290
   Biology see Science 290
   Black Authors 290
   Blacks In Literature 291
   Censorship 292

Children	293
Christianity see Religion	294
Comedy/Humor	294
Condemned Books	295
Critical Theory	295
Culture	296
Customs see Culture	296
Darwinism see Science	296
Detective Stories see Mystery and Suspense	297
Dialectical Materialism see Marxism	297
Eroticism	297
Ethnic	297
European War see War	298
Evolution see Science	298
Existentialism	298
Expatriate see Authors in Exile	298
Fantasy see Science Fiction and Fantasy	298
Film	298
Foreign Country	298
Gay see Homosexuality	299
Gothic and Horror	299
Great War see War	300
Hero	300
History	300
Homosexuality	302
Horror see Gothic and Horror	302
Humanism	302
Humor see Comedy/Humor	302
Imagery	302
Imperialism see Politics	302
Journalism see Publications	303
Lesbianism see Homosexuality	303
Lost Generation see War	303
Love	303
Magazines see Publications	303
Marxism	303
Melodrama see Sentimentalism	303
Metaphysics see Philosophy	304
Militarism see War	304
Morality/Ethics	304
Movies see Film	304
Mystery/Suspense	304
Mysticism	305
Mythology	305
Nationalism see Politics	306
Naturalism	306

Newspapers see Publications	307
Novel	307
Obscenity	307
Parody see Satire	308
Periodicals see Publications	308
Philosophy	308
Picaresque see Hero	309
Politics	309
Popular Fiction	310
Pornography see Obscenity	310
Propaganda see Politics	310
Psychoanalysis see Psychology	310
Psychology	310
Psychosexuality see Sexuality	312
Publications	312
Pulp Magazines see Publications	312
Race Relations	312
Realism	312
Reference Works	313
Regionalism	315
Religion	318
Religious Humanism see Religion	319
Revolution see Politics, Marxism	319
Romanticism	319
Satire	321
Science	322
Science Fiction-Fantasy	322
Sentimentalism	323
Sexuality	323
Short Story (As Subject)	324
Socialism see Marxism	324
Society	324
Sociology see Culture	327
Stream of Consciousness see Psychology	327
Structuralism	327
Suspense see Mystery and Suspense	328
Symbolism	328
Technique	
General	328
Criticism	329
Fiction	329
Non-Fiction	331
Style (Analysis Of)	331
Reference	331
Technology see Science	331

Tradition see Culture	332
Transcendentalism	332
Violence see Society	332
War	332
Women	333
Women In Literature	335
World War see War	336
Reference-Bibliographies	336

MAIN LISTING SECTION

AARON, DANIEL. Writers on the Left;Episodes in American Literary Communism. Harcourt, NY. 1961 460p. 15.00Hdbd. LC61-13349.

ABBATT, WILLIAM. The Colloquial Who's Who;Contributors who have used pen-names, initials, etc. (1600-1924). Gale, Detroit. 1974. 15.00Hdbd. ISBN 0-8103-3956-0. LC 78-159865.

ABBE, GEORGE, Ed. Stephen Vincent Benet on Writing. Stephen Greene Pr., Brattleboro, VT. 1964. 111p. LC 63-13865.

ABRAMOWITZ, MOLLY. Elie Wiesel:a Bibliography. Scarecrow Pr., Metuchen, NJ. 1974. 6.50Hdbd. ISBN 0-8108-0731-9. LC74-17166.

ABRAMS, MEYER H. Mirror and the Lamp. Oxford Univ. Pr. 1953. 17.50Hdbd. ISBN 0-19-500465-5.

ABRAMS, M.H. Natural Supernaturalism;Tradition and Revolution in Romantic Literature. Norton. 1973. 3.95Pa. ISBN 0-393-00609-3.

ADAMS, MAURIANNE. Autobiography;The Bobbs-Merrill Series in Composition and Rhetoric. Bobbs-Merrill, Indianapolis. 1968. 64p. 1.00Pa.

ADAMS, RICHARD P. Faulkner: Myth and Motion. Princeton Univ. Pr., Princeton, NJ. 1968. 260p. 9.50 Hdbd. ISBN 0-691-06141-6.

ADAMS, STEPHEN D. James Purdy. Barnes and Noble, NY. 1976. 166p. 12.00Hdbd. ISBN 0-06-490014-2.

AHNEBRINK, LARS. The Beginnings of Naturalism in American Fiction; 1891-1903. Russell and Russell, NY. 1950(1961). 505p. 16.00Hdbd. ISBN 0-8462-0105-4. LC61-13093.

AICHINGER, PETER. The American Soldier in Fiction;1880-1963. Iowa State Univ. Pr. 1975. 143p. 7.50 Hdbd. ISBN 0-8138-0100-1.

ALDISS, BRIAN WILSON. Billion Year Spree;The True History of Science Fiction. Schocken Books, Garden City, NY. 1974. 339p. 2.95 Pa. ISBN 0-8052-0450-4.

ALDRIDGE, JOHN W. Critiques and Essays on Modern Fiction;1920-1951;Representing the Achievement of Modern American and British Critics. Ronald Pr., NY. 1952. 610p. LC 52-6180.

CHICOREL INDEX SERIES   15

ALBRECHT, MILTON C. Sociology of Art and Literature;A Reader. Praeger. 1970. 15.00Hdbd. ISBN 0-275-54630-6. LC70-7685.

ALDRIDGE, JOHN W. After the Lost Generation;A Critical Study of the Writers of Two Wars. Books for Libraries Pr., Freeport, NY. 1951 (1971).263 p. 10.75Hdbd. ISBN 0-8369-2141-0. LC 79-142602.

ALDRIDGE, JOHN W. In Search of Heresy;American Literature in an Age of Conformity. Kennikat Pr., Port Washington, NY. 1956(1967). 208p. LC 67-16254.

ALEXANDER, LOUIS. Beyond the Facts;A Guide to the Art of Feature Writing. Gulf Pub., Houston. 1975. 263p. 8.95.

ALLEN, GAY WILSON. Melville and His World. Viking Pr., NY. 1971. 144p. 10.00Hdbd. ISBN 0-670-46740-5. LC 77-117066.

ALLEN, L. DAVID. Science Fiction; an Introduction. 1973. 187p. 1.95Pa. ISBN 0-8220-1169-7.

ALLEN, MARY. The Necessary Blankness;Women in Major American Fiction of the Sixties. 8.95Hdbd.

ALLEN, RICHARD STANLEY. Detective Fiction;Crime and Compromise. Harcourt, NY. 1974. 481p. 4.95 Pa. ISBN 0-15-517408-8.

ALLEN, WALTER. Contemporary Novelists. St. Martin's Pr., NY. 1976. 1650p. 35.00Hdbd.

ALLEN, WALTER. The Modern Novel;In Britain and the United States. Dutton, NY. 1964. 346p. 1.95.

Pa. ISBN 0-525-47167-7. LC 63-7045.

ALLIBONE, Samuel Austin. A Critical Dictionary of English Literature and British and American Authors, Living and Deceased, from the Earliest Accounts to the latter half of the Nineteenth Century. Gale, Detroit. 1965. 3140p. 84.00Hdbd. LC 67-295.

ALPERT, HOLLIS. Censorship;For and Against. Hart. 1971. 7.95Hdbd. ISBN 0-8055-1095-8. 2.95Pa. ISBN 0-8055-0120-7

ALTERTON, MARGARET. Origins of Poe's Critical Theory. Russell and Russell, NY. 1965. 7.00Hdbd. ISBN 0-8462-0540-8.

ALTICK, RICHARD D. The Art of Literary Research. W. W. Norton, NY. 1963. 276p. 5.50Hdbd. ISBN 0-393-09590-8. LC 63-8025.

ALTICK, RICHARD D. Selective Bibliography for the Study of English and American Literature. Macmillan, NY. 1971. 164p. 3.50Pa. LC 75-132867.

AMERICAN LIBRARY ASSOCIATION. Freedom of Inquiry;Supporting the Library Bill of Rights. 1965. 1.75Pa. ISBN 0-8389-3033-6. LC 65-24954.

AMES, VAN METER. Aesthetics of the Novel. Gordian Pr., NY. 1928(1966). 221p. 6.00. ISBN 0-87752-003-8. LC 66-29460.

AMIS, KINGSLEY. New Maps of Hell; A Survey of Science Fiction. Harcourt, NY. 1960. 161p. LC 60-5441.

ANDERSON, CARL L. Poe in Northlight;The Scandinavian Response to His Life and Work. Duke. 1973. 5.75 ISBN 0-8223-0275-6.

ANDERSON, CHARLES R. Melville in the South Seas. Columbia Univ. Pr. NY. 1939(1967). 522p. 12.50Hdbd. ISBN 0-231-01058-3. LC 39-8153.

ANDERSON, FREDERICK. Mark Twain;The Critical Heritage. Barnes and Nobel, NY. 347p.

ANDERSON, QUENTIN. Henry James. John Calder, London. 1958. 369p.

ANDERSON, SHERWOOD. Sherwood Anderson;Dimensions of His Literary Art;A Collection of Critical Essays. Michigan State Univ. Pr. 1976. 141p. 9.50Hdbd. ISBN 0-87013-204-0. LC 76-25796.

ANDERSON, SHERWOOD. The Writer's Book. Scarecrow Pr., Metuchen, NJ. 1975. 355p. 16.00Hdbd. ISBN 0-8108-0737-8. LC 74-22088.

ANDREACH, ROBERT F. The Slain and Resurrected God;Conrad, Ford, and the Christian Myth. New York Univ. Pr., NY. 1970. 245p. 8.95Hdbd. ISBN 0-8147-0456-5. LC 70-11517. 2.95Pa. ISBN 0-8147-0493-X.

ANDREAS, OSBORN. Henry James and the Expanding Horizon;A Study of the Meaning and Basic Themes of James's Fiction. Greenwood Pr., NY. 1948. 179p. 9.00Hdbd. ISBN 0-8371-2133-7.

ANDREWS, KENNETH R. Nook Farm;Mark Twain's Hartford Circle. Harvard Univ. Pr., Mass. 1950(1967). 288p. LC 67-26658.

ANGOFF, ALLAN, Ed. American Writing Today;Its Independence and Vigor. Books for Libraries Pr., Freeport, NY. 1957. 433p. 16.50Hdbd. ISBN 0-8369-2030-9. LC 74-134144.

ANGOFF, CHARLES. The Tone of the Twenties and Other Essays. A. S. Barnes and Co., NY. 1966. 245p. 2.98Pa. ISBN 0-498-06404-2. LC 66-14772.

ANTHONY, GERALDINE. John Coulter. Twayne Pub., Canada. 1976. 7.50Hdbd. ISBN 0-8057-6240-X. LC 76-10728.

APPEL, ALFRED. Nabokov's Dark Cinema. Oxford Univ. Pr., NY. 1974. 324p. 14.95Hdbd. LC 74-79617.

APPEL, PAUL P. Ed. Homage to Sherwood Anderson. Appel. 1970. 10.00Hdbd. ISBN 0-911858-02-4. LC 77-105304.

AQUINO, JOHN. Science Fiction as Literature. National Ed. Assoc., Wash. 1976. 2.50Pa. ISBN 0-8106-1804-4. LC 76-10715.

ARGYLE, BARRY. An Introduction to the Australian Novel;1830-1930. Oxford, NY. 1972. 265p.

ARGYLE, BARRY. Patrick White. Barnes and Noble, NY. 1967. 109p. 2.25Pa.

ARMITAGE, A. D., and Nancy Tudor. Canadian Essay and Literature Index. Univ. of Toronto Pr. 1975. 27.50Hdbd. ISBN 0-8020-4518-9. LC 75-7703.

ARMSTRONG, JOHN. Paradise Myth. Oxford Univ. Pr., NY. 1969. 8.00 Hdbd. ISBN 0-19-212175-8.

ARMSTRONG, JUDITH. The Novel of Adultery. Barnes and Noble, NY. 1976. 182p. 21.50. ISBN 0-06-490203-X. LC 76-15793.

ARNOLD, LLOYD R. High on the Wild with Hemingway. Caxton Printers, Caldwell, ID. 1968. 343p. 6.75Hdbd. ISBN 0-87004-008-1. LC 68-15029.

ARVIN, NEWTON. Herman Melville; A Critical Biography. Viking, NY. 1957. 1.85Pa.

ARVIN, NEWTON. Nathaniel Hawthorne. Russell and Russell. 1960. 10.00Hdbd.

ASH, BRIAN. Faces of the Future; the Lessons of Science Fiction. Taplinger Pub. Co. 1975. 213p. 8.95Hdbd. ISBN 0-8008-2583-7. LC 74-21697.

ASSELINEAU, ROGER. The Literary Reputation of Hemingway in Europe. New York Univ. Pr., NY. 1965. 210p.

ASSELINEAU, ROGER. The Merrill Studies in The House of the Seven Gables. Charles E. Merrill Pub., Columbus, OH. 1971. 1.75Pa. ISBN 0-675-09277-9.

ASTRO, RICHARD, and Jackson J. Benson. Hemingway In Our Time. Oregon State Univ. Pr., Corvallis, OR. 1974. 214p. 8.00Hdbd. ISBN 0-87071-445-7. LC 73-18428.

ASTRO, RICHARD. John Steinbeck and Edward F. Ricketts;The Shaping of a Novelist. Univ. of Minn. Pr. Minneapolis, MN. 1973. 259p. 12.95 Hdbd. ISBN 0-8166-0704-4. LC 73-87252.

ASTRO, RICHARD. Ed. Steinbeck; The Man and His Work. Ore. State Pr., Corvallis, OR. 1971. 183p. 5.00 ISBN 0-87071-443-0. LC 76-632182.

AUCHINCLOSS, LOUIS. Edith Wharton;A Woman in Her Time. Viking Pr., NY. 1971. 191p. ISBN 670-28911-6. LC 77-146606.

AUCHINCLOSS, LOUIS. Pioneers and Caretakers;A Study of 9 American Novelists. Univ. of Minn. Pr., Minneapolis, MN. 1965. 202p. 5.95 Pa. ISBN 0-8166-0344-8. LC 65-17016.

AUCHINCLOSS, LOUIS. Reading Henry James. Univ. of Minn. Pr., Minneapolis, MN. 1975. 181p. 8.95Hdbd. ISBN 0-8166-0744-3. LC 74-25934.

AUERBACH, ERICH. Mimesis;The Representation of Reality in Western Literature. Princeton Univ. Pr., Princeton, NJ. 1946(1953). 563p. 13.50 Hdbd. ISBN 0-691-06078-9. LC 52-3152. 3.45Pa. ISBN 091-01269-5-124.

AUSTEN, ROGER. The Homosexual Novel in America. Bobbs-Merrill. 8.95. ISBN 0-672-52287-X.

B

BABB, HOWARD S. Essays in Stylistic Analysis. Harcourt, NY. 1972. 7.50 Pa. ISBN 0-15-522902-8.

BABBITT, IRVING. Spanish Character and Other Essays. Houghton, Mifflin Co., Boston. 1940. 360p.

BACKMAN, MELVIN. Faulkner; The Major Years; A Critical Study. Indiana Univ. Pr., Bloomington. 1966. 212p. 6.75Hdbd. ISBN 0-253-32140-9. 1.95Pa. ISBN 0-253-20089-X.

BADER, A.L., Ed. To the Young Writer; Hopwood Lectures, Second Series. Univ. of Mich. Pr. 1965. 196p. 1.95Pa. ISBN 0-472-06102-X. LC 65-14374.

BAETZHOLD, HOWARD G. Mark Twain and John Bull. Indiana Univ. Pr. Bloomington. 1970. 394p. 15.00 Hdbd. ISBN 0-253-15025-6. LC 73-103928.

BAIRD, NEWTON D., and Robert Greenwood. An Annotated Bibliography of California Fiction; 1664-1970. Talisman Literary, Georgetown, CA. 1971. 521p. 20.00Hdbd. LC 72-176607.

BAKER, CARLOS, Ed. Ernest Hemingway; Critiques of Four Major Novels. Scribner's, NY. 1962. 199p. 2.95Pa. ISBN 0-684-41157-1.

BAKER, CARLOS, Ed. Hemingway and His Critics; An International Anthology. Hill and Wang, NY. 1961. 298p. 1.95Pa. ISBN 0-8090-5455-8.

BAKER, CARLOS. Hemingway; The Writer as Artist. Princeton Univ. Pr., Princeton, NJ. 1963. 379p. 12.50 Hdbd. ISBN 0-691-06231-5. 2.95Pa. ISBN 0-691-01305-5.

BAKER, HOUSTON A., JR. Black Literature in America. McGraw-Hill, NY. 1971. LC 72-143442.

BAKER, HOUSTON A., JR. Singers of Daybreak; Studies in Black American Literature. Howard Univ. Pr. Washington. 1974. 6.95Hdbd. ISBN 0-88258-017-5. LC 74-11006.

BAKER, R.P. A History of English-Canadian Literature. Gordon Pr. 39.95Hdbd. ISBN 0-8390-0324-5.

BAKER, RAY P. History of English-Canadian Literature to the Confederation; Its Relation to the Literature of Great Britain and the U.S. Russell. 1920(1968)8.50Hdbd. ISBN 0-8462-1160-2. LC 68-2567.

BAKER, RONALD L. Folklore in the

Writings of Rowland B. Robinson. Bowling Green Univ. Pr., Bowling Green, OH. 1973. 240p. ISBN 0-87972-038-7. LC 74-186630.

BALAKIAN, NONA, and Charles Simmons, Eds. The Creative Present; Notes on Contemporary American Fiction. Doubleday, NY. 1963. 265p. LC 63-11628. Rev. Ed. Gordian Pr., NY. 1972. 8.50. ISBN 0-87752-158-1.

BALDANZA, FRANK. Mark Twain; An Introduction and Interpretation. Barnes and Noble, NY. 1961. 150p. 1.25Pa.

BALL, JOHN, et. al. The Mystery Story; An Appreciation. Publisher's Inc. 1976. 11.95Hdbd. ISBN 0-89163-019-8. LC 76-7110.

BALLSTADT, CARL, Ed. The Search for English-Canadian Literature; An Anthology of Critical Articles from the Nineteenth and Early Twentieth Centuries. Univ. of Toronto Pr. 1975. 15.00Hdbd. ISBN 0-8020-2177-8. LC 75-15779. 5.95Pa. ISBN 0-8020-6263-6.

BANK, STANLEY. American Romanticism; A Shape for Fiction. G. P. Putnam, NY. 1969. 345p. LC 69-18164

BANTA, MARTHA. Henry James and the Occult; The Great Extention. Indiana Univ. Pr., Bloomington, IN. 1972. 273p. 9.50Hdbd. ISBN 0-253-32732-6.

BARFIELD, O. Romanticism Comes of Age. Anthroposophic. 2.50Pa. ISBN 0-85440-185-7.

BARGER, JAMES. Ernest Hemingway; American Literary Giant. SamHar Pr., Charlotteville, NY. 1975.
2.29Pa. LC 75-33830.

BARNES, JOHN, Ed. Writer in Australia; A Collection of Literary Documents 1856-1964. Oxford Univ. Pr. 1969. 13.50Hdbd. ISBN 0-19-550036-9

BARNES, MELVYN P. The Best Detective Fiction; A Guide from Godwin to the Present. Linnet Books, Hamden, CT. 1975. 7.00Hdbd. ISBN 0-208-01376-8. LC 75-22344.

BARNES, MYRA EDWARDS. Linguistics and Languages in Science Fiction-Fantasy. Arno Pr., NY. 1975. 196p. 11.00Hdbd. ISBN 0-405-06319-9 LC 74-17864.

BARNETT, JAMES HARWOOD. Divorce and the American Divorce Novel 1858-1937; A Study in Literary Reflections of Social Influences. Russell and Russell, NY. 1939(1968)168p 8.00. ISBN 0-8462-1070-3. LC 68-10900.

BARNETT, LOUISE K. The Ignoble Savage; American Literary Racism, 1790-1890. Greenwood Pr., Westport, CT. 1975. 13.95Hdbd. ISBN 0-8371-8281-6. LC 75-16964.

BARNET, SYLVAN. Barnet and Stubbs's Practical Guide to Writing. Little, Brown, Boston. 1975. 319p. 4.95Pa. LC 74-26405.

BARNET, SYLVAN. A Short Guide to Writing About Literature. Little, Brown, Boston. 1975. 244p. 3.95Pa. ISBN 0-316-08205-8.

BARNS, FLORENCE. Texas Writers of Today. Gryphon Books, Ann Arbor, MI. 1971. 513p. 23.50Hdbd. LC 70-157491.

BARSON, ALFRED T. A Way of Seeing;A Critical Study of James Agee. Univ. of Mass. Pr. 1971. 9.50Hdbd. ISBN 0-87023-094-8. LC 75-181365.

BARTH, ROBERT J., S.J. Ed. Religious Perspectives in Faulkner's Fiction;Yoknapatawpha and Beyond. Univ. of Notre Dame Pr., Notre Dame, London. 1972. 233p. 8.95Hdbd. ISBN 0-268-00464-1.

BARZUN, JACQUES. Simple and Direct;A Rhetoric for Writers. Harper and Row, NY. 1975. 212p. 10.00Hdbd. ISBN 0-06-010236-5. LC 75-6328.

BASLER, ROY P. Sex, Symbolism and Psychology in Literature. Octagon. 1967. 10.50Hdbd. ISBN 0-374-90437-5.

BASSAN, MAURICE, Ed. Stephen Crane;A Collection of Critical Essays. Prentice-Hall, Englewood Cliffs, NJ. 1967. 5.95. ISBN 0-13-188888-9.

BASSETT, JOHN. William Faulkner; An Annotated Checklist of Criticism. David Lewis, NY. 1972. 551p. 18.50Hdbd. LC 72-89960.

BASSETT, JOHN, Ed. William Faulkner;The Critical Heritage. Routledge and K. Paul, Boston. 1975. 422p. 28.00Hdbd. ISBN 0-7100-8124-3. LC 75-31884.

BATESON, FREDERICK WILSE, and Marilyn R. Mumford. A Guide to English and American Literature. Gordian Pr., NY. 1976. 15.00Hdbd. ISBN 0-87752-186-7. LC 76-19083.

BAUDELAIRE, CHARLES P. Baudelaire on Poe;Critical Papers. Bald Eagle Pr., PA. 1952. 4.00. ISBN 0-910196-04-4.

BAUMANN, Michael L. B. Traven; An Introduction. Univ. of New Mexico Pr., Albuquerque, NM. 1976. 9.95 Hdbd. ISBN 0-8263-0412-5. LC 75-40832.

BAUMBACH, JONATHAN. The Landscape of Nightmare;Studies in the Contemporary American Novel. NY Univ. Pr., NY. 173p. 6.95Hdbd. ISBN 0-8147-0031-4. LC 65-11761. 1.95Pa. ISBN 0-8147-0032-2.

BAYM, NINA. The Shape of Hawthorne's Career. Cornell Univ. Pr., Ithaca, NY. 1976. 15.00Hdbd. ISBN 0-8014-0996-9. LC 75-36994.

BEACH, JOSEPH WARREN. American Fiction;1920-1940. Russell and Russell, NY. 1941(1960). 371p. 11.00Hdbd. ISBN 0-8462-0119-4. LC 60-8197.

BEACH, JOSEPH WARREN. The Method of Henry James. Albert Saifer, Philadelphia. 1954. 218p. 6.00Hdbd. ISBN 0-87556-020-2. 3.00Pa. ISBN 0-87556-151-9.

BEACH, JOSEPH W. Obsessive Images. Greenwood. 1973. 17.25Hdbd. ISBN 0-8371-7079-6. LC 73-11620.

BEACH, JOSEPH WARREN. The Twentieth Century Novel;Studies in Technique. Appleton-Century-Crofts, NY. 1932. 569p. 8.50Hdbd. ISBN 0-8462-0120-8.

BEARD, JAMES FRANKLIN, Ed. The Letters and Journals of James Fenimore Cooper;Vol. I. Harvard Univ. Pr., Cambridge, MA. 1960. 444p. 25.00Hdbd. ISBN 0-674-52550-7. LC 60-5388.

BEARD, JAMES FRANKLIN, Ed. The Letters and Journals of James

BEARD

Fenimore Cooper;Vol.II.Harvard Univ.Pr.,Cambridge,MA.1960.420p 25.00Hdbd.ISBN 0-674-52550-7.LC 60-5388.

BEARD,JAMES FRANKLIN,Ed.The Letters and Journals of James Fenimore Cooper;Vol.III.Harvard Univ.Pr.,Cambridge,MA.1964.466p. 25.00Hdbd.ISBN 0-674-52551-5.LC 60-5388.

BEARD,JAMES FRANKLIN,Ed.The Letters and Journals of James Fenimore Cooper;Vol.IV.Harvard Univ.Pr.,Cambridge,MA.1964.508p. 25.00Hdbd.ISBN 0-674-52551-5.LC 60-5388.

BEARS,JAMES FRANKLIN,Ed.The Letters and Journals of James Fenimore Cooper;Vols.V and VI.Harvard Univ.Pr.,Cambridge,MA.1968 460p.ISBN 0-674-52552-3.LC 60-5388.

BEASLEY,DAVID.The Canadian Don Quixote.228p.10.95Hdbd.ISBN 0-88984-022-9.6.95Pa.ISBN 0-88984-020-2.

BEATSON,PETER.The Eye in the Mandala;Patrick White;A Vision of Man and God.Barnes and Noble,NY. 1976.18.50Hdbd.ISBN 0-06-490331-1. LC 76-13072.

BEAUVOIR,SIMONE DE.The Second Sex.Bantam,NY.1970.1.25Pa.

BECK,WARREN.Man in Motion.Univ. of Wisconsin Pr.,Madison,WI. 1961.203p.2.50Pa.ISBN 0-299-02414-8.

BECK,WARREN A., and Myles L. Clowers.Understanding American History through Fiction.McGraw-Hill,NY.1975.Vol.1.4.95Pa.ISBN 0-0704217-9.Vol.2.4.95Pa.ISBN 0-07-004218-7.LC 74-11266.

BECKER, JOHN E.Hawthorne's Historical Allegory;An Examination of the American Conscience.Kennikat Pr.,Pt. Wash.,NY.1971.9.95Hdbd. ISBN 0-8046-9002-2.LC 78-139350.

BECKER,GEORGE JOSEPH.John Dos Passos.F.Unger Pub.Co.1974. 133p.6.00.LC 74-78437.

BEJA,MORRIS.Epiphany in the Modern Novel.Univ. of Wash.Pr.,Seattle,WA.1971.255p.9.75Hdbd.ISBN 0-295-95081-1.LC 71-117725.

BELKIND,ALLEN.Dos Passos;the Critics,and the Writer's Intention. Preface,Harry T. Moore.Southern Illinois Univ.Pr.,Carbondale and Edwardsville,IL.Feffer and Simons, London.1971.288p.8.95Hdbd.ISBN 0-8093-05224.LC 70-156782.

BELL,MICHAEL DAVITT.Hawthorne and the Historical Romance of New England.Princeton Univ.Pr., Princeton,NJ.1971.9.00Hdbd.ISBN 0-691-06136X.LC 72-148169.

BELL,MILLICENT.Edith Wharton and Henry James;The Story of Their Friendship.George Braziller,NY. 1965.384p.6.50.ISBN 0-8076-0295-7.LC 65-10196.

BELL,MILLICENT.Hawthorne's View of the Artist.State Univ.of NY Pr.1962.6.00.ISBN 0-87395-008-9.

BELLAMY,GLADYS CARMEN.Martk Twain as a Literary Artist.Univ. of Oklahoma Pr.,Norman,OK. 1950(1969).396p.8.95Hdbd.ISBN 0-8061-0211-X.

22   CHICOREL INDEX SERIES

BELLAMY, JOE DAVID. The New Fiction;Interviews with Innovative American Writers. Univ. of Illinois Pr., Urbana, IL. 1974. 7.95Hdbd. ISBN 0-252-00430-2. LC 74-14841.

BELLMAN, SAMUEL IRVING. Marjorie Kinnan Rawlings. Twayne Pub. NY. 1974. 7.50Hdbd. ISBN 0-8057-0610-0.

BELMONT, GEORGES. Henry Miller in Conversation. Quadrangle Books, Chicago. 1969(1972). 103p. ISBN 0-8129-0248-3. LC 73-185062.

BENNETT, JAMES R. Studies in Prose Style;A Historical Approach. Chandler Pub. 1972. 8.00Hdbd.

BENNETT, MILDRED R. The World of Willa Cather. Univ. of Nebraska Pr., Lincoln. 1951(1961)285p. 1.95Pa. ISBN 0-8032-5013-4, 112. LC 61-7235.

BENOIT, RAYMOND. Single Nature's Double Name;The Collectedness of the Conflicting in British and American Romanticism. Humanities. 1973. 13.00Hdbd. ISBN 90-279-2599-2.

BENSON, JACKSON J., Ed. The Short Stories of Ernest Hemingway; Critical Essays. Duke Univ. Pr., Durham, NC. 1975. 375p. 11.75Hdbd. ISBN 0-8223-0320-5. LC 74-75815.

BENSON, FREDERICK R. Writers in Arms;The Literary Impact of the Spanish Civil War. NY Univ. Pr., NY. 1967. 3.95Pa. ISBN 0-8147-0960-5. 9.75Hdbd. ISBN 0-8147-0035-7.

BERBRICH, JOAN D. Three Voices from Paumanok;The Influence of Long Island on James Fenimore Cooper, William Cullen Bryant, Walt Whitman. Ira J. Friedman, Inc., Port Washington, NY. 1965(1969). 225p. 8.75Hdbd. ISBN 0-87198-081-9.

BERGER, MORROE. Real and Imagined Worlds;The Novel and Social Science. Harvard Univ. Pr., Cambridge, MA. 15.00Hdbd. ISBN 0-674-45441-3. LC 76-27375.

BERGON, FRANK. Stephen Crane's Artistry. Columbia Univ. Pr., NY. 1975. 10.00Hdbd. ISBN 0-231-03905-0. LC 75-19159.

BERNSTEIN, JOHN. Pacifism and Rebellion in the Writings of Herman Melville. Folcroft Library Editions. Folcroft, PA. 1974. 20.00Hdbd. ISBN 0-8414-3295-3. LC 74-26813.

BERRYMAN, JOHN. Stephen Crane. The World Publishing Co., NY. 1950 (1962). 347p. LC 62-10788.

BERTHOFF, WARNER. The Example of Melville. Princeton Univ. Pr., Princeton, NJ. 1962. 218p.

BERTHOFF, WARNER. The Ferment of Realism;American Literature, 1884-1919. Free Pr., NY. 1965. 330p. 7.50. LC 65-23115.

BERTHOFF, WARNER. Fictions and Events;Essays in Criticism and Literary History. E.P. Dutton, NY. 1971. 349p. 10.00Hdbd. ISBN 0-525-10470-4. LC 78-133582.

BEWLEY, MARIUS. The Eccentric Design;Form in the Classic American Novel. Columbia Univ. Pr., NY. 1959. 321p. 2.45Pa. ISBN 0-231-08542-742. LC 59-13769.

BEWLEY, MARIUS. Masks and Mirrors. Atheneum, NY. 1949(1970). 364p 10.00Hdbd. ISBN 0-689-10308-5.

BICKLEY, ROBERT BRUCE. The Method of Melville's Short Fiction. Duke Univ. Pr.,Durham, NC. 1975. 142 p. 7.75Hdbd. ISBN 0-8223-0334-5. LC 74-28904.

BIGSBY, C. W. E. The Black American Writer;Vol. I:Fiction. Penguin, Baltimore, MD. 1969(1971). 1.45Pa. ISBN 0-14-021225-6, A1225.

BIKLE, LUCY LEFFINGWELL CABLE. George W. Cable;His Life and Letters.Russell and Russell, NY. 1928(1967). 306p. 8.50Hdbd. ISBN 0-8462-0976-4. LC 66-27039.

BIRKHEAD, EDITH. The Tale of Terror;A Study of the Gothic Romance. Russell and Russell, NY. 1921(1963). 241p. 10.00Hdbd. ISBN 0-8462-0388-X. LC 63-15149.

BLACK, MICHAEL H. The Literature of Fidelity. Barnes and Noble, NY. 1975. 216p. 16.00Hdbd. ISBN 0-06-490440-7. LC 75-2868.

BLACKMUR, R. P. Dirty Hands or the True-Born Censor. Folcroft. 1930. 10.00Hdbd.

BLACKMUR, R. P. The Lion and the Honeycomb;Essays in Solicitude and Critique. Harcourt, NY. 1935(1955) 309p. LC 55-5638.

BLACKMUR, R. P. New Criticism in the United States. Folcroft, Folcroft, PA. 1959(1975). 25.00Hdbd. LC 75-32579.

BLACKMUR, R. P. A Primer of Ignorance. Ed. by Joseph Frank. Harcourt, NY. 1967. 273p. LC 67-10757.

BLAIR, EVERETTA LOVE. Jesse Stuart;His Life and Works. Univ. of South Carolina Pr. 1967. 8.95Hdbd.

BLAIR, WALTER, et al. American Literature;A Brief History. Scott, Foresman, Glenview, IL. 1974. 359p. 4.75Pa. ISBN 0-673-05931-6. LC 73-88913.

BLAKE, FAY M. The Strike in the American Novel. Scarecrow Pr., Metuchen, NJ. 1972. 292p. 7.50Hdbd. ISBN 0-8108-0481-6. LC 72-623.

BLAKE, L. J. Australian Writers. Verry. 1968. 9.50Hdbd.

BLAKE, NELSON MANFRED. Novelists' America;Fiction as History, 1910-1940. Syracuse Univ. Pr., NY. 1969. 279p. 6.95Hdbd. ISBN 0-8156-2129-9. 2.95Pa. ISBN 0-8156-2147-7.

BLANCK, JACOB. Bibliography of American Literature;Vol. 1; Henry Adams to Donn Byrne. Yale Univ. Pr., New Haven, CT. 1955. 474p. 24.00Hdbd. ISBN 0-300-00310-2. LC 54-5283.

BLANCK, JACOB. Bibliography of American Literature;Vol. 2; George W. Cable to Timothy Dwight. Yale Univ. Pr., New Haven, CT. 1957. 534p 25.00Hdbd. ISBN 0-300-00311-0. LC 54-5283.

BLANCK, JACOB. Bibliography of American Literature;Vol. 3;Edward Eggleston to Bret Harte. Yale Univ. Pr., New Haven, CT. 1959. 482p. 25.00Hdbd. ISBN 0-300-00312-9. LC 54-5283.

BLANCK, JACOB. Bibliography of American Literature;Vol. 4;Nathaniel Hawthorne to Joseph Holt Ingraham. Yale Univ. Pr., New Haven, CT. 1963. 495p. 25.00Hdbd. ISBN 0-300-

BLANCK, JACOB. Bibliography of American Literature;Vol. 5;Washington Irving to Henry Wadsworth Longfellow. Yale Univ. Pr., New Haven, CT. 1969. 643p. 25. 00Hdbd. ISBN 0-300-01099-0. LC 54-5283.

BLANCK, JACOB. Bibliography of American Literature;Vol. 6;Augustus Baldwin Longstreet to Thomas William Parsons. Yale Univ. Pr., New Haven, CT. 1973. 594p. 30. 00Hdbd. ISBN 0-300-01618-2. LC 54-5283.

BLASING, MUTLU KONUK. The Art of Life;Studies in American Autobiographical Literature. Univ. of Texas Pr. Austin, TX. 1977. 11. 95Hdbd. ISBN 0-292-70315-5. LC 76-20760.

BLEIKASTEN, ANDRE. The Most Splendid Failure;Faulkner's The Sound and The Fury. Indiana Univ. Pr., Bloomington, IN. 1976. 12. 50Hdbd. ISBN 0-253-33877-8. LC 75-22638.

BLISH, JAMES, Ed. The Issue at Hand;Studies in Contemporary Magazine Science Fiction by William Atheling, Jr. Advent Pub., Chicago, IL. 1964(1970).136p. ISBN 911682-09-0. LC 65-2533.

BLISH, JAMES, Ed. More Issues at Hand;Studies in Contemporary Science by William Atheling, Jr. Advent Pub., Chicago, IL. 1970(1971). 154p. ISBN 0-911682-104. LC 72-115400.

BLOCK, HASKELL M. Naturalistic Triptych;The Fictive and the Real in Zola, Mann and Dreiser. Phila. Bk. Co. 1970. 2. 95Pa.

BLOOM, HAROLD. Ringers in the Tower. Univ. of Chicago Pr. 1973. 3. 45 Pa. ISBN 0-2206049.1971. 12. 75Hdbd. ISBN 0-226-06048-9.

BOYDE, PATRICK. Dante's Style in His Lyric Poetry. Indiana Univ. Pr. 1967. 1. 25Pa. ISBN 0-253-20106-3. LC 67-24518.

BLOOMFIELD, MORTON W. The Interpretation of Narrative;Theory and Practice. Harvard Univ. Pr., Cambridge, MA. 1970. 287p. 8. 50Pa. ISBN 0-674-37521-1. LC 77-122214.

BLOTNER, JOSEPH. The Modern American Political Novel;1900-1960. Univ. of Texas Pr., Austin. 1966(1967). 424p. 8. 50. ISBN 0-292-73607-X. LC 65-27533.

BLOUNT, MARGARET. Animal Land;The Creatures of Children's Fiction. Wm. Morrow, NY. 1974(1975). 336p. 8. 95Hdbd. ISBN 0-688-00272-2. LC 74-19775.

BLUES, THOMAS. Mark Twain and the Community. Univ. of Kentucky Pr., Louisville, KY. 1970. 84p. 4. 95. ISBN 0-8131-1201-X. LC 73-94063.

BLUESTEIN, GENE. The Voice of the Folk;Folklore and American Literary Theory. Univ. of Mass. Pr., Amherst, MA. 1972. 170p. 9. 00Hdbd.

BOAS, GEORGE. Romanticism in America. Russell and Russell, NY. 1940(1968). 202p. 8. 50Hdbd. ISBN 0-8462-0126-7. LC 61-13777.

BODE, CARL, Ed. The New Mencken Letters. Dial Pr. NY. 1976. 19. 95Hdbd. ISBN 0-8037-1379-7. LC 76-44850.

BODE, CARL. Ralph Waldo Emerson;A Profile. Hill and Wang, NY. 1969. 199p. 1. 95Pa. ISBN 0-8090-0207-8. LC 68-9298.

BOLGER, STEPHEN. The Irish Character in American Fiction;1830-1860. Arno Pr., NY. 1976. 14.00Hdbd. ISBN 0-405-09320-9. LC 76-6323.

BONAPARTE, MARIE. Life and Works of Edgar Allan Poe;A Psycho-Analytic Interpretation. Humanities Pr. 1949(1971)749p. ISBN 0-391-00086-1.

BONE, ROBERT. The Negro Novel in America. Yale Univ. Pr., New Haven, CT. 1958(1965). 289p. 8.50Hdbd. ISBN 0-300-00316-1. LC 58-11249. 2.95Pa. ISBN 0-300-00024-3.

BOON, JAMES A. From Symbolism to Structuralism;Levi-Strauss in a Literary Tradition. Harper-Row. 1972. 11.00Hdbd. ISBN 0-06-136086-4. LC 72-75621. 3.95Pa. ISBN 0-06-131736-5.

BORNSTEIN, GEORGE, Ed. Romantic and Modern;Revaluations of Literary Tradition. Univ. of Pittsburgh Pr., Pittsburgh. 1977. 11.95Hdbd. ISBN 0-8229-3322-5. LC 76-6658.

BOROWITZ, ALBERT. Innocence and Arsenic;Studies in Crime and Literature. Harper and Row, NY. 1977. 10.95Hdbd. ISBN 0-06-010413-9. LC 76-27267.

BOULTON, MARJORIE. The Anatomy of the Novel. Routledge and K. Paul, London. 1975. 189p. 10.95Hdbd. ISBN 0-7100-8135-9. LC 75-324097. 5.00Pa. ISBN 0-7100-8136-7.

BOURINOT, J. G., et al. Our Intellectual Strength and Weakness;English-Canadian Literature;French-Canadian Literature. Univ. of Toronto Pr. 1973. 12.50Hdbd. ISBN 0-8020-1950-1. 3.95Pa. ISBN 0-8020-6175-3.

BROOKS, VAN WYCK. History of a Literary Radical and Other Essays. Biblo and Tannen, NY. 1920(1969). 343p. LC 69-17713.

BOVA, BENJAMIN. Notes to a Science Fiction Writer. Scribner, NY. 1975. 177p. 6.95. ISBN 0-684-14434-4. LC 75-8343.

BOVA, BENJAMIN. Through Eyes of Wonder;Science Fiction and Science. Addison-Wesley, Reading, MA. 1975. 5.75. ISBN 0-201-09206-9. LC 74-13893.

BOWDEN, EDWIN T. The Dungeon of the Heart;Human Isolation and the American Novel. Macmillan Co., NY 1961. 175p. LC 61-8262.

BOWDEN, EDWIN T. James Thurber;A Bibliography. Ohio State Univ. Pr., 1969. 353p. 10.00Hdbd. ISBN 0-8142-0025-7. LC 68-20365.

BOWDEN, EDWIN T. The Themes of Henry James;A System of Observation through the Visual Arts. Archon Books, NY. 1956(1969)117p. 4.25Pa. ISBN 0-208-00723-7.

BOWEN, MERLIN. The Long Encounter;Self and Experience in the Writings of Herman Melville. Univ. of Chicago Pr., Chicago. 1960. 282p. 1.95Pa. ISBN 0-226-06835-8.

BOWKER, ALAN, Ed. The Social Criticism of Stephen Leacock;The Unsolved Riddle of Social Justice and Other Essays. Univ. of Toronto Pr. 1973. 145p. 3.95Pa. ISBN 0-8020-6201-6. LC 73-79860.

BOWRA, CECIL M. Heritage of Symbolism. St. Martin Pr., NY. 1943. 12.95Hdbd.

BOWRON, BERNARD R., JR. Henry B. Fuller of Chicago;The Ordeal of a Genteel Realist in Ungenteel America. Greenwood Pr., Westport, CT. 1974. 12.50Hdbd. ISBN 0-8371-5820-6. LC 70-140915.

BOYD, JOHN D., S.J. The Function of Mimesis and Its Decline. Harvard Univ. Pr., Cambridge, MA. 1968. 317p 9.00Hdbd. ISBN 0-674-32700-4. LC 28691.

BOYERS, ROBERT. Excursions;Selected Literary Essays. Kennikat Pr. Port Washington, NY. 1976. 12.50Hdbd. ISBN 0-8046-9148-7. LC 76-22547.

BRADBURY, RAY. Zen and the Art of Writing;and, The Joy of Writing;Two Essays. Capra Pr., Santa Barbara, CA. 1973. 34p. 2.50Pa. ISBN 0-012264-79-9.

BRADLEY, EDWARD SCULLEY. The American Tradition in Literature. Grosset and Dunlap. NY. 1974. 10.50 Hdbd. LC 73-14129.

BRAINE, JOHN. Writing a Novel. Coward, McCann and Geoghegan, NY. 1974. 223p. 7.95Hdbd. ISBN 0-698-10584-2. LC 73-93771.

BRANCH, EDGAR. A Bibliography of James T. Farrell's Writings;1921-1957. Univ. of Pennsylvania Pr., Philadelphia. 1959. 142p. 9.00Hdbd. ISBN 0-8122-7179-3. LC 58-10532.

BRANCH, EDGAR MARQUESS. The Literary Apprenticeship of Mark Twain;With Selections From His Apprentice Writing. Russell and Russell, NY. 1950(1966). 325p. LC 66-24672.

BRANCH, WATSON GAILEY. Melville, The Critical Heritage. Routledge and K. Paul, London. 1974. 444p. 22.50Hdbd. ISBN 0-7100-7774-2. LC 73-86570.

BRANDEN, NATHANIEL. Who is Ayn Rand?;An Analysis of the Novels of Ayn Rand. Random, NY. 1962. 239p. 6.95. ISBN 0-394-45179-1. LC 62-10336.

BRANTLEY, JOHN D. The Fiction of John Dos Passos. Mouton, The Hague, Paris. 1968. 136p.

BRASCH, ILA WALES. A Comprehensive Annotated Bibliography of American Black English. Louisiana St. Univ. Pr. 1974. 289p. 15.00Hdbd. ISBN 0-8071-0069-2. LC 73-83908.

BRASHEAR, MINNIE M., AND Robert M. Rodney. The Art Humor and Humanity of Mark Twain. Univ. of Oklahoma Pr., Norman, OK. 1959. 423p.

BRAUDY, LEO. Norman Mailer;A Collection of Critical Essays. Prentice-Hall, Englewood Cliffs, NJ. 1972. 185p. 5.95. ISBN 0-13-545533-2.

BRAWEELL, WILLIAM. Melville's Religious Thought;An Essay in Interpretation. Octagon Books, NY. 1973. 154p. 8.25Hdbd. ISBN 0-374-90945-8. LC 73-324.

BREMNER, ROBERT H., Ed. Essays on History and Literature. Ohio St. Univ. Pr. 1966. 5.00Pa. ISBN 0-8142-0029-X. LC 66-22733.

BRENNI, VITO J. William Dean Howells;A Bibliography. Scarecrow Pr. Metuchen, NJ. 1973. 212p. ISBN 0-8108 LC 73-4855.

BRETNOR, REGINALD, Ed. The Craft of Science Fiction; A Symposium on Writing Science Fiction and Science Fantasy. Harper and Row, NY. 1975. 288p. 8.95Hdbd. ISBN 0-06-010461-9. LC 75-23872.

BRETNOR, REGINALD, Ed. Science Fiction, Today and Tomorrow. Penguin Books, Baltimore, MD. 1974(1975). 2.95Pa. ISBN 0-14-003921-X, 3921.

BRIGGS, JULIA. Night Visitors; The Rise and Fall of the English Ghost Story. 1977. 240p. 6.95Hdbd. ISBN 0-571-11113-0.

BRIGNANO, RUSSELL CARL. Black Americans in Autobiography; An annotated Bibliography of Autobiographies and Autobiographical Books Written since the Civil War. Duke Univ. Pr., Durham, NC. 1974. 118p. 5.75. LC 73-92535.

BRINNIN, JOHN MALCOLM. Dylan Thomas in America; An Intimate Journal. Little, Brown, Boston. 1955. 303p. LC 55-10768.

BRINNIN, JOHN MALCOLM. The Third Rose; Gertrude Stein and Her World. Little, Brown, Boston. 1959. 427p. 7.50Hdbd. LC 59-13732.

BRISSENDEN, R. F. Patrick White. British Bk. Ctr. 1966. 3.95Hdbd. 1.95Pa.

BREGENZER, DON MARSHALL, Ed. Round Table in Poictesme; A Symposium. Gordon Pr., NY. 1924(1975). 34.95Hdbd. ISBN 0-87968-234-5. LC 75-11379.

BRODERICK, DOROTHY M. Image of the Black in Children's Fiction. R. R. Bowker Co., NY. 1973. 219p. 12.50.

BRODHEAD, RICHARD H. Hawthorne, Melville; and the Novel. Univ. of Chicago Pr., Chicago. 1976. 216p. 12.00Hdbd. ISBN 0-226-07522-2. LC 75-5071.

BRODTKORB, PAUL, JR. Ishmael's White World; A Phenomenological Reading of Moby Dick. Yale Univ. Pr., New Haven, CT. 1965. 170p.

BROOKS, CLEANTH. American Literature; The Makers and the Making. St. Martin's Pr., NY. 1973(1974). Vol. 1. 11.95Hdbd. 8.98Pa. Vol. 2. 12.95Hdbd. 9.95Pa. LC 72-95981.

BROOKS, CLEANTH. William Faulkner; The Yoknapatawpha Country. Yale Univ. Pr. 1963. 10.00Hdbd. 2.95Pa.

BROOKS, CLEANTH. The Hidden God; Studies in Hemingway, Faulkner, Yeats, Eliot, and Warren. Yale Univ. Pr., New Haven, CT. 1963. 136p. 5.00Hdbd. ISBN 0-300-00327-7. LC 63-9308. 1.45Pa. ISBN 0-300-0025-1, Y87.

BROOKS, PETER. The Melodramatic Imagination; Balzac, Henry James, Melodrama, and the Mode of Excess. Yale Univ. Pr. New Haven, CT. 1976. 235p. 15.00Hdbd. ISBN 0-300-02001-5. LC 75-43305.

BROOKS, VAN WYCK. Howells; His Life and World. Dutton. 1959. 5.00.

BROOKS, VAN WYCK. The Malady of the Ideal; Obermann, Maurice de Guerin and Amiel. Univ. of Pennsylvania Pr., Philadelphia. 1947. 88p.

BROOKS, VAN WYCK. The World of Washington Irving. E. P. Dutton, NY. 1950. 514p.

BROUGHTON, PANTHEA REID. William Faulkner;The Abstract and the Actual. Louisiana State Univ. Pr. 1974. 222p. 7.95Hdbd. ISBN 0-8071-0083-8. LC 74-77324.

BROWN, ARTHUR W. Margaret Fuller. Twayne Pub., NY. 1964. 159p. 2.45Pa. LC 63-20612.

BROWN, CLARENCE ARTHUR. The Achievement of American Criticism; Representative Selections from Three Hundred Years of American Criticism. Ronald Pr., NY. 1954. 724p. LC 54-6962.

BROWN, DEMING. Soviet Attitudes Toward American Writing. Princeton Univ. Pr., Princeton, NJ. 1962. 338p. 11.50Hdbd. ISBN 0-691-08712-1. LC 62-11954.

BROWN, DOUGLAS. The Enduring Legacy;Biblical Dimensions in Modern Literature. Scribner, NY. 1975. 389p. 5.26Pa. ISBN 0-684-13848-4. LC 74-13863.

BROWN, EDWARD K. Willa Cather; A Critical Biography. Alfred A. Knopf, NY. 1953(1967). 351p. 5.95Pa. ISBN 0-394-45196-1. LC 52-12204.

BROWN, HERBERT ROSS. The Sentimental Novel in America;1789-1860. Books for Libraries Pr., Freeport, NY. 1940(1970). 407p. 14.50Hdbd. ISBN 0-8369-1490-2. LC 75-107107685.

BROWN, HUNTINGTON. Prose Styles;Five Primary Types. Univ. of Minn. Pr., Minneapolis. 1966. 149p. 4.50Pa. ISBN 0-8166-0375-8. LC 66-12925.

BROWN, JOHN RUSSEL, Ed., and Bernard Harris. The American Novel and the Nineteen Twenties. Edward Arnold, London. Crane, Russak, NY. 269p.

BROWNE, NINA E. A Bibliography of Nathaniel Hawthorne. Houghton, Mifflin, NY. 1905(1968)215p.

BROWNE, RAY B. Melville's Drive to Humanism. Purdue Univ. Studies. Lafayette, IN. 1971. 394p. 7.50Hdbd. ISBN 0-911198-27-X. LC 76-151514.

BROWNELL, W. C. Criticism;An Essay on Function, Form and Method. Kennikat Pr., Port Washington, NY. 1914(1967). 85p. LC 67-27579.

BROWNING, PRESTON M. Flannery O'Connor. Southern Illinois Univ. Pr., Carbondale, IL. 1974. 6.95Hdbd. ISBN 0-8093-0672-7. LC 74-8849.

BRUCCOLI, MATTHEW J. Apparatus for F. Scott Fitzgerald's The Great Gatsby (Under the Red, White and Blue). 1974. 140p. 14.95Trade. 50.00Deluxe. LC 74-4142.

BRUCCOLI, MATTHEW J. The Composition of Tender is the Night;A Study of the Manuscripts. Univ. of Pittsburgh Pr., Pittsburgh. 1963. 252p. 6.00. ISBN 0-8229-30560.

BRUCCOLI, MATTHEW J. F. Scott Fitzgerald;A Descriptive Bibliography. Univ. of Pittsburgh Pr. 1972. 369p. 19.95Hdbd. ISBN 0-8229-3239-3. LC 77-181395.

BRUCCOLI, MATTHEW J., and C.E. Frazer Clark, Jr., Eds. First Printings of American Authors;Contributions Toward Descriptive Checklists, Vol. 1. Gale Research Co., Detroit. 1977. ISBN 0-8103-0933-5.

LC 74-11756.

BRUCCOLI, MATTHEW J. Hemingway at Auction;1930-1973. Gale Research, Detroit. 1973. 286p. 25.00Hdbd. LC 73-178294.

BRUCCOLI, MATTHEW J. John O'Hara;A Checklist. Random House, NY. 1972. 136p. ISBN 0-394-46991-7.

BRUCCOLI, MATTHEW J. Kenneth Millar/Ross Macdonald;A Checklist. Gale, Detroit. 1971. 86p. 8.50Hdbd. LC 77-39690.

BRUSHWOOD, JOHN S. The Spanish American Novel;A Twentieth-Century Survey. Univ. of Texas Pr., Austin. 1975. 15.95Hdbd. ISBN 0-292-77515-6. LC 74-32429.

BRUSS, ELIZABETH W. Autobiographical Acts;The Changing Situation of a Literary Genre. John Hopkins Univ. Pr., Baltimore. 1976. 10.00Hdbd. ISBN 0-8018-1821-4. LC 76-13460.

BRYAN, MARGARET B. Writing about Literature and Film. Harcourt, NY. 1975. 192p. 3.95Pa. ISBN 0-15-597854-3. LC 75-3528.

BRYANT, JERRY H. The Open Decision;The Contemporary American Novel and Its Intellectual Background. Free Pr., NY. 1970. 415p. 8.95Hdbd. LC 79-128473.

BRYER, JACKSON R., and Eugene Harding. Hamlin Garland and the Critics;An Annotated Bibliography. Whitston Pub. Co., Troy, NY. 1973. 282p. 12.50Hdbd. ISBN 0-87875-020-7. LC 75-183300.

BRYER, JACKSON R. The Critical Reputation of F. Scott Fitzgerald;A Bibliographical Study. Archon Books, CT. 1967. 434p. 15.00Hdbd. ISBN 0-208-00412-2, 2. LC 67-24031.

BRYER, JACKSON R. Fifteen Modern American Authors;A Survey of Research and Criticism. Duke Univ. Pr. Durham, NC. 1969. 493p. ISBN 0-8223-0208-X. LC 78-83720.

BRYLOWSKI, WALTER. Faulkner's Olympian Laugh;Myth in the Novels. Wayne State Univ. Pr., Detroit. 1968. 236p. 8.95. ISBN 0-8143-1328-0.

BUCK, GERTRUDE. The Metaphor; A Study in the Psychology or Rhetoric. Folcroft, Folcroft, PA. 1974. 10.00Hdbd. LC 74-9847.

BUCK, PEARL S., and Theodore F. Harris. For Spacious Skies;Journey in Dialogue. John Day Co., NY. 1966. 221p. 6.95. ISBN 0-381-98059-6, A-28260. LC 66-18781.

BUELL, LAWRENCE. Literary Transcendentalism;Style and Vision in the American Renaissance. Cornell Univ. Pr., Ithaca, NY. 1973(1975). 336p. 3.45Pa. ISBN 0-8014-9152. LC 73-8409.

BUITENHUIS, PETER. The Grasping Imagination;The American Writings of Henry James. Univ. of Toronto Pr. Toronto, Ont. 1970. 288p. 17.50Hdbd. ISBN 0-8020-5244-4. LC 79-149323. 5.00Pa. ISBN 0-8020-6225-3.

BUITENHUIS, PETER. Twentieth Century Interpretations of The Portrait of A Lady;A Collection of Critical Essays. Prentice-Hall, Englewood Cliffs, NJ. 1968. 122p.

BURACK, A.S. Techniques of Novel Writing. Writer, Inc., Boston. 1973.

305p. 8.95Hdbd. ISBN 0-87116-000-5. LC 72-95433.

BURACK, A.S. Writing Detective and Mystery Fiction. Writer, Inc., Boston. 1945(1967)280p. 6.95Hdbd. ISBN 0-87116-004-8. LC 67-13424.

BURBANK, REX. Sherwood Anderson. Twayne. 1964. 6.95. ISBN 0-8057-0020-X.

BURGESS, ANTHONY. The Novel Now. W.W. Norton, NY. 1967. 224p. LC 67-24015.

BURKE, KENNETH. The Philosophy of Literary Form Studies in Symbolic Action. Univ. of Calif. Pr., Berkeley. 1974. 463p. 4.95Pa. ISBN 0-520-02483-4. LC 72-93526.

BURNETT, HALLIE. Fiction Writer's Handbook. Harper and Row, NY. 1975. 200p. 7.95. ISBN 0-06-010574-7. LC 74-1797.

BURNS, SHANNON. An Annotated Bibliography of Texts on Writing Skills Grammar and Usage, Composition, Rhetoric, and Technical Writing. Garland Publ, NY. 1975(1976). 23.00Hdbd. ISBN 0-8240-9968-0. LC 75-24096.

BURROUGHS, JOHN. Literary Values and Other Papers;Emerson, Thoreau. R. West, Haverton, PA. 1903(1973). 10.00Hdbd.

BURROWS, DAVID J., et al. Myths and Motifs in Literature. Free Pr., Riverside, NJ. 1973. 5.96Pa. LC 72-90506.

BUTCHER, PHILIP. George W. Cable;The Northampton Years. Columbia Univ. Pr., NY. 1959. 286p. LC 59-6213.

BUTLER, CHRISTOPHER. Number Symbolism. Routledge and Kegan. 1970. 7.00Hdbd. ISBN 0-7100-6766-6.

BUTWIN, JOSEPH, and Frances Butwin. Sholom Aleichem. Twayne, Boston. 1977. 8.50Hdbd.

C

CADY, EDWIN H. The Light of Common Day;Realism in American Fiction. Indiana Univ. Pr., Bloomington, IL. 1971. 224p. 8.95Hdbd. ISBN 0-253-33430-6. LC 70-159725.

CADY, EDWIN H. Stephen Crane. Twayne, NY. 1962. 6.50Hdbd. ISBN 0-8057-0168-0. Coll. and Univ. Pr., New Haven, CT. 2.45Pa.

CADY, EDWIN H., and Lester G. Wells. Stephen Crane's Love Letters to Nellie Crouse. Syracuse Univ. Pr., Syracuse, NY. 1954. 87p. LC 54-9916.

CADY, EDWIN H. William Dean Howells;Dean of American Letters. Syracuse Univ. Pr. Vol.1. 1956. 4.00. Vol. 2. 1958. 5.00.

CALDWELL, ERSKINE. Call It Experience;The Years of Learning How to Write. Duell, Sloan and Pearce, NY 1951. 239p. LC 51-10412.

CALLAHAN, JOHN F. The Illusions of a Nation;Myth and History in the Novels of F. Scott Fitzgerald. Univ. of Illinois Pr., Urbana, IL. 1972. 221p. 7.95Hdbd. ISBN 0-252-00232-6. LC 77-174778.

CALLOUD, JEAN. Structural Analysis of the Narrative. Fortress. 1976. 3.95Pa. ISBN 0-8006-1503-4. LC 75-37158.

CALLOW, JAMES T., and Robert J. Reilly. Guide to American Literature from Emily Dickinson to the Present. Barnes and Noble, NY. 1977. 272p. 12.50Hdbd. ISBN 0-06-480133-0. LC75-39903.

CALLOW, JAMES T., and Robert J. Reilly. Guide to American Literature from its Beginnings through Walt Whitman. Barnes and Noble, NY. 1976. 244p. 3.95Pa. ISBN0-06-460165-X. LC75-29621.

CALHOUN, RICHARD J., Ed. James Dickey;The Expansive Imagination; A Collection of Critical Essays. Everett/Edwards, DeLand, FL. 1973. 231 p. 12.00Hdbd. ISBN 0-912112-00-X. LC 72-90914.

CAMERON, ELEANOR. The Green and Burning Tree;On the Writing and Enjoyment of Children's Books. Little, Brown, Boston, MA. 1969. 377p. 6.95Hdbd.

CAMERON, KENNETH WALTER. Ralph Waldo Emerson's Reading. Haskell House, NY. 1941(1966). 44p. 8.96 Hdbd. ISBN 0-8383-0518-0. LC 68-55159.

CAMPBELL, FRANK D., JR. John D. MacDonald and the Colorful World of Travis McGee. Borgo Pr., San Bernadino, CA. 1977. 1.95Pa. ISBN 0-89370-208-0. LC 77-773.

CAMPBELL, HARRY MODEAN, and Ruel E. Foster. Elizabeth Madox Roberts; American Novelist. Univ. of Oklahoma Pr., Norman, OK. 283p. 8.95Hdbd. ISBN 0-8061-0355-8. LC 56-11237.

CAMPBELL, HILBERT H., and Charles E. Modlin, Eds. Sherwood Anderson; Centennial Studies. Whitston Pub., Troy, NY. 1976. 275p. 12.50Hdbd. ISBN 0-87875-093-2. LC 76-21468.

CAMPBELL, LOUISE, Ed. Letters to Louise; Theodore Dreiser's Letters to Louise Campbell. Univ. of Pennsylvania Pr., Philadelphia, PA. 1959. 123p. LC 59-6698.

CANBY, HENRY SEIDEL. Turne West, Turn East; Mark Twain and Henry James. Biblo and Tannen. 1965. 7.50Hdbd.

CANTRELL, LEON. Modern Australian Prose; A Guide to Information Sources. Gale. 18.00. ISBN 0-8103-1243-3. LC 74-11536.

CANTWELL, ROBERT. Nathaniel Hawthorne; The American Years. Rinehart, NY. 1948. 499p.

CARDWELL, GUY A., Ed. Discussions of Mark Twain. D.C. Heath, Boston, MA. 1963. 130p.

CARGILL, OSCAR. Toward a Pluralistic Criticism. Southern Illinois Univ. Pr., Carbondale, IL. 1965. 205p. 6.95Hdbd. ISBN 0-8093-0179-2.

CARLSON, ERIC W. Introduction to Poe; A Thematic Reader. Foresman, Glenview, IL. 1967. 4.15Pa. ISBN 0-673-05421-7.

CARPENTER, FREDERIC IVES. Emerson Handbook. Hendricks House, NY. 1953. 268p.

CARR, JOHN. Kite-Flying and Other Irrational Acts; Conversations with Twelve Southern Writers. Louisiana State Univ. Pr., Baton Rouge, LA. 1972. 288p. 10.00Hdbd. ISBN 0-8071-0242-3. LC 72-79328.

CARRINGTON, GEORGE C., JR. The Dramatic Unity of "Huckleberry Finn". Ohio State Univ. Pr., Columbus, OH. 1976. 12.00Hdbd. ISBN 0-8142-0238-1. LC76-939.

CARTER, EVERETT. The American Idea; The Literary Reaction to American Optimism. Univ. of North Carolina Pr., Chapel Hill, NC. 1976(1977)14.95Hdbd. ISBN 0-8078-1278-X. LC 76-13867.

CARTER, EVERETT. Howells and the Age of Realism. Shoe String. 1954(1966. 12.50Hdbd. ISBN 0-208-00447-5.

CARY, JOYCE. Art and Reality; Ways of the Creative Process. Anchor Books, Garden City, NY. 1958(1961). 199p.

CARY, NORMAN REED. Christian Criticism in the Twentieth Century; Theological Approaches to Literature. Kennikat Pr., Port Washington, NY. 1975. 9.95Hdbd. ISBN 0-8046-9104-5. LC 75-37785.

CASSADY, CAROLYN. Heart Beat; My Life with Jack and Neal. Creative Arts Book Co., Berkeley, CA. 1976.

CASSILL, RONALD VERLIN. Writing Fiction. Prentice-Hall, Englewood Cliffs, NJ. 2nd Ed. 1975. 174p. 7.95Hdbd. ISBN 0-13-970111-7. LC75-12535. 2.95Pa. ISBN 0-13-970103-6.

CAVELL, STANLEY. The Senses of Walden. Viking Pr., NY. 1972. 5.95Hdbd. ISBN 0-670-63357-7. 1.95Pa. ISBN 0-670-00404-9, C404.

CAZAMIAN, LOUIS. Criticism in the Making. Folcroft Library Editions, Folcroft, PA. 1929(1977). 20.00Hdbd. ISBN 0-8414-3588-X.

CHADWICK, CHARLES. Symbolism; Critical Idiom;Ser. Vol. 16. Barnes and Noble, NY. 1971. 2.75Pa. ISBN 0-416-60900-7.

CHAMBERS, ROBERT D. Sinclair Ross and Ernest Buckler;Studies in Canadian Literature Ser. McGill-Queens Univ. Pr. 1975. 2.35Pa. ISBN 0-7735-0240-8.

CHANDLER, ELIZABETH LATHROP. A Study of the Sources of the Tales and Romances Written by Nathaniel Hawthorne before 1853. Folcroft, Folcroft, PA. 1926(1975). 64p. 12.50Hdbd. ISBN 0-8414-3645-2. LC 75-9569.

CHANKIN, DONALD O. Anonymity and Death;The Fiction of B. Traven. Pennsylvania State Univ. Pr., Univ. Park, PA. 1975. 142p. 9.50Hdbd. ISBN 0-271-01190-4. LC 75-1376.

CHAPMAN, ABRAHAM. Jewish-American Literature;An Anthology of Fiction, Poetry, Autobiography and Criticism. New American Library, NY. 1974. 727p. 2.25Pa. LC 74-81014.

CHAPMAN, ABRAHAM. Literature of the American Indians;Views and Interpretations;A Gathering of Indian Memories, Symbolic Contexts, and Literary Criticism. Meridian, NY. 1975. 357p. 3.95Pa. LC 75-13683.

CHAPMAN, RAYMOND. Linguistics and Literature;An Introduction to Literary Stylistics. Littlefield. 1973. 1.50Pa. ISBN 0-8226-0267-9.

CHARTERS, ANN. Kerouac;A Biography. Warner, NY. 1974. 416p. 1.95Pa.

CHARVAT, WILLIAM. The Origins of American Critical Thought;1810-1835. A. S. Barnes, NY. 1936(1961). 218p. 1.65Pa. ISBN 0-498-04042-9.

CHASE, RICHARD. The American Novel and Its Tradition. Doubleday, Garden City, NY. 1957. 266p. 1.95Pa. ISBN 0-385-09322-5. LC 57-11412.

CHASE, RICHARD, Ed. Melville;A Collection of Critical Essays. Prentice-Hall, Englewood Cliffs, NJ. 1962. 168p. 5.95 Hdbd. 1.95Pa.

CHASE, RICHARD. Herman Melville; A Critical Study. MacMillan, NY. 1949. 306p.

CHATMAN, SEYMOUR, Ed. Literary Style Symposium. Oxford Univ. Pr., 1971. 15.00Hdbd. ISBN 0-19-501345-X. 4.00Pa. ISBN 0-19-501348-4.

CHERRY, RICHARD L., and Robert J. Conley, Bernard A. Hirsch. The Essay;Structure and Purpose. Houghton Mifflin, Boston, Ma. 1975. 473p. 5.95Pa. ISBN 0-395-18610-2. LC 74-19660.

CHESNUTT, HELEN M. Charles Waddell Chesnutt;Pioneer of the Color Line. Univ. of NC Pr., Chapel Hill. 1952. 324p. 5.95. ISBN 0-8078-0621-8.

CHEVIGNY, BELL GALE. The Woman and the Myth;Margaret Fuller's Life and Writings. Feminist Pr., Old Westbury, NY. 1976. 6.50Pa. ISBN 0-912670-43-6. LC 76-19030.

CHIARI, JOSEPH. Symbolisme from Poe to Mallarme;The Growth of a Myth. Gordian. 1970. 8.50Hdbd. ISBN 0-87752-020-8. LC 76-114096.

CHOAT, JOSEPH H. Ralph Waldo Emerson. Folcroft, PA. 1973. 5.50

CHRISTY, A. E. The Orient in American Transcendentalism;A Study of Emerson, Thoreau and Alcott. Gordon Pr., NY. 34.95.

CHRISTY, ARTHUR. Orient in American Transcendentalism;A Study of Emerson, Thoreau and Alcott. Octagon, NY. 1963. 14.00. ISBN 0-374-91539-3.

CHUPACK, HENRY. James Purdy. Twayne Pub., Boston, MA. 1975. 144p. 7.50Hdbd. ISBN 0-8057-0601-1. LC 74-22438.

CHURCHILL, ALLEN. The Literary Decade. Prentice-Hall, Englewood Cliffs, NJ. 1971. 328p. 9.95Hdbd. ISBN 0-13-537522-3. LC 73-152312.

CHURCHILL, E. RICHARD, and Linda R. Churchill, Edward H. Blair, and Kay Reynolds Blair. Fun with American Literature. Abingdon Pr., NY. 1968. 254p. 4.95Pa. ISBN 0-687-13787-X. LC 68-11470.

CLACK, DORIS H. Black Literature Resources;Analysis and Organization. M. Dekker, NY. 1975. 207p. 17.50 Hdbd. ISBN 0-8247-6307-6. LC 75-23582.

CLAIR, JOHN A. The Ironic Dimension in the Fiction of Henry James. Duquesne Pr., Pittsburgh, PA. 1965. 140p. 6.00Pa. ISBN 0-8207-0060-6.

CLARESON, THOMAS D. Science Fiction Criticism;An Annotated Checklist. Kent State Univ. Pr., Kent, OH. 1972. 225p. 7.00Hdbd. ISBN 0-87338-123-8. LC 71-181084.

CLARK, C. E. FRAZER, JR. Hawthorne at Auction;1894-1971. Gale, Detroit, MI. 1972. 419p. 25.00Hdbd. LC 70-38939.

CLARK, JOHN R., and Anna L. Motto, Eds. Satire;That Blasted Art. Putnam. 1975. 3.95Pa. ISBN 0-399-50312-9.

CLARKE, JOHN HENRIK, Ed. William Styron's Nat Turner;Ten Black Writers Respond. Beacon Pr., Boston, MA. 1968. 120p. 4.95Hdbd. ISBN 0-8070-6426-2. LC 68-27519. 1.95Pa. ISBN 0-8070-6427-0.

CLIFFORD, GAY. The Transformations of Allegory. Routledge and K. Paul, Boston, MA. 1974. 132p. ISBN 0-7100-7976. LC 74-84170.

CLOR, HARRY M. Censorship and Freedom of Expression. Rand. 2.95 Pa. ISBN 0-528-65611-2.

CLOR, HARRY M. Obscenity and Public Morality;Censorship in a Liberal Society. Univ. of Chicago Pr., Chicago, IL. 1969. 10.50Hdbd. ISBN 0-226-11033-8. LC 69-16772.

CLUYSENAAR, ANNE. Aspects of Literary Stylistics. St. Martin's Pr., NY. 1976. 11.95Hdbd.

COAN, OTIS W., and Richard G. Lillard. America in Fiction; An Annotated List of Novels That Interpret Aspects of Life in the United States, Canada, and Mexico. Pacific Books, Palo Alto, CA. 1941(1967). 232p. 7.95 Hdbd. ISBN 0-87015-155-X. LC 66-28118.

COCKCROFT, THOMAS G. L. Index to the Weird Fiction Magazines. Arno Pr., NY. 1962(1975). 7.00Hdbd. ISBN 0-405-06322-9. LC 74-15955.

COCKSHUT, A.O.J. Truth to Life; The Art of Biography in the Nineteenth Century. Harvest. 3.95Pa. ISBN 0-15-691385-2.

COHEN, HENNIG, Ed., and William B. Dillingham. Humor of the Old Southwest. Univ. of Georgia Pr., Athens, GA. 1964(1975). 427p. 4.50Pa. ISBN 0-8203-0358-5. LC 74-13512.

COHEN, HENNIG, Ed. Landmarks of American Writing. Basic Books, NY. 1969. 298p. 8.50Hdbd. ISBN 0-465-03776-3. LC 70-78456.

COHN, JILL WILSON. Writing; The Personal Voice. Harcourt, NY. 1975. 214p. 4.95Pa. ISBN 0-15-597787. LC 74-33749.

COHN, LOUIS HENRY. A Bibliography of the Works of Ernest Hemingway. Haskell House, NY. 1931(1973). 116p. 8.95Hdbd. ISBN 0-8383-1694-8. LC 73-2635.

COINDREAU, MAURICE EDGAR, George McMillan Reeves, Ed. and Trans. The Time of William Faulkner; A French View of Modern American Fiction; Essays by Maurice Edgar Coindreau. Univ. of So. Carolina Pr., Columbia, SC. 1931(1971). 226p. 14.95Hdbd. ISBN 0-87249-212-5. LC 74-144804.

COLE, WALTER R., Ed. A Checklist of Science-Fiction Anthologies. Arno Pr., NY. 1964(1974). 21.00Hdbd. ISBN 0-405-06323-7. LC 74-15956.

COLES, ROBERT. Irony in the Mind's Life; Essays on Novels by James Agee, Elizabeth Bowen and George Eliot. Univ. Pr. of Virginia. 1974. 9.-75Hdbd. ISBN 0-8139-0550-8. LC 74-5260.

COLUM, PADRAIC, and Margaret Freeman Cabell, Carl Van Vechten. Between Friends; Letters of James Branch Cabell and Others. Harcourt, NY. 1962. 304p. LC 60-10935.

COMERCHERO, VICTOR. Nathanael West; The Ironic Prophet. Syracuse Univ. Pr. 1964. 189p. 5.95Pa. ISBN 0-8156-2071-3. LC 64-23342.

COOK, RICHARD M. Carson McCullers. Ungar, NY. 1975. 150p. 7.00Hdbd. ISBN 0-8044-2128-5. LC 75-2789.

COOK, SYLVIA JENKINS. From Tobacco Road to Route 66; The Southern Poor White in Fiction. Univ. of North Carolina Pr., Chapel Hill, NC. 1976. 11.95Hdbd. ISBN 0-8078-1264-1. LC 75-35822.

COOKE, GEORGE WILLIS. Ralph Waldo Emerson; His Life, Writings and Philosophy. Folcroft, Folcroft, PA. 1882(1974). 25.00Hdbd. LC 74-8996.

COOKE, M.G. Modern Black Novelists; A Collection of Critical Essays. Prentice-Hall, Englewood Cliffs, NJ. 1971. 219p. 5.95Pa. ISBN 0-13-588004-1. LC 70-163856.

COOLEY, THOMAS. Educated Lives; The Rise of Modern Autobiography in America. Ohio State Univ. Pr. 1977. 190p. 12.00Hdbd. ISBN 0-8142-0263-2. LC 76-28952.

COOPER, L. Aristotelian Theory of Comedy. Kraus. 1922 Repro. 14.00Hdbd. ISBN 0-527-19420-4.

COOPERMAN, STANLEY. World War I and the American Novel. Johns Hopkins Pr., Baltimore, MD. 1970. 10.00 Hdbd. ISBN 0-8018-0138-9. LC 66-28506. 2.45Pa. ISBN 0-8018-1151-1.

COPELAND, CAROLYN FAUNCE. Language and Time and Gertrude Stein. Univ. of Iowa Pr., Iowa City, IO. 1975. 8.95Hdbd. ISBN 0-87745-059-5. 4.95Pa. ISBN 0-87745-062-5.

CORE, GEORGE, Ed. Southern Fiction Today; Renascence and Beyond. Univ. of Georgia Pr., Athens, GA. 1969. 102p. 5.25Pa. ISBN 0-8203-0164-7. LC 68-58324.

CORNELL, KENNETH. Symbolist Movement. Archon. 1951(1970). 10.00Hdbd. ISBN 0-208-00947-7. LC 70-121755.

CORNILLON, SUSAN KOPPELMAN, Ed. Images of Women in Fiction Feminist Perspectives. Bowling Green Univ. Popular Pr., Bowling Green, OH. 1972. 399p. 10.00Hdbd.

CORNWELL, ETHEL F. The "Still Point". Rutgers Univ. Pr. New Brunswick, NJ. 261p. LC 62-18948.

COTNAM, JACQUES. Contemporary Quebec. McClelland and Stewart, Canada. 1973. 2.95Pa. ISBN 0-7710-2249-2.

COTTON, GERALD B., and Hilda Mary McGill. Fiction Guides. Clive Bingley, London. 1967. 126p.

COUGHLAN, ROBERT. The Private World of William Faulkner. Cooper Square, NY. 1954(1972)151p. 5.00. ISBN 0-8154-0424-7. LC 72-78474.

COVICI, PASCAL, JR. Mark Twain's Humor; The Image of a World. Southern Methodist Pr., Dallas, TX. 1962. 226p. 5.95. ISBN 0-87074-034-2. LC 62-13274.

COVO, JACQUELINE. The Blinking Eye; Ralph Waldo Ellison and his American, French, German and Italian Critics; 1952-1971. Scarecrow Pr. Metuchen, NJ. 1974. 214p. 6.50. ISBN 0-8108-0736-X. LC 74-13042.

COWAN, MICHAEL H. Twentieth Century Interpretations of The Sound and the Fury; A Collection of Critical Essays. Prentice-Hall, Englewood Cliffs, NJ. 1968. 114p. 6.95. ISBN 0-13-823211-3.

COWIE, ALEXANDER. The Rise of the American Novel. American Book, NY. 1951(1958). 877p.

COWLEY, MALCOLM, Ed. After the Genteel Tradition; American Writers 1910-1930. Southern Univ. Pr., Carbondale, IL. 1936(1967). 210p. LC 64-11608.

COWLEY, MALCOLM. Exile's Return; A Literary Odyssey of the 1920s. Viking Pr., NY. 1934(1965). 322p. 2.75 Pa. ISBN 0-670-00004-3, C4.

COWLEY, MALCOLM. The Literary Situation. Viking Pr., NY. 1954(1966). 259p. 1.65Pa. ISBN 0-670-00038-8, C38. LC 54-7984.

COWLEY, MALCOLM. Think Back on Us;A Contemporary Chronicle of the 1930's. Southern Illinois Univ. Pr. Carbondale, IL. 400p.

COX, C. B. The Free Spirit;A Study of Liberal Humanism. Oxford Univ. Pr., NY. 1963. 195p.

COX, JAMES M. Mark Twain;The Fate of Humor. Princeton Univ. Pr., Princeton, NJ. 1966. 321p.

COX, MARTHA HEASLEY, and Wayne Chatterton. Twayne, Boston, MA. 1975. 163p. 7. 50Hdbd. ISBN 0-8057-0014-5. LC 74-19223.

COXE, LOUIS OSBORNE. Enabling Acts;Essays in Criticism. Univ. of Missouri Pr., Columbia, MO. 1976. 10.50Hdbd. ISBN 0-8262-0200-4. LC 76-4485.

CRAIG, ALEC. Above All Liberties. Books for Libraries. 1942 Repro. 11.00Hdbd. ISBN 0-8369-2547-4. LC 70-37839.

CRAIG, DAVID, Ed. Marxists on Literature;An Anthology. Penguin Books, Baltimore, MD. 1975. 527p. 5.95 Pa. ISBN 0-14-021809-2. LC 76-351933.

CRAIG, DAVID. The Real Foundation; Literature and Social Change. Oxford Univ. Pr. 1974. 8.95Hdbd. ISBN 0-19-519752-6.

CRANFILL, THOMAS MABRY, and Robert Lanier Clark, Jr. An Anatomy of The Turn of The Screw. Gordian Pr., NY. 1965(1971). 7.50Hdbd. ISBN 0-87752-151-4.

CREWS, FREDERICK C. Out of My System;Psychoanalysis, Idealogy, and Critical Method. Oxford Univ. Pr., NY. 1975. 214p. 10.00Hdbd. ISBN 0-19-501947-4. LC 75-7361.

CREWS, FREDERICK, Ed. Psychoanalysis and Literary Process. Winthrop Pub., Cambridge, MA. 1970. 296p. LC 76-119025.

CREWS, FREDERICK C. The Sins of the Fathers;Hawthorne's Psychological Themes. Oxford Univ. Pr., NY. 1966. 1.75Pa. ISBN 0-19-500798-0. LC 66-16011.

CREWS, FREDERICK C. The Tragedy of Manners;Moral Drama in the Later Novels of Henry James. Archon Books. 1957(1971). 114p. 5.00Pa. ISBN 0-208-01047-5. LC 77-131376.

CRISLER, JESSE E., and Joseph R. McElrath, Jr. Frank Norris;A Reference Guide. G. K. Hall, Boston, MA. 1973. 145p. 12.50Hdbd. ISBN 0-8161-1097-2.

CROSLAND, ANDREW T. A Concordance to The Great Gatsby. Gale Research Co., Detroit, MI. 1974. 35.00 Hdbd. ISBN 0-8103-1005-8. LC 74-11607.

CROTHERS, GEORGE D. Ed. Invitattion to Learning;English and American Novels. Basic Books, Inc., NY. 1966. 356p. LC 66-10405.

CROWLEY, J. DONALD. Hawthorne; The Critical Heritage. Barnes and Noble, NY. 1976. 170p. ISBN 389-04055.

CROWLEY, JOSEPH DONALD. Nathaniel Hawthorne;A Collection of Criticism. McGraw-Hill, NY. 1974. 2.25Pa. ISBN 0-07-014768-X. LC 74-22440.

CULLEN, JOHN B., and Floyd C. Watkins. Old Times in the Faulkner Country. Univ. of North Carolina Pr., Chapel Hill, NC. 1961. 132p. 3.95Pa. ISBN 0-8078-0807-5.

CULLER, JONATHAN D. Structuralist Poetics;Structuralism, Linguistics, and the Study of Literature. Cornell Univ. Pr., Ithaca, NY. 1975. 301p. 13.50Hdbd. ISBN 0-8014-0928-4 LC 74-11608.

CULP, D. W. Ed. Twentieth Century Negro Literature;A Cyclopedia of Thought on the Vital Topics Relating to the American Negro by One Hundred of America's Greatest Negroes. Arno Pr., NY. 1902. 20.00Hdbd. ISBN 0-405-01856-8. LC 69-18586.

CURLEY, DOROTHY NYREN, et al. Modern American Literature;Supplement to the Fourth Edition. Ungar. 1976. 605p. 25.00Hdbd. ISBN 0-8044-3050-0. LC 76-76599.

CURNOW, WYSTAN. Essays on New Zealand Literature. Heinemann Educational Bks., Auckland, NZ. 1973. 192p. 7.00Pa. ISBN 0-435-18195-5. LC 74-179530.

CURRIE, ROBERT. Genius;An Ideology in Literature. Schocken Books, NY. 1974. 222p. 10.00Hdbd. ISBN 0-8052-3563-9. LC 74-8635.

CURRY, PEGGY SIMSON. Creating Fiction from Experience. The Writer, Inc., Boston, MA. 1964(1967). 148p. LC 64-12149.

D

DAICHES, DAVID. Literature and Society. Haskell House, NY. 1938(1970). 287p. LC 74-95422.

DAILY, JAY E. The Anatomy of Censorship. 1973. 14.50Hdbd. ISBN 0-8247-6065-4.

DANBY, LEWIS M. The Indians of Yoknapatawpha;A Study in Literature and History. Louisiana State Univ. Pr., Baton Rouge, LA. 1974. 163p. 6.95.

DAUBER, KENNETH. Rediscovering Hawthorne. Princeton Univ. Pr., Princeton, NJ. 1977. 13.00Hdbd. ISBN 0-691-06323-0. LC 76-45893.

DAVENPORT, BASIL. Inquiry into Science Fiction. Longmans, Green, NY. 1955. 87p. LC 55-8306.

DAVIDSON, EDWARD H. Poe;A Critical Study. Belknap Pr. of Harvard Univ. Pr., Cambridge, MA. 1957(1966). 296p. 5.00. LC 57-12965.

DAVIDSON, EDWARD HUTCHINS. Hawthorne's Last Phase. Archon Books. Hamden, CT. 1949(1967). 6.75Hdbd. ISBN 0-208-00297-9.

DAVIS, ARTHUR PAUL. From the Dark Tower;Afro-American Writers (1900 to 1960). Howard Univ. Pr., Washington. 1974. 306p. 10.95Hdbd. ISBN 0-88258-004-3. LC 73-88969.

DAVIS, ARTHUR P., Comp., and Michael W. Peplow. The New Negro Renaissance;An Anthology. Holt, Rinehart, NY. 1975. 10.00Hdbd. ISBN 0-03-014066-8. LC 75-2238.

DAVIS, DAVID BRION. Homicide in American Fiction;1798-1860;A Study in Social Values. Cornell Univ. Pr., Ithaca, NY. 1957(1968). 346p. 2.45Pa. ISBN 0-8014-0101-1.

DAVIS, MERRELL R. Melville's Mardi;A Chartless Voyage. Archon Books, Hamden, CT. 1952(1967). 240p. 6.50Hdbd. ISBN 0-208-0069-0.

DAVIS, ROBERT H., and Arthur B. Maurice. The Caliph of Bagdad. D. Appleton, NY, London. 1931. 411p.

DAVIS, ROBERT MURRAY, Ed., Steinbeck;A Collection of Critical Essays. Prentice-Hall, Englewood Cliffs, NJ. 1972. 183p. 1.95Pa. ISBN 0-13-846642-4.

DAVIS, MERRELL R., and William H. Gilman, Eds. The Letters of Herman Melville. Yale Univ. Pr., New Haven, CT. 1960. 398p.

DAY, A. GROVE. Eleanor Dark. Twayne. 1976. 7.95Hdbd. ISBN 0-8057-6224-8. LC 75-23369.

DAY, MARTIN STEEL. A Handbook of American Literature. Univ. of Queensland Pr., St. Lucia, Quebec. 1975. 661p. 28.60Hdbd. ISBN 0-7022-0770-5. LC 76-366251.

DE CAMP, LYON SPRAGUE. Literary Swordsmen and Sorcerers; The Makers of Heroic Fantasy. Arkham House, Sauk City, WI. 1976. 313p. 10.00 Hdbd. ISBN 0-87054-076-9. LC 76-17991.

DE CAMP, LYON SPRAGUE. Lovecraft; A Biography. Doubleday, Garden City, NY. 1975. 5.95. ISBN 0-385-00578-4. LC 74-9483.

DEEGAN, DOROTHY YOST. The Stereotype of The Single Woman in American Novels; A Social Study with Implications for the Education of Women. Octagon Books, NY. 1951. 252p. LC 69-16754.

DE FALCO, JOSEPH. The Hero in Hemingway's Short Stories. Univ. of Pittsburgh Pr., PA. 1963. 226p.

DE GRAZIA, EDWARD. Censorship Landmarks. Bowker. 1969. 23.00Hdbdg. ISBN 0-8352-0207-0. LC 71-79424.

DE JOVINE, F. ANTHONY. The Young Hero in American Fiction; A Motif for Teaching Literature. Appleton, Div. Meredith, NY. 1971. 176p. 4.95.

DEKKER, GEORGE. James Fenimore Cooper; The American Scott. Barnes and Noble, NY. 1967.

DEKKER, GEORGE, and John P. McWilliams, Eds. Fenimore Cooper; The Critical Heritage. Routledge and Kegan Paul, Boston, MA. 1973. 173p. 15.50Hdbd. ISBN 0-7100-7635-5.

DE MOTT, ROBERT J., and Sanford E. Marovitz, Eds. Artful Thunder; Versions of the Romantic Tradition in American Literature, in Honor of Howard P. Vincent. Kent State Univ. Pr., Kent, OH. 1975. 312p. 12.50Hdbd. ISBN 0-87338-172-6. LC 74-21886.

DE MILLE, GEORGE E. Literary Criticism in America; A Preliminary Survey. Russell and Russell, NY. 1931(1967). 288p. 10.00Hdbd. ISBN 0-8462-0812-1. LC 66-24685.

DEODENE, FRANK, and William P. French. Black American Fiction since 1952; A Preliminary Checklist. Chatham Bookseller, Chatham, NJ. 1970. 25p. LC 78-96384.

DENNY, MARGARET and William H. Gilman, Eds. The American Writer and the European Tradition. Haskell House, NY. 1950(1968). 192p. LC 68-24936.

DERLETH, AUGUST. Concord Rebel; A Life of Henry David Thoreau. Chilton Book, NY. 1962. 213p. LC 62-15166.

DERLETH, AUGUST, and Donald Wandrei. H.P. Lovecraft; Selected Letters; 1929-1931. Arkham, Sauk City, WI. 1971. 451p.

DERLETH, AUGUST. Some Notes on H.P. Lovecraft. Folcroft, Folcroft, PA. 1959(1973). 5.50. LC 73-16283.

DERLETH, AUGUST. Writing Fiction. Greenwood Pr., Westport, CT. 1946 (1971) 201p. ISBN 8371-4694-1.

DERRICK, CHRISTOPHER. The Writings of Novels. The Writer, Boston, MA. 1969. 192p. ISBN 87116-014-5. LC 70-79488.

DETWEILER, ROBERT. Four Spiritual Crises in Mid-Century American Fiction. Univ. of Florida Pr., Gainesville, FL. 1963(1968)53p. LC 64-63316.

DE VOTO, BERNARD, Ed. The Portable Mark Twain. Viking, NY. 1946 (1971). 10.00Hdbd. ISBN 670-73341-5. 4.25Pa. ISBN 670-01020-0. LC 46-6686.

DE VOTO, BERNARD. The World of Fiction. Houghton Mifflin, Boston, MA. 1950. 299p. 5.95. ISBN 0-87116-016-1.

DIAMOND, ARLYN, and Lee R. Edwards. The Authority of Experience; Essays in Feminist Criticism. Univ. of Mass. Pr., Amherst, MA. 1977. 15.00Hdbd. ISBN 0-87023-220-7. LC 76-8755.

DICK, BERNARD F. The Apostate Angel;A Critical Study of Gore Vidal. Random House, NY. 1974. 6.95Hdbd. ISBN 0-394-48108-9. LC 73-20533.

DICKENS, ROBERT. Thoreau;The Complete Individualist. Exposition Pr., NY. 1974. 122p. 6.00. ISBN 0-682-47863-6. LC 73-91092.

DICKINSON, A. T., JR. American Historical Fiction;Second Edition. Scarecrow Pr., NY. 1963. 364p. LC 58-7803.

DICKINSON, DONALD C. A Bio-Bibliography of Langston Hughes;1902-1967. Shoe String Pr. 1972. 14.00Hdbd. ISBN 0-208-01269-9. LC 70-181877.

DICKINSON, H. T., Ed. Politics and Literature in the Eighteenth Century. Rowman. 1974. 7.75Hdbd. ISBN 0-87471-405-2. 4.00Pa. ISBN 0-87471-400-1.

DILLINGHAM, WILLIAM B. An Artist in the Rigging;The Early Work of Herman Melville. Univ. of Georgia Pr., Athens, GA. 1972. 177p. 8.50 Hdbd. ISBN 0-8203-0276-7.

DILLON, JOHN MILTON. Edgar Allan Poe;His Genius and Character. Haskell House, NY. 1911(1974). 9.95 Hdbd. ISBN 0-8383-2069-4. LC 74-3420.

DINGLE, HERBERT. Science and Literary Criticism. Folcroft, Folcroft, PA. 1949(1974). 12.50Hdbd. ISBN 0-8414-3799-8. LC 74-16039.

DJWA, SANDRA. E.J. Pratt;The Evolutionary Vision. McGill-Queens Univ. Pr., Canada. 1974. 2.35Pa. ISBN 0-7735-0199-1.

DOIG, IVAN, Comp. The Streets We Have Come Down;Literature of the City. Hayden, Rochelle Park, NJ. 1975. 214p. 4.25Pa. ISBN 0-8104-5823-3. LC 74-17213.

DOLAN, PAUL J. Of War and War's Alarms;Fiction and Politics in the Modern World. Free Pr., NY. 1975 (1976). 192p. 9.95Hdbs. ISBN 0-02-907500-9. LC 75-11287.

DONALDSON, NORMAN. In Search of Dr. Thorndyke;The Story of R. Austin Freeman's Great Scientific Investigator and His Creator. Bowling Green Univ. Pr., Bowling Green, OH. 1971. 288p. 3.00Pa. LC 72-147819.

DONALDSON, SCOTT. By Force of Will;The Life and Art of Ernest Hemingway. Viking Pr., NY. 1977. 12.50 Hdbd. ISBN 0-670-19824-2. LC 76-18306.

DONOGHUE, DENIS. Thieves of Fire. Oxford Univ. Pr., NY. 1974. 139p. 6.95Hdbd. ISBN 0-19-519775-5. LC 74-75763.

DONOHUE, AGNESS MC NEILL, Ed. A Casebook on the Hawthorne Question. Thomas Y. Crowell, NY. 1969. 3.95Pa. ISBN 0-690-17851-4.

DONOVAN, JOSEPHINE, Ed. Feminist Literary Criticism;Explorations in Theory. Univ. Pr. of Kentucky, Lexington, KY. 1975. 81p. 4.00Pa. ISBN 0-8131-1334-2. LC 75-12081.

DOUGLAS, ANN. The Feminization of American Culture. Knopf, NY. 15.00Hdbd. ISBN 0-394-40532-3.

DOUBLEDAY, NEAL FRANK. Variety of Attempt;British and American Fiction in the Early Nineteenth Century. Univ. of Nebraska Pr., Lincoln, NB. 1976. 12.95Hdbd. ISBN 0-8032-0876-6. LC 75-38057.

DOWNS, ROBERT B., Ed. First Freedom;Liberty and Justice in the World of Books and Reading. Ala. 1960. 9.95Hdbd. ISBN 0-8389-0030-5. LC 59-13653.

DOYLE, PAUL A. Guide to Basic Information Sources in English Literature. Halsted Pr., NY. 1976. 10.95 Hdbd. ISBN 0-470-15011-4. LC 75-43260.

DRAKEFORD, JOHN W., and Jack Hamm. Pornography;The Sexual Mirage. Nelson. 1973. 6.95Hdbd. ISBN 0-8407-5051-X. 2.95Pa. ISBN 0-8407-5559-7.

DRYDEN, EDGAR A. Nathaniel Hawthorne;The Poetics of Enchantment. Cornell Univ. Pr., Ithaca, NY. 1977. 10.00Hdbd. ISBN 0-8014-1028-2. LC 76-28010.

DUCKETT, MARGARET. Mark Twain and Bret Harte. Univ. of Oklahoma Pr., Norman, OK. 1964. 365p. LC 64-21709.

DUDLEY, EDWARD, and Maxmillian E. Novak, Eds. The Wild Man Within; An Image in Western Thought from the Renaissance to Romanticism. Univ. of Pittsburgh Pr., PA. 1972. 11.95Hdbd. ISBN 0-8229-3246-6. LC 72-77191.

DUFFEY, BERNARD. The Chicago Renaissance in American Letters; A Critical History. Michigan State Univ. Pr. 1956. 285p. LC 54-11828.

DUNCAN, HUGH DALZIEL. Language and Literature in Society;A Sociological Essay on Theory and Method in the Interpretation of Linguistic Symbols;With a Bibliographical Guide to the Sociology of Literature. Bedminster Pr., NY. 1953(1961)262p. 6.50Hdbd. ISBN 0-87087-005-X.

DUNCAN, JEFFREY L. The Power and Form of Emerson's Thought. Univ. Pr. of Virginia, Charlottesville, VA. 1973. 105p. 6.75Hdbd. ISBN 0-8139-0510-9. LC 73-85043.

DUNLAP, GEORGE ARTHUR. The City in the American Novel;1789-1900;A Study of American Novels Portraying Contemporary Conditions in New York, Philadelphia and Boston. Russell, NY. 1934(1965)LC 65-17889.

DUNNING, STEPHEN. Teaching Literature to Adolescents;Short Stories. Scott, Foresman, Glenview, IL. 1968. 161p. 2.25Pa.

DUPEE, FREDERICK W. Henry James. Sloane, 1951. 5.75Hdbd. Dell, NY. 1.95Pa.

DUTTON, G., Ed. Literature of Australia. Peter Smith. 5.00Hdbd. ISBN 0-8446-2017-3.

DUTTON, GEOFFREY. Patrick White. Folcroft, Folcroft, PA. 1962. 7.50 Hdbd. ISBN 0-8414-3749-1. LC 74-9788.

DYCE, J.R. Patrick White As Playwright. Univ. of Queensland Pr. 11.10Hdbd. ISBN 0-7022-0854-X.

E

EAGLETON, TERENCE. Criticism and Ideology;A Study in Marxist Literary Theory. Humanities Pr., Atlantic Highlands, NJ. 1976. 13.00Hdbd. ISBN 0-391-00664-9. LC 76-40251.

EAKIN, PAUL JOHN. The New England Girl;Cultural Ideals in Hawthorne, Stowe, Howells, and James. Univ. of Georgia Pr., Athens, GA. 1976. 252 p. 11.00Hdbd. ISBN 0-8203-0398-4. LC 74-18583.

EARLY, JAMES. The Making of Go Down, Moses. Southern Methodist Univ. Pr., Dallas, TX. 1972. 127p. 5.95 ISBN 0-87074-003-2. LC 72-80404.

EARNEST, ERNEST. The Single Vision;The Alienation of American Intellectuals. NY Univ. Pr., NY. 1970. 241 p. Hdbd. ISBN 8147-0459-X. Pa. ISBN 8147-0460-3. LC 78-116132.

EASTMAN, MAX. Artists in Uniform. Octagon. 1972. 12.00Hdbd. ISBN 0-374-92453-8.

EASTMAN, MAX. The Literary Mind;Its Place in an Age of Science. Octagon, NY. 1931(1969). 343p. LC 72-75992.

EBLE, KENNETH E., Ed. Howells; A Century of Criticism. Southern Methodist Univ. Pr., Dallas, TX. 1962. 247p. 5.95. ISBN 0-87074-050-4.

EBLE, KENNETH E., Ed. F. Scott Fitzgerald;A Collection of Criticism. McGraw-Hill, NY. 1973. 152p. 1.95 Pa.

ECKLEY, WILTON. Harriette Arnow. Twayne, NY. 1974. 138p. 6.50Hdbd. ISBN 0-8057-0023-4. LC 73-18406.

ECKLEY, WILTON. T. S. Stribling. Twayne, Boston, MA. 1975. 127p. 6.95 Hdbd. ISBN 0-8057-7151-4. LC 75-1096.

ECKMAN, FERN MARJA. The Furious Passage of James Baldwin. M. Evans, NY. 1966. 254p. LC 66-11165.

EDEL, LEON. The Modern Psychological Novel. Grosset and Dunlap, NY 1955. 210p. 5.00. ISBN 0-8446-2020-3.

EDEL, LEON, Ed. Henry James;The Future of the Novel;Essays on the Art of Fiction. Vintage, NY. 1956. 286p.

EDEL, LEON. Henry James;The Untried Years. J. B. Lippincott, NY. 1953. 350p. LC 53-5421.

EDEL, LEON, Ed. Letters;Henry James. Harvard Univ. Pr., Cambridge,

EDEL, LEON. Henry James;The Conquest of London. J. B. Lippincott;NY 1962. 465p. LC 53-5421.

EDEL, LEON. Henry James;The Middle Years. J. B. Lippincott, NY. 1962. 408p. LC 53-5421.

EDEL, LEON, Ed. Henry James;A Collection of Critical Essays. Prentice-Hall, Englewood Cliffs, NJ. 1963. 186p. 5.95. ISBN 0-13-509349-X.

EDEL, LEON. Henry James;The Treacherous Years. J. B. Lippincott, NY. 1969. 381p. LC 53-5421.

EDEL, LEON. Henry James;The Master. J. B. Lippincott, NY. 591p. ISBN 0-397-00733-7. LC 53-5421.

EDEL, LEON. The Modern Psychological Novel. Grosset and Dunlap, NY. 1955. 210p. 5.00. ISBN 0-8446-2020-3.

EDGAR, PELHAM. Henry James;Man and Author. Russell and Russell, NY. 1927(1964). 251p. 11.00Hdbd. ISBN 0-8462-0416-9.

EDMISTON, SUSAN, and Linda D. Cirino. Literary New York;A History and Guide. Houghton, Mifflin, Boston, MA. 1976. 12.95Hdbd. 6.95Pa.

EDWARDS, CLIFFORD D. Conrad Richter's Ohio Trilogy;Its Ideas, Themes, and Relationship to Literary Tradition. Mouton, The Hague, Netherlands. 1970. 210p. LC 79-85902.

EDWARDS, JOHN. A Preliminary Checklist of the Writings of Ezra Pound, Especially his Contributions to Periodicals. Folcroft Lib. Eds., Folcroft, PA. 1974. 8.50Hdbd. ISBN 0-8414-3915-X. LC 74-22321.

EGAN, MICHAEL. Henry James;The Ibsen Years. Barnes and Noble, NY. 1973. 8.50Hdbd. ISBN 0-06-491910-2.

EGOFF, SHEILA A. The Republic of Childhood;A Critical Guide to Canadian Children's Literature in English. Oxford Univ. Pr., NY. 1975. 335p. 10.95Pa. ISBN 0-19-540231-6. LC 75-329954.

EGRI, LAJOS. The Art of Creative Writing. Citadel Pr., NY. 1965. 224p. LC 65-16192.

EICHELBERGER, CLAYTON L. Published Comment on William Dean Howells through 1920;A Research Bibliography. G. K. Hall, Boston, MA. 1976. 23.00Hdbd. ISBN 0-8161-1078-6. LC 76-2030.

ELDER, MARJORIE J. Nathaniel Hawthorne;Transcendental Symbolist. Ohio Univ. Pr., Akron, OH. 1969. 8.00 Hdbd. 2.75Pa. ISBN 0-8214-0051-7. LC 69-18476.

ELGIN, SUZETTE HADEN. Pouring Down Words. Prentice-Hall, Englewood, NJ. 1975. 233p. 5.95Pa. ISBN 0-13-686857. LC 74-22139.

ELIAS, ROBERT H., Ed. Letters of Theodore Dreiser;A Selection;Volumes 1-3. Univ. of Pennsylvania Pr., Philadelphia, PA. 1959. 389p. Vol. 1. 759p. Vol. 2. 1067p. Vol. 3. LC 58-8203.

ELIAS, ROBERT H. Theodore Dreiser;Apostle of Nature. Knopf, NY. 1949(1970). 359p. 12.50Hdbd. 3.45Pa. ISBN 0-8014-0603-X.

ENCYCLOPEDIA of World Literature in the 20th Century. Ungar, NY. 1975. 48.00. ISBN 0-8044-3091-8.

ELIOT, THOMAS STEARNS. What is a Classic? Haskell House, NY. 1944 (1974) 7.95Hdbd. ISBN 0-8383-2059-7. LC 74-4089.

ELKINS, A.C., JR., Ed. The Romantic Movement; Bibliography; 1936-1970; A Master Cumulation from ELH, Philological Quarterly, and English Notes. Pierian Pr., Ann Arbor, MI. 1973. 3289p. 160.00Hdbd. ISBN 0-87650-025-4. LC 77-172773.

ELLIOTT, ROBERT C. Power of Satire; Magic, Ritual, Art. Princeton Univ. Pr., Princeton, NJ. 1960. 3.95 Pa. ISBN 0-691-01276-8, 61.

ELLMANN, MARY. Thinking About Women. Harcourt, NY. 1968. 2.65Pa.

ELLMANN, RICHARD. Golden Codgers; Biographical Speculations. Oxford Univ. Pr., NY. 1973. 193p. 7.95 Hdbd. ISBN 0-19-211827-7. LC 73-86067.

EMANUAL, JAMES A. Langston Hughes. Twayne. 1967. 7.50Hdbd. ISBN 0-8057-0388-8.

EMERSON, EVERETT, Ed. American Literature; 1764-1789; The Revolutionary Years. Univ. of Wisconsin Pr., Madison, WI. 1977. 15.00Hdbd. ISBN 0-299-07270-3. LC 75-32073.

EMRICH, WILHELM. Literary Revolution and Modern Society and Other Essays. Ungar. 1971. 7.50Hdbd. LC 70-125963.

ENGEL, MONROE, Ed. Uses of Literature. Harvard Univ. Pr., Cambridge, MA. 1973. 290p. 12.50Hdbd. LC 73-82627.

ENKVIST, NILS E., et al. Linguistics and Style. Oxford Univ. Pr., NY. 1964. 4.50Pa. ISBN 0-19-437016-X.

ENSOR, ALLISON. Mark Twain and the Bible. Univ. of Kentucky Pr., Lxington, KY. 1969. 130p. 4.75Pa. ISBN 0-8131-1181-1.

ENZENSBERGER, HANS. The Consciousness Industry; On Literature, Politics and the Media. Seabury Pr. NY. 1974. 184p. 6.95Hdbd. ISBN 0-8164-9185-2. LC 73-17873.

ERICSON, EDWARD E., JR., and Georg B. TENNYSON, Eds. Religion and Modern Literature; An Anthology. Eerdmans, Grand Rapids. 1974. 4.95Pa. LC 74-13237.

ERNST, M.L., and A. Lindey. The Censor Marches On. DaCapo. 1971. 19.50Hdbd. ISBN 0-306-70295-9. LC 73-164512.

ERNST, M.L., and W. Seagle. To the Pure; A Study of Obscenity and the Censor. Kraus. 1928. 17.00Hdbd. ISBN 0-527-2765-2. LC 28-30424.

ERNST, MORRIS L., and Alan U. Schwartz. Censorship. Macmillan, NY. 1964. 6.95.

ERSKINE, JOHN. Leading American Novelists. Books for Libraries Pr., Freeport, NY. 1910(1966). 378p. LC 67-22091.

ERSKINE, JOHN. The Literary Discipline. Books for Libraries Pr., Freeport, NY. 1923(1969). 231p. ISBN 8369-1252-8. LC 74-90635.

ETULAIN, RICHARD W., and Michael T. Marsden. The Popular Western; Essays Toward a Definition. Bowling Green Univ. Pr., Bowling

Green, OH. 1974. 111p. 2.00Pa.

ETULAIN, RICHARD W. Western American Literature; A Bibliography of Interpretive Books and Articles. Dakota Pr., Vermillion, SD. 1972. 137p. 4.00Pa. ISBN 0-88249-010-9. LC 72-78188.

EVERSON, IDA GERTRUDE. George Henry Calvert; American Literary Pioneer. Columbia Univ. Pr., NY. 1944. 330p. 13.00Hdbd. ISBN 0-374-92644-1.

FABRE, MICHEL. The Unfinished Quest of Richard Wright. Wm. Morrow and Co., NY. 1973. 652p. Hdbd. ISBN 0-688-00163-7. Pa. ISBN 0-688-05163-4. LC 73-7227.

FADIMAN, REGINA K. Faulkner's Light in August. Univ. Pr. of Virginia. Charlottesville, VA. 1975. 231p. 12.50Hdbd. ISBN 0-8139-0584-2. LC 74-8242.

FAGIN, N. BRYLLION. The Histrionic Mr. Poe. Johns Hopkins Pr., Baltimore, MD. 1949(1967). 289p. 10.00 Hdbd. ISBN 0-8018-0193-1.

FALK, ROBERT, Ed. Literature and Ideas in America;Essays in Memory of Harry Hayden Clark. Ohio Univ. Pr., Athens, OH. 1975. 243p. 10.00Hdbd. ISBN 0-8214-0180-7. LC 74-27708.

FALK, ROBERT. The Victorian Mode in American Fiction;1865-1885. Michigan St. Univ. Pr., East Lansing, MI. 1964(1965). 188p. LC 64-21643.

FALKNER, MURRY C. The Falkners of Mississippi;A Memoir. Louisiana St. Univ. Pr., Baton Rouge, LA. 1967. 205p. 5.95. LC 67-24417.

FANNING, MICHAEL. France and Sherwood Anderson;Paris Notebook; 1921. Louisiana St. Univ. Pr., Baton Rouge, LA. 1976. 7.95Hdbd. ISBN 0-8071-0176-1. LC 74-27189.

FARR, FINIS. Margaret Mitchell of Atlanta. Avon, NY. 1965(1974). 283p. 1.75Pa.

FASS, BARBARA. La Belle Dame sans Merci and the Aesthetics of Rommanticism. Wayne St. Univ. Pr., Detroit, MI. 1974. 311p. 15.95Hdbd. ISBN 0-8143-1509-7. LC 73-8365.

FATOUT, PAUL. Mark Twain on the Lecture Circuit. Indiana Univ. Pr., Bloomington, IN. 1960(1966). 321p. 5.00Hdbd. ISBN 0-8446-1177-8. 2.85 Pa.

FAULKNER, JOHN. My Brother Bill; An Affectionate Reminiscence. Trident Pr., NY. 1963. 277p. LC 63-13769.

FAUST, BERTHA. Hawthorne's Contemporaneous Reputation;A Study of Literary Opinion in American and England;1828-1864. Octagon, NY. 1968. 7.50Hdbd. ISBN 0-374-92717-0.

FEIDELSON, CHARLES, JR., and Paul Brodtkorb, Jr., Eds. Interpretations of American Literature.

Oxford Univ.Pr.,NY.1959(1967)386p. LC 59-9818.

FEIDELSON,CHARLES,JR. Symbolism and American Literature. Univ. of Chicago Pr., Chicago,IL.1953. 355p.6.00.ISBN 0-226-24023-1.

FEIED,FREDERICK.No Pie in the Sky;The Hobo as American Cultural Hero in the Works of Jack London, John Dos Passos,and Jack Kerouac. Citadel Pr.,NY.1964.95p.LC 64-21892.

FEINBERG,LEONARD.Introduction to Satire.Iowa St.Univ.Pr.,Ames, IA.1967.293p.6.95Hdbd.ISBN 0-8138-1379-1.3.50Pa.ISBN 0-8138-1378-6.

FEINBERG,LEONARD.The Satirist; His Temperament, Motivation, and Influence.Iowa St.Univ.Pr.,Ames, IA.1963.370p.5.95.ISBN 0-8138-1380-8.

FENNIMORE,KEITH J. Booth Tarkington. Twayne,NY.1974.167p.ISBN 0-8057-0715-8.LC 73-16403.

FENTON,CHARLES A. The Apprenticeship of Ernest Hemingway;The Early Years.Octagon,NY.1954(1975) 302p.13.00Hdbd.ISBN 0-374-92737-5.LC 75-11784.

FERGUSON,JOHN DE LANCEY.American Literature in Spain.AMS Pr. NY.1916(1966).267p.9.00Hdbd.ISBN 0-404-02377-0.

FERGUSON,JOHN DE LANCEY.Mark Twain;Man and Legend.Russell and Russell,NY.1943(1965).352p.LC 66-15430.

FETHERLING,DOUG.The Five Lives of Ben Hecht.Lester and Orpen. 1977.10.00Hdbd.ISBN 0-919630-85-5.

FICK,LEONARD J.The Light Beyond;A Study of Hawthorne's Theology. Folcroft Lib.,Folcroft,PA.1955(1974).15.00Hdbd.LC 74-8995.

FIEDLER,LESLIE.The Collected Essays of Leslie Fiedler;Vol.II.Stein and Day,NY.1971.560p.LC 76-122420.

FIEDLER,LESLIE A. Love and Death in the American Novel.Stein and Day,NY.Rev.Ed.1966(1973)512p.LC 66-14948.

FIEDLER,LESLIE A. The Return of the Vanishing American.Stein and Day,NY.1968.192p.LC 68-15433.

FIEDLER,LESLIE A. Waiting for the End.Stein and Day,NY.1964.256p. LC 64-13673.

FIELD,ANDREW.Nabokov;A Bibliography.McGraw-Hill,NY.1973.249p. 15.00Hdbd.ISBN 0-07-02680-5.LC 72-10473.

FIELD,ELINOR WHITNEY,Ed. Horn Book Reflections on Children's Books and Reading;Selected from Eighteen Years of "The Horn Book Magazine"-1949-1966.Horn Book,Inc., Boston,MA.1969.367p.3.50Pa.

FIELD,LESLIE A.,and Joyce W. Field,Eds.Bernard Malamud and the Critics.New York Univ.Pr.,NY. Univ.of London Pr.,London.1970. 353p.10.00Hdbd.3.50Pa.ISBN 0-8147-2552-X.

FIELD,LESLIE A.,and Joyce W. Field,Eds.Bernard Malamud;A Collection of Critical Essays.Prentice-Hall,Englewood Cliffs,NJ.1975.179p.

6.95Hdbd. ISBN 0-13-548032-9. LC 74-23353. 2.95Pa. ISBN 0-13-548024-8.

FIELD, LESLIE A. Ed. Thomas Wolfe;Three Decades of Criticism. New York Univ. Pr., NY. 1968. 304p. 9.95 Hdbd. 2.45Pa. ISBN 0-8147-0147-7. LC 68-13024.

FIELD, LOUISE MAUNSELL. Ellen Glasgow;Novelist of the Old and the New South;An Appreciation. Folcroft Lib. Editions, Folcroft, PA. 1923(1974) 5.50. LC 74-11118.

FINKELSTEIN, DOROTHEE METLITSKY. Melville's Orienda. Octagon, NY. 1971. 317p.

FIRKINS, OSCAR W. William Dean Howells;A Study. Harvard Univ. Pr., Cambridge, MA. 1924(1963). 356p. 8.50 Hdbd. ISBN 0-8462-0346-4.

FIRMAGE, GEORGE JAMES. A Check-list of the Published Writings of Gertrude Stein. Folcroft, Folcroft, PA. 1974. 4.50Pa. LC 74-16361.

FISCHER, JOHN, and Robert B. Silvers, Eds. Writing in America. Rutgers Univ. Pr., New Brunswick, NJ. 1960. 178p. LC 60-9692.

FISHER, MARGERY TURNER. Who's Who in Children's Books. Holt, Rinehart, NY. 1975. 19.95hdbd. ISBN 0-03-015091-4. LC 75-5463.

FISKE, MARJORIE. Book Selection and Censorship;A Study of School and Public Libraries in California. Univ. of Calif. Pr. 1968. 9.00Hdbd. ISBN 0-520-00418-3.

FITZ GERALD, GREGORY. Modern Satiric Stories;The Impropriety Principle. Scott F. 1971. 5.95Pa. ISBN 0-673-05881-6.

FLETCHER, RICHARD M. Edgar Allen Poe, 1809-1849;Criticism and Interpretation. Humanities Pr. 13.75 Pa.

FLETCHER, RICHARD M. The Stylistic Development of Edgar Allan Poe. Mouton, The Hague. 1973.192p. LC 72-94467.

FLIBBERT, JOSEPH. Melville and the Art of Burlesque. Rodopi, Amsterdam. 1974. 165p. ISBN 9-06-203268-0. LC 74-80748.

FLORY, CLAUDE REHERD. Economic Criticism in American Fiction; 1792 to 1900. Russell and Russell, NY. 1937. 261p. LC 68-25075.

FOERSTER, NORMAN. Image of America;Our Literature from Puritanism to the Space Age. Univ. of Notre Dame Pr., Notre Dame, IN. 1934 (1962). 152p. 2.25Pa. ISBN 0-268-00127-8.

FOERSTER, NORMAN. The Intellectual Heritage of Thoreau. Folcroft, Folcroft, PA. 1974. 5.00. LC 74-19264.

FOERSTER, NORMAN, Ed. The Reinterpretation of American Literature;Some Contributions Toward the Understanding of its Historical Development. Russell and Russell, NY. 1928(1959). 213p. LC 59-6876.

FOGLE, RICHARD HARTER. Hawthorne's Fiction;The Light and The Dark. Univ. of Oklahoma Pr., Norman. 1964. 5.50. ISBN 0-8061-0256-X.

FOGLE, RICHARD HARTER. Melville's Shorter Tales. Univ. of Georgia Pr., Norman, OK. 1960. 150p. 4.95. ISBN 0-8061-0451-1.

FOGLE, RICHARD HARTER. The Permanent Pleasure; Essays on Classics of Romanticism. Univ. of Georgia Pr., Athens, GA. 1974. 225p. 8.50Hdbd. ISBN 0-8203-0311-9. LC 72-86784.

FOGLE, RICHARD HARTER, Comp. Romantic Poets and Prose Writers. AHM Pub. 1967. 2.95Pa. ISBN 0-88295-513-6. LC 66-29743.

FOLSOM, JAMES K. The American Western Novel. College & Univ. Pr., New Haven, CT. 224p.

FOLSOM, JAMES K. Man's Accidents and God's Purposes; Multiplicity in Hawthorne's Fiction. College and Univ. Pr., New Haven, CT. 1963. 6.00 Hdbd. 1.95Pa.

FORD, FORD MADOX. It Was the Nightingale. Octagon, NY. 1933(1975) 381 p. 13.50Hdbd. ISBN 0-374-92782-0. LC 75-5832.

FORD, FORD MADOX. Portraits From Life; Memories and Criticisms of Henry James, Joseph Conrad, Thomas Hardy, H. G. Wells, Stephen Crane, D. H. Lawrence, John Galsworthy, Ivan Turgenev, W. H. Hudson, Theodore Dreiser, Algernon Charles Swinburne. Greenwood Pr., Westport, CT. 1937(1974). 227p. 13.50Hdbd. ISBN 0-8371-7405-8. LC 74-2553.

FORD, HUGH. Published in Paris; American and British Writers, Printers, and Publishers in Paris, 1920-1939. Macmillan, NY. 1975. 14.95Hdbd. ISBN 0-02-539600- . LC 74-14584.

FORD, MARGARET PATRICIA, and Suzanne Kincaid. Who's Who in Faulkner. Louisiana State Univ. Pr., Baton Rouge, LA. 1963. 118p. 3.75, 1.75 Pa. ISBN 0-8071-0449-3.

FORD, NICK AARON. The Contemporary Negro Novel; A Study in Race Relations. McGrath, College Park, MD. 1936(1968). 108p. 9.50Hdbd. ISBN 0-8434-0027-7. LC 77-632.

FORST, LILIAN R. Romanticism in Perspective. Humanities. 1970. 12.00 Hdbd. ISBN 0-396-00003-9.

FORSYTHE, ROBERT STANLEY. Bernard DeVoto; A New Force in American Letters. Folcroft, Folcroft, PA. 1928(1974). 5.00. LC 74-17306.

FOSSUM, ROBERT H. Hawthorne's Inviolable Circle; The Problem of Time. Everett/Edwards, Deland, FL. 1972. 12.00Hdbd. LC 74-172791.

FOSTER, EDWARD HALSEY. Catharine Maria Sedgwick. Twayne, NY. 1973(1974). 5.50. ISBN 0-8057-0658-5. LC 73-14674.

FOSTER, EDWARD HALSEY. The Civilized Wilderness; Backgrounds in American Romantic Literature, 1817-1860. Free Pr., NY. 1975. 220p. 11.95Hdbd. ISBN 0-02-910350-9. LC 74-33091.

FOSTER, EDWARD. Mary E. Wilkins Freeman. Hendricks House, NY. 1956. 229p. 6.00.

FOSTER, JEANNETTE H. Sex Variant Women in Literature. Vantage, NY. 1956.

FOSTER, RICHARD. The New Romantics;A Reappraisal of the New Criticism. Kennikat Pr., Port Washington, NY.1962(1973). 238p. ISBN 0-8046-1696-5. LC 72-85288.

FOSTER, RICHARD, Ed. Six American Novelists of the Nineteenth Century;An Introduction. Univ. of Minnesota Pr., Minneapolis, MN. 1960(1968) 270p. LC 68-17305.

FOSTER-HARRIS, WILLIAM. The Basic Formulas of Fiction. Univ. of Oklahoma Pr., Norman, OK. 1944(1960).

FOWLER, DOUGLAS. Reading Nabakov. Cornell Univ. Pr., Ithaca, NY. 1974. 224p. 9.97Hdbd. ISBN 0-8014-0828-8. LC 73-20798.

FOWLER, ROGER. Essays on Style and Language;Linguistic and Critical Approaches to Literary Style. Humanities. 1970. 9.50Hdbd. 4.75Pa.

FOWLER, ROGER, Ed. Style and Structure in Literature;Essays in the New Stylistics. Cornell Univ. Pr., Ithaca, NY. 1975. 262p. 13.50Hdbd. ISBN 0-8014-0949-7. LC 74-24277.

FOWLIE, WALLACE, and Henry Miller. Letters of Henry Miller and Wallace Fowlie. Grove Pr., NY. 1975. 184p. 9.50Hdbd. ISBN 0-394-49737-6. LC 74-24859.

FOWLIE, WALLACE. Love in Literature;Studies in Symbolic Expression. Indiana Univ. Pr. 1965. 10.00Hdbd. ISBN 0-8369-2589-0. LC 70-37836. 1.65Pa. ISBN 0-253-20074-1. LC 65-11792.

FRAIBERG, LOUIS. Psychoanalysis and American Literary Criticism. Wayne State Univ. Pr., Detroit, MI. 1960. 263p. LC 59-11980.

FRANCHERE, RUTH. Jack London; The Pursuit of a Dream. Thomas Y. Crowell, NY. 1962. 264p. LC 62-16542.

FRANCHERE, RUTH. Stephen Crane;The Story of an American Writer. Thomas Y. Crowell, NY. 1961. 4.50. ISBN 0-690-77423-0.

FRANK, NEAL. Hawthorne's Early Tales;A Critical Study. Duke Univ. Pr., Durham, NC. 1972.

FRANKLIN, BENJAMIN. Anais Nin; A Bibliography. Kent State Univ. Pr. Kent, OH. 1973(1974). 115p. 6.50Hdbd. ISBN 0-87338-137-8. LC 72-619701.

FRANKLIN, H. BRUCE. Future Perfect;American Science Fiction of the Nineteenth Century. Oxford Univ. Pr. NY. 1966. 402p. LC 66-14475.

FRANKLIN, H. BRUCE. The Wake of the Gods;Melville's Mythology. Stanford Univ. Pr., Stanford, CA. 1963. 236p. 7.50Hdbd. ISBN 0-8047-0138-5. 2.95Pa.

FREEMAN, D.C. Linguistics and Literary Style. HR&W. 1970. 7.95Hdbd. ISBN 0-03-080800-6.

FREEMAN, JOHN. Herman Melville. Haskell House, NY. 1974. 11.95Hdbd. ISBN 0-8383-1733-2. LC 73-18099.

FRENCH, WARREN G., and Walter E. Kidd, Eds. American Winners of the Nobel Literary Prize. Univ. of Oklahoma Pr., Norman, OK. 1968. 248p. LC 67-24622.

FRENCH, WARREN, Ed. A Companion to The Grapes of Wrath. Augustus M. Kelley, Clifton. 1963(1972). 243p 10.00Hdbd. ISBN 0-678-03156-8.

FRENCH, WARREN, Ed. The Fifties; Fiction, Poetry, Drama. Everett/Edwards, Deland, FL. 1970. 316p. LC 73-125030.

FRENCH, WARREN, Ed. The Forties; Fiction, Poetry, Drama. Everett/Edwards, Deland, FL. 1969. 330p. LC 69-10440.

FRENCH, WARREN. John Steinbeck. Twayne, NY. 1961. 190p. 7.95Hdbd. ISBN 0-8057-0693-3. LC 74-16017. 2.45Pa.

FRENCH, WARREN. The Social Novel; At the End of an Era. Southern Illinois Univ. Pr., Carbondale, IL. 1966. 212p. LC 66-10056.

FRENCH, WARREN, Ed. The Twenties; Fiction, Poetry, Drama. Everett/Edwards, Deland, FL. 1975. 12.00Hdbd. ISBN 0-912112-05-0. LC 74-24534.

FRIEDERICH, WERNER P. Australia in Western Imaginative Prose Writings; 1600-1960. Univ. of North Carolina Pr. 1967. 7.50Hdbd. ISBN 0-8078-7040-4.

FRIEDMAN, LENEMAJA. Shirley Jackson. Twayne, Boston, MA. 1975. 182p. 7.95Hdbd. ISBN 0-8057-0402-7. LC 74-31244.

FRIEDMAN, MAURICE. Problematic Rebel; Melville, Dostoievsky, Kafka, Camus. Univ. of Chicago Pr. 1970. 3.95Pa. ISBN 0-226-26396-7.

FRIEDMAN, MELVIN J., Ed. The Added Dimension; The Art and Mind of Flannery O'Connor. Forham Univ. Pr., NY. 1966. 6.95Hdbd.

FRIEDMAN, MELVIN J. William Styron. Bowling Green Univ. Pr., Bowling Green, OH. 1974. 72p. 2.50Pa. ISBN 0-97972-071-9. LC 74-16889.

FRIEDMAN, NORMAN. Form and Meaning in Fiction. Univ. of Georgia Pr., Athens, GA. 1975. 420p. 14.00Hdbd. ISBN 0-8203-0357-7. LC 73-90843.

FROHOCK, W. M. The Novel of Violence in America. Southern Methodist Univ. Pr., Dallas, TX. 1950(1951). 238p. LC 57-14767.

FROHOCK, W. M. Strangers to this Ground; Cultural Diversity in Contemporary American Writing. Southern Methodist Univ. Pr., Dallas, TX. 1961. 180p. 4.50. LC 61-17183.

FRYE, NORTHROP. Anatomy of Criticism; Four Essays. Princeton Univ. Pr., Princeton, NJ. 1957. 383p. LC 56-8380.

FRYE, NORTHROP. The Critical Path; An Essay on the Social Context of Literary Criticism. Indiana Univ. Pr. Bloomington, IN. 1971. 174p. 5.95. ISBN 253-31568-9. LC 70-143246.

FRYE, NORTHROP. The Educated Imagination. Indiana Univ. Pr., Bloomington, IN. 1964. 156p. 4.50. LC 64-18815.

FRYE, NORTHROP. Myth and Symbol; Critical Approaches and Applications. Univ. of Nebraska Pr. 1963. 2.25 Pa. ISBN 0-8032-5065-7. LC 63-9960.

FRYE, NORTHROP. The Secular Scripture; A Study of the Structure of Romance. Harvard Univ. Pr., Cambridge, MA. 1976. 199p. 8.95Hdbd. ISBN 0-674-79675-6. LC 75-37627.

FRYE, NORTHROP. The Stubborn Structure; Essays on Criticism and Society. Cornell Univ. Pr., Ithaca, NY. 1970. 316p. 8.50Hdbd. ISBN 0-8014-0583-1. LC 73-127776.

FRYE, NORTHROP. The Well-Tempered Critic. Indiana Univ. Pr., Bloomington, IN. 1963. 160p. 4.50. LC 63-9716.

FULLER, EDMUND. Man in Modern Fiction; Some Minority Opinions on Contemporary American Writing. Random House, NY. 1949. 171p. LC 58-7764.

FURST, LILIAN R. Romanticism. Methuen, London. 1976. 84p. 3.50Pa. ISBN 0-416-83920-7. LC 76-378017.

FURST, LILIAN R. Romanticism in Perspective. Humanities. 1970. 12.00 Hdbd. ISBN 0-39-00003-9.

G

GADO, FRANK, Ed. First Person;Conversations on Writers and Writing with Glenway Wescott,John Dos Passos,Robert Penn Warren,John Updike,John Barth, Robert Coover. Union Coll. Pr., Schenectady, NY. 1973. 159p. 9.50Hdbd. ISBN 0-912756-03-9. 3.95Pa.ISBN 0-912756-04-7. LC 73-84601.

GAER, JOSEPH, Ed. Bret Harte;Bibliography and Biographical Data. Burt Franklin, NY. 1935(1968). 189p.

GAER, JOSEPH, Ed. Frank Norris(Benjamin Franklin Norris)Bibliography and Biographical Data. Folcroft, Folcroft, PA. 1934(1974). 9.95Hdbd. LC 74-16033.

GAER, JOSEPH, Ed. Upton Sinclair; Bibliography and Biographical Data. B. Franklin, NY. 1971. 54p. 12.50Hdbd. ISBN 0-8337-1262-4. LC 79-156117.

GALE, ROBERT L. The Caught Image;Figurative Language in the Fiction of Henry James. Univ. of North Carolina Pr., Chapel Hill, NC. 1964. 266p. Reprint Folcroft, Folcroft, PA. 1975. 20.00Hdbd. ISBN 0-8414-5342-X. LC 75-30855.

GALE, ROBERT L. Plots and Characters in the Fiction and Sketches of Nathaniel Hawthorne. Archon, Hamden, CT. 1968.

GALE, ROBERT L. Plots and Characters in the Fiction of Henry James. Archon, Hamden, CT. 1965. 207p. ISBN 0-208-00500-5.

GALLAGHER, EDWARD JOSEPH. Early Puritan Writers;A Reference Guide;William Bradford, John Cotton, Thomas Hooker, Edward Johnson, Richard Mather, Thomas Shepard. G. K. Hall, Boston, MA. 1976. 20.00Hdbd. ISBN 0-8161-1196-0. LC 76-2498.

GANZEL, DEWEY. Mark Twain Abroad;The Cruise of the "Quaker City". Univ. of Chicago Pr., Chicago, IL. 1968. 330p. 7.95Hdbd. ISBN 0-226-28145-0. LC 68-16691.

GARD, ROGER, Ed. Henry James;The Critical Heritage. Barnes and Noble, NY. 1968. 565p.

GARNETT, RICHARD. Life of Ralph Waldo Emerson. Haskell House, NY. 1974. 12.95Hdbd. ISBN 0-8383-1775-8. LC 73-21630.

GASTON, EDWIN W., JR. Conrad Richter. Twayne, NY. 1965. 176p. LC 65-13001.

GASTON, EDWIN W., JR. The Early Novel of the Southwest. Univ. of New Mexico Pr., Albequerque, NM. 1961. 318p. LC 61-11693.

GAYLE, ADDISON, JR. The Way of the New World;The Black Novel in America. Anchor Pr., Garden City, NY. 1975. 339p. 10.00Hdbd. ISBN 0-385-04103-9.3.50Pa. LC 74-9449.

GEISMAR, MAXWELL. Henry James and The Jacobites. Houghton Mifflin, Boston, MA. 1963. 463p.

GEISMAR, MAXWELL. The Last of the Provincials;The American Novel;1915-1925. Houghton Mifflin, Boston, MA. 1943. 404p. 7.50Hdbd. ISBN 0-395-07723-0.

GEISMAR, MAXWELL. Mark Twain; An American Prophet. Houghton Mifflin, Boston, MA. 1970. 564p. 10.00Hdbd. LC 71-108681.

GEISMAR, MAXWELL, Ed. Mark Twain and the Three R's;Race, Religion, Revolution-and Related Matters. Bobbs-Merrill, Indianapolis, IN. 1973. 260p. 8.50Hdbd. ISBN 0-672-51705-1. LC 72-9882.

GEISMAR, MAXWELL. Rebels and Ancestors;The American Novel;1800-1915. Houghton Mifflin, Boston, MA. 1953. 435p. LC 53-5730.

GEISMAR, MAXWELL. Writers in Crisis;The American Novel;1925-1940. Houghton Mifflin, Boston, MA. 1942. 308p. 6.95Hdbd. ISBN 0-395-07726-5.

GEIST, STANLEY. Herman Melville; The Tragic Vision and The Heroic Ideal. Octagon, NY. 1966. 76p.

GELFANT, BLANCHE HOUSMAN. The American City Novel. Univ. of Oklahoma Pr., Norman, OK. 1954. 289p. ISBN 8061-0293-4. LC 54-5936.

GELLENS, JAY, Ed. Twentieth Century Interpretations of A Farewell to Arms;A Collection of Critical Essays. Prentice-Hall, Englewood Cliffs, NY. 1970. 120p.

GERBER, JOHN C., Ed. Twentieth Century Interpretations of The Scarlet Letter. Prentice-Hall, Englewood Cliffs, NJ. 1968. 4.95. ISBN 0-13-791582-9.

GERBER, PHILIP L. Plots and Characters in the Fiction of Theodore Dreiser. Archon, Hamden, CT. 1976. 15.00Hdbd. LC 76-54792.

GERBER, PHILIP L. Theodore Dreiser. Twayne, NY. 1964. 220p.

GERBER, PHILIP L. Willa Cather. Twayne, NY. 1975. 187p. 7.50Hdbd. ISBN 0-8057-7155-7. LC 75-2287.

GERSTENBERGER, DONNA, and George Hendrick. The American Novel;1789-1959;A Checklist of Twentieth-Century Criticism. Alan Swallow, Denver, CO. 1961. 333p. 2.50Pa. LC 61-9356.

GERSTENBERGER, DONNA, and George Hendrick. The American Novel; A Checklist of Twentieth Century; Criticism on Novels Written Since 1789;Volume II:Criticism Written 1960-1968. Swallow Pr., Chicago, IL. 1970. 459p. 2.50Pa. LC 61-9356.

GIBSON, DONALD B. The Fiction of Stephen Crane. Southern Illinois Univ. Pr., Carbondale, IL. 1968.

GILBERTSON, CATHERINE. Harriet Beecher Stowe. Kennikat Pr., Port Washington, NY. 1937(1968). 330p. LC 67-27599.

GILKES, LILLIAN. Cora Crane; A Biography of Mrs. Stephen Crane. Indiana Univ. Pr., Bloomington, IN. 1960. 416p. LC 59-13548.

GILMAN, RICHARD. The Confusion of Realms. Random House, NY. 1963. 272p. LC 69-16444.

GINDIN, JAMES. Harvest of a Quiet Eye; The Novel of Compassion. Indiana Univ. Pr., Bloomington, IN. 1971. 370p. 13.95Hdbd. ISBN 253-32705-9. LC 75-135006.

GLECKNER, ROBERT, and Gerald Enscoe, Eds. Romanticism; Points of View. Wayne St. Univ. Pr. 1975. 5.95 Pa. ISBN 0-8143-1543-7. LC 75-4682.

GLEIM, WILLIAM S. The Meaning of Moby Dick. Russell and Russell, NY. 1938. 149p.

GLICK, WENDELL, Ed. The Recognition of Henry David Thoreau; Selected Criticism Since 1848. Univ. of Michigan Pr., Ann Arbor, MI. 1969.

GLICKSBERG, CHARLES. The Literature of Commitment. Bucknell Univ. Pr., Lewisburg, PA. 1975. 24.50Hdbd ISBN 0-8387-1685-7. LC 75-5148.

GLICKSBERG, CHARLES. The Literature of Nihilism. Bucknell Univ. Pr. Lewisburg, PA. 1975. 354p. 17.50Hdbd. ISBN 0-8387-1520-6. LC 74-203.

GLICKSBERG, CHARLES. Tragic Vision in Twentieth Century Literature. So. Ill. Univ. Pr. 1963. 6.95Hdbd. ISBN 0-8093-0091-5. LC 63-8904.

GLOSTER, HUGH M. Negro Voices in American Fiction. Univ. of North Carolina Pr., Chapel Hill, NC. 1948.

GOBLE, NEIL. Asimov Analyzed. Mirage Pr., Baltimore, MD. 1972. 174p. 5.95Hdbd. LC 73-169988.

GNAROWSKI, MICHAEL. Leonard Cohen; The Artist and His Critics. McGraw-Hill, NY. 1976. 169p. 11.95Hdbd. ISBN 0-07-082179-8. 4.95Pa. ISBN 0-07-082180-1. LC 76-383877.

GOHDES, CLARENCE. American Literature in Nineteenth Century England. Southern Illinois Univ. Pr., Carbondale, IL. 1944. 191p.

GOHDES, CLARENCE. Bibliographical Guide to the Study of the Literature of the U.S.A.; Third Edition. Duke Univ. Pr., Durham, NC. 1970. 134p. ISBN 0-8223-0234-9. LC 79-110576.

GOHDES, CLARENCE. Literature and Theater of the States and Regions of the U.S.A.; An Historical Bibliography. Duke Univ. Pr., Durham, NC. 1967. 276p. 10.00Hdbd. ISBN 0-404-02854-3. LC 66-30584.

GOING, WILLIAM THORNBURY. Essays on Alabama Literature. Univ. of Alabama Pr. 1975. 176p. 6.75Hdbd. ISBN 0-8173-7318-7. LC 73-22586.

GOLD, JOSEPH. William Faulkner; A Study in Humanism From Metaphor to Discourse. Univ. of Oklahoma Pr., Norman, OK. 1966. 205p. 5.95. ISBN 0-8061-0706-5.

GOLDBERG, ISAAC. The Man Mencken; A Biographical and Critical Survey. AMS Pr., NY. 1925(1968). 388p. LC 68-54271.

GOLDMAN, ARNOLD, Ed. Twentieth Century Interpretations of Absalom, Absalom!;A Collection of Critical Essays. Prentice-Hall, Englewood Cliffs, NJ. 1971. 120p.

GOLDMAN, SHERLI EVENS. Mary McCarthy;A Bibliography. Harcourt, NY. 1968. 80p. 4.50. ISBN 0-15-15775-7. LC 68-12574.

GOLDSMITH, DAVID H. Kurt Vonnegut;Fantasist of Fire and Ice. Popular Pr., Bowling Gr. Univ., Bowling Green, OH. 50p. 1.50Pa.

GOLDSTEIN, JEFFREY H., and Paul E. McGhee, Eds. The Psychology of Humor;Theoretical Perspectives and Empirical Issues. Academic, NY. 1972. 294p. 11.95Hdbd. ISBN 0-12-288950-9. LC 71-187246.

GOLDSTEIN, MICHAEL J., et al. Pornography and Sexual Deviance. Univ. of Calif. Pr. 1973. 7.95Hdbd. ISBN 0-520-02406-0. 2.45Pa. ISBN 0-520-02619-5.

GOLDSTONE, ADRIAN H., and John R. Payne. John Steinbeck;A Bibliographical Catalogue of the Adrian H. Goldstone Collection. Univ. of Texas, Austin, TX. 1974. 240p. 17.50Hdbd. LC 73-620234.

GOLDSHALK, WILLIAM LEIGH. In Quest of Cabell;Five Exploratory Essays. Revisionist Pr., NY. 1975. 97p. 34.95Hdbd. ISBN 0-87700-217-7. LC 74-50.

GOODE, JOHN, Ed. The Air of Reality;New Essays on Henry James. Methuen, London. 1972. 368p.

GOODMAN, PAUL. The Structure of Literature. Univ. of Chicago Pr., Chicago Pr., Chicago, IL. 1954. 280p. 2.45Pa. ISBN 0-226-30327-6.

GORDON, DAVID J. Literary Art and the Unconscious. Louisiana State Univ. Pr., Baton Rouge, LA. 1976. 10.95 Hdbd. ISBN 0-8071-0197-4. LC 27662.

GORDON, MICHAEL. Juvenile Delinquency in the American Novel;1905-1965;A Study in the Sociology of Literature. Bowling Green Univ. Pr., Bowling Green, OH. 1971. 145p.

GORDON, WILLIAM A. The Mind and Art of Henry Miller. Louisiana State Univ. Pr., Baton Rouge, LA. 1967. 232 p. LC 67-12215.

GORDON, WILLIAM A. Writer and Critic;A Correspondence with Henry Miller. Louisiana St. Univ. Pr., Baton Rouge, LA. 1968. 88p. LC 68-15427.

GORMAN, HERBERT. Hawthorne;A Study in Solitude. Biblo and Tannen, NY. 1966.

GOSSETT, LOUISE Y. Violence in Recent Southern Fiction. Duke Univ. Pr., Durham, NC. 1965(1966)207p. 2.75Pa. LC 65-13656.

GOTTESMAN, RONALD. The Literary Manuscripts of Upton Sinclair. Ohio State Univ. Pr., Columbus, OH. 1973. 470p. 12.50Hdbd. ISBN 0-8142-0169-5. LC 72-751.

GOTTESMAN, RONALD. Upton Sinclair;An Annotated Checklist. Kent State Univ. Pr., Kent, OH. 1973. 544p. 15.00Hdbd. ISBN 0-87338-114-9. LC 72-634010.

GOULD, JAMES A., and John J. Iorio

Love, Sex and Identity. Boyd and Fraser. 1972. 3.95Pa. ISBN 0-87835-033-0. LC 78-176093.

GOVE, PHILIP BABCOCK. The Imaginary Voyage in Prose Fiction. Arno Pr., NY. 1974. 445p. 25.00Hdbd. ISBN 0-405-06328-8. LC 74-15972.

GRAHAM, GEORGE KENNETH. Henry James;The Drama of Fulfilment. an Approach to the Novels. Clarendon Pr. 1975. 234p. 18.25Hdbd. ISBN 0-19-812058-3. LC 75-322597.

GRAHAM, JOHN, Comp. The Merrill Studies in A Farewell to Arms. Merrill, Columbus, OH. 1971. 105p.

GRAHAM, SHEILAH. The Real F.Scott Fitzgerald;Thirty-Five Years Later. Warner Books, NY. 1976. 311p. LC 74-18880.

GRANT, DAMIAN. Realism. Barnes and Noble, NY. 1970. 2.75Pa. ISBN 0-416-17820-0.

GRAVES, ROBERT, and Alan Hodge. The Reader Over Your Shoulder;A Handbook for Writers of English Prose. Collier, NY. 1966. 446p.

GRAY, GENNISON. Style;The Problem and Its Solution. Humanities. 1969. 10.50Hdbd. ISBN 90-279-0441-3.

GRAY, RICHARD J. The Literature of Memory;Modern Writers of the American South. Johns Hopkins Univ. Pr., Baltimore, MD. 1976. 16.00Hdbd. LC 76-18941.

GRAY, W. B. How to Measure Readability. Dorrance, Philadelphia, PA. 1975. 22p. 3.50Pa. ISBN 0-8059-1996-1. LC 73-94389.

GREBSTEIN, SHELDON NORMAN. Sinclair Lewis. Twayne, NY. 1962. 192p.

GREEN, DOROTHY. Ulysses Bound; Henry Handel Richardson and Her Fiction. International Scholarly Book Service;Australian National Univ. Pr., Australia. 1973. 582p. 15.00Hdbd. ISBN 0-7081-0239-5. LC 72-87433.

GREEN, ELIZABETH LAY. The Negro in Contemporary American Literature;An Outline for Individual and Group Study. McGrath, College Park, MD. 1928(1968). 92p. 9.50Hdbd. ISBN 0-8434-0028-5. LC 68-4428.

GREEN, HENRY M. Australian Literature;1900-1950. Melbourne Univ. Pr., 1963. 3.00Pa. ISBN 0-522-83620-8.

GREEN, MARTIN. Re-Appraisals; Some Commonsense Readings in American Literature. W. W. Norton, NY. 1963. 250p. LC 65-18775.

GREEN, MARTIN. Transatlantic Patterns. Basic Books, NY. 1977. 15.00 Hdbd. ISBN 0-465-08688-8. LC 74-78305.

GREEN, ROGER LANCELYN. Into Other Worlds;Space-Flight in Fiction from Lucian to Lewis. Arno, NY. 1958(1975). 190p. 10.00Hdbd. ISBN 0-405-06329-6. LC 74-15976.

GREEN, ROSE BASILE. The Italian-American Novel;A Document of the Interaction of Two Cultures. Fairleigh Dickinson Univ. Pr., Rutherford, NJ. 1974. 415p. 18.00Hdbd. ISBN 0-8386-1287-3. LC 72-11081.

GREGG, EDITH W., Ed. One First Love;The Letters of Ellen Louisa Tucker to Ralph Waldo Emerson. Harvard Univ. Pr., Cambridge, MA. 1962. 208p. LC 62-19215.

GREGOR, IAN, and Brian Nicholas. The Moral and the Story. Faber and Faber. 1962. 8.95Hdbd. ISBN 0-571-04454-9.

GREGORY, HORACE. Spirit of Time and Place;Collected Essays of Horace Gregory. W.W. Norton, NY. 1973. 316p. 8.95Hdbd. ISBN 0-393-04265-0. LC 72-10090.

GREINER, DONALD J. Comic Terror;The Novels of John Hawkes. Memphis State Univ. Pr. 1973. 260p. 7.50 Hdbd. ISBN 0-87870-017-X. LC 73-81555.

GREJDA, EDWARD S. The Common Continent of Men;Racial Equality in the Writings of Herman Melville. Kennikat Pr., NY. 1974. 7.95Hdbd. ISBN 0-8046-9073-1. LC 74-80067.

GRENANDER, M.E. Ambrose Bierce. Twayne, NY. 7.50Hdbd. ISBN 0-8057-0056-0.

GRIBBEN, LENORE S. Who's Whodunit. University of North Carolina Pr., Chapel Hill, NC. 1969. 174p.

GRIFFIN, MARTIN I.J. Frank R. Stockton;A Critical Biography. Kennikat Pr., Port Washington, NY. 1939 (1965). 7.00Hdbd. ISBN 0-8046-0185-2. LC 65-18606.

GRIFFIN, ROBERT J., Ed. Twentieth Century Interpretations of Arrowsmith. Prentice-Hall, Englewood Cliffs, NJ. 1968. 118p. 1.25Pa. ISBN 0-13-046672-7.

GRISMER, R.L. Cervantes;A Bibliography. Kraus. Repro. 1946 Ed. Vol. 1. 14.00Hdbd. ISBN 0-527-36200-X. Vol. 2. 24.00Hdbd. ISBN 0-527-36201-8.

GRISMER, RAYMOND LEONARD. A Reference Index to Twelve Thousand Spanish American Authors;A Guide to Bibliographies and Bio-bibliographies. H.W. Wilson, NY. 1939 (1971). 150p. 9.00Hdbd. ISBN 0-87917-011-3. LC 72-165655.

GROS, LOUIS KENNETH. Literary Interpretations of Biblical Narratives. Abingdon Pr., Nashville, TN. 1974. 6.95Pa. ISBN 0-687-22131-5. LC 74-12400.

GROSS, HARVEY. Contrived Corridor;History and Fatality in Modern Literature. Univ. of Michigan Pr. 1972. 7.95Hdbd. ISBN 0-472-39390-1. LC 74-163621.

GROSS, SEYMOUR L., and John Edward Hardy, Eds. Images of the Negro in American Literature;Patterns of Literary Criticism;No. 5. Univ. of Chicago Pr., Chicago, IL. 1966. 321p. 6.50Hdbd. 2.95Pa.

GROSS, SEYMOUR L., Ed. Nathaniel Hawthorne;The House of the Seven Gables;An Authoritative Text;Backgrounds and Sources;Essays in Criticism. W.W. Norton, NY. 1967. 6.00 Hdbd. ISBN 0-393-04287. 2.45Pa.

GROSS, SEYMOUR L., Ed. A Scarlet Letter Handbook. Wadsworth, Belmont, CA. 1960. 2.95Pa.

GROSS, THEODORE L., and Stanley Wertheim. Hawthorne, Melville, Stephen Crane; A Critical Bibliography. The Free Press, NY. 1971. 301p. 8.95 Hdbd. LC 75-142364.

GROVER, DORYS C. Vardis Fisher; The Novelist as Poet. Revisionist Pr. NY. 1973. 140p. 29.95Hdbd. ISBN 0-87700-197-9. LC 73-78795.

GROVER, DORYS C. A Solitary Voice; Vardis Fisher. Revisionist Pr., NY. 1973. 72p. 24.95Hdbd. ISBN 0-87700-198-7. LC 73-6255.

GROVER, PHILIP. Henry James and the French Novel. Barnes and Noble, NY. 1973. 221p. 10.50Hdbd. ISBN 0-06-492568-4. LC 74-155335.

GRUBER, FRANK. Zane Grey; A Biography. World Publishing, Cleveland, OH. 1970. 284p. 6.95Hdbd. LC 75-75879.

GRUMBACH, DORIS. The Company She Kept. Coward-McCann, NY. 1967. 218p. 6.00. LC 66-26531.

GRUNWALD, HENRY A., Ed. Salinger; A Critical and Personal Portrait. Harper, NY. 1962. 4.95Hdbd. 1.75 Pa.

GUERARD, ALBERT J. The Triumph of the Novel; Dickens, Dostoevsky, Faulkner. Oxford Univ. Pr., NY. 1976 365p. 13.95Hdbd. ISBN 0-19-502066-9. LC 75-46357.

GUETTI, JAMES. The Limits of Metaphor; A Study of Melville, Conrad, and Faulkner. Cornell Univ. Pr., Ithaca, NY. 1967. 196p. LC 67-10489.

GULLASON, THOMAS A. Stephen Crane's Career; Perspectives and Evaluation. NYU Pr., NY. 1971. 10.00Hd bd. ISBN 0-8147-2952-5.

GULLIVER, LUCILLE. Louisa May Alcott; A Bibliography. B. Franklin, NY. 1973. 15.50Hdbd. ISBN 0-8337-1490-2. LC 76-102858.

GULLIVER, LUCILLE. Louisa May Alcott; A Bibliography. Gordon Pr., NY. 35.00Hdbd. ISBN 0-8490-0559-0.

GUNN, DREWEY W. American and British Writers in Mexico; 1556-1973. University of Texas Pr., Austin, TX. 1974. 301p. 12.50Hdbd. ISBN 0-292-70307-4. LC 74-8840.

GUNN, JAMES. Alternate Worlds. Printice-Hall, Englewood Cliffs, NJ. 1975. 29.95Hdbd. ISBN 0-13-023267-X. LC 75-8561.

GUREWITCH, MORTON L. Comedy; The Irrational Vision. Cornell Univ. Pr., Ithaca, NY. 1975. 245p. 10.00Hd bd. ISBN 0-8014-0843-1. LC 74-15186.

GURIAN, JAY. Western American Writing; Tradition and Promise. Everett/Edwards, DeLand, FL. 1975. 153p. 12.00Hdbd. ISBN 0-912112-04-2. LC 74-82195.

GURKO, LEO. Ernest Hemingway and the Pursuit of Heroism. Crowell, NY. 1969. 256p. 3.50Pa. ISBN 0-8152-0211-3. LC 68-21604.

GURKO, LEO. Thomas Wolfe; Beyond the Romantic Ego. Crowell, NY. 1975. 183p. 5.95Hdbd. ISBN 0-690-00751-5. LC 74-34204.

GUTH, DOROTHY LOBRANO, Ed. Letters of E. B. White. Harper, NY.

1976.15.00Hdbd.ISBN 0-06-014601-X. LC 73-18660.

GUTTENBERG, BARNETT. Web of Being;The Novels of Robert Penn Warren. Vanderbilt Univ. Pr., Nashville, TN.1975.73p.9.95Hdbd. LC 74-26892.

H

HAAS, ROBERT BARTLETT. A Catalogue of the Published and Unpublished Writings of Gertrude Stein, exhibited in the Yale University Library 22 February to 29 March 1941. Folcroft, Folcroft, PA. 1941(1974). 12.50Hdbd. LC 74-16094.

HACKETT, ALICE PAYNE, and James Henry Burke. 80 Years of Best Sellers;1895-1975. R.R. Bowker, NY. 1977.

HACKETT, FRANCIS. On American Books;A Symposium by Five American Critics as Printed in the London Nation. Folcroft, Folcroft, PA. 19-20(1974)5.00Hdbd. LC 74-16347.

HADGRAFT, CECIL. Queensland and Its Writers. Univ. of Queensland Pr. 1959. 4.30Pa. ISBN 0-7022-0366-1.

HAINES, CHARLES. Edgar A. Poe; His Writings and Influence. Franklin Watts, NY. 1974. 99p. 4.95Hdbd. ISBN 0-531-02737-6. LC 74-3352.

HALL, ERNEST JACKSON. The Satirical Element in the American Novel. Haskell House, NY. 1966. 89p.

HALL, JAMES. The Lunatic Giant in the Drawing Room;The British and American Novel since 1930. Indiana Univ. Pr., Bloomington, IN. 1968. 242 p. LC 68-14602.

HALL, LAWRENCE SARGENT. Hawthorne;Critic of Society. Peter Smith, Gloucester, MA. 1966. 200p.

HALL, LAWRENCE SARGENT. How Thinking is Written;An Analytic Approach to Writing. Greenwood Pr., Westport, CT. 1963(1975). 312p. 15.00 Hdbd. ISBN 0-8371-6059-6. LC 73-21176.

HALPERIN, JOHN, Ed. The Theory of the Novel;New Essays. Oxford Univ. Pr., NY. 1974. 396p. 10.95Hdbd.

HAMBLETON, RONALD. Mazo DeLa Roche of Jalna. Hawthorn, NY. 1966. 239p. LC 66-22660.

HANNEMAN, AUDRE. Ernest Hemingway;A Comprehensive Bibliography. Princeton Univ. Pr., Princeton, NJ. 1967. 568p. LC 67-14409.

HANDY, WILLIAM J. Modern Fiction;A Formalist Approach. Southern Illinois Univ. Pr., Carbondale, IL. 1971. 165p. ISBN 0-8093-0525-9. LC 71-156785.

HARAP, LOUIS. The Image of the Jew in American Literature;From

Early Republic to Mass Immigration. Jewish Publication Society of America, Philadelphia, PA. 1974. 586 p. 10.00Hdbd. ISBN 0-8276-0054-2. LC 74-12887.

HARDWICK, ELIZABETH. A View of My Own;Essays in Literature and Society. Farrar, NY. 1951(1962)214p. LC 62-16277.

HARDY, BARBARA. The Appropriate Form;An Essay on the Novel. Northwestern Univ. Pr. 1971. 218p. ISBN 0-8101-0335-4.

HARDY, BARBARA NATHAN. Tellers and Listeners;The Narrative Imagination. Athlone Pr., London. 1975. 279p. 16.00Hdbd. ISBN 0-485-11153-5. LC 76-352274.

HARDY, JOHN EDWARD. Katherine Anne Porter. Frederick Ungar, NY. 1973. 160p. ISBN 0-8044-2351-2. LC 72-79929.

HARDY, JOHN EDWARD. Man in the Modern Novel. Univ. of Washington Pr., Seattle and London. 1964. 228p. LC 64-12899.

HARDWICK, ELIZABETH. Seduction and Betrayal;Women and Literature. Vintage, NY. 1974(1975). 1.95Pa. LC 74-19117.

HARNSBERGER, CAROLINE THOMAS. Mark Twain;Family Man. Citadel Pr., NY. 296p.

HARPER, HOWARD M., JR. Desperate Faith;A Study of Bellow, Salinger, Mailer, Baldwin and Updike. Univ. of North Carolina Pr., Chapel Hill, NC. 1967. 200p. LC 67-17034.

HARPER, RALPH. The World of the Thriller. Johns Hopkins Univ. Pr., Baltimore, MD. 1974. 2.45Pa. ISBN 0-8018-1710-2. LC 74-24791.

HARRIS, CHARLES B. Contemporary American Novelists of the Absurd. College and Univ. Pr., New Haven, CT. 1971. 159p. LC 70-147308.

HARRIS, JANET. A Century of American History in Fiction;Kenneth Roberts'Novels. Gordon Pr., NY. 1976. 29.95Hdbd. ISBN 0-87968-455-0. LC 76-16528.

HARRIS, LEON. Upton Sinclair;American Rebel. Crowell, NY. 1975. 435 p. 12.95Hdbd. ISBN 0-690-00671-3. LC 74-23582.

HARRIS, THEODORE F., in consultation with Pearl S. Buck. Pearl S. Buck;A Biography. John Day, NY. 1933(1969). 381p. 7.95Hdbd. LC 68-9456.

HARRIS, THEODORE F., in consultation with Pearl S. Buck. Pearl S. Buck;A Biography;Volume Two;Her Philosophy as Expressed in Her Letters. John Day, NY. 372p.

HARRISON, DICK. Unnamed Country. U. of Alberta Pr. 1977. 10.00Hdbd. ISBN 0-88864-019-6.

HARRISON, JAMES A. Ed. The Last Letters of Edgar Allan Poe to Sarah Helen Whitman. Folcroft, Folcroft, PA. 1974. 15.00Hdbd. ISBN 0-8414-4899-X. LC 74-26841.

HART, JAMES DAVID. The Popular Book;A History of America's Literary Taste. Greenwood Pr., Westport, CT. 1950(1976). 22.00Hdbd. ISBN 0-8371-8694-3. LC 75-40925.

HARTLEY, L. P. The Novelist's Responsibility. Hamish Hamilton, London. 1967. 216p.

HARVEY, ALEXANDER. William Dean Howells;A Study of the Achievement of a Literary Artist. Folcroft, Folcroft, PA. 1973. 267p. 12.50Hdbd. LC 73-4378.

HARWELL, RICHARD, Ed. Margaret Mitchell's Gone with the Wind Letters;1936-1949. Macmillan, NY. 1976. 12.95Hdbd. ISBN 0-02-548650-0. LC 76-13190.

HALSAM, GERALD W. Jack Schaefer. Boise State Univ., Boise, ID. 1975(1976)46p. 1.50Pa. ISBN 0-88430-019-6. LC 75-29981.

HALSAM, GERALD W., Ed. Western Writing. Univ. of New Mexico Pr., 1974. 156p. 3.50. ISBN 0-8263-0353-6. LC 74-83389.

HASSAN, IHAB. Contemporary American Literature;1945-1972;An Introduction. Frederick Ungar, NY. 194p.

HAASAN, IHAB. The Literature of Silence;Henry Miller and Samuel Beckett. Alfred A. Knopf, NY. 1967(1968). 225p. LC 67-15808.

HASSAN, IHAB. Radical Innocence; Studies in the Contemporary American Novel. Harper and Row, NY. 1966. 361p. LC 61-7146.

HASSLER, KENNETH WAYNE, Comp. Mark Twain, Dean of American Humorists. SamHar Pr., Charlotteville, NY. 1975. 2.29Pa. LC 75-16279.

HASTINGS, GEORGE EVERETT. The Life and Works of Francis Hopkinson. Russell and Russell, NY. 1955(1968)516p. LC 68-11334.

HATZFELD, HELMUT A. Critical Bibliography of New Stylistics Applied to the Romance Literature. Johnson Repro. 1966. 14.00Hdbd. ISBN 0-384-21775-3.

HAUCK, RICHARD BOYD. A Cheerful Nihilism;Confidence and "The Absurd"in American Humorous Fiction.Indiana Univ. Pr., Bloomington, IN. 269p.

HAVILAND, VIRGINIA. Children and Literature;Views and Reviews. Scott, Foresman, Glenview, IL. 1973. 461p. 4.95Pa.

HAVLICE, PATRICIA PATE. Index to Literary Biography. Scarecrow Pr., Metuchen, NJ. 1974. 9.00Hdbd. ISBN 0-8108-0745-9. LC 74-8315.

HAWTHORN, JEREMY. Identity and Relationship;A Contribution to Marxist Theory of Literary Criticism. Norwood Editions, Norwood, PA. 1972(1974). 15.00Hdbd. LC 74-13257.

HAWTHORNE, JULIAN. Hawthorne and His Circle. Archon, NY. 1903(1968). 371p. LC 68-20382.

HAWTHORNE, JULIAN. Nathaniel Hawthoren and His Wife;A Biography. Vol.1. Archon, NY. 1968. 505p. LC 68-20383.

HAYASHI, TETSUMARO. John Steinbeck;A Concise Bibliography;(1930-65). Scarecrow Pr., Metuchen, NJ. 1967. 164p. LC 67-10184.

HAYASHI, TETSUMARO, Ed. John Steinbeck;A Dictionary of His Fictional Characters. Scarecrow Pr., Metuchen, NJ. 1976. 222p. 9.00Hdbd.

ISBN 0-8108-0948-6. LC 76-14803.

HAYASHI, TETSUMARO. A New Steinbeck Bibliography 1929-1971. Scarecrow Pr., Metuchen, NJ. 1973. 225p. 8.50Hdbd. ISBN 0-8108-0647-9.

HAYASHI, TETSUMARO, Ed. Steinbeck's Literary Dimension;A Guide to Comparative Studies. Scarecrow Pr., Metuchen, NJ. 1973. 191p. 6.00 Hdbd. ISBN 0-0108-0550-2.

HAYASHI, TETSUMARO, Ed. A Study Guide to Steinbeck;A Handbook to His Major Works. Scarecrow Pr., Metuchen, NJ. 1974. 316p. 10.00Hdbd. ISBN 0-8108-0706-8.

HAYFORD, HARRISON, and Hershel Parker, Eds. Herman Melville;Moby-Dick;An Authoritative Text, Reviews and Letters by Melville;Analogues and Sources;Criticism. W.W. Norton, NY. 1967. 728p.

HAYTER, ALETHEA. Opium and the Romantic Imagination. Univ. of California Pr. 1968. 3.45Pa. ISBN 0-520-01746-3. LC 68-29700.

HEARTMAN, CHARLES FREDERICK, and James R. Canny, Comp. A Bibliography of First Printings of the Writings of Edgar Allen Poe. Kraus Reprint, NY. 1972. 294p. 15.00 Hdbd. LC 44-7988.

HEDGES, WILLIAM L. Washington Irving;An American Study;1802-1832. Johns Hopkins Pr., Baltimore, MD. 1965. 274p.

HEILBRUN, CAROLYN G. Toward A Recognition of Androgyny. Harper and Row, NY. 1973(1974). 189p. 2.45Pa ISBN 0-06-090378-3.

HEILMAN, ROBERT BECHTOLD. America in English Fiction;1760-1800; The Influences of the American Revolution. Octagon, NY. 1968. LC 68-28261.

HEINTZ, ANN CHRISTINE. Persuasion. Loyola Univ. Pr., Chicago, IL. 1974. 224p. 3.20Pa. LC 75-306229.

HEINEY, DONALD. Recent American Literature. Barron's Ed. Series, Woodbury, NY. 609p.

HEINEY, DONALD, and Lenthiel H. Downs. Recent American Literature to 1930. Barron's Ed. Series, Woodbury, NY. 1973. 374p. 2.95Pa. ISBN 0-8120-0449-3. LC 73-75772.

HELLMAN, GEORGE S. Washington Irving Esquire;Ambassador at Large From the New World to the Old. Knopf, NY. 355p.

HEMINGWAY, LEICESTER. My Brother, Ernest Hemingway. World Pub. 1962. 5.95Hdbd. Fawcett. .75Pa.

HEMINGWAY, MARCELLINE. At the Hemingways;A Family Portrait. Little. 1962. 5.95Hdbd.

HEMMINGHAUS, EDGAR. Mark Twain in Germany. AMS Pr., NY. 1966. 170p.

HEMMINGS, FREDERICK. The Age of Realism. Penguin, Baltimore, MD. 1974. 414p. 3.50Pa. ISBN 0-14-021779-7. LC 74-193355.

HENDERSON, ARCHIBALD. Mark Twain. Haskell House, NY. 1974. 13. 95Hdbd. ISBN 0-8383-1742-1. LC 74-10996.

HENDERSON, HARRY B. Versions

of the Past;the Historical Imagination in American Fiction. Oxford Univ. Pr., 1974. 344p. 12.50Hdbd. ISBN 0-19-501810-9. LC 74-79624.

HENDRICK, GEORGE. Katherine Anne Porter. Twayne, NY. 1965. 176p. LC 65-18909.

HENRY, JEANNETTE, Ed. American Indian Reader;Literature. Indian Historian Pr., San Francisco, CA. 1973 249p. 3.00Pa.

HEPWORTH, BRIAN. The Rise of Romanticism. Dufour. 15.95Hdbd. ISBN 0-85635-112-1.

HERBERT, THOMAS WALTER. Moby Dick and Calvinism;A World Dismantled. Rutgers Univ. Pr., New Brunswick, NJ. 1977. 12.50Hdbd. ISBN 0-8135-0829-0. LC 76-56252.

HERMAN, LINDA, and Beth Stiel. Corpus Delicti of Mystery Fiction;Or, A Guide to the Body of the Case. Scarecrow Pr., Metuchen, NJ. 1974. 6.50Hdbd. ISBN 0-8108-0770-X. LC 74-16319.

HERSEY, JOHN RICHARD, Ed. Ralph Ellison;A Collection of Critical Essays. Prentice-Hall, Englewood Cliffs, NJ. 1973(1974). 5.95Hdbd. ISBN 0-13-274357-4. LC 73-16224.

HESELTINE, HARRY P. Xavier Herbert. Oxford Univ. Pr. NY. 1973. 52p. 1.15Pa. ISBN 0-19-550409-7. LC 74-175347.

HETHERINGTON, HUGH W. Melville's Reviewers;British and American 1846-1891. Russell and Russell, NY. 1961(1975. 304p. 20.00Hdbd. LC 73-86720.

HETHERINGTON, JOHN. Forty-Two Faces. Books for Libraries Pr., Freeport, NY. 250p. LC 73-75719.

HEWITT, CECIL R., Ed. Does Pornography Matter?Books for Libraries, Freeport, NY. 1961. 9.50Hdbd. ISBN 0-8369-2651-X. LC 71-152175.

HIATT, MARY P. Artful Balance;The Parallel Structures of Style. Teachers Coll. 1975. 12.50Hdbd. ISBN 0-8077-2487-4. 6.50Pa. ISBN 0-8077-248-6.

HICKS, GRANVILLE, and Jack Alan Robbins. Literary Horizons;A Quarter Century of American Fiction. New York Univ. Pr., NY. 1970. 290p. ISBN 0-8147-3354-9. LC 72-133011.

HICKS, JOHN H. Thoreau in Our Season. Univ. of Massachusetts Pr., Amherst, MA. 180p. 9.00Hdbd.

HIGGINS, JOHN A. F. Scott Fitzgerald;A Study of the Stories. St. John's Univ. Pr. 1971. LC 70-129840.

HIGGINSON, THOMAS WENTWORTH. Margaret Fuller Ossoli. Greenwood Pr., NY. 1968. 323p. LC 68-57609.

HIGHET, GILBERT. Anatomy of Satire. Princeton Univ. Pr. 1962. 10.50 Hdbd. ISBN 0-691-06005-3. 3.95Pa. ISBN 0-691-01306-3.

HIGHET, GILBERT. Explorations. Oxford Univ. Pr., NY. 1971. 383p. LC 74-142798.

HIGHSMITH, PATRICIA. Plotting and Writing Suspense Fiction. The Writer, Boston, MA. 1966. 149p.

HILDICK, WALLACE. Thirteen Types of Narrative. Clarkson N. Potter,

NY.1970.136p. LC 73-123391.

HILDICK, WALLACE. Word for Word; The Rewriting of Fiction. Norton. 1966. 1.95Pa. ISBN 0-393-09674-2.

HILDRETH, MARGARET HOLBROOK. Harriet Beecher Stowe;A Bibliography. Archon, Hamden, CT. 1976. 257p. 17.50Hdbd. ISBN 0-208-01596-5. LC 76-14425.

HILFER, ANTHONY CHANNEL. The Revolt from the Village; 1915-1930. Univ. of North Carolina Pr., Chapel Hill, NC. 1969. 275p. LC 72-75976.

HILL, HAMLIN LEWIS. Mark Twain; God's Fool. Harper and Row, NY. 1973(1975). 308p. 3.95Pa. ISBN 0-06-090391-0. LC 72-9754.

HILL, HAMLIN. Mark Twain and Elisha Bliss. Univ. of Missouri Pr., Columbia, MO. 1964. 214p. LC 64-17646.

HILLEGAS, MARK R. The Future as Nightmare;H.G.Wells and the Antiutopians. Oxford Univ. Pr., NY. 1967. 200p. LC 67-28128.

HILLWAY, TYRUS. Herman Mellville. Twayne, NY. 1963. 176p.

HILLWAY, TYRUS, and Luther S. Mansfield. Moby-Dick;Centennial Essays. Southern Methodist Univ. Pr., Dallas, TX. 1953. 182p.

HINDUS, MILTON. F.Scott Fitzgerald;An Introduction and Interpretation. Holt, Rinehart, NY. 1968. 129p.

HIPKISS, ROBERT A. Jack Kerouac; Prophet of the New Romanticism;A Critical Study of the Published Works of Kerouac and a Comparison of them to those of J.D.Salinger, James Purdy, John Knowles, and Ken Kesey. Regents Pr. of Kansas, Lawrence, KS. 1976. 150p. 10.50Hdbd. ISBN 0-7006-0151-1. LC 76-14817.

HIRSCHFELDER, ARLENE B., Comp. American Indian and Eskimo Authors;A Comprehensive Bibliography. Assn. on American Indian Affairs, Dist. by Interbook, NY. 1973. 99p. 4.00Pa. LC 82109.

HOBSON, FRED C. The Serpent in Eden;H.L.Mencken and the South. Univ. of North Carolina Pr.,Chapel Hill, NC. 1974. 8.95Hdbd. ISBN 0-8078-1224-2. LC 73-15674.

HOCKS, RICHARD A. Henry James and Pragmatistic Thought;A Study in the Relationship Between the Philosophy of William James and the Literary Art of Henry James. Univ. of North Carolina Pr., Chapel Hill, NC. 1974. 9.95Hdbd. ISBN 0-8078-1225-0. LC 73-16271.

HODGART, MATTHEW. Satire. McGraw, NY. 1969. 2.95Pa. ISBN 0-07-029121-7.

HOELTJE, HUBERT H. Inward Sky; The Mind and Heart of Nathaniel Hawthorne. Duke Univ. Pr.,Durham,NC. 1962. 579p. LC 62-10052.

HOELTJE, HUBERT. Sheltering Tree;A Story of the Friendship of Ralph Waldo Emerson and Amos Bronson Alcott. Kennikat Pr., Port Washington, NY. 1965. 209p. LC 65-27109.

HOFFMANN, CHARLES G. The Short Novels of Henry James. Bookman, NY. 1957. 143p.

HOFFMAN, DANIEL. Form and Fable in American Fiction. Oxford Univ. Pr. 1961(1965)368p. LC 61-8371.

HOFFMAN, FREDERICK J. The Great Gatsby;A Study. Scribner's, NY. 1962. 338p.

HOFFMAN, FREDERICK J. The Twenties;American Writing in the Postwar Decade. Free Pr., NY. 516p. LC 62-17574.

HOFFMAN, FREDERICK J. William Faulkner. Twayne, NY. 1966. 160p.

HOFFMAN, FREDERICK J., and Olga W. Vickery, Eds. William Faulkner;Three Decades of Criticism. Michigan State Univ. Pr., 1960. 428p.

HOFFMAN, MICHAEL J. Gertrude Stein. Twayne, Boston, MA. 1976. 7.50 Hdbd. ISBN 0-8057-7168-9. LC 76-2661.

HOFFMAN, MICHAEL J. The Subversive Vision;American Romanticism in Literature. Kennikat Pr., Port Washington, NY. 1972. 160p. ISBN 0-8046-9032-4. LC 72-91174.

HOLBROOK, DAVID, Ed. The Case Against Pornography. Open Court, 1973. 9.95Hdbd. ISBN 0-91205-28-4.

HOLBROOK, DAVID. Quest for Love. Univ. of Ala. Pr. 1965. 10.00Hdbd. ISBN 0-8173-7305-5. LC 65-24879.

HOLDER, ALAN. Three Voyagers in Search of Europe;A Study of Henry James, Ezra Pound, and T.S. Eliot. Univ. of Pennsylvania Pr., Philadelphia, PA. 1966. 396p. LC 64-24513.

HOLDER-BARELL, ALEXANDER. The Development of Imagery and its Functional Significance in Henry James's Novels. Haskell House, NY. 1966. 215p.

HOLLAND, LAURENCE BEDWELL. The Expense of Vision;Essays on the Craft of Henry James. Princeton Univ. Pr., Princeton, NJ. 1964. 414p.

HOLLAND, NORMAN NORWOOD. The Dynamics of Literary Response. Norton, NY. 1975. 4.45Pa. ISBN 0-393-00790-1. LC 75-23485.

HOLLIDAY, CARL. A History of Southern Literature. Kennikat Pr., Port Washington, NY. 1906(1969)406p. LC 68-26281.

HOLLOWAY, JEAN. Hamlin Garland; A Biography. Books for Libraries, Freeport, NY. 1960(1972). 15.50Hdbd. ISBN 0-8369-5802-0.

HOLLOWELL, JOHN. Fact and Fiction;the New Journalism and the Nonfiction Novel. Univ. of North Carolina Pr., Chapel Hill. 1977. 11.95 Hdbd. ISBN 0-8078-1281-1. LC 76-20826.

HOLMAN, C. HUGH., Comp. The American Novel Through Henry James. Appleton-Century Crofts, NY. 1966. 102p. LC 66-24253.

HOLMAN, C. HUGH, and Sue Fields Ross, Eds. The Letters of Thomas Wolfe to His Mother. Univ. of North Carolina Pr., Chapel Hill, NY. 1943 (1968). 320p. LC 68-14361.

HOLMAN, CLARENCE HUGH. The Loneliness at the Core;Studies in Thomas Wolfe. Louisiana State Univ. Pr., Baton Rouge, LA. 1975. 184p. 8.95Hdbd. ISBN 0-8071-0085-4. LC 74-77325.

HOLMAN, HUGH C. Three Modes of Modern Fiction. Univ. of Georgia Pr. Athens, GA. 1966. 95p. LC 66-19490.

HOLMAN, HUGH C. The World of Thomas Wolfe. Scribner's, NY. 1962. 187p.

HOLMES, OLIVER WENDELL. Ralph Waldo Emerson. Houghton, Mifflin, Boston, MA. Republished Gale, Detroit, MI. 1967. 441p. LC 67-23884.

HOLT, GUY. A Bibliography of the Writings of James Branch Cabell. Haskell House, NY. 1972. 73p. 7.95 Hdbd. ISBN 0-8383-1424-4. LC 72-757.

HOLTON, MILNE. Cylinder of Vision; The Fiction and Journalistic Writings of Stephen Crane. Louisiana State Univ. Pr., Baton Rouge, LA. 1972. 10.95Hdbd. ISBN 0-8071-0045-5. LC 79-181358.

HOPE, A. D. Australian Literature; 1950-62. Melbourne Univ. Pr. 1963. 3.00Pa. ISBN 0-522-83636-4.

HOPKINS, KENNETH. Portraits in Satire. Scholarly. 1958. 16.00Hdbd. ISBN 0-403-01330-5. LC 71-161941.

HOPKINS, LEE BENNETT. More Books by More People; Interviews with Sixty-Five Authors of Books for Children. Citation Pr., NY. 1974. 410p. 8.95Hdbd. ISBN 0-590-07357-5. LC 73-87223. 4.95Pa. ISBN 0-590-09401-7.

HORGAN, PAUL. Approaches to Writing. Farrar, Straus, NY. 1974. 233p. 3.25Pa. ISBN 0-374-51158-6. LC 74-7305.

HOSILLOS, LUCILA V. Philippine-American Literary Relations; 1898-1941. Oriole Editions, NY. 1968(1976). 200p. 12.50Hdbd. ISBN 0-88211-054-3. LC 75-85114.

HOTCHKISS, JEANETTE. American Historical Fiction and Biography for Children and Young People. Scarecrow Pr., Metuchen, NJ. 1973. 318p. 7.50Hdbd. ISBN 0-8108-0650-9. LC 73-13715.

HOTCHNER, A. E. Papa Hemingway; A Personal Memoir. Random, NY. 1966. 5.95Hdbd. Bantam. 1.25Pa.

HOUGH, GEORGE A. News Writing. Houghton-Mifflin, Boston, MA. 1975. 221p. 9.95Hdbd. ISBN 0-395-18597-1. LC 74-17877. 5.95Pa.

HOUGH, ROBERT L. The Quiet Rebel; William Dean Howells as Social Commentator. Univ. of Nebraska Pr. Lincoln, NB. 1959. 137p.

HOUSE, KAY SEYMOUR. Cooper's Americans. Ohio State Univ. Pr., 1965(1966). 6.25Hdbd. ISBN 0-8142-0065-6.

HOVEY, RICHARD B. Hemingway; The Inward Terrain. Univ. of Washington Pr., Seattle, WA. 1968. 248p.

HOWARD, DAVID, Ed., et al. Tradition and Tolerance in Nineteenth-Century Fiction. Routledge and Kegan Paul, London. 1966. 281p.

HOWARD, LEON. Herman Melville; A Biography. Univ. of California Pr., Berkeley and Los Angeles, CA. 1967. 354p.

HOWARD, LEON. Literature and the American Tradition. Doubleday, Garden City, NY. 1960. 318p.

HOWARTH, WILLIAM L., Ed. Twentieth Century Interpretations of Poe's Tales. Prentice-Hall. 1971. 1.45Pa. ISBN 0-13-684647-5. LC 69-15337.

HOWE, IRVING. The Critical Point on Literature and Culture. Horizon Pr., NY. 1973. 232p. ISBN 0-8180-1161-0. LC 73-85276.

HOWE, IRVING, Ed. Edith Wharton; A Collection of Critical Essays. Prentice-Hall, Englewood Cliffs, NJ. 1962. 180p. 1.95Pa.

HOWE, IRVING, Ed. The Idea of the Modern in Literature and the Arts. Horizon Pr., NY. 1967. 317p. LC 68-54188.

HOWE, IRVING. Sherwood Anderson. Stanford Univ. Pr. 1951. 8.50Hdbd. ISBN 0-8047-0236-5. 2.95Pa. ISBN 0-8047-0237-3.

HOWE, IRVING. William Faulkner; A Critical Study. Random House, NY. 1952. 299p.

HOWE, JULIA WARD. Love-Letters of Margaret Fuller;1845-1846. Greenwood Pr., NY. 1903(1969). 228p. LC 69-14023.

HOWE, JULIA WARD. Margaret Fuller;Marchesa Ossoli. Haskell House, NY. 1968. 298p. LC 68-24938.

HOWELLS, W. D. Literary Friends and Acquaintance;A Personal Retrospect of American Authorship. Indiana Univ. Pr., Bloomington, IN. 1968. 297p. LC 68-29523.

HOWELLS, WILLIAM DEAN. My Mark Twain Reminiscences and Criticisms. Louisiana State Univ. Pr., Baton Rouge, LA. 1938(1967). 189p. LC 67-21374.

HOWELLS, WILLIAM DEAN. Years of my Youth, and Three Essays. Indiana Univ. Pr., Bloomington, IN. 1975. 420p. 20.00Hdbd. ISBN 0-253-36850-2. LC 78-166119.

HOYT, CHARLES ALVA, Ed. Minor American Novelists. Southern Illinois Univ. Pr., Carbondale, IL. 1970. 140p. ISBN 0-8093-0447-3. LC 70-86184.

HOYT, EDWIN. A Gentlemen of Broadway;The Story of Damon Runyon. Little. 1964. 6.50Hdbd.

HOYT, OLGA G., and Edwin P. Hoyt. Censorship in America. Seabury. 1970. 6.95Hdbd. ISBN 0-8164-3013-6. LC 73-125833.

HSU, KAI-YU, Comp. Asian-American Authors. Houghton-Mifflin, Boston, MA. 1976. 184p. 3.08Pa. ISBN 0-395-12701-7. LC 76-367678.

HUBBELL, JAY B. South and Southwest;Literary Essays and Reminiscences. Duke Univ. Pr., Durham, NC. 1965. 369p. LC 65-26839.

HUBBELL, JAY B. The South in American Literature;1607-1900. Duke Univ. Pr. 1954(1967). 988p. LC 54-9434.

HUBBELL, JAY B. Southern Life in Fiction. Univ. of Georgia Pr., Athens, GA. 1960. 99p. LC 60-9898.

HUBBELL, JAY B. Who Are the Major American Writers? Duke Univ. Pr., Durham, NC. 1972. 344p. ISBN 0-8223-0289-6. LC 72-17202.

HUDGENS, BETTY LENHARDT, Comp. Kurt Vonnegut, Jr.;A Checklist. Gale Research, Detroit, MI. 1972. 67p.

HUDSON, THEODORE R. From LeRoi Jones to Amiri Baraka;The Literary Works. Duke Univ. Pr., Durham, NC. 1973. 222p. 7.95Hdbd. ISBN 0-8223-0296-9. LC 72-97096. 4.75 Pa.

HUFF, MARY NANCE, Comp. Robert Penn Warren;A Bibliography. David Lewis, NY. 1968. 171p. LC 68-28007.

HULME, T. E. Notes on Language and Style. Folcroft, Folcroft, Pa. 1929. 7.50Hdbd.

HULME, T. E. Notes on Language and Style;Studies in Comparative Literature. Haskell. 1974. 7.95Hdbd. ISBN 0-838-2017-1. LC 74-1105.

HUMPHREY, ROBERT. Stream of Consciousness in the Modern Novel. Univ. of California Pr., Berkeley and Los Angeles. 1954(1968). 129p. LC 54-6673.

HUMPHREYS, A. R. Herman Melville. Barnes and Noble, NY. 1962. 2.50Pa.

HUNKING, ELIZABETH MORSE WALSH. The Picturesque English of Henry James;A Collection of Quotations. Dorrance, Philadelphia, PA. 1976. 74p. 3.95. ISBN 0-8059-2310-1

HUNT, JOHN WESLEY. William Faulkner;Art in Theological Tension. Haskell, NY. 1965(1973). 184p. 10.95 Hdbd. ISBN 0-8383-1658-1. LC 72-6942.

HUNTER, JAMES. B. F. Skinner and Contemporary Literature;An Analysis of Lolita;Cancer Ward;Steppenwolf;Portnoy's Complaint from the Viewpoint of Skinner's Psychology. Gordon Pr. 1975. 34.95Hdbd. ISBN 0-87968-689-8.

HUXLEY, ALDOUS. Literature and Science. Harper-Row, NY. 1963. 10.00 Hdbd. ISBN 0-06-012090-8.

HYDE, H. MONTGOMERY. Henry James at Home. Farrar, Straus, NY. 322p. LC 68-14920.

HYNEMAN, ESTHER F. Edgar Allan Poe;An Annotated Bibliography of Books and Articles in English;1827-1973. G. K. Hall, Boston, MA. 1974. 19.50Hdbd. ISBN 0-8161-1104-9. LC 74-16359.

I

IFKOVIC, EDWARD, Comp. American Letter;Immigrant and Ethnic. Prentice-Hall, Englewood Cliffs, NJ. 1975. 6.95 Hdbd. ISBN 0-13-027896-3. LC 74-23351.

INGARDEN, ROMAN. Trans. by Ruth Ann Crowley and Kenneth R. Olson. The Cognition of the Literary Work of Art. Northwestern Univ. Pr., Evanston, IL. 1973. 436p. 15.00Hdbd. ISBN 0-8101-0424-5. LC 73-80117.

INGE, M. THOMAS, Ed. Ellen Glasgow;Centennial Essays. Univ. Pr. of Virginia, Charlottesville, VA. 1974 (1975). 9.75Hdbd. ISBN 0-8139-0620-2. LC 75-15976.

INGE, M. THOMAS, Ed. The Frontier Humorists;Critical Views. Archon, Hamden, CT. 1975. 331p. 15.00Hdbd. ISBN 0-208-01509-4. LC 75-12698.

IRMSCHER, WILLIAM F. The Nature of Literature;Writing on Literary Topics. Holt, Rinehart, NY. 1975. 190p. 3.95Pa. ISBN 0-03-013286-X. LC 74-22085.

IRVING, PIERRE M. Life and Letters of Washington Irving. Vol. I. G. P. Putnam, NY. 1863. Republished Gale, Detroit, MI. 1967. 463p. LC 67-23893.

IRVING, PIERRE M. The Life and Letters of Washington Irving. Vol. II. G. P. Putnam, NY. 1863. Republished Gale, Detroit, MI. 1967. 492p. LC 67-23893.

IRVING, PIERRE M. The Life and Letters of Washington Irving. Vol. III. G. P. Putnam, NY. 1864. Republished Gale, Detroit, MI. 1967. 403p. LC 67-23893.

IRVING, PIERRE M. The Life and Letters of Washington Irving. Vol. IV. G. P. Putnam, NY. 1864. Republished Gale, Detroit, MI. 1967. 450p. LC 67-23893.

IRWIN, JOHN T. Doubling and Incest/Repetition and Revenge;A Speculative Reading of Faulkner. Johns Hopkins Univ. Pr., Baltimore, MD. 1975. 183p. 8.95Hdbd. ISBN 0-8018-1722-6. LC 75-11341.

IRWIN, LEONARD BETRAM, Comp. A Guide to Historical Fiction for the Use of Schools, Libraries and the General Reader. McKinley, Brooklawn, NJ. 1971. 225p. 10.00Hdbd. ISBN 0-910942-26-9. LC 70-31631.

ISLE, WALTER. Experiments in Form;Henry James's Novels. Harvard Univ. Pr., Cambridge, MA. 1968. 247p.

J

JACKSON, BLYDEN. The Waiting Years;Essays on American Negro Literature. Louisiana State Univ. Pr., Baton Rouge, LA. 1976. 10.00Hdbd. ISBN 0-8071-0173-7. LC 74-82001.

JACKSON, THOMAS H., Ed. Twentieth Century Interpretations of Miss Lonelyhearts. Prentice-Hall, Englewood Cliffs, NJ. 1971. 112p.

JACOBS, WILLIAM JAY. Edgar Allan Poe;Genius in Torment. McGraw-Hill, NY. 1975. 135p. 5.72Hdbd. ISBN 0-07-032158-2. LC 74-32010.

JAMES, HENRY. Hawthorne. Cornell Univ. Pr., Ithaca, NY.

JAMES, HENRY. The Middle Years; 1843-1916. Scribner's, NY. 1917. 119p.

JAMES, HENRY. Notes of a Son and Brother. Scribner's, NY. 1914. 515p.

JAMES, HENRY. The Question of our Speech;The Lesson of Balzac;Two Lectures. Folcroft, Folcroft, PA. 1905(1974). 7.75Hdbd. ISBN 0-8414-5335-7. LC 74-28338.

JAMES, PHILIP BRUTTON. Children's Books of Yesterday. Gale, Detroit, MI. 1975(1976). 12.50Hdbd. ISBN 0-8103-4135-2. LC 79-174059.

JAMESON, FREDRIC. Marxism and Form;Twentieth-Century Dialectical Theories of Literature. Princeton Univ. Pr., Princeton, NJ. 1971(1974). 432p. ISBN 0-691-01311-X. LC 71-155962.

JAN, ISABELLE. On Children's Literature. Schocken, NY. 1974. 189p. 6.00Hdbd. ISBN 0-8052-3564-7.

JANSSENS, G. A. M. The American Literary Review;A Critical History; 1920-1950. Mouton, The Hague, Paris. 1968. 341p.

JASEN, DAVID A. P. G. Wodehouse; A Portrait of a Master. Mason and Lipscomb, NY. 1974. ISBN 0-88405-010-6. LC &3-84879.

JEFFERSON, D. W. Henry James and the Modern Reader. St. Martin's Pr., NY. 1964. 240p.

JEHLEN, MYRA. Class and Character in Faulkner's South. Columbia Univ. Pr., NY. 9.00Hdbd. ISBN 0-231-04011-3. LC 76-3519.

JESSUP, JOSEPHINE LURIE. Faith of Our Feminists. Biblo. 1950.

JOBES, KATHARINE T., Ed. Twentieth Century Interpretations of The

Old Man and The Sea;A Collection of Critical Essays. Prentice-Hall, Englewood Cliffs, NJ. 1968. 120p.

JOHNSON, JAMES GIBSON. Southern Fiction Prior to 1860;An Attempt at a First-Hand Bibliography. Phaeton Pr., NY. 1909(1968). 126p. LC 67-30804.

JOHNSON, JAMES WELDON. Along This Way;The Autobiography of James Weldon Johnson. Viking Pr., NY. 1933(1961). 418p. LC 33-29189.

JOHNSON, MERLE DE VORE. A Bibliography of the Works of Mark Twain, Samuel Langhorne Clemens. Greenwood, Westport, CT. 1935(1972). 274p. 12.00Hdbd. ISBN 0-8371-5610-6. LC 71-138153.

JOHNSON, PAMELA HANSFORD. The Art of Thomas Wolfe. Scribner's, NY. 1963. 170p.

JOHNSON, R. L. The American Heritage of James Norman Hall. Dorrance, Philadelphia, PA. 1969. 4.95Hdbd. ISBN 0-8059-1377-7.

JOHNSON, ROSSITER. A Dictionary of Famous Names in Fiction, Drama, Poetry, History and Art. Gale, Detroit, MI. 1974. 411p. 17.50Hdbd. LC 75-167012.

JOHNSTON, ALVA. The Case of Erle Stanley Gardner. William Morrow, NY. 1947. 87p.

JOHNSTON, GRAHAME. Annals of Australian Literature. Oxford Univ. Pr. 1970. 7.25Hdbd. ISBN 0-19-550315-5.

JOHNSTON, JOHANNA. The Heart That Would Not Hold;A Biography of Washington Irving. M. Evans, NY. 1971. 376p. LC 72-122822.

JOHNSTON, JOHANNA. Runaway to Heaven;The Story of Harriet Beecher Stowe. Doubleday, Garden City, NY. 490p.

JONES, D. G. Butterfly on Rock;A Study of Themes and Images in Canadian Literature. Univ. of Toronto Pr. 1970. 4.75Pa. LC 75-133438.

JONES, GRANVILLE M. Henry James's Psychology of Experience;Innocence, Responsibility and Renunciation in the Fiction of Henry James. Mouton, The Hague. 1975. 310p. 26.00 LC 74-75036.

JONES, HOWARD MUMFORD, and Richard M. Ludwig. Guide to American Literature and Its Backgrounds Since 1890. Harvard Univ. Pr., Cambridge, MA. 1972. 264p. 2.95Pa. ISBN 0-674-36753-7. LC 72-85143.

JONES, HOWARD MUMFORD. Jeffersonianism and the American Novel. Teachers College Pr., Columbia Univ., NY. 1966. 77p. LC 66-28267.

JONES, HOWARD MUMFORD. The Theory of American Literature. Cornell Univ. Pr., Ithaca, NY. 1948 (1965). 225p. LC 48-11948.

JONES, JOSEPH, Ed. Image of Australia. Univ. of Texas Pr. 1962. 7.50 Hdbd. ISBN 0-292-73269-4.

JONES, JOSEPH JAY. Radical Cousins;Nineteenth Century American and Australian Writers. Univ. of Queensland Pr., St. Lucia, Qld. 1976. 132p. 12.00Hdbd. ISBN 0-7022-1223-7. LC 77-351511.

JONES, PETER G. War and the Novelist;Appraising the American War Novel. Univ. of Missouri Pr., Columbia, MO. 1976. 12.50Hdbd. ISBN 0-8262-0211-X. LC 76-23268.

JONES, W. T. Romantic Syndrome; Toward a New Method in Cultural Anthropology and History of Ideas. Humanities. 1961. 15.50.

JORDAN, ALICE MABEL. From Rollo to Tom Sawyer, and Other Papers. Horn, Boston, MA. 1948(1974).160p. 3.50Pa.

K

KABLER, ERICH. Trans. by Richard Winston and Clara Winston. The Inward Turn of Narrative. Princeton Univ. Pr., Princeton, NJ. 1973. 9.50 Hdbd. ISBN 0-691-09891-3. LC 72-4036.

KALLSEN, LOREN J., Ed. Kentucky Tragedy;A Problem in Romantic Attitudes. Bobbs. 1963. 4.50Pa. ISBN 0-672-60662-3. LC 63-12190.

KAMMAN, WILLIAM FREDERIC. Socialism in German American Literature. Hyperion Pr., Westport, CT. 1917(1975). 12.50Hdbd. ISBN 0-88355-232-9. LC 75-328.

KAPLAN, JUSTIN. Mark Twain and His World. Simon and Schuster, NY. 1974. 224p. 19.95Hdbd. ISBN 0-671-21462-4. LC 72-87659.

KAPLAN, JUSTIN. Mr. Clemens and Mark Twain;A Biography. Simon and Schuster, NY. 1966. 7.95Hdbd.

KAPLAN, MORTON, and Robert Kloss. The Unspoken Motive;A Guide to Pyschoanalytic Literary Criticism. The Free Pr., NY. 1973. 323p. LC 79-163609.

KARANIKAS, ALEXANDER. Tillers of a Myth;Southern Agrarians as Social and Literary Critics. Univ. of Wisconsin Pr., Madison, WI. 1966. 251p. LC 66-11802.

KAROLIDES, NICHOLAS J. The Pioneer in the American Novel;1900-1950. Univ. of Oklahoma Pr., Norman, OK. 324p.

KARTIGANER, DONALD M., and Malcolm A. Griffith. Theories of American Literature. Macmillan, NY. 1972. 438p. LC 78-150070.

KATES, GEORGE N. Willa Cather in Europe;Her Own Story of the First Journey. Knopf, NY. 1956. 4.95Hdbd. 178p. ISBN 0-394-45197-X. LC 56-10906.

KAUL, A.N. The American Vision; Actual and Ideal Society in Nineteenth-Century Fiction. Yale Univ. Pr., New Haven, CT. 1963. 340p. LC 63-9309.

KAUL, A.N. Hawthorne;A Collection of Critical Essays. Prentice-Hall, Englewood Cliffs, NJ. 1966.

KAZIN, ALFRED. Bright Book of Life;American Novelists and Storytellers from Hemingway to Mailer. Dell, NY. 1974. 334p. 2.95Pa. LC 72-13748.

KAZIN, ALFRED, Ed. F. Scott Fitzgerald; The Man and His Work. Collier-Macmillan, London. Collier, NY. 1951(1966). 221p.

KAZIN, ALFRED. On Native Grounds; An Interpretation of Modern American Prose, Literature. Harcourt, Brace. NY. 1947. 541p.

KAZIN, ALFRED, Ed. The Open Form; Essays for our Time. Harcourt, Brace, NY. 1965. 397p. LC 65-14914.

KAZIN, ALFRED, and Charles Shapiro, Eds. The Stature of Theodore Dreiser; A Critical Survey of the Man and His Work. Indiana Univ. Pr., Bloomington, IN. 1955. 303p.

KEET, ALFRED E. Stephen Crane; In Memoriam. Folcroft, Folcroft, PA. 4.50Hdbd.

KEGAN, ROBERT. The Sweeter Welcome; Voices for a Vision of Affirmation; Bellow, Malamud and Martin Buber. Humanities Pr., Needham Heights, MA. 1976. 169p. 4.95Hdbd. ISBN 0-911628-25-8. LC 76-55860.

KEHLER, DOROTHEA. Problems in Literary Research; A Guide to Selected Reference Works. Scarecrow Pr., Metuchen, NJ. 1975. 160p. 6.00 Hdbd. ISBN 0-8108-0841-2. LC 75-16427.

KEILEY, JARVIS. Edgar Allen Poe; A Probe. Prometheus Pr., NY. 1927. Haskell House, NY. 1974. 7.95Hdbd. ISBN 0-8383-2065-1. LC 74-4051.

KELLEY, CORNELIA PULSIFER. The Early Development of Henry James. Univ. of Illinois Pr., Urbana, IL. 1965. 319p.

KELLOGG, GRACE. The Two Lives of Edith Wharton; The Woman and Her Work. Appleton, NY. 1965. 432p. LC 65-11638.

KELLOGG, JEAN DEFREES. Dark Prophets of Hope; Dostoevsky, Sartre, Camus, Faulkner. Loyola Univ. Pr., Chicago, IL. 1975. 200p. 8.35Hdbd. ISBN 0-8294-0234-9. LC 75-5697. 5.95Pa. ISBN 0-8294-0243-8.

KELLY, WILLIAM W. Ellen Glasgow; A Bibliography. Univ. Pr. of Virginia, Charlottesville, VA. 1964. 330p.

KEMP, PETER. Muriel Spark. Barnes and Noble, NY. 1975. 167p. 12.50 Hdbd. ISBN 0-06-493619-8. LC 75-310316.

KENNARD, JEAN E. Number and Nightmare; Forms of Fantasy in Contemporary Fiction. Archon, Hamden, CT. 1975. 244p. 10.00Hdbd. ISBN 0-208-01486-1. LC 74-28448.

KENNEDY, ARTHUR G., and Donald B. Sands. A Concise Bibliography for Students of English. Stanford Univ. Pr., Stanford, CA. 1972. 300p. Hdbd. ISBN 0-8047-0804-5. LC 77-183889. Pa. ISBN 0-8047-0813-4.

KENNELL, RUTH EPPERSON. Theodore Dreiser and The Soviet Union; 1927-1945; A First-Hand Chronicle. International, NY. 1969. 320p.

KENNER, HUGH. A Homemade World. Knopf, NY. 1974(1975). 7.95Hdbd. ISBN 0-394-49102. LC 74-7759.

KENNER, HUGH. Studies in Change; A Book of the Short Story. Prentice-Hall, Englewood Cliffs, NJ. 1965. 238p. LC 65-10148.

KERNAN, ALVIN B. Plot of Satire. Yale Univ. Pr. 1965. 11.50Hdbd. ISBN 0-300-00621-7.

KERR, ELIZABETH MARGARET. Bibliography of the Sequence Novel. Octagon, NY. 1950(1973). 126p. 7.50 Hdbd. ISBN 0-374-94568-3. LC 70-159201.

KESSELRING, MARION LOUISE. Hawthorne's Reading;1828-1850;A Transcription and Identification of Titles Recorded in the Charge-Books of the Salem Athenaeum. Haskell, NY. 1976. 10.95Hdbd. ISBN 0-8383-2076-7. LC 75-22074.

KESTERSON, DAVID B. Josh Billings(Henry Wheeler Shaw). Twayne, NY. 1973(1974). 157p. 5.50Hdbd. ISBN 0-8057-0058-7. LC 73-1985.

KETTERER, DAVID. New Worlds of Old;The Apocalyptic Imagination, Science Fiction and American Literature. Anchor Pr./Doubleday, Garden City, NY. 1974. 347p. ISBN 0-385-00470-2. LC 72-96278.

KIELL, NORMAN. Varieties of Sexual Experience;Psychosexuality in Literature. International Univ. Pr., NY. 1976. 753p. 25.00Hdbd. ISBN 0-8236-6725-1. LC 74-21187.

KIERNAN, BRIAN. Images of Society and Nature;Seven Essays on Australian Novels. Oxford Univ. Pr. 1971. 187p.

KIERNAN, ROBERT F. Katherine Anne Porter and Carson McCullers;A Reference Guide. G. K. Hall, Boston, MA. 1976. 19.00Hdbd. ISBN 0-8161-7806-2. LC 76-2357.

KILLIGREW MICHAEL, Ed. Your Mirror to My Times;The Selected Autobiographies and Impressions of Ford Madox Ford. Holt, Rinehart, NY. 1971. 392p. LC 74-138884.

KILLINGER, JOHN. Hemingway and the Dead Gods;A Study in Existentialism. University of Kentucky Pr. 1960. 114p.

KINGSTON, CAROLYN T. The Tragic Mode in Children's Literature. Teachers College Pr., NY. 1974. 177 p. 5.95Hdbd. LC 73-14665.

KINSELLA, PAUL. The Technique of Writing. Harcourt, NY. 1975. 337p. 4.95Pa. ISBN 0-15-589726-8. LC 74-28512.

KIRBY, DAVID K. American Fiction to 1900;A Guide to Information Sources. Gale, Detroit, MI. 1975. ISBN 0-8103-1210-7. LC 73-16982.

KIRK, CLARA MARBURG. W. D. Howells;Traveler from Altruria;1889-1894. Rutgers Univ. Pr., New Brunswick, NJ. 1962. 148p. LC 62-13762.

KIRK, JOHN FOSTER. A Supplement to Allibone's Critical Dictionary of English Literature and British and American Authors. Gale, Detroit, MI. 1965. 1562p. 43.00Hdbd. LC 67-296.

KLEIN, HOLGER, Ed. The First World War in Fiction;A Collection of Critical Essays. Barnes and Noble, NY. 1976. 22.50Hdbd. ISBN 0-06-493792-5. LC 76-28822.

KLIMO, VERNON, and Will Oursler. Hemingway and Jake;An Extraordinary Friendship. Popular Library, NY. 1973. 223p. 1.25Pa. LC 72-76180(Hdbd Ed.)

KLINCK, CARL F., Ed. Literary History of Canada;Canadian Literature in English. 3 Vols. Univ. of Toronto Pr. 1976. Set 35.00Pa. ISBN 0-8020-6265-2. Each 8.95Pa. Vol. 1 ISBN 0-8020-6276-8. Vol. 2 ISBN 0-8020-6277-6. Vol. 3 ISBN 0-8020-6278-4.

KLINCK, CARL F., Ed. Literary History of Canada;Canadian Literature in English. 3Vols. Univ. of Toronto Pr. 1976. Vol. 1. 25.00Hdbd. ISBN 0-8020-2211-1. Vol. 2. 25.00Hdbd. ISBN 0-8020-2213-8. Vol. 3. 20.00Hdbd. ISBN 0-8020-2214-6.

KLINKOWITZ, JEROME. Literary Disruptions;The Making of a Post-Contemporary American Fiction. Univ. of Illinois, Urbana, IL. 1975. 241p. 7.95Hdbd. ISBN 0-252-00514-7. LC 75-4806.

KLINKOWITZ, JEROME, and John Somer, Eds. The Vonnegut Statement. Dell, NY. 1973. 286p. 2.65Pa.

KLOTMAN, PHYLLIS R. Another Man Gone;The Black Runner in Contemporary Afro-American Literature. Kennikat Pr., Port Washington, NY. 1976. 9.95Hdbd. ISBN 0-8046-9149-5. LC 76-18826.

KNIGHT, DAMON. In Search of Wonder;Essays on Modern Science Fiction. Advent, Chicago, IL. 1967. 306p. LC 67-4260.

KNIGHT, GRANT C. The Strenuous Age in American Literature. Univ. of North Carolina Pr., Chapel Hill, NC. 1954. 270p.

KNOLL, ROBERT E., Ed. Conversations with Wright Morris;Critical Views and Responses. Univ. of Nebraska Pr., Lincoln, NB. 1977. 10.95Hdbd. ISBN 0-8032-0904-5. LC 76-25497. 3.95Pa. ISBN 0-8032-5854-2.

KNOTT, WILLIAM C. The Craft of Fiction. Reston;A Prentice-Hall Co., Reston, VA. 1973. 149p. Hdbd. ISBN 0-87909-157-6. LC 72-90504. Pa. ISBN 0-87909-156-8.

KNOX, RONALD A. Essays in Satire. Kennikat Pr., Port Washington, NY. 1928(1968). 287p. LC 68-26297.

KOLB, HAROLD H., JR. Illusion of Life;American Realism As a Literary Form. Univ. Pr. of Virginia. 1969. 7.50Hdbd. ISBN 0-8139-0286-X. LC 76-93186.

KOLODNY, ANNETTE. The Lay of the Land;Metaphor as Experience and History in American Life and Letters. Univ. of North Carolina Pr. Chapel Hill, NC. 1975. 8.95Hdbd. ISBN 0-8078-1241-2. LC 74-23950.

KONVITZ, MILTON R., Ed. The Recognition of Ralph Waldo Emerson; Selected Criticism Since 1837. Univ. of Michigan Pr. 1972. 8.50Hdbd. ISBN 0-472-08508-5. LC 74-185152.

KOONTZ, DEAN R. Writing Popular Fiction. Writer's Digest, Cincinnati, OH. 1972. 233p. ISBN 0-911654-21-6. LC 72-92664.

KORSHIN, PAUL J., Ed. Studies in Change and Revolution. British Book Center. 1975. 12.50Pa. ISBN 0-8277-4314-9.

KORT, WESLEY A. Narrative Elements and Religious Meanings. Fortress Pr., Philadelphia, PA. 1975. 118p. 3.95. ISBN 0-8006-1433-X. LC 75-15257.

KOSTELANETZ, RICHARD. The End of Intelligent Writing;Literary Politics in America.Sheed and Ward; NY.1974.480p.12.95Hdbd.ISBN 0-8362-0554-5.LC 73-9098.

KOSTELANETZ, RICHARD, Ed.Younger Critics of North America;Essays on Literature and the Arts.Margins.1976.205p.5.00Pa.

KRAFT, JAMES.The Early Tales of Henry James.Southern Illinois Univ. Pr., Carbondale and Edwardsville, IL.1969.143p.

KRAMER, VICTOR A. James Agee. Twayne.1975.7.50Hdbd.ISBN 0-8057-0006-4.LC 74-23882.

KRAWITZ, HENRY. A Post-Symbolist Bibliography.Scarecrow Pr., Metuchen,NJ.1973.284p.7.50Hdbd. ISBN 0-8018-0594-4.LC 73-1181.

KRIM, SEYMOUR.Shake it for the World, Smartass.Dial Pr.,NY.1970. 376p.LC 74-80500.

KROOK, DOROTHEA. The Ordeal of Consciousness in Henry James.Cambridge Univ.Pr., Cambridge, MA. 1963(1968).422p.

KRUTCH, JOSEPH WOOD. Edgar Allan Poe;A Study in Genius.Knopf,NY. 1926.244p.

KRUTCH, JOSEPH WOOD.Henry David Thoreau.William Morrow,NY. 1948(1974).2.95Pa.ISBN 0-688-06774-3.LC 73-16724.

KUEHL, JOHN, and Jackson R. Bryer, Eds.Dear Scott/Dear Max;The Fitzgerald-Perkins Correspondence. Scribner's,NY.1971.282p.ISBN 6841-2373-8.LC 76-143940.

KUEHL, JOHN RICHARD. John Hawkes and the Craft of Conflict.Rutgers Univ. Pr., New Brunswick,NJ. 1975.195p.10.00Hdbd.ISBN 0-8315-0802-9.LC 74-34088.

KUHLMANN,SUSAN.Knave, Fool, and Genius;The Confidence Man as He Appears in Nineteenth-Century American Fiction.Univ.of North Carolina Pr., Chapel Hill,NC.1973.142 p.ISBN 0-8078-1208-0.LC 73-493.

KUNKEL, FRANCIS LEO.Passion and the Passion;Sex and Religion in Modern Literature.Westminster Pr. Philadelphia, PA.1975.206p.4.95Pa. ISBN 0-664-24778-4.LC 75-20085.

KVAM, WAYNE E. Hemingway in Germany;The Fiction, the Legend, and the Critics.Ohio Univ.Pr., Athens,OH.1973.214p.ISBN 8214-0126-2.LC 79-181689.

KYTLE,RAY,Comp., and Juanita Lyons.The Wrought Response;Reading and Writing about Literature. Dickenson, Encino, CA.1976.238p. 6.95Hdbd.ISBN 0-8221-0183-1.LC 76-3850.

L

LA BEAU, DENNIS, Ed. Children's Authors and Illustrators;An Index to Biographical Dictionaries. Gale, Detroit, MI. 1976. 15.00Hdbd. ISBN 0-8103-1078-3. LC 76-23534.

LABOR, EARLE. Jack London. Twayne, NY. 1974. 179p. 6.50Hdbd. ISBN 0-8057-0455-8. LC 73-2363.

LA FRANCE, MARSTON, Ed. Patterns of Commitment in American Literature. Univ. of Toronto Pr., Canada. 1967. 210p.

LA FRANCE, MARSTON. Reading of Stephen Crane. Oxford Univ. Pr. 1971. 9.50Hdbd. ISBN 0-19-812011-7.

LA HOOD, MARVIN J., Ed. Tender is the Night;Essays in Criticism. Indiana Univ. Pr., Bloomington, IN. 1969. 208p.

LANDSBERG, MELVIN. Dos Passos' Path to U.S.A.;A Political Biography;1912-1936. Colorado Univ. Pr., Boulder, CO. 1972. 292p. ISBN 87081-018-9. LC 72-75880.

LANGFELD, WILLIAM R., and Philip C. Blackburn, H.L. Kleinfield. Washington Irving;A Bibliography. Kennikat Pr., Port Washington, NY. 1933(1968). 32p. LC 67-27617.

LANGFORD, RICHARD E., and Guy Owen, William E. Taylor, Eds. Essays in Modern American Literature. Stetson Univ. Pr., DeLand, FL. 1963. 122p.

LANSBURY, CORAL. Already in Australia;The Evocation of Australia in Nineteenth Century English Literature. Melbourne Univ. Pr. 1970. 17.50Hdbd. ISBN 0-522-83979-7.

LARRICK, NANCY. A Parent's Guide to Children's Reading. Doubleday, Garden City, NY. 1975. 8.95Hdbd. ISBN 0-385-02564-5. LC 74-18815.

LARSEN, ERLING. James Agee. Univ. of Miami Pr. 1971. 1.25Pa. ISBN 0-8166-0599-8.

LASER, MARVIN, and Norman Fruman, Eds. Studies in J.D. Salinger. Odyssey. 1963. 2.25Pa.

LATHAM, AARON. Crazy Sundays; F. Scott Fitzgerald in Hollywood. Viking Pr., NY. 1971. 308p. LC 70-132860.

LATHROP, GEORGE PARSONS. Study of Hawthorne. James R. Osgood, Boston, MA. 1876. Repub. Scholarly Pr., St. Clair Shores, MI. 1970.

LAURENSON, DIANA T., and Alan Swingewood. The Sociology of Literature. Schocken, NY. 1972. 281p. LC 72-79743.

LAWALL, SARAH N. Critics of Consciousness;The Existential Structures of Literature. Harvard Univ. Pr. Cambridge, MA. 1968. 281p.

LAWRENCE, D. H. Studies in Classic American Literature. Viking Pr., NY. 1961(1968). 177p.

LAWSON, ALAN. Patrick White. Oxford Univ. Pr. 1974. 7.50Pa. ISBN 0-19-550453-4.

LAWSON, RICHARD H. Edith Wharton. Frederick Ungar, NY. 8.00Hdbd.

LEARY, LEWIS, Ed. American Literary Essays. Crowell, NY. 1960. 318p. LC 60-6316.

LEARY, LEWIS, Ed. Mark Twain's Letters to Mary. Columbia Univ. Pr. NY. 1961. 138p. LC 61-7714.

LEARY, LEWIS GASTON. Soundings; Some Early American Writers. Univ. of Georgia Pr., Athens, GA. 1975. 332p. 14.00Hdbd. ISBN 0-8203-0350-X. LC 73-90847.

LEARY, LEWIS GASTON. William Faulkner of Yoknapatawpha County. Crowell, NY. 1973. 214p. 4.50Hdbd. ISBN 0-690-89173-3. LC 72-7551.

LEAVIS, F. R. Anna Karenina and Other Essays. Pantheon, Div. Random House, NY. 1933(1967). 248p. LC 67-25426.

LEAVIS, FRANK. For Continuity. Folcroft, Folcroft, PA. 1974. 13.00Hdbd. ISBN 0-8414-5676-3. LC 74-22143.

LEAVIS, F. R. The Great Tradition; George Eliot, Henry James, Joseph Conrad. NY Univ. Pr., NY. 248p.

LEAVIS, FRANK RAYMOND. Mass Civilisation and Minority Culture. Folcroft, Folcroft, PA. 1930(1974). 7.50Hdbd. ISBN 0-8414-5730-1. LC 74-20677.

LEAVIS, FRANK RAYMOND, Ed. Towards Standards of Criticism;Selections from The Calendar of Modern Letters;1925-7. Folcroft, Folcroft, PA. 1974. 8.95Hdbd. ISBN 0-8414-5678-X. LC 74-22147.

LEBOWITZ, ALAN. Progress Into Silence;A Study of Melville's Heroes. Indiana Univ. Pr., Bloomington, IN. 1970. 240p.

LEBOWITZ, NAOMI. The Imagination of Loving;Henry James's Legacy to the Novel. Wayne State Univ. Pr., Detroit, MI. 1965. 184p.

LE CLAIR, ROBERT C. Young Henry James;1843-1870. Bookman, NY. 1955. 469p.

LEE, ALFRED PYLE. A Bibliography of Christopher Morley. Gryphon, Ann Arbor, MI. 1935(1971). 277p. 15.00 Hdbd. LC 70-152251.

LEE, LAWRENCE L. Vladimir Nabokov. Twayne, Boston, MA. 1976. 7.95 Hdbd. ISBN 0-8057-7166-2.

LEE, ROBERT EDSON. From West to East;Studies in the Literature of the American West. Univ. of Illinois Pr., Urbana, IL. 1966. 172p. LC 66-18825.

LEE, VERNON. The Handling of Words;And Other Studies in Literary

Psychology. Univ. of Nebraska Pr., Lincoln, NB. 1968(1969). 315p. LC 68-13649.

LEEMING, GLENDA. Who's Who in Henry James. Taplinger, NY. 1976. 120p. 7.95Hdbd. ISBN 0-8008-8626-7. LC 75-34783.

LEGGETT, JOHN. Ross and Tom;Two American Tragedies. Simon and Schuster, NY. 1974. 447p. ISBN 671-21733-X. LC 74-118.

LEHAN, RICHARD. A Dangerous Crossing;French Literary Existentialism and the Modern American Novel. Southern Illinois Univ. Pr., Carbondale and Edwardsville, IL. 1973. 198p. ISBN 0-8093-0607-7. LC 72-10233.

LEHAN, RICHARD D. F. Scott Fitzgerald and the Craft of Fiction. Southern Illinois Univ. Pr., Carbondale and Edwardsville, IL. 1967. 206p.

LEHAN, RICHARD. Theodore Dreiser;His World and His Novels. Southern Illinois Univ. Pr., Carbondale and Edwardsville, IL. 1969. 280p.

LEISY, ERNEST E. The American Historical Novel. Univ. of Oklahoma Pr., Norman. 1950. 280p.

LE ROY, GAYLORD C., and Ursula Beitz, Eds. Preserve and Create;Essays in Marxist Literary Criticism. Humanities Pr., NY. 1973. 276p. ISBN 391-00233-3. LC 72-75793.

LEVANT, HOWARD. The Novels of John Steinbeck;A Critical Study. Univ. of Missouri Pr. 1974. 304p. 12.50 Hdbd. ISBN 0-8262-0164-4. LC 74-76251.

LEVERENCE, JOHN. Irving Wallace A Writer's Profile. Popular Pr., Bowling Green, OH. 1974. 454p. ISBN 0-87972-063-8. LC 73-93855.

LEVIN, DAVID, Ed. Emerson;Prophecy, Metamorphosis, and Influence; Selected Papers from the English Institute. Columbia Univ. Pr., NY. 1975. 8.50Hdbd. ISBN 0-231-04000-8 LC 75-17704.

LEVIN, DAVID. In Defense of Historical Literature. Hill and Wang. 1967. 3.95Hdbd. ISBN 0-8090-5750-6.

LEVIN, HARRY. The Power of Blackness;Hawthorne, Poe, Melville. Knopf;Random House, NY. 1958(1967). 263p. 1.45Pa. ISBN 0-394-70090-2.

LEVINE, GEORGE, and David Leverenz, Eds. Mindful Pleasures;Essays on Thomas Pynchon. Little, Brown, Boston, MA. 1976. 9.95Hdbd. ISBN 0-316-52230- . LC76-21279. 4.95Pa.

LEVINS, LYNN GARTRELL. Faulkner's Heroic Design;The Yoknapatawpha Novels. Univ. of Georgia Pr., Athens, GA. 1976. 202p. 9.00Hdbd. ISBN 0-8203-0374-7. LC 74-18585.

LEWIS, CLAUDIA. Writing for Young Children. Simon and Schuster, NY. 1954. 115p. 3.00. LC 54-5809.

LEWIS, EDITH. Willa Cather;A Personal Record. Univ. of Nebraska Pr., Lincoln, NB. 1953(1976). 2.95Pa. ISBN 0-8032-5849-6. LC 76-17551.

LEWIS, FELICE F. Literature, Obscenity and Law. Southern Illinois Univ. Pr. 1976. 12.50Hdbd. ISBN 0-8093-0749-9. LC 75-42094.

LEWIS, GERALD E. Up Here in Maine. Pittsfield. 1974. 3.75Pa. LC 74-

LEWIS, RICHARD. WARRINGTON BALDWIN. Edith Wharton;A Biography. Harper and Row,NY.1975.15.00 Hdbd.ISBN 0-06-012603-5.LC 74-1833.

LEWIS, ROBERT W., JR. Hemingway on Lov. Univ. of Texas Pr., Austin, TX. 1965. 252p.

LEWIS, R.W.B. Trials of the Word; Essays in American Literature and the Humanistic Tradition. Yale Univ. Pr., New Haven, CT. 1965(1966). 235p. LC 65-22331.

LEWIS, WYNDHAM. Men Without Art. Russell and Russell, NY. 1934(1964). 303p. LC 64-13930.

LEWIS, WYNDHAM. Time and Western Man. Beacon Pr., Beacon Hill, Boston, MA. 1957. 469p. LC 57-9207.

LEWIS, WYNDHAM. The Writer and the Absolute. Greenwood Pr., Westport, CT. 1975. 202p. 12.00Hdbd. ISBN 0-8371-8098-8. LC 75-7240.

LEYBURN, ELLEN DOUGLASS. Strange Alloy;The Relation of Comedy to Tragedy in the Fiction of Henry James. Univ. of North Carolina Pr., Chapel Hill, NC. 1968. 180p.

LEYDA, JAY. The Melville Log;A Documentary Life of Herman Melville;1819-1891. Vol.1. Gordian Pr., NY. 1969. 494p. LC 73-81564.

LEYDA, JAY. The Melville Log;A Documentary Life of Herman Melville;1819-1891. Vol.2. Harcourt, Brace, NY. 1951. 899p.

LIEBER, TODD M. Endless Experiments;Essays on the Heroic Experience in American Romanticism. Ohio State Univ. Pr. 1973. 8.00Hdbd. ISBN 0-8142-0180-6. LC 72-10658.

LIEBERMAN, ELIAS. The American Short Story;A Study of the Influence of Locality in its Development. AMS Pr., NY. 1970. 183p. LC 71-128995.

LIGHT, MARTIN, Comp. The Merrill Studies in Babbitt. Merrill, Columbus, OH. 1971. 116p.

LIGHT, MARTIN. The Quixotic Vision of Sinclair Lewis. Purdue Univ. Pr., West Lafayette, IN. 1975. 162p. 6.50Hdbd. ISBN 0-911198-40-7. LC 74-82792.

LILJEGREN, STEN B. Revolt Against Romanticism in American Literature;As Evidenced in the Works of S. L. Clemens. Haskell. 1969. 7.95Hdbd. ISBN 0-8383-0583-0. LC 65-15896.

LINDAUER, MARTIN S. The Psychological Study of Literature;Limitations, Possibilities, and Accomplishments. Nelson-Hall, Chicago, IL. 1974. 254p. 11.00Hdbd. ISBN 0-911012-74-5. LC 73-80499.

LINDBERG, GARY H. Edith Wharton and the Novel of Manners. Univ. Pr. of Virginia, Charlottesville, VA. 1975. 186p. 11.50Hdbd. ISBN 0-8139-0563-X. LC 75-17504.

LINSON, CORWIN K. My Stephen Crane. Syracuse Univ. Pr. 1958. 115p. LC 58-9279.

LINTOT, BERNARD. Literature and Science;Balzac, Goethe, Flaubert, Zola, Chehkov, Proust. R. West. 1955. 35.00Hdbd.

LISCA, PETER. The Wide World of

John Steinbeck.Rutgers Univ.Pr., New Brunswick,NJ.1958.326p.9.00 Hdbd.ISBN 0-8135-0281-0.

LITTLEJOHN,DAVID.Back on White;A Critical Survey of Writing by American Negroes.Viking,NY.1966.

LITZ,A.WALTON,Ed.Modern American Fiction;Essays in Criticism. Oxford Univ.Pr.,NY.1963.365p.

LIVELY,ROBERT A.Fiction Fights The Civil War.Univ.of North Carolina Pr.,Chapel Hill,NC.1957.230p.

LOCKRIDGE,ERNEST,Ed.Twentieth Century Interpretations of The Great Gatsby;A Collection of Critical Essays.Prentice-Hall,Englewood Cliffs,NJ.1968.118p.

LONDON,JOAN.Jack London and His Times;An Unconventional Biography.Univ.of Washington Pr.,Seattle,WA.1939(1968).385p.LC 39-33408.

LONG,E.HUDSON.Mark Twain Handbook.Hendricks House,NY.1957. 454p.

LONG,E.HUDSON.O.Henry;The Man and His Work.A.S.Barnes,NY. 1960.158p.

LONG,FRANK BELKNAP.Howard Phillips Lovecraft;Dreamer on the Nightside.Arkham House,Sauk City, WI.1975.237p.8.50Hdbd.ISBN 0-87054-068-8.LC 74-18652.

LONGLEY,JOHN LEWIS,JR.The Tragic Mask;A Study of Faulkner's Heroes.Univ.of North Carolina Pr., Chapel Hill,NC.1963.242p.

LONSDALE,BERNARD J.Children Experience Literature.Random House,NY.1973.525p.9.95Hdbd.

LORCH,FRED W.The Trouble Begins at Eight;Mark Twain's Lecture Tours.Iowa State Univ.Pr.,Ames, IA.1968.375p.LC 68-17493.

LOSHE,LILLIE DEMING.The Early American Novel;1789-1830.Frederick Ungar,NY.1958(1966).131p. LC 58-9337.

LOWENTHAL,LEO.Literature,Popular Culture,and Society.Pacific Books,Palo Alto,CA.1968.169p. LC 61-13532.

LUBBOCK,PERCY.The Craft of Fiction.Viking Pr.,NY.1957(1968). 274p.LC 57-3468.

LUBBOCK,PERCY.Portrait of Edith Wharton.Appleton-Century,NY. 1947.Reprint Kraus Co.,NY.1969. 249p.LC 47-31175.

LUCCOCK,HALFORD E.American Mirror;Social,Ethical and Religious Aspects of American Literature; 1930-1940.Cooper Sq.1971.9.00Hdbd. ISBN 0-8154-0385-2.LC 75-156806.

LUDINGTON,TOWNSEND,Ed.The Fourteenth Chronicle;Letters and Diaries of John Dos Passos.Gambit, Boston,MA.1973.662p.15.00Hdbd. ISBN 0-87645-073-7.LC 72-94006.

LUKACS,GEORG.Trans.Hannah and Stanley Mitchell.The Historical Novel.Merlin Pr.,London.1962(1965). 363p.

LUKACS,GEORG.Realism in Our Time.Harper-Row,NY.1971.2.25Pa. ISBN 0-06-131603-2.

LUKACS, GEORG. Realism in Our Time;Literature and the Class Struggle. Peter Smith. 4.50Hdbd. ISBN 0-8446-4576-1.

LUKENS, REBECCA J. A Critical Handbook of Children's Literature. Foresman, Glenview, IL. 1976. 4.50 Pa. ISBN 0-673-15007-0. LC 75-35858.

LUNDBLAD, JANE. Nathaniel Hawthorne and European Literary Tradition. Russell and Russell, NY. 1965.

LUNDBLAD, JANE. Nathaniel Hawthorne and the Tradition of Gothic Romance. Haskell House, NY. 1964. 146p.

LUNDQUIST, JAMES. Chester Himes. Ungar, NY. 1976. 166p. 7.00Hdbd. ISBN 0-8044-2561-2. LC 75-42864.

LUNDQUIST, JAMES. Sinclair Lewis. Ungar, NY. 1973. 150p.

LUNDQUIST, JAMES. Theodore Dreiser. Ungar, NY. 1974. 150p. ISBN 0-8044-2563-9. LC 73-84600.

LUNDWALL, SAM J. Science Fiction; What it's All About. Ace Books, NY. 1971(1975). 256p. 1.50Pa. LC 72-459336.

LUTWACK, LEONARD. Heroic Fiction;The Epic Tradition and American Novels of the Twentieth Century. Southern Illinois Univ. Pr., Carbondale, IL. 1971. 174p. LC 78-156784.

LYDENBERG, JOHN, Ed. Dreiser;A Collection of Critical Essays. Prentice-Hall, Englewood Cliffs, NJ. 1971. 182p.

LYNCH, WILLIAM F. Christ and Apollo;The Dimensions of the Literary Imagination. Univ. of Notre Dame Pr., Notre Dame. 1960(1975). 8.95Hdbd. ISBN 0-268-00711-X. LC 75-19873. 3.25Pa. ISBN 0-268-00712-8.

LYNN, KENNETH S. Mark Twain and Southwestern Humor. Little, Brown, Boston, MA. 1959. 300p.

LYNN, KENNETH S. Visions of America;Eleven Literary Historical Essays. Greenwood Pr., Westport, CT. 205p.

LYON, THOMAS J. Frank Waters. Twayne, NY. 1973. 166p. 5.50Hdbd. LC 72-13369.

LYONS, JOHN O. The College Novel in America. Southern Illinois Univ. Pr., Carbondale, IL. 208p. LC 62-17619.

M

MC ALEER, JOHN J. Theodore Dreiser;An Introduction and Interpretation. Barnes and Noble, NY. 1968. 180p.

MC ARTHUR, PETER. Stephen Leacok. Folcroft, Folcroft, PA. 1923(1974). 10. 00Hdbd. LC 74-19412.

MC AULEY, JAMES. The Grammar of the Real;Selected Prose;1959-1974. Oxford Univ. Pr. 1976. 20. 00Hdbd. ISBN 0-19-550480-1.

MAC CANN, DONNARAE, and Olga Richard. The Child's First Books; A Critical Study of Pictures and Tests. Wilson Co., Bronx, NY. 1973. 135 p. 10. 00Hdbd.

MC CARTHY, HAROLD T. The Expatriate Perspective;American Novelists and the Idea of America. Fairleigh Dickinson Univ. Pr., Rutherford, Madison, Teaneck, NJ. 1974. 244p. ISBN 0-8386-1150-8. LC 74-418.

MC CARTHY, HAROLD T. Henry James;The Creative Process. Fairleigh Dickinson Univ. Pr., Rutherford, Madison, Teaneck, NJ. 1958. 172p.

MC CARTHY, MARY. Memories of a Catholic Girlhood. Heinemann, London, Melbourne, Toronto. 1957. 226p.

MC CARTHY, MARY. On the Contrary;Articles of Belief. Noonday, NY. 1962.

MC CARTHY, MARY. The Writing on the Wall and Other Literary Essays. Harcourt, NY. 1962(1970). 213p. LC 70-100498.

MC CARTNEY, FREDERICK A. Australian Literary Essays. R. West. 1958(1973). 10. 00Hdbd.

MC CLELLAN, GRANT S. Censorship in the United States. Wilson. 1967. 5. 25Hdbd. ISBN 0-8242-0096-9.

MC CLINTOCK, JAMES I. White Logic;Jack London's Short Stories. Wolf House, Grand Rapids, MI. 1975. 10. 00Hdbd. ISBN 0-915046-22-9. LC 74-84862.

MCCORMACK, THOMAS, Ed. Afterwords;Novelists on Their Novels. Harper-Row, NY. 1969. 231p. LC 68-28208.

MCCORMICK, JOHN. Catastrophe and Imagination;An Interpretation of the Recent English and American Novel. Folcroft, Folcroft, PA. 1974. 20. 00Hdbd. LC 74-19298.

MC CORMICK, JOHN. The Middle Distance;A Comparative History of American Imaginative Literature; 1919-1932. Free Pr., NY. 1971. 256p. LC 76-139233.

MC CRACKEN, ELIZABETH. The Feminine in Fiction. Folcroft, Folcroft, PA. 1918(1974). 15.00Hdbd. LC 74-7185.

MAC CULLOCH, CLARE. The Neglected Genre. Alive Pr., Canada. 1973. 2.95Pa. ISBN 0-919568-14-9.

MC DANIEL, JOHN N. The Fiction of Philip Roth. Haddonfield House, Haddonfield, NJ. 1974. 10.00HDBD. ISBN 0-88366-002-4. LC 74-8804.

MC DONALD, EDWARD DAVID. A Bibliography of the Writings of Theodore Dreiser. Folcroft, Folcroft, PA. 1974. 15.00Hdbd. LC 74-19299.

MC DONOUGH, IRMA, Ed. Canadian Books for Children. Univ. of Toronto Pr., Toronto/Buffalo. 1976. 112p. 7.50 Pa. ISBN 0-8020-4533-2. LC 76-3276.

MC DOWELL, FREDERICK P. W. Elizabeth Madox Roberts. Twayne, NY. 1963. 176p. LC 63-10955.

MC ELDERRY, BRUCE R., JR. Henry James. Twayne, NY. 1965. 192p.

MC ELDERRY, BRUCE R., JR. Thomas Wolfe. Twayne, NY. 1964. 207p.

MC FARLAND, DOROTHY TUCK. Flannery O'Connor. Ungar, NY. 1976. 132p. 7.00Hdbd. ISBN 0-8044-2609-0. LC 74-78443.

MC GARRY, DANIEL D., and Sarah Harriman White. World Historical Fiction Guide;An Annotated Chronological, Geographical and Topical List of Selected Historical Novels. Scarecrow Pr., Metuchen, NJ. 1973. 629p. 15.00Hdbd. ISBN 0-8108-0616-9. LC 73-4367.

MC HANEY, THOMAS L. William Faulkner;A Reference Guide. G. K. Hall, Boston, MA. 1976. 30.00Hdbd. ISBN 0-8161-1132-4. LC 76-2490.

MC HANEY, THOMAS L. William Faulkner's The Wild Palms;A Study. Univ. Pr. of Mississippi, Jackson, MS. 1975. 209p. 12.50Hdbd. ISBN 0-87805-070-1. LC 75-3648.

MC HUGH, VINCENT. Primer of the Novel. Random House, NY. 1950. 308p.

MC INTOSH, JAMES. Thoreau as Romantic Naturalist;His Shifting Stance Toward Nature. Cornell Univ. Pr. Ithaca, NY. 1974. 310p. 12.50Hdbd. ISBN 0-8014-0807-5. LC 73-8412.

MC LACHLAN, BRUCE. Censorship; A Study of the Censorship of Books, Films and Plays in New Zealand. Intl. Pubns. Serv. 1974. 3.00Pa. ISBN 0-8002-0088-8.

MC CLEARY, DOROTHY. Creative Fiction Writing. The Writer, Inc., Boston, MA. 1947. 148p.

MAC LEOD, ANNE. A Moral Tale; Children's Fiction and American Culture;1820-1860. Archon, Hamden, CT. 1975. 196p. 10.00Hdbd. ISBN 0-208-01552-3. LC 75-12533.

MC MASTER, HELEN NEILL. Margaret Fuller as a Literary Critic. Folcroft, Folcroft, PA. 1928(1974). 100p. 10.00Hdbd. ISBN 0-377-00019-1. LC 74-20532.

MC MICHAEL, GEORGE. Journey to Obscurity;The Life of Octave Thanet. Univ. of Nebraska Pr., Lincoln, NB. 1965. 259p. LC 64-19852.

MAC MILLAN, DOUGALD. Transition;The Story of a Literary Era;1927-1938. Braziller, NY. 1976. 12.50Hdbd. ISBN 8076-0780-0.

MC MURRAY, WILLIAM. The Literary Realism of William Dean Howells. Southern Illinois Univ. Pr., Carbondale. 1967. 147p.

MC NAMEE, LAWRENCE. Dissertations in English and American Literature;Theses Accepted by American, British and German Universities; 1865-1964. Bowker, NY. 1968. 1124p. 17.50Hdbd. LC 68-27446.

MC NAMEE, LAWRENCE. Dissertations in English and American Literature;Supplement One;Theses Accepted by American, British and German Universities;1964-1968. Bowker, NY. 1969. 450p. ISBN 8352-0280-1. LC 68-27446.

MC NEIR, WALDO, and Leo B. Levy, Eds. Studies in American Literature. Books for Libraries Pr., Plainview, NY. 1960(1974). 177p. ISBN 0-518-10152-5. LC 74-999.

MC NULTY, JOHN BARD. Modes of Literature. Houghton-Mifflin, Boston, MA. 1977. 630p. 11.50Pa. ISBN 0-394-24249-5. LC 76-10896. 0.95Inst. Manual. ISBN 0-395-24248-7.

MC PHERSON, HUGO. Hawthorne as Myth-Maker;A Study in Imagination. Univ. of Toronto Pr., Ontario, Canada. 1969.

MC WILLIAMS, JOHN P., JR. Political Justice in a Republic;James Fenimore Cooper's America. Univ. of California Pr., Berkeley, CA. 1972.

MACAULEY, ROBIE, and George Lanning. Technique in Fiction. Harper and Row, NY. 1964. 227p. LC 64-12803.

MACSHANE, FRANK. Raymond Chandler. Dutton, NY. 1976. 10.95Hdbd. LC 75-38791.

MACY, JOHN ALBERT, Ed. American Writers on American Literature; by 37 Contemporary Writers. Greenwood Pr., Westport, CT. 1931(1974). 539p. 24.50Hdbd. ISBN 0-8371-7350-7. LC 73-22753.

MADDEN, DAVID, Ed. Nathanael West;The Cheaters and the Cheated;A Collection of Critical Essays. Everett/Edwards, Deland, FL. 1973. 346p.

MADDEN, DAVID, Ed. Remembering James Agee. La State Univ. Pr. 1974. 8.95Hdbd. ISBN 0-8071-0086-2. LC 74-77326.

MADDEN, DAVID, Ed. Tough Guy Writers of the Thirties. Southern Illinois Univ. Pr., Carbondale, IL. 1968. 247p.

MAGNY, CLAUDE-EDMONDE. Trans. by Eleanor Hochman. The Age of the American Novel;The Film Aesthetic of Fiction Between the Two Wars. Ungar, NY. 1972. 239p. ISBN 0-8044-2586-8. LC 77-178166.

MAILER, NORMAN. Existential Errands. Little-Brown, Boston, MA. 1963(1972). 365p. LC 76-175-476.

MAIER, NORMAN RAYMOND FREDERICK, and H. Willard Reninger.

A Psychological Approach to Literary Criticism. Norwood Editions, Norwood, Pa. 1933(1975). 154p. 20.00Hdbd. ISBN 0-88305-426-4. LC 73-15974.

MAJOR, CLARENCE. The Dark and Feeling; Black American Writers and Their Work. Third Press, NY. 1974. 153p. 6.95Hdbd. ISBN 0-89388-118-X. LC 73-83162.

MAJOR, MABEL, and T.M. Pearce. Southwest Heritage; A Literary History with Bibliographies. Univ. of New Mexico Pr., Albuquerque, NM. 1972. 364p. 12.00Hdbd. 4.95Pa.

MAKSYM, TOM, Ed. Short World Biographies. Globe, NY. 1973. 342p. 3.20Pa.

MALE, ROY R. Hawthorne's Tragic Vision. Norton, NY. 1959.

MALIN, IRVING, Ed. Contemporary American-Jewish Literature; Critical Essays. Indiana Univ. Pr., Bloomington, IN. 1973. 302p. ISBN 0-253-31420-8. LC 72-75393.

MALIN, IRVING. Nathanael West's Novels. Southern Illinois Univ. Pr., Carbondale, IL. 1972. 141p.

MANCHESTER, WILLIAM. H.L. Mencken; Disturber of the Peace. Collier, NY. 1950, 51(1962). 382p.

MANDEL, ELI. Another Time. Press Porcepic. 1977. 15.00Hdbd. ISBN 0-88878-076-1. 4.95Pa. ISBN 0-88878-077-X.

MANDEL, ELI. Contexts of Canadian Criticism. Univ. of Chicago Pr., Chicago, IL. 1971. 12.50Hdbd. ISBN 0-226-50298-8. LC 78-143280.

MANTZ, HAROLD ELMER. French Criticism of American Literature Before 1850. AMS Press, NY. 1966. 165p.

MARCUS, STEVEN. Representations; Essays on Literature and Society. Random House, NY. 1975, 1976. 12.95 Hdbd. ISBN 0-394-49559-4. LC 75-10252.

MARGOLIES, EDWARD. Native Sons; A Critical Study of Twentieth-Century Negro American Authors. Lippincott, Philadelphia, PA. 1968. 209p. 1.95Pa.

MARGULIS, JOEL B. An Awareness of Language. Winthrop, Cambridge, MA. 1975. 148p. 5.95Pa. ISBN 0-87626-050-4. LC 74-34203.

MARKLE, JOYCE B. Fighters and Lovers; Theme in the Novels of John Updike. New York Univ. Pr., NY. 1973. 205p. 8.95Hdbd. ISBN 0-8147-5361-2. LC 72-96469.

MARKOW-TOTEVY, GEORGES. Henry James. Crowell. 128p. 1.95Pa. ISBN 0-308-60048-7.

MARKS, BARRY A., Ed. Mark Twain's Huckleberry Finn. D.C. Heath, Boston, MA. 1959. 108p.

MARKS, LESTER JAY. Thematic Design in the Novels of John Steinbeck. Mouton, The Hague, Paris. 1971. 144p. 13.75Hdbd. LC 68-24621.

MARPLE, ALICE. Iowa Authors and Their Works; A Contribution toward a Bibliography. Gale, Detroit, MI. 1976. 22.50Hdbd. ISBN 0-8103-4287-1. LC 72-174076.

MARTIN, EVANS J. America; The

View from Europe. San Francisco Book Co. 1977. 139p. 8.95Hdbd. ISBN 0-913374-50-4. LC 76-40688. 3.95Pa. ISBN 0-913374-51-2.

MARTIN, JAY. Harvests of Change; American Literature;1865-1914. Prentice-Hall, Englewood Cliffs, NJ. 1967. LC 67-14850.

MARTIN, JAY, Ed. Nathanael West; A Collection of Critical Essays. Prentice-Hall, Englewood Cliffs, NJ. 1971. 176p.

MARTIN, TERENCE. Nathaniel Hawthorne. Twayne U.S. Author Series No. 75. Twayne Pub., NY. 1965.

MASINTON, CHARLES G. J.P. Donleavy;The Style of His Sadness and Humor. Bowling Green Univ. Pr., Bowling Green, OH. 1975. 75p. 3.00 Pa. ISBN 0-87972-103-0. LC 75-930.

MASON, BOBBIE ANN. The Girl Sleuth. Feminist Pr., Old Westbury, NY. 1974. 2.00. ISBN 0-912670-17-3. LC 74-22313.

MASON, BOBBIE A. Nabokov's Garden;A Study of Ada. Ardis. 1974. 8.95 Hdbd. ISBN 0-88233-052-7. 3.25Pa. ISBN 0-88233-053-5.

MASON, RONALD. The Spirit Above the Dust;A Study of Herman Melville. Appel, Mamaroneck, NY. 1972. 269p.

MASSEY, IRVING J. Uncreating World;Romanticism and the Object. Indiana Univ. Pr. 1970. 7.50Hdbd. ISBN 0-253-18993-4. LC 77-126213.

MASSEY, LINTON R., Comp. "Man Working," 1919-1962;William Faulkner;A Catalogue of the William Faulkner Collections at the University of Virginia. Bibliographical Society of the Univ. of Virginia, Charlottesville, VA. 1968. 250p. LC 68-19477.

MASTERS, EDGAR LEE. Across Spoon River;An Autobiography. Octagon Books, NY. 1969. 426p. LC 70-96162.

MASTERS, EDGAR LEE. Mark Twain;A Portrait. Biblo and Tannen, NY. 1966. 259p. LC 66-15216.

MATTHIESSEN, F.O. Henry James; The Major Phase. Oxford Univ. Pr., NY. 1963. 190p.

MATTHIESSEN, FRANCIS OTTO. Sarah Orne Jewett. Peter Smith, Gloucester, MA. 1965. 159p.

MATTHIESSEN, F.O. Theodore Dreiser. Delta, NY. 1951(1966). 267p.

MAURICE, ARTHUR BARTLETT. New York in Fiction. Friedman, Port Washington, NY. 1969. 231p. LC 68-28930.

MAVES, CARL. Sensuous Pessimism;Italy in the Work of Henry James. Indiana Univ. Pr., Bloomington, IN. 1973. 169p.

MAXWELL, D.E.S. Herman Melville. Routledge and Kegan Paul, London and Humanities Pr., NY. 1968. 101p.

MAY, CHARLES E., Ed. Short Story Theories. Ohio Univ. Pr., Athens, OH. 1976. 10.00Hdbd. 4.25Pa.

MAY, JOHN R. The Pruning Word; The Parables of Flannery O'Connor. Univ. of Notre Dame Pr., Notre Dame, IN. 1976. 178p. 10.95Hdbd. ISBN 0-268-01518-X. LC 75-19878.

MAY, JOHN R. Toward a New Earth; Apocalypse in the American Novel. Univ. of Notre Dame Pr., Notre Dame, IN. 1972. 254p. LC 72-3510.

MAY, ROLLO, Ed. Symbolism in Religion and Literature. Braziller. 6.95 Hdbd. ISBN 0-8076-0115-2. LC 59-8842. 2.95Pa. ISBN 0-8076-0376-7.

MAYFIELD, SARA. The Constant Circle; H. L. Mencken and His Friends. Delacorte, NY. 1968. 307p. LC 68-16641.

MAYFIELD, SARA. Exiles from Paradise; Zelda and Scott Fitzgerald. Delacorte Pr., NY. 1971. 309p. LC 76-137744.

MAYS, BENJAMIN E. The Negro's God; As Reflected in His Literature. Russell and Russell, NY. 1938(1968). 269p. LC 68-26870.

MEAD, EDWIN D. The Influence of Emerson. Folcroft, Folcroft, PA. 1903(1972). 25.00Hdbd.

MEEKER, JOSEPH W. The Comedy of Survival; Studies in Literary Ecology. Scribner, NY. 1974. 217p. 8.95 Hdbd. ISBN 0-684-13711-9. LC 74-1002.

MELLOW, JAMES R. Charmed Circle; Gertrude Stein and Company. Praeger, NY. 1974. 528p. 12.50Hdbd. LC 73-7473.

MENCKEN, H. L. Happy Days; 1880-1892. Knopf, NY. 1968. 313p.

MEREDITH, ROBERT C., and John D. Fitzgerald. The Professional Story Writer and His Art. Crowell, NY. 1963. LC 63-9201.

MERIWETHER, JAMES B. Ed. A Faulkner Miscellany. Univ. Pr. of Mississippi. 1974. 166p. 8.50Hdbd. ISBN 0-87805-051-5. LC 73-87167.

MERIWETHER, JAMES B. The Literary Career of William Faulkner; A Bibliographical Study. Univ. of South Carolina Pr., Columbia, SC. 1961 (1971). 192p. ISBN 6-87249-213-3. LC 79-149488.

MERIWETHER, JAMES B., Comp. The Merrill Studies in The Sound and the Fury. Merrill Pub., Columbus, OH. 1970. 156p.

MERRY, BRUCE. Anatomy of the Spy Thriller. 1977. 200p. 14.95Hdbd. ISBN 0-7735-0316-1.

MERSAND, JOSEPH. Traditions in American Literature; A Study of Jewish Characters and Authors. Kennikat Pr., Port Washington, NY. 1968. 247p. LC 68-26240.

MERWIN, HENRY CHILDS. The Life of Bret Harte; With Some Account of the California Pioneers. Univ. Pr. Cambridge; Houghton Mifflin, Boston, MA. 1911. Repub. Gale, Detroit, MI. 1967. 362p. LC 67-23887.

METZGER, CHARLES R. Emerson and Greenough; Transcendental Pioneers of an American Esthetic. Greenwood. 1971. 8.50Hdbd. ISBN 0-8371-5756-0. LC 74-139140.

MEYER, ROY WILLARD. The Middle Western Farm Novel in the Twentieth Century. Univ. of Nebraska Pr. Lincoln, NB. 1964(1974). 265p. 2.45Pa. ISBN 0-8032-5798-8. LC 64-17221.

MICHAUD, REGIS. The American Novel Today; A Social and Psychological Study. Kennikat Pr., Port Washington, NY. 293p.

MICHAUD, REGIS. Emerson;The Enraptured Yankee. R. West. 1930(1973). 10.00Hdbd.

MICHEL, PIERRE. James Gould Cozzens. Twayne, NY. 1974. 7.50Hdbd. ISBN 0-8057-0163-X. LC 73-17017.

MICHEL, PIERRE. James Gould Cozzens;An Annotated Checklist. Kent State Univ. Pr., Kent, OH. 1971. 123p. 6.50Hdbd. LC 75-169068.

MIGNON, CHARLES W. Emerson's Essays;Notes. Cliffs Notes, Lincoln, NB. 1975. 78p. 1.25Pa. ISBN 0-8220-0429-1. LC 75-315891.

MILES, JOSEPHINE. Ralph Waldo Emerson;Pamphlets on American Writers;No. 41. Univ. of Minn. Pr. 1964. 1.25Pa. ISBN 0-8166-0333-2.

MILES, ROBERT. First Principles of the Essay. Harper and Row, NY. 1975. 267p. 4.95Pa. ISBN 0-06-044439-8. LC 74-11768.

MILES, ROSALIND. The Fiction of Sex;Themes and Functions of Sex Difference in the Modern Novel. Barnes and Noble, NY. 1974(1975). 208p. 12.00Hdbd. ISBN 0-06-494822-6. LC 75-307038.

MILFORD, NANCY. Zelda;A Biography. Harper and Row, NY. 1962. 424p. LC 66-20742.

MILLER, E. MORRIS. Australian Literature;1795-1938. 2 vols. Sydney Univ. Pr., Sydney, Aust. 1940(1975). 66.00Hdbd. Set. ISBN 0-424-06700-5.

MILLER, EDWIN HAVILAND. Melville. G. Braziller, NY. 1975. 382p. 15.00Hdbd. ISBN 0-8076-0787-8. LC75-7958.

MILLER, HENRY. The Books in My Life. New Directions, NY. 1969. 316p. LC 71-88728.

MILLER, HENRY. Henry Miller on Writing. New Directions, NY. 1939(1964). 216p. LC 64-10675.

MILLER, HENRY. Reflections on the Death of Mishima. Capra Pr. 1972. 2.75Pa. ISBN 0-912264-38-1.

MILLER, HENRY. Stand Still Like the Hummingbird. New Directions, NY. 1962. 194p. LC 62-10408.

MILLER, HENRY. Sunday After the War. New Directions, NY. 1944. 300p.

MILLER, HENRY. The Wisdom of the Heart. New Directions, NY. 1941 (1960). 250p.

MILLER, JAMES E., JR. F. Scott Fitzgerald;His Art and His Technique. New York Univ. Pr., NY. 1967. 173p.

MILLER, JAMES E., JR. A Reader's Guide to Herman Melville. Farrar, Straus, NY. 1962. 266p.

MILLER, JAMES E., JR. Quests Surd and Absurd;Essays in American Literature. Univ. of Chicago Pr., Chicago, IL. 1967. 271p. LC 67-25520.

MILLER, MARJORIE M. Isaac Asimov;A Checklist of Works Published in the United States;March 1939-May 1972. Kent State Univ. Pr., Kent, OH. 1972. 98p. 6.50Hdbd. ISBN 0-87338-126-2. LC 72-76948.

MILLER, WAYNE CHARLES. An Armed America;Its Face in Fiction;A History of the American Novel. New York Univ. Pr., NY. and Univ. of London Pr., London. 1970. 294p. ISBN 8147-0473-5. LC 75-111521.

MILLETT, FRED B. Contemporary American Authors;A Critical Survey and 219 Bio-Bibliographies. Harcourt, Brace, NY. 1940. 716p.

MILLETT, KATE. Sexual Politics. Ballantine Books, NY. 1978. ISBN 0-345-27534-9. LC 70-103769.

MILLGATE, MICHAEL. The Achievement of William Faulkner. Random House, NY. 1966. 344p.

MILLGATE, MICHAEL. American Social Fiction;James to Cozzens. Barnes and Noble, NY. 1964(1967). 217p. LC 64-5659.

MILLS, GORDON. Hamlet's Castle; The Study of Literature As a Social Experience. Univ. of Texas Pr. 1976. 14.95Hdbd. ISBN 0-292-73005-5. LC 76-8020.

MILLS, NICOLAUS. American and English Fiction in the Nineteenth Century;An Antigenre Critique and Comparison. Indiana Univ. Pr., Bloomington, IN. 1973. 150p. ISBN 0-253-30590-X. LC 72-85853.

MILNE, GORDON. The American Political Novel. Univ. of Oklahoma Pr., Norman, OK. 1966. LC 66-13417.

MILNE, GORDON. The Sense of Society;A History of the American Novel of Manners. Fairleigh Dickinson Univ. Pr., Rutherford, NJ. 1977. 12.50 Hdbd. ISBN 0-8386-1927-4. LC 76-748.

MILTON, JOHN R., Comp. The Literature of South Dakota. Dakota Pr., Vermillion, SD. 1976. 395 p. 10.00Hdbd. ISBN 0-88249-023-0. LC 73-13468.

MINER, EARL ROY. The Japanese Tradition in British and American Literature. Greenwood Pr., Westport, CT. 1976. 16.50 Hdbd. ISBN 0-8371-8818-0. LC 76-3698.

MINER, WARD L. The World of William Faulkner. Cooper Sq. Pub., NY. 1963. 170p.

MINNIGERODE, MEADE. Some Personal Letters of Herman Melville and a Bibliography. Books for Libraries Pr., Freeport, NY. 1922(1969). 194p. LC 78-75511.

MINTER, DAVID L., Ed. Twentieth Century Interpretations of Light in August;A Collection of Critical Essays. Prentice-Hall, Englewood Cliffs, NJ. 1969. 120p.

MIRON, DAN. Sholem Aleykhem;Person, Persons, Presence. Yivo Inst., NY. 1972. 1.50Pa. ISBN 0-914512-02. LC 73-161969.

MIRON, DAN. A Traveler Disguised; A Study in the Rise of Modern Yiddish Fiction in the Nineteenth Century. Schocken, NY. 1973. 347p. 10.95 Hdbd. ISBN 0-8052-3499-3. LC 72-95663.

MIRRIELEES, EDITH RONALD. Story Writing. The Writer, Boston, MA. 1947(1966). ISBN 0-87116-075-7. LC 72-6277.

MITCHELL, EDWARD, Ed. Henry Miller;Three Decades of Criticism. New York Univ. Pr., NY. 1971. 216p.

6.00Hdbd. ISBN 8147-5356-6. LC 78-181513. 4.00Pa. ISBN 8147-5357-4.

MIZENER, ARTHUR, Ed. F. Scott Fitzgerald; A collection of Critical Essays. Twentieth Century Views Series. Prentice-Hall, Englewood Cliffs, NJ. 1963. 174p. 5.95Hdbd. 1.95Pa.

MIZENER, ARTHUR. The Far Side of Paradise; A Biography of F. Scott Fitzgerald. Houghton Mifflin, Boston, MA. 1965. 416p.

MIZENER, ARTHUR. The Saddest Story; A Biography of Ford Madox Ford. World Pub., NY. 1971. 615p. LC 73-124285.

MIZENER, ARTHUR. Scott Fitzgerald and His World. G.P. Putnam's Sons, NY. 1972. 128p. LC 72-189992.

MIZENER, ARTHUR. The Sense of Life in the Modern Novel. Houghton Mifflin, Boston, MA. 1963. 291p. LC 62-11483.

MIZENER, ARTHUR. Twelve Great American Novels. New American Library, NY. 1967. 204p. LC 67-24788.

MIZENER, SHARON FUSSELMAN. Manhattan Transients; A Critical Essay. Exposition Pr., Hicksville, NY. 1977. 48p. 4.50. ISBN 0-682-48734-1. LC 76-50294.

MOERS, ELLEN. Literary Women. Doubleday, NY. 1975. 10.00Hdbd. ISBN 0-385-07427-1. LC 74-33686.

MOERS, ELLEN. Two Dreisers. Viking Pr., NY. 1969. 366p.

MONTGOMERY, CONSTANCE CAPPEL. Hemingway in Michigan. Fleet Pub., NY. 1966. 224p.

MOON, ERIC, Ed. Book Selection and Censorship in the Sixties. Bowker. 1969. 12.75Hdbd. ISBN 0-8352-0205-4. LC 78-79423.

MOONEY, HARRY J., JR. The Fiction and Criticism of Katherine Anne Porter. Univ. of Pittsburgh Pr. 1957 (1967). 65p. LC 57-9404.

MOORE, HARRY T. Henry James. Viking Pr., NY. 1974. 128p. LC 73-21499.

MOORE, MAXINE. The Lonely Game; Melville, Mardi, and the Almanac. Univ. of Missouri Pr., Columbia, MS. 1975. 15.00Hdbd. ISBN 0-8262-0175-X. LC 75-8578.

MOORE, T. INGLIS. Social Patterns in Australian Literature. Univ. of Calif. Pr. 1971. 13.75Hdbd. ISBN 0-520-0182-1. LC 71-133027.

MORAVIA, ALBERTO. Man as an End; A Defense of Humanism; Literary, Social and Political Essays. Transl. by Bernard Wall. Greenwood Pr., Westport, CT. 1965(1976). 14.50 Hdbd. ISBN 0-8371-8019-8. LC 75-391.

MORE, PAUL ELMER. Shelburne Essays on American Literature. Harcourt, NY. 1963. 280p. LC 63-19640.

MOREAU, GENEVIEVE. The Restless Journey of James Agee. Trans. Miriam Kleiger. Morrow, NY. 1977. 10.95 Hdbd. ISBN 0-688-03141-2. LC 76-25832.

MORGAN, H. WAYNE. American Writers in Rebellion; From Mark Twain to Dreiser. Hill and Wang, NY. 1965(1969). 205p. Hdbd. ISBN 8090-

2590-6. LC 65-24713. Pa. ISBN 8090-0077-6.

MORLEY, PATRICIA A. The Comedians;Hugh Hood and Rudy Wiebe. Clarke, Irwin, Toronto, Vancouver, Canada. 1977. 130p. ISBN 0-7720-1051-X.

MORLEY, PATRICIA. The Mystery of Unity;Theme and Technique in the Novels of Patrick White. McGill, Queens Univ. Pr. 1972. 9.50Hdbd. ISBN 0-7735-0112-6.

MORRELL, DAVID. John Barth;An Introduction. Pennsylvania St. Univ. Pr., University Park, PA. 1976. 10.00 Hdbd. ISBN 0-271-01220-X. LC 75-27284.

MORRIS, ROBERT K., and Irving Malin. The Achievement of William Styron. Univ. of Georgia Pr., Athens, GA. 1975. 280p. 12.00Hdbd. ISBN 0-8203-0351-8. LC 74-75942.

MORRIS, WESLEY. Toward a New Historicism. Princeton Univ. Pr., Princeton, NJ. 1972. 11.00Hdbd. ISBN 0-691-06223-4. LC 77-166384.

MORRIS, WRIGHT. The Territory Ahead. Atheneum, NY. 1963. 247p.

MORRISON, CLAUDIA C. Freud and the Critic;The Early Use of Depth Psychology in Literary Criticism. Univ. of North Carolina Pr., Chapel Hill, NC. 1968. 248p. LC 68-54948.

MORSE, GRANT W. Complete Guide to Organizing and Documenting Research Papers. Fleet, NY. 1974. 156p. 15.00Hdbd. ISBN 0-8303-0129-1. LC 73-83969.

MORSE, J. MITCHELL. Prejudice and Literature. Temple Univ. Pr., Philadelphia, PA.

MORTON, DONALD E. Vladimir Nabokov. Ungar, NY. 1974. 164p. 6.00Hd bd. ISBN 0-8044-2638-4. LC 74-76128.

MOSELEY, JAMES G. A Complex Inheritance/The Idea of Self-Transcendence in the Theology of Henry James, Sr., and the Novels of Henry James. American Acad. of Religion, Missoula, MT. 1975. ISBN 0-89130-000-7. LC 75-8955.

MOSKOWITZ, SAMUEL. Explorers of the Infinite;Shapers of Science Fiction. Hyperion Pr., Westport, CT. 1974. 353p. 9.75Hdbd. ISBN 0 88355-130-6. LC 73-15068.

MOSKOWITZ, SAMUEL. The Immortal Storm;A History of Science Fiction Fandom. Hyperion Pr., Westport, CT. 1954(1973). 8.95Hdbd. ISBN 0-88355-131-4. LC 73-15069.

MOSKOWITZ, SAMUEL. Seekers of Tomorrow;Masters of Modern Science Fiction. Hyperion Pr., Westport, CT. 1974. 441p. 11.50Hdbd. ISBN 0-88355-129-2. LC 73-15073.

MOSS, SIDNEY P. Poe's Literary Battles;The Critic in the Context of His Literary Milieu. Duke. 1963. 7.75 Hdbd. ISBN 0-8223-0119-9. Southern Illinois Univ. Pr. 1969. 2.85Pa. ISBN 0-8093-0351-5. LC 63-9010.

MOSS, SIDNEY P. Poe's Major Crisis;His Libel Suit and New York's Literary World. Duke. 1970. 7.75Hdbd. ISBN 0-8223-0217-9.

MOYLES, R. G. English-Canadian Literature to 1900;A Guide to Information Sources. Gale, Detroit, IL. 1976. 346p. 18.00Hdbd. LC 73-16986.

MUDRICK, MARVIN. On Culture and Literature. Horizon Pr., NY. 1970. 252p. Hdbd. ISBN 0-8180-1150-5. LC 77-92717. Pa. ISBN 0-8180-1156-4.

MUELLER, GUSTAV E. Philosophy of Literature. Philosophical Library, NY. 1948. 226p.

MULLER, HERBERT J. Thomas Wolfe. New Directions, Norfolk, CT. 1947. 196p.

MUMFORD, LEWIS. The Golden Day; A Study in American Literature and Culture. Dover, NY. 1957(1968). 144p. LC 68-17395.

MUMFORD, LEWIS. Herman Melville; A Study of His Life and Vision. Harcourt, NY. 1956(1962). 4.50Hdbd. 2.45Pa.

MUNSON, GORHAM BERT. Waldo Frank; A Study. Folcroft, Folcroft, PA. 1923(1975). 10.00Hdbd. ISBN 0-8414-6124-4. LC 75-23023.

MURRY, JOHN MIDDLETON. Unprofessional Essays. Greenwood Pr., Westport, CT. 1975. 11.50Hdbd. ISBN 0-8371-8099-6. LC 75-7241.

MYERS, ANDREW B., Comp. The Worlds of Washington Irving; 1783-1859; From an Exhibition of Rare Book and Manuscript Materials in the Special Collections of the New York Public Library. Sleepy Hollow Restorations, Tarrytown, NY. 1974. 134p.

MYERS, CAROL FAIRBANKS. Women in Literature; Criticism of the Seventies. Scarecrow Pr., Metuchen, NJ. 1976. 10.00Hdbd. ISBN 0-8108-0885-4. LC 75-35757.

MYERSON, JOEL, and Arthur Miller, Jr. Melville Dissertations; An Annotated Directory. Melville Society of America. 1972. 57p. 4.00Pa.

MURPHY, JOHN J. Five Essays on Willa Cather; The Merrimack Symposium. Merrimack College, Andover, MA. 1974. 142p. 2.50Pa. LC 74-78413.

N

NABOKOV, VLADIMIR. Speak, Memory;An Autobiography Revisited.Putnam's Sons,NY. 316p. LC 66-23330.

NABOKOV, VLADIMIR. Strong Opinions. McGraw-Hill,NY. 335p. ISBN 0-07-045737-9. LC 73-6604.

NAGEL, JAMES, Comp. Critical Essays on Catch-22. Dickenson, Encino, CA. 1974. 179p. ISBN 0-8221-0088-6. LC 73-88119.

NAHAL, CHAMAN. The Narrative Pattern in Ernest Hemingway's Fiction. Vikas Pub.,Delhi;London.1971. 245p.

NANCE, WILLIAM L. Katherine Anne Porter and the Art of Rejection. Univ. of North Carolina Pr., Chapel Hill,NC. 1963(1964). 258p. LC 64-22525.

NELSON, GERALD B. Ten Versions of America. Knopf,NY. 1972. 201p. ISBN 0-399-466-10-1. LC 72-171129.

NETTELS, ELSA. James and Conrad. Univ. of Georgia Pr., Athens, GA. 1977. 289p. 12.00Hdbd. ISBN 0-8203-0408-5. LC 76-2897.

NEUFELDT, LEONARD NICK. Ralph Waldo Emerson;New Appraisals and Symposium. Transcendental Books,Hartford, CT. 1973. 12.50Hdbd. LC 74-154357.

NEUMANN, ALFRED R., and David V. Erdman, Eds. Literature and the Other Arts;A Select Bibliography; 1952-1958. Norwood, Norwood, PA. 1959(1974). 5.50Hdbd. LC 74-9588.

NEVINS, FRANCIS M., JR.,Ed. The Mystery Writer's Art. Bowling Green Univ. Popular Pr., Bowling Green,OH. 1970. 338p. LC 77-147820.

NEVINS, FRANCIS M., JR. Royal Bloodline;Ellery Queen, Author and Detective. Bowling Green Univ. Pr., Bowling Green, OH. 1974. 288p. 9.95 Hdbd. ISBN 0-87972-066-2. LC 73-89839.

NEVIUS, BLAKE, Comp. The American Novel;Sinclair Lewis to the Present. Appleton-Century-Crofts,NY. 1970. 126p. 1.95Pa.

NEVIUS, BLAKE. Edith Wharton;A Study of Her Fiction. Univ. of California Pr., Berkeley, CA. 1953(1976). 271p. 14.25Hdbd. ISBN 0-520-03180-6.

NEVIUS, BLAKE. Robert Herrick; The Development of a Novelist. Univ. of California Pr., Berkeley, CA.

1962. 9. 50Hdbd. ISBN 0-520-00926-6.

NEW ENGLAND SCIENCE FICTION ASSOCIATION. Index to the Science Fiction Magazines;1966-1970. 1971. 82p.

NEW YORK CITY PUBLIC LIBRARY.No Crystal Stair;A Bibliography of Black Literature. NY. 1971. 63p. 2. 00Pa. LC 72-175979.

NICHOLS, MARY SARGEANT GOVE. Reminiscences of Edgar Allan Poe. Haskell House, NY. 1931(1974). 7. 95 Hdbd. ISBN 0-8383-2068-6. LC 74-4041.

NIELD, JONATHAN. A Guide to Best Historical Novels and Tales. Putnam, NY. 1904. Milford House, Boston, MA. 1973. 15. 00Hdbd. ISBN 0-87821-062-8. LC 73-12361.

NILON, CHARLES H. Faulkner and the Negro. Citadel Pr. 1965. 1. 75Pa.

NIN, ANAIS. The Novel of the Future. Macmillan, NY. Collier-Macmillan, London. 214p. 5. 95Hdbd. LC 68-8710.

NIST, JOHN, Ed. Style in English. The Bobbs-Merrill Series in Composition and Rhetoric. Bobbs-Merrill, Indianapolis, IN. 1969. 61p. 1. 00Pa.

NNOLIM, CHARLES E. Melville's "Benito Cereno";A Study in Meaning of Name Symbolism. New Voices, NY. 1974. 68p. 4. 95Pa. ISBN 0-911024-13-1. LC 74-80979.

NOBLE, DAVID W. The Eternal Adam and the New World Garden;The Central Myth in the American Novel Since 1830. Braziller, NY. 1968. 226p. LC 68-12889.

NOEL, THOMAS. Theories of the Fable in the Eighteenth Century. Columbia Univ. Pr., NY. 1975. 177p. 9. 00Hdbd. ISBN 0-231-03858. LC 74-23251.

NOLTE, WILLIAM H., Ed. H. L. Mencken's Smart Set Criticism. Cornell Univ. Pr., Ithaca, NY. 1968. 349p. LC 68-16387.

NORDLOH, DAVID J.William Dean Howells. Years of my Youth, and Three Essays. Indiana Univ. Pr., Bloomington, IN. 1974. 20. 00Hdbd. ISBN 0-253-36850-2. LC 78-166119.

NORMAND, JEAN. Nathaniel Hawthorne;An Approach to an Analysis of Artistic Creation. Transl. by Derek Coltman. Pr. of Case Western Reserve Univ., Cleveland, OH. 1970.

NORRIS, FRANK. The Responsibilities of the Novelist;and Other Literary Essays. Greenwood Pr., NY. 1902(1968) 311p. LC 69-10143.

NORTHEY, MARGOT. The Haunted Wilderness;The Gothic and Grotesque in Canadian Fiction. Univ. of Toronto Pr., Canada. 1977. 12. 50Hdbd. 4. 95Pa.

NORTON, CHARLES A. Melville Davisson Post;Man of Many Mysteries. Bowling Green Univ. Pr., Bowling Green, OH. 1974. 261p. 8. 95Hdbd. ISBN 0-87972-056-5. LC 73-83359. 3. 95Pa. ISBN 0-87972-060-3.

NORTON, RICTOR. The Homosexual Literary Tradition. Revisionist Pr., NY. 1974. 399p. 34. 95Hdbd. ISBN 0-87700-204-5.

NOWELL, ELIZABETH, Ed. The Letters of Thomas Wolfe. Scribner's, NY. 1956. 797p. LC 56-9880.

NYE, RUSSEL B., Ed. New Dimensions in Popular Culture. Bowling Green Univ. Pr., Bowling Green, OH. 1972. Hdbd. ISBN 0-87972-046-8. LC 72-88412. Pa. ISBN 0-87972-047-6.

O

OATES, JOYCE CAROL. New Heaven, New Earth;The Visionary Experience in Literature. Vanguard Pr., NY. 1974. 307p. 10. 00Hdbd. ISBN 0-8149-0743-1. LC 74-76438.

OBOLER, ELI. The Fear of the Word;Censorship and Sex. Scarecrow. 1974. 10. 00Hdbd. ISBN 0-8108-0724-6.

O'BRIEN, EDWARD JOSEPH HARRINGTON. The Advance of the American Short Story. Folcroft, Folcroft, PA. 1974. 20. 00Hdbd. ISBN 0-8414-6500-2. LC 74-23658.

O'BRIEN, JOHN. Interviews with Black Writers. Liveright, NY. 1973. 274p. 8. 95Hdbd. ISBN 0-87140-561-X. LC 72-97488.

O'BRIEN, JOHN, Comp. No Signs From Heaven;Theological Tradition and the Modern Literary Imagination. Dell, NY. 1975. 317p. 1. 75Pa.

O'CONNOR, EVANGELINE MARIA (JOHNSON). An Analytical Index to the Works of Nathaniel Hawthorne, with a Sketch of His Life. Houghton Mifflin, Boston, MA. 1882. Gale, Detroit, IL. 1967. 294p. 6. 00Hdbd. LC 66-27844.

O'CONNOR, FLANNERY. Mystery and Manners;Occasional Prose, Selected and Edited by Sally and Robert Fitzgerald. Farrar, Straus, NY. 237p. LC 69-15409.

O'CONNOR, RICHARD. Ambrose Bierce;A Biography. Little, Brown, Boston, MA. 1967. 333p. 6. 95 Hdbd. LC 67-11229.

O'CONNOR, RICHARD. Bret Harte; A Biography. Little, Brown, Boston, MA. 1966. 6. 95Hdbd.

O'CONNOR, RICHARD. Jack London; A Biography. Little, Brown, Boston, MA. 1964. 6. 95Hdbd.

O'CONNOR, WILLIAM VAN. The Grotesque;An American Genre and Other Essays. Southern Illinois Univ. Pr. Carbondale, IL. 1962. 231p. LC 62-15004.

O'CONNOR, WILLIAM VAN, Ed. Seven Modern American Novelists. Univ. of Minnesota Pr., Minneapolis, MN. 1959(1966). 302p. LC 64-18175.

O'CONNOR, WILLIAM VAN. The Tangled Fire of William Faulkner. Gordian Pr., NY. 1968. 182p.

O'DANIEL, THERMAN B. James Baldwin;A Critical Evaluation. Howard

Univ. Pr., Washington. 1975. 8.95Hdbd. ISBN 0-88258-047-7. LC 74-30006.

O'DANIEL, THERMAN B., Ed. Langston Hughes;Black Genius;A Critical Evaluation. Morrow. 1972. 5.95Hdbd. ISBN 0-688-06043-9. 2.95Pa.

ODIER, DANIEL. The Job;Interviews with William S. Burroughs. Random House, NY. 1974. 224p. 2.95Pa. ISBN 0-8021-0057-0. LC 73-20495.

O'DONNELL, BERNARD. Analysis of Prose Style to Determine Authorship of the O'Ruddy, a Novel by Stephen Crane and Robert Barr. Humanities. 1970. 9.25Pa. Text Ed. LC 72-114576.

O'DONOVAN, MICHAEL. Towards an Appreciation of Literature. Folcroft, Folcroft, PA. 1945(1974). 58p. 7.75Hdbd. LC 74-11154.

O'FAOLAIN, SEAN. The Short Story. Devin-Adair, NY. 1951(1964). 370p.

O'FAOLAIN, SEAN. The Vanishing Hero;Studies in Novelists of the Twenties. Books for Libraries Pr., Freeport, NY. 1956(1971). 204p. ISBN 0-8369-2065-1. LC 71-142686.

OHLIN, PETER. Agee. Astor-Honor. 1965. 10.00Hdbd. ISBN 0-8392-1146-5. 3.95Pa. ISBN 0-8392-5011-8.

OLANDER, JOSEPH D., and Martin Harry Greenberg, Eds. Arthur C. Clarke. Taplinger, NY. 1977. 9.95Hdbd. ISBN 0-8008-0402-3. LC 76-11052. 4.50Pa.

OLANDER, JOSEPH D., and Martin Harry Greenberg, Eds. Isaac Asimov. Taplinger, NY. 1977. 9.95Hdbd. ISBN 0-8008-4257-X. LC 76-11053. 4.50Pa. ISBN 0-8008-4258-8.

OLDERMAN, RAYMOND M. Beyond the Waste Land;A Study of the American Novel in the Nineteen-Sixties. Yale Univ. Pr., New Haven, CT. 1972. 258p. ISBN 0-300-01543-7. LC 73-182210.

OLIVER, GRACE A. A Study of Maria Edgeworth;With Notices of Her Father and Friends. 571p.

OLSON, ELDER, Ed. Aristotle's Poetics and English Literature. Univ. of Toronto Pr. 1965. 6.50Hdbd. ISBN 0-8020-1343-0. LC 67-71627. 2.45Pa. ISBN 0-8020-1344-9.

O'NEILL, JOHN P. Workable Design; Action and Situation in the Fiction of Henry James. Kennikat Pr., Port Washington, NY. 1973. 152p.

ORTON, VREST. Dreiserana;A Book About His Books. Folcroft, Folcroft, PA. 1929(1973). 7.75Hdbd. LC 73-12077.

OSTERWEIS, ROLLIN G. The Myth of the Lost Cause;1865-1900. Archon. 1973. ISBN 0-208-01318-0.

OSTERWEIS, ROLLIN. Romanticism and Nationalism in the Old South. Peter Smith. 5.00Hdbd. ISBN 0-8446-1335-5. Louisiana State Univ. Pr. 1967. 2.25Pa. ISBN 0-8071-0121-4. LC 49-7620.

OSTROM, JOHN WARD, Ed. The Letters of Edgar Allan Poe, 2 Volumes. Gordian Pr., NY. 1948(1966). 730p. LC 66-20025.

OWEN, JEAN Z. Professional Fiction Writing;A Practical Guide to

Modern Techniques. The Writer, Boston, MA. 1974. 133p. ISBN 0-87116-015-3. LC 77-188589.

OWINGS, MARK, and Jack L. Chalker. The Revised H. P. Lovecraft Bibliography. Mirage Pr., Baltimore, MD. 1973. 43p. 3.50Pa. ISBN 0-88358-010-1. LC 72-85408.

P

PACEY, DESMOND. Creative Writing in Canada;A Short History of English-Canadian Literature. Greenwood. 1961(1976). 18. 00Hdbd. ISBN 0-8371-9013-4. LC 76-23210.

PACEY, DESMOND, Ed. The Letters of Frederick Philip Grove. Univ. of Toronto Pr., Canada. 1975. 25. 00Hdbd. ISBN 0-8020-5311-4. LC 74-75828.

PAGE, SALLY R. Faulkner's Women; Characterization and Meaning. Everett/Edwards, Deland, FL. 1972. 233p.

PALEY, ALAN L. Edgar Allan Poe; American Poet and Mystery Writer. SamHar Pr., Charlotteville, NY. 1975. 2. 29Pa. LC 75-16318.

PALMER, FLORENCE K. The Confession Writer's Handbook. Writer's Digest, Cincinnati, OH. 1975. 6. 95Hdbd. ISBN 0-911654-29-1. LC 75-30884.

PALMER, VANCE. Legend of the Nineties. Melbourne Univ. Pr. 1966. 4.50 Hdbd. ISBN 0-522-83690-9.

PANICHAS, GEORGE ANDREW. The Politics of Twentieth-Century Novelists. Crowell, NY. 1974. 375p. 4. 50 Pa. ISBN 0-8152-0366-7. LC 75-115914.

PANSHIN, ALEXEI, and Cory Panshin. SF in Dimension;A Book of Explorations. Advent, Chicago, IL. 1976. 342p. 10. 00Hdbd. ISBN 0-911682-21-X. LC 76-21424.

PAPASHVILY, HELEN WAITE. All The Happy Endings;A Study of the Domestic Novel in America, the Women who Wrote it, the Women who Read it in the Nineteenth Century. Kennikat Pr., Port Washington, NY. 1956(1972). 231p. ISBN 0-8046-1497-0. LC 76-153255.

PARKER, DOROTHY. The Portable Dorothy Parker. Viking Pr., NY. 1944(1973). 5. 95Hdbd. ISBN 670-54016-1. LC 74-180479. 3. 95Pa. ISBN 670-01074-X.

PARKER, HERSHEL, Ed. Herman Melville;The Confidence-Man;His Masquerade. W. W. Norton, NY. 1971. 376p.

PARKER, HERSHEL, Ed. The Recognition of Herman Melville;Selected Criticism Since 1846. Univ. of Michigan Pr., Ann Arbor, MI. 364p.

PARKS, EDD WINFIELD. Ante-Bellum;Southern Literary Critics. Univ. of Georgia Pr., Athens, GA. 1962. 358p. LC 62-22136.

PARKS, EDD WINFIELD. Edgar Allan Poe As Literary Critic. Univ. of Georgia Pr. 1964. 5.00Hdbd. ISBN 0-8203-0055-1.

PARRINGTON, VERNON LOUIS. Main Currents in American Thought;An Interpretation of American Literature From The Beginnings to 1920. Harcourt, Brace, NY. 429p.

PATERSON, JOHN. The Novel as Faith;The Gospel According to James, Hardy, Conrad, Joyce, Lawrence and Virginia Woolf. Gambit, Boston, MA. 1973. 348p. ISBN 0-87645-075-3. LC 74-137016.

PATRIDES, C. A., Ed. Aspects of Time. Univ. of Toronto Pr., Buffalo, NY. 1976. 270p. 25.00Hdbd. ISBN 0-8020-2232-4. LC 76-367818.

PATROUCH, JOSEPH F. The Science Fiction of Isaac Asimov. Doubleday, Garden City, NY. 1974. 283p. 6.95Hdbd. ISBN 0-385-08696-2. LC 74-5534.

PATTEE, FRED LEWIS. The Development of the American Short Story; An Historical Survey. Biblo and Tannen, NY. 1966. 388p. LC 66-13477.

PATTEE, FRED LEWIS. The First Century of American Literature;1770-1870. Cooper Square Pub., NY. 1966. 613p.

PATTEE, FRED LEWIS. A History of American Literature Since 1870. Cooper Square Pub., NY. 1968. 449p.

PATTERSON, MARGARET C. Literary Research Guide. Gale, Detroit, MI. 1975. 18.50Hdbd. ISBN 0-8103-1102-X. LC 75-13925.

PAUL, SHERMAN, Ed. Six Classic American Writers;An Introduction. Univ. of Minnesota Pr., Minneapolis, MN. 1961(1970). 271p. ISBN 0-8166-0586-6. LC 71-120808.

PEARCE, ROY HARVEY. Historicism Once More;Problems and Occasions for the American Scholar. Princeton Univ. Pr., Princeton, NJ. 1969. 357p. LC 68-56317.

PEARSON, BILL. Fretful Sleepers and Other Essays. Heinemann, London. 1974. 168p. 12.00Hdbd. ISBN 0-8002-0089-6. LC 75-312566.

PEARSON, CAROL, and Katherine Pope. Who Am I This Time?;Female Portraits in British and American Literature. McGraw-Hill, NY. 1976. 288p. 5.95 Pa.

PEARSON, EDMUND. Dime Novels; or, Following An Old Trail in Popular Literature. Kennikat Pr., Port Washington, NY. 1968. 280p. LC 67-27632.

PECK, H. DANIEL. A World by Itself; The Pastoral Moment in Cooper's Fiction. Yale Univ. Pr., New Haven, CT. 1977. 12.50Hdbd. ISBN 0-300-02027-9. LC 76-25868.

PECKHAM, MORSE, Ed. Romanticism;The Culture of the Nineteenth Century. Braziller. 1965. 6.95Hdbd. ISBN 0-8076-0314-7.

PEDEN, WILLIAM HARWOOD. The American Short Story;Continuity and Change;1940-1975. Houghton-Mifflin, 1975. 7.95Hdbd. ISBN 0-395-20720-7. LC 75-23089.

PEDEN, WILLIAM HARWOOD. The American Short Story;Front Line in the National Defense of Literature.

Houghton Mifflin, Boston, MA. 213p. LC 64-17360.

PEET, LOUIS HARMAN. Handy Book of American Authors. Gale, Detroit, MI. 1971. 317p. 14.00Hdbd. LC 75-156928.

PENDO, STEPHEN. Raymond Chandler on Screen;His Novels Into Film. Scarecrow Pr., Metuchen, NJ. 1976. 10.00Hdbd. ISBN 0-8108-0931-1. LC 76-9855.

PENZOLDT, PETER. The Supernatural in Fiction. Humanities Pr., NY. 1952(1965). 271p. LC 65-25277.

PERCIVAL, M.O. A Reading of Moby Dick. Octagon, NY. 1967. 135p.

PERKINS, MICHAEL. The Secret Record;Modern Erotic Literature. Morrow, NY. 1976. 7.95Hdbd. ISBN 0-688-0213-8. LC 76-18832.

PEROSA, SERGIO. The Art of F. Scott Fitzgerald. Transl. by Charles Matz and the Author. Univ. of Michigan Pr., Ann Arbor, MI. 1965. 239p.

PERRY, DICK. Reflections of Jesse Stuart on a Land of Many Moods. McGraw-Hill, NY. 1971. 7.95Hdbd. ISBN 0-07-049450-9.

PERRY, MARGARET. Silence to the Drums;A Survey of the Literature of the Harlem Renaissance. Greenwood Pr., Westport, CT. 1976. 12.50 Hdbd. ISBN 0-8371-7847-9. LC 74-19806.

PETERSON, DALE L. The Clement Vision;Poetic Realism in Turgenev and James. Kennikat Pr., Port Washington, NY. 1975. 9.95Hdbd. ISBN 0-8046-9107-X. LC 75-31614.

PETTER, HENRI. The Early American Novel. Ohio State Univ. Pr. 500p. LC 73-114737.

PETTIT, ARTHUR G. Mark Twain and the South. Univ. Pr. of Kentucky, Lexington, KY. 1974. 223p. 9.75Hdbd. ISBN 0-8131-1310-5. LC 73-86405.

PEYRE, HENRI. Historical and Critical Essays. Univ. of Nebraska Pr. 1968. 12.50Hdbd. ISBN 0-8032-0145-1. LC 68-12702.

PEYRE, HENRI. What is Romanticism? Univ. of Alabama Pr. 1976. 9.75 Hdbd. ISBN 0-8173-7003-X. LC 75-42374.

PFEIFFER, JOHN R. Fantasy and Science Fiction;A Critical Guide. Filter Pr., Palmer Lake, CO. 1971. 64p. ISBN 0-910584-25-7.

PHELAN, JOHN, Ed. Communications Control;Readings in the Motives and Structures of Censorship. Sheed and Ward, NY. 1969. 238p. 6.50Hdbd.

PHELPS, ARTHUR L. Canadian Writers. Books for Libraries. Repro. of 1951 Ed. 9.25Hdbd. ISBN 0-8369-2617-X.

PHILBRICK, THOMAS. James Fenimore Cooper and the Development of American Sea Fiction. Harvard Univ. Pr., Cambridge, MA. 1961.

PHILLIPS, LE ROY. A Bibliography of the Writings of Henry James. Milford House, Boston, MA. 1906(1974). 20.00Hdbd. ISBN 0-87821-247-7. LC 73-19941.

PHILLIPS, MARY ELIZABETH. James Fenimore Cooper. Folcroft, Folcroft, PA. 1974. 35.00. LC 74-9802.

PICHASKE, DAVID R. Writing Sense; A Handbook of Composition. Free Pr. NY. 1975. 330p. 2.95. ISBN 0-02-925170-2. LC 74-15134.

PICKERING, JAMES H., Ed. The World Turned Upside Down; Prose and Poetry of the American Revolution. Kennikat Pr., Port Washington, NY. 1975. 271p. 12.95Hdbd. ISBN 0-8046-9082-0. LC 75-15551.

PIERATT, ASA B., JR., and Jerome Klinkowitz. Kurt Vonnegut Jr., A Descriptive Bibliography and Annotated Secondary Checklist. Archon, Hamden, CT. 1974. 10.00Hdbd. ISBN 0-208-01449-7. LC 74-11295.

PILKINGTON, WILLIAM T. My Blood's Country; Studies in Southwestern Literature. Texas Christian Univ. Pr. Fort Worth, TX. 1973. 211p. 3.50Pa. LC 72-95053.

PINSKER, SANFORD. The Comedy that "hoits"; An Essay on the Fiction of Philip Roth. Univ. of Missouri Pr., Columbia, MO. 1975. 121p. 5.00Pa. ISBN 0-8262-0181-4. LC 75-16210.

PIPER, HENRY DAN. F. Scott Fitzgerald; A Critical Portrait. Holt, Rinehart, NY. 1965. 344p.

PIPER, HENRY DAN, Ed. Think Back on Us; A Contemporary Chronicle of the 1930's by Malcolm Cowley. Southern Illinois Univ. Pr., Carbondale, IL. 1967. 400p. LC 67-10024.

PIRIE, GORDON. Henry James. Rowman and Littlefield, Totowa, NJ. 1974 (1975). 152p. 6.00Hdbd. ISBN 0-87471-611-X. LC 75-308403.

PIZER, DONALD. The Novels of Theodore Dreiser; A Critical Study. Univ. of Minnesota Pr., Minneapolis, MN. 1976. 382p. 20.00Hdbd. ISBN 0-8166-0768-0. LC 75-20769.

PIZER, DONALD, Ed. The Literary Criticism of Frank Norris. Univ. of Texas Pr., Austin, TX. 1964. 247p. LC 63-17618.

PIZER, DONALD. Realism and Naturalism; In Nineteenth-Century American Literature. Southern Illinois Univ. Pr., Carbondale, IL. 1966(1967). 176p. LC 66-10058.

PODHORETZ, NORMAN. Doings and Undoings; The Fifties and After in American Writing. Farrar, Straus, NY. 1953(1966). 371p. LC 64-12358.

POETS AND WRITERS, INC. A Directory of American Fiction Writers. Poets and Writers, Inc., NY. 1975. 10.00Hdbd. ISBN 0-913734-04-7. LC 75-25710. 5.00Pa. ISBN 0-913734-05-5.

POHL, FREDERIK, Ed. The Science Fiction Scroll of Honor. Random House, NY. 1975. 8.95Hdbd. ISBN 0-394-48677-3. LC 75-10340.

POIRIER, RICHARD. The Comic Sense of Henry James; A Study of the Early Novels. Oxford Univ. Pr., NY. 1967. 260p.

POIRIER, RICHARD. A World Elsewhere; The Place of Style in American Literature. Oxford Univ. Pr., NY. 1966. 257p. LC 66-24438.

POLLARD, ARTHUR. Satire. Methuen. 1970. 2.75Pa. ISBN 0-416-17240-7.

POLLARD, RICHARD N., and Hazel M. (Batzer) Pollard. From Human Sentience to Drama; Principles of Critical Analysis;Tragic and Comedic. Ohio Univ.Pr.,Athens,OH.1974.310 p.10.00Hdbd.ISBN 0-8214-0135-1.LC 73-85447.

POLLOCK,THOMAS CLARK.The Nature of Literature;Its Relation to Science, Language and Human Experience.Gordian Pr.,NY.1942(1965). 218p.LC 65-25135.

POMMER,HENRY F.Emerson's First Marriage.Southern Illinois Univ. Pr.,Carbondale,IL.1967.126p.LC 67-22023.

POPS,MARTIN LEONARD.The Melville Archetype.Kent State Univ.Pr. Kent,OH.1970.287p.

PORGES,IRWIN.Edgar Allan Poe. Chilton Bks.,Philadelphia,PA.1963 (1965).191p.LC 63-21333.

PORGES,IRWIN,in Collab.with Edgar Rice Burroughs,Inc.Edgar Rice Burroughs;The Man and His Works. Brigham Young Univ.Pr.,Provo,UT. 1975.14.95Hdbd.ISBN 0-8425-0079-0.LC 75-15980.

PORTE,JOEL.The Romance in America;Studies in Cooper,Poe,Hawthorne, Melville and James.Wesleyan Univ.Pr.,Middletown,CT.1969. 235p.LC 69-17795.

PORTER,BERNARD H.The First Publications of F.Scott Fitzgerald. Quality Books.1965.11p.

PORTER,KATHERINE ANNE.The Collected Essays and Occasional Writings of Katherine Anne Porter. Delta.1923(1970).196p.2.95Pa.

POWELL,LAWRENCE CLARK.Books;West,Southwest;Essays on Writers, Their Books, and Their Land. Greenwood Pr.,Westport,CT.1957 (1974).157p.9.75Hdbd.ISBN 0-8371-7545-3.LC 74-6711.

POWELL,LAWRENCE CLARK.Southwest Classics;The Creative Literature of the Arid Lands;Essays on the Book and Their Writers.Ritchie Pr.,Los Angeles,CA.1974.370 p.12.95Hdbd.ISBN 0-378-07751-1. LC 73-89437.

POWERS,LYALL H.,Ed.Henry James's Major Novels;Essays in Criticism.Michigan State Univ.Pr.,East Lansing,MI.1973.461p.

POWERS,LYALL H.Henry James and the Naturalist Movement.Michigan State Univ.Pr.,East Lansing, MI.1971.200p.

POWNALL,DAVID E.Articles on Twentieth Century Literature;An Annotated Bibliography;1954 to 1970. Kraus-Thomson,NY.1973.195.00Hdbd.(7 Volumes).ISBN 0-527-72150-6.LC 73-6588.

PRAGER,ARTHUR.Rascals at Large;or,The Clue in the Old Nostalgia. Doubleday,Garden City,NY.1971.334 p.LC 70-158350.

PRAWER,SIEGBERT SALOMON. Karl Marx and World Literature. Clarendon Pr.1976.446p.19.50Hdbd. ISBN 0-19-815745-2.LC 76-383940.

PRICKWETT,S.Romanticism and Religion.Cambridge Univ.Pr.1976. 21.95Hdbd.ISBN 0-521-21072-0.LC 75-2254.

PRITCHARD,JOHN PAUL.Criticism in America;An Account of the Development of Critical Techniques from the Early Period of the Republic to the Middle Years of the Twentieth Century. University of Oklahoma Pr. Norman, OK. 1956. 325p. LC 56-5992.

PRITCHARD, JOHN PAUL. Return to the Fountains;Some Classical Sources of American Criticism. Octagon, NY. 1966. 271p. LC 66-18041.

PROFFER, CARL R., Ed. Soviet Criticism of American Literature in the Sixties;An Anthology. Ardis, Ann Arbor, MI. 1972. ISBN 0-88233-012-8.

ticism of American Literature in the Sixties;An Anthology. Ardis, Ann Arbor, MI. 1972. ISBN 0-88233-012-8.

PULLAR, PHILIPPA. Frank Harris; A Biography. Simon and Schuster, NY. 1975. 9.95Hdbd. ISBN 0-671-22091-8. LC 75-23352.

PUTT, S. GORLEY. Henry James;A Reader's Guide. Cornell Univ. Pr Ithaca, NY. 1966. 432p.

QUICK, DOROTHY. Enchantment; A Little Girl's Friendship with Mark Twain. Univ. of Oklahoma Pr., Norman, OK. 1961. 221p. LC 61-15143.

QUINN, ARTHUR HOBSON. American Fiction; An Historical and Critical Survey. Appleton-Century, NY. 1936(1964). 805p.

QUINN, ARTHUR H. Edgar Allan Poe; A Critical Biography. Meredith(Appleton). 1941. 10.00Hdbd.

QUINN, ARTHUR H., and Richard H. Hart. Letters and Documents in the Enoch Pratt Free Library/Edgar Allan Poe. Norwood Editions, Norwood, PA. 1941(1975). 15.00Hdbd. ISBN 0-88305-525-2. LC 75-33016.

R

RABAN, JONATHAN. The Technique of Modern Fiction;Essays in Practical Criticism. Univ. of Notre Dame Pr.1968(1969).199p. LC 71-75153.

RABKIN, ERIC S. The Fantastic in Literature. Princeton Univ.Pr., Princeton, NJ.1976.234p.12.50Hdbd. ISBN 0-691-06301-X. LC 75-30201.

RAHV, PHILIP. Literature and the Sixth Sense. Houghton-Mifflin, Boston, MA. 1969. 445p. LC 70-79390.

RAHV, PHILIP. Literature in America;An Anthology of Literary Criticism. Meridian Books, World Pub.Co., Cleveland and NY.1957.452p. LC 57-10840.

RALEIGH, JOHN HENRY. Time, Place, and Idea;Essays on the Novel. Southern Illinois Univ.Pr., Carbondale, IL.1968.176p. LC 68-10116.

RAMPERSAD, ARNOLD. Melville's Israel Potter;A Pilgrimage and Progress. Bowling Green Univ.Pr., Bowling Green, OH.1969.128p.

RAMSAY, ROBERT L., and Frances G. Emberson. A Mark Twain Lexicon. Russell and Russell, NY.1963.

RAND, AYN. The Romantic Manifesto;A Philosophy of Literature. World Pub., NY and Cleveland.1962(1969).201p.5.50. LC 77-93469.

RANSOME, ARTHUR. Edgar Allan Poe;A Critical Study. Haskell House, NY.1973.12.95Hdbd. ISBN 0-8383-1548-8. LC 72-3534.

RAO, V. RAMAKRISHNA. Emerson; His Muse and Message. Folcroft, Folcroft, PA. Repro.1938.20.00Hdbd.

RATNER, MARC L. William Styron. Twayne, NY.1972.6.95Hdbd. LC 70-169623.

RAY, DAVID, and Robert M. Farnsworth, Eds. Richard Wright;Impressions and Perspectives. Univ. of Michigan Pr., Ann Arbor, MI.1973.207p. 7.95Hdbd. ISBN 0-472-09189. LC 74-163565.

RAYNOLDS, ROBERT. Thomas Wolfe;Memoir of a Friendship. Univ. of Texas Pr., Austin, TX.154p. LC 65-23163.

READER'S ADVISER;A Layman's Guide to Literature. Bowker, NY.1974.23.50Hdbd. ISBN 0-8352-0781-1. LC 57-13277.

REAVER, J. RUSSELL. Emerson as

Mythmaker. Univ. of Florida Pr., Gainesville, FL. 1954. 2.00Pa. ISBN 0-8130-0195-1.

REED, JOSEPH W., JR. Faulkner's Narrative. Yale Univ. Pr., New Haven, CT. 1973. 303p.

REED, PETER J. Kurt Vonnegut, Jr. Crowell, NY. Hdbd. ISBN 0-690-01048-6. LC 75-24870. Pa. ISBN 0-690-01049-4.

REED, WALTER L. Meditations on the Hero; A Study of the Romantic Hero in Nineteenth-Century Fiction. Yale Univ. Pr., New Haven, CT. 1974. 207p. 11.95Hdbd. ISBN 0-300-01735-9. LC 74-77068.

REES, ROBERT A., and Earl N. Harbert, Eds. Fifteen American Authors Before 1900; Bibliographic Essays on Research and Criticism. Univ. of Wisconsin Pr., Milwaukee, WI. 1971. 442p. ISBN 0-299-05910-3. LC 77-157395.

REEVES, PASCHAL, Ed. Thomas Wolfe and The Glass of Time. Univ. of Georgia Pr., Athens, GA. 1971. 166p.

REGINALD, R., Ed. Contemporary Science Fiction Authors. Arno, NY. 1975. 65p. 20.00Hdbd. ISBN 0-405-06332-6. LC 74-16517.

REID, RANDALL. The Fiction of Nathanael West; No Redeemer, No Promised Land. Univ. of Chicago Pr., Chicago, IL. 1967. 174p.

REIGELMAN, MILTON M. The Midland; A Venture in Literary Regionalism. Univ. of Iowa Pr., Iowa City, IA. 1975. 4.95Pa. ISBN 0-87745-054-4. LC 75-28219.

ROMANTICISM. Harper-Row, NY. 3.75Pa.

REYNOLDS, MICHAEL S. Hemingway's First War; The Making of A Farewell to Arms. Princeton Univ. Pr. Princeton, NJ. 1976. 13.50Hdbd. ISBN 0-691-06302-8. LC 75-30202.

RICE, HOWARD CROSBY. Rudyard Kipling in New England. Haskell House, NY. 1973. 7.95Hdbd. ISBN 0-8383-1635-2. LC 72-6747.

RICHARDS, IVOR ARMSTRONG. Beyond. Harcourt Brace, NY. 1974. 201p. 8.50Hdbd. LC 73-18249.

RICHARDSON, KENNETH E. Force and Faith in the Novels of William Faulkner. Mouton, The Hague, Paris. 1967. 187p.

RICHARDSON, ROBERT. Literature and Film. Indiana Univ. Pr., Bloomington, IN. 1969. 149p. 4.95.

RICHMAN, SIDNEY. Bernard Malamud. Twayne, NY. 1966. 160p.

RICKELS, MILTON. George Washington Harris. Twayne, NY. 1965. 5.50 Hdbd. 2.45Pa.

RICKELS, MILTON. Thomas Bangs Thorpe; Humorist of the Old Southwest. Louisiana State Univ. Pr., Baton Rouge, LA. 1962. 275p. LC 62-8018.

RICKS, BEATRICE, and Joseph D. Adams, Comp. Herman Melville; A Reference Bibliography; 1900-1972; with Selected Nineteenth-Century Materials. G. K. Hall, Boston, MA. 1973. 532p. ISBN 0-8161-1036-0. LC 72-14197.

RICOEUR, PAUL. The Rule of Metaphor. Univ. of Toronto Pr. 1977. 448p. 22.50Hdbd. ISBN 0-8020-5326-2.

RIDEOUT, WALTER B. The Radical Novel in the United States;1900-1954; Some Interrelations of Literature and Society. Harvard Univ. Pr., Cambridge, MA. 1965. 339p. LC 56-10162.

RIDEOUT, WALTER B., Ed. Sherwood Anderson;A Collection of Critical Essays. P-H. 1974. 7.95Hdbd. ISBN 0-13-036558-0. 2.45Pa. ISBN 0-13-036533-5.

RIGHTER, WILLIAM. Myth and Literature. Routledge and Paul, Boston, MA. 1975. 132p. 10.95Hdbd. ISBN 0-7100-8137-5. LC 75-319878.

RINGE, DONALD A. James Fenimore Cooper. Twayne, NY. 1962.

RIST, RAY C., Ed. Pornography Controversy;Changing Moral Standards in American Life. Transaction Books. 1974. 9.95. ISBN 0-87855-093-3. LC 73-92813. 3.95Pa. ISBN 0-87855-587-0.

RIVERS, WILLIAM L. Writing, Craft and Art. Prentice-Hall, Englewood Cliffs, NJ. 1975. 6.95Hdbd. ISBN 0-13-970210-5. LC 74-26703. Pa. ISBN 0-13-970202-4.

ROBB, MARY COOPER. William Faulkner;An Estimate of His Contribution to the Modern American Novel. Univ. of Pittsburgh Pr. 1957. 70p.

ROBBINS, JACK ALAN, Ed. Granville Hicks in the New Masses. Kennikat Pr., Port Washington, NY. 1974. 437p. 17.50Hdbd. ISBN 0-8046-9042-1. LC 73-83265.

ROBBINS, JACK ALAN, Ed. Literary Essays;1954-1974/James T. Farrell. Kennikat Pr., Port Washington, NY. 1976. 147p. 9.95Hdbd. ISBN 0-8046-9125-8. LC 76-17588.

ROBERTS, EDGAR V. Writing Themes About Literature. Prentice-Hall, Englewood Cliffs, NJ. 1964(1969, 1973) 297p. Hdbd. ISBN 0-13-970731-X. Pa. ISBN 0-13-970723-9. LC 72-8508.

ROBINS, ELIZABETH. Theatre and Friendship;Some Henry James Letters. Jonathan Cape, London. 1932. 311p.

ROBINSON, FORREST GLEN, and Margaret G. Robinson. Wallace Stegner. Twayne, Boston, MA. 1977. 8.50 Hdbd. ISBN 0-8057-7182-4. LC 76-54313.

ROCKWELL, F.A. How to Write Nonfiction that Sells. H. Regnery Co., Chicago, IL. 1975. 5.95Pa. ISBN 0-8092-8200-3. LC 75-13241.

ROCKWELL, F.A. How to Write Plots that Sell. H. Regnery Co., Chicago, IL. 1975. 279p. 10.00Hdbd. LC 74-23408. 4.95Pa.

ROCKWELL, F.A. Modern Fiction Techniques. The Writer, Boston, MA. 1962(1969). 292p. LC 62-14074.

RODGERS, BERNARD F., JR. Philip Roth;A Bibliography. Scarecrow Pr. Metuchen, NJ. 1974. 104p. ISBN 0-8108-0754-8. LC 74-16224.

ROGERS, DOUGLAS G. Sherwood Anderson;A Selective, Annotated Bibliography. Scarecrow Pr., Metuchen, NJ. 1976. 157p. 6.00Hdbd. ISBN 0-8108-0900-1. LC 75-45225.

ROGERS, FRANKLIN R. Mark Twain's Burlesque Patterns;As Seen in the Novels and Narratives;1855-1885. Southern Methodist Univ.Pr.,Dallas TX.1960.189p.

ROGERS,KATHERINE.The Troublesome Helpmate.Univ.of Washington Pr.,Seattle,WA.1966.2.95Pa.

RONALD,ANN.Zane Grey.Boise State Univ.,Boise,ID.1975(1976).46p. 1.50Pa.ISBN 0-88430-016-1.LC 75-7010.

ROSA,ALFRED E.,Ed.Contemporary Fiction in America and England; 1950-1970;A Guide to Information Sources.Gale,Detroit,MI.1976.18.00 Hdbd.ISBN 0-8103-1219-0.LV 73-16990.

ROSE,ALAN HENRY.Demonic Vision;Racial Fantasy and Southern Fiction.Archon,Hamden,CT.1976.12.-50Hdbd.ISBN 0-208-01582-5.LC 76-12088.

ROSE,ELLEN CRONAN.The Tree Outside the Window;Doris Lessing's Children of Violence.Univ.Pr.of New England,Ann Arbor.11.00Hdbd. ISBN 0-8357-0189-1.LC 76-44671.

ROSE,MARK,Ed.Science Fiction; A Collection of Critical Essays.Prentice-Hall,Englewood Cliffs,NJ.1976.7.95Hdbd.LC 76-19008.2.95Pa.

ROSELLE,DANIEL.Transformations,2;Understanding American History Through Science Fiction.Fawcett,Greenwich,CT.1974.143p.1.25Pa. LC 74-18012.

ROSENBLATT,ROGER.Black Fiction.Harvard Univ.Pr.,Cambridge, MA.1974.211p.8.50Hdbd.ISBN 0-674-07620-6.LC 74-81387.

ROSENFELT,DEBORAH SILVERTON,Ed.Strong Women;An Annoted Bibliography of Literature for the High School Classroom.Feminist Pr.,Westbury,NY.1976.56p.1.95Pa. LC 76-375218.

ROSS,LILLIAN B.Portrait of Hemingway.Simon and Schuster,NY.1961.2.50.Avon,NY.1964..60Pa.

ROSS,RALPH GILBERT,Ed.Makers of American Thought;An Introduction to Seven American Writers.Univ.of Minnesota Pr.,Minneapolis, MN.1974.301p.10.50Hdbd.ISBN 0-8166-0712-5.LC 74-78993.

ROSS,T.J.Film and the Liberal Arts.Holt,Rinehart,NY.1970.419p. 4.95.

ROTTENSTEINER,FRANZ.The Science Fiction Book.Seabury Pr.,NY. 1975.160p.14.95Hdbd.ISBN 0-8164-9169-0.LC 73-17886.

ROUTH,H.V.Money,Morals and Manners As Revealed in Modern Literature.Gordon Pr.35.00Hdbd.ISBN 0-8490-0662-7.

ROVIT,EARL.Ernest Hemingway. Twayne,NY.1963.192p.

RUBIN,LOUIS D.,JR,Ed.A Bibliographical Guide to the Study of Southern Literature.Louisiana State Univ.Pr.,Baton Rouge,LA.1969.368p. 10.00Hdbd.3.25Pa.

RUBIN,LOUIS D.,JR.The Comic Imagination in American Literature. Rutgers Univ.Pr.,New Brunswick, NJ.1973.430p.ISBN 0-8135-0758-8. LC 73-7921.

RUBIN, LOUIS D., JR. The Curious Death of the Novel;Essays in American Literature. Louisiana State Univ. Pr., Baton Rouge, LA. 1967(1969). 302p. LC 67-26970.

RUBIN, LOUIS D., JR. The Faraway Country;Writers of the Modern South. Univ. of Washington Pr., Seattle, WA. 1963. 256p. LC 63-19632.

RUBIN, LOUIS D., JR., Ed. South;Modern Southern Literature in its Cultural Setting. Greenwood Pr., Westport, CT. 1961(1974). 16.00Hdbd. ISBN 0-8371-7224-1. LC 73-16744.

RUBIN, LOUIS D., JR., and C. Hugh Holman, Eds. Southern Literary Study;Problems and Possibilities. Univ. of North Carolina Pr., Chapel Hill, NC. 1975. 12.50Hdbd. ISBN 0-8078-1252-8. LC 75-11553.

RUBIN, LOUIS D., JR., and Robert D. Jacobs, Eds. Southern Renascence; The Literature of the Modern South. Johns Hopkins Pr., Baltimore, MD. 1953. 444p.

RUBIN, LOUIS D., JR. Thomas Wolfe;The Weather of His Youth. Louisiana State Univ. Pr., Baton Rouge, LA. 1955. 183p.

RUDICH, NORMAN, Ed. Weapons of Criticism;Marxism in America and the Literary Tradition. Ramparts Pr. Palo Alto, CA. 1976. 389p. 14.00Pa. ISBN 0-87867-056-4. LC 74-9178.

RUDMAN, MASHA KABAKOW. Children's Literature;An Issues Approach. Heath, Lexington, MA. 1976. 433p. 11.95Hdbd. ISBN 0-669-00322-0. LC 72-28958. 6.95Pa.

RULAND, RICHARD. America in Modern European Literature;From Image to Metaphor. New York Univ. Pr. 1976. 197p. 12.50Hdbd. ISBN 0-8147-7364-8. LC 74-29376.

RULAND, RICHARD, Ed. The Native Muse;Theories of American Literature;Volume 1. E. P. Dutton, NY. 1972. 465p. LC 70-95496.

RULAND, RICHARD. The Rediscovery of American Literature;Premises of Critical Taste;1900-1940. Harvard Univ. Pr., Cambridge, MA. 1967. 329p. LC 67-20880.

RULAND, RICHARD, Ed. The Spirit of Place. Dutton, NY. 1975. 10.00Hdbd. LC 75-14009. 3.45Pa.

RULAND, VERNON. Horizons of Criticism;An Assessment of Religious-Literary Options. American Library Assoc., Chicago, IL. 1975. 265p. 14.95 Hdbd. ISBN 0-8389-0196-4. LC 75-20162. 7.50Pa.

RULE, JANE. Lesbian Images. Doubleday, Garden City, NY. 1975. 246p. 8.50Hdbd. ISBN 0-385-04255-8. LC 74-18829.

RUNYAN, HARRY. A Faulkner Glossary. Citadel Pr., NY. 1964. 310p.

RUOTOLO, LUCIO P. Six Existential Heroes;The Politics of Faith. Harvard Univ. Pr., Cambridge, MA. 1973. 261p. ISBN 674-81025-2. LC 72-86386.

RUSSELL, FRANCIS. Three Studies in Twentieth Century Obscurity. Gordon Pr. 1973. 34.95Hdbd. ISBN 0-87968-046-6.

RUSSELL, FRANCIS. Three Studies in Twentieth Century Obscurity;Joyce, Kafka, Gertrude Stein. Haskell.

1969. 9.95Hdbd. ISBN 0-8383-0678-0.
LC 68-658.

RUSK, RALPH L. The Life of Ralph Waldo Emerson. Columbia Univ. Pr., NY. 1957. 592p.

RYSSEL, FRITZ HEINRICH. Thomas Wolfe. Ungar, NY. 1972. 117p.

S

SACHS, VIOLA. The Myth of America;Essays in the Structures of Literary Imagination. Mouton, The Hague. 1974. 162p. 8.25Hdbd. LC 72-93158.

SAITO, GEORGE, and Philip Williams. Soseki and Salinger;American Students on Japanese Fiction. Japan Publications. 3.95Pa.

SALZMAN, JACK, Ed. Theodore Dreiser;The Critical Reception. David Lewis, NY. 1972. 741p.

SAMPSON, EDWARD C. E. B. White. Twayne, NY. 1974. 190p. 7.50Hdbd. ISBN 0-8057-0787-5. LC 73-21582.

SAMUEL, MAURICE. World of Sholom Aleichem. Knopf. 1943. 10.00Hdbd. ISBN 0-394-45269-0.

SAMUEL, MAURICE. The World of Sholom Aleichem. Random, NY. 1973. 2.45Pa. ISBN 0-394-71899-2.

SAMUELS, CHARLES THOMAS. The Ambiguity of Henry James. Univ. of Illinois Pr., Chicago, IL. 1971. 235p.

SAMUELS, LEE. A Hemingway Check List. Scribner's, NY. 1951. 63p.

SANDERLIN, GEORGE. Washington Irving;As Others Saw Him. Coward, McCann and Geoghegan, NY. 1975. 128p. 5.95Hdbd. ISBN 0-698-20296-1. LC 74-79701.

SANDERS, CHARLES. The Scope of Satire. Scott F. 1971. 5.95Pa. ISBN 0-673-05887-5.

SANFORD, MARCELLINE HEMINGWAY. At The Hemingways;A Family portrait. Little, Brown, Boston, MA. 1961(1962). 244p. LC 62-10529.

SARASON, BERTRAM D. Hemingway and The Sun Set. Bruccoli Clark, Microcard Editions, Washington, DC. 1972. 279p.

SAROYAN, WILLIAM. Places Where I've Done Time. Praeger, NY. 1972. 182p. LC 70-178227.

SAUL, GEORGE BRANDON. In Praise of the Half-Forgotten and Other Essays. Bucknell Univ. Pr., Lewisburg. 1976. 6.95Hdbd. ISBN 0-8387-1824-8. LC 75-18926.

SAVAGE, ARTHUR W. How to Analyze The Short Story. Branden Pr., Boston, MA. 1971. 5.95Hdbd. 89p.

SCHAEFER, MARTHA. The Writing Process, Step by Step. Winthrop, Cambridge, MA. 1975. 328p. 4.95Pa.

ISBN 0-87626-873-4. LC 74-32463.

SCHATT, STANLEY. Kurt Vonnegut, Jr. Twayne, Boston, MA. 1976. 7.95 Hdbd. ISBN 0-8057-7176-X. LC 76-41754.

SCHMERLING, HILDA L. Finger of God;Religious Thought and Themes in Literature from Chaucer to Kafka. Gordon Pr., NY. 1977. 39.95Hdbd. ISBN 0-8490-1358-5. LC 76-54842.

SCHMITTER, DEAN MORGAN, Ed. Mark Twain;A Collection of Criticism. McGraw-Hill, NY. 1974. 150p. 2.45Pa. ISBN 0-07-055394-7. LC 74-19111.

SCHNEIDER, DANIEL J. Symbolism; The Manichean Vision;A Study in the Art of James, Conrad, Woolf and Stevens. Univ. of Nebraska Pr., Lincoln, NB. 1975. 235p. 10.95Hdbd. ISBN 0-8032-0847-2. LC 74-12841.

SCHNEIDER, ROBERT W. Five Novelists of the Progressive Era. Columbia Univ. Pr., NY. 1965. 290p. LC 65-12110.

SCHOLES, ROBERT, and Eric Rabkin. Science Fiction;History, Science, Vision. Oxford Univ. Pr. 10.00Hdbd. ISBN 0-19-502173-8. 2.95Pa. ISBN 0-19-502174-6.

SCHOLES, ROBERT. Structural Fabulation;An Essay on the Fiction of the Future. Univ. of Notre Dame Pr., 1975. 60p. 2.95Pa. ISBN 0-298-00571-0. LC 74-30167.

SCHOLES, ROBERT. Structuralism in Literature;An Introduction. 230p. 11.00Hdbd. ISBN 01750-2. LC 73-90578. 2.95Pa. ISBN 01850-9.

SCHORER, MARK. Sinclair Lewis; An American Life. McGraw-Hill, NY. 1961. 2.98Pa. Dell. 1963. 3.75Pa. Univ. of Minnesota Pr. 1963. .65Pa.

SCHORER, MARK, Ed. Sinclair Lewis;A Collection of Critical Essays. Twentieth Century Views Series. Prentice-Hall, Englewood Cliffs, NJ. 1962. 174p. 5.95Hdbd. 1.95Pa.

SCHORER, MARK. The World We Imagine;Selected Essays by Mark Schorer. Farrar, Straus, NY. 1968. 402p. LC 68-14917.

SCHROEDER, THEODORE A. Free Speech;Bibliography. B. Franklin. 1969. 20.00Hdbd. ISBN 0-8337-3171-8.

SCHUBERT, LELAND. Hawthorne, the Artist;Fine-Art Devices in Fiction. Russell and Russell, NY. 44p.

SCHULBERG, BUDD. The Four Seasons of Success. Doubleday, Garden City, NY. 1972. 203p. ISBN 0-385-00510-5. LC 72-76202.

SCHULZ, MAX F. Black Humor Fiction of the Sixties;A Pluralistic Definition of Man and His World. Ohio Univ. Pr., Athens, OH. 1973. 156p. ISBN 8214-0125-4. LC 72-85538.

SCHULZ, MAX F. Bruce Jay Friedman. Twayne, NY. 1974. 164p. 5.50Hdbd. ISBN 0-8057-0290-3. LC 72-9347.

SCHULZ, MAX F. Radical Sophistication;Studies in Contemporary Jewish-American Novelists. Ohio Univ. Pr., Athens, OH. 224p.

SCHWARTZ, ELIAS. The Forms of Feeling;Toward a Mimetic Theory of Literature. Kennikat Pr., Port Washington, NY. 1972. 124p. LC 74-189561.

SCHWARZSCHILD, BETTINA. Not-Right House;Essays on James Purdy. Univ. of Missouri Pr.1968.2.50Pa. ISBN 0-8262-8217-2.

SCOTT, ARTHUR L. Mark Twain At Large. Henry Regnery, Chicago, IL. 1969.342p.7.50Hdbd. LC 69-15705.

SCOTT, JAMES B. Djuna Barnes. Twayne, Boston, MA.1976.6.95Hdbd. ISBN 0-8057-7153-0. LC 75-45214.

SCOTT, NATHAN A., JR., Ed. Adversity and Grace;Studies in Recent American Literature. Univ. of Chicago Pr., Chicago, IL.1968.269p. LC 68-16717.

SCOTT, WILLIAM THOMPSON. Chesterton, and Other Essays. Folcroft, Folcroft, PA.1912(1974).20.00Hdbd. LC 74-18300.

SCOTTO, ROBERT M. Three Contemporary American Novelists;An Annotated Bibliography of Works by and About John Hawkes, Joseph Heller and Thomas Pynchon. Garland Pub.1976.20.00Hdbd.ISBN 0-8240-9948-6.

SEALTS, MERTON M., JR. Comp. The Early Lives of Melville;Nineteenth-Century Biographical Sketches and Their Authors. Univ. of Wisconsin Pr., Madison, WI. 1974.12.50Hdbd. ISBN 0-299-06570-7. LC 74-5906.

SEALTS, MERTON M., JR. Melville as Lecturer. Harvard Univ. Pr., Cambridge, MA.1957.202p. LC 58-5542.

SEALTS, MERTON M., JR. Melville's Reading;A Check-List of Books Owned and Borrowed. Univ. of Wisconsin Pr., Madison, WI.1966.134p. LC 66-22850.

SEARLE, WILLIAM. The Saint and the Skeptics;Joan of Arc in the Work of Mark Twain, Anatole France, and Bernard Shaw. Wayne State Univ. Pr., Detroit, MI.1975.12.50Hdbd. ISBN 0-8143-1541-0. LC 75-26709.

SEARS, SALLIE. the Negative Imagination;Form and Perspective in the Novels of Henry James. Cornell Univ. Pr., Ithaca, NY.1968.231p.

SEDGWICK, WILLIAM ELLERY. Herman Melville;The Tragedy of Mind. Russell and Russell, NY.1944.255p.

SEELYE, JOHN. Melville;The Ironic Diagram. Northwestern Univ. Pr., Evanston.1970.177p.

SEGAL, ORA. The Lucid Reflector; The Observer in Henry James' Fiction. Yale Univ. Pr., New Haven, CT. 1969.265p.

SEIB, KENNETH. James Agee;Promise and Fulfillment. Univ. of Pittsburgh Pr., Pittsburgh, PA.1968.2.95 Pa. ISBN 0-8229-5171-1. LC 68-21634.

SELTZER, LEON F. The Vision of Melville and Conrad;A Comparative Study. Ohio Univ. Pr., Athens, OH. 1970.132p.

SEMMLER, CLEMENT. Art of Brian James;And Other Essays on Australian Literature. Humanities.1972. 9.25Hdbd.

SEMMLER, CLEMENT, Ed. Twentieth Century Australian Literary Criticism. Oxford Univ. Pr.1967.12.50 Hdbd. ISBN 0-19-550258-2.

SENIOR, JOHN. Way Down and Out; The Occult and Symbolist Literature.

Greenwood. 1968. ISBN 0-8371-0218-9. LC 68-23326.

SEVIGG, RICHARD. Lawrence, Hardy and American Literature. Oxford Univ. Pr. 1972. 16. 25Hdbd. ISBN 0-19-212552-4.

SEWARD, WILLIAM. My Friend Ernest Hemingway;An Affectionate Reminiscence. A.S. Barnes, South Brunswick and NY. 1969. 69p.

SEWARD, WILLIAM W., JR. Contrasts in Modern Writers;Some Aspects of British and American Fiction Since Mid-Century. Frederick Fell, NY. 1963. 184p. LC 63-14280.

SEYERSTED, PER. Kate Chopin;A Critical Biography. Universitetsforlaget, Oslo and Louisiana State Univ. Pr., Baton Rouge, LA. 1969. 246p. ISBN 8071-0915-0. LC 77-88740.

SEYMOUR-SMITH, MARTIN. Funk and Wagnalls Guide to Modern World Literature. Crowell. 1973. 17. 50Hdbd. ISBN 0-308-10079-4.

SEYMOUR-SMITH, MARTIN. Who's Who in Twentieth-Century Literature. Holt, Rinehart, NY. 1976. 12. 95Hdbd. ISBN 0-03-013926-0. LC 75-21470.

SEYPPEL, JOACHIM. William Faulkner. Ungar, NY. 1971. 120p.

SHANKS, EDWARD. Edgar Allen Poe. Folcroft, Folcroft, PA. 1974. 20. 00Hdbd. ISBN 0-8414-7745-0. LC 74-5139.

SHANLEY, J. LYNDON. The Making of Walden with the Text of the First Version. Univ. of Chicago Pr., Chicago, IL. 1957.

SHAPIRO, CHARLES. Theodore Dreiser;Our Bitter Patriot. Southern Illinois Univ. Pr., Carbondale, IL. 1962. 137p.

SHAPIRO, CHARLES, Ed. Twelve Original Essays on Great American Novels. Wayne State Univ. Pr., Detroit, MI. 1958. 289p. LC 57-13316.

SHARP, SISTER M. CORONA. The Confidante in Henry James. Univ. of Notre Dame Pr. 1963. 305p.

SHARPLESS, F. PARVIN. Symbol and Myth in Modern Literature. Hayden. 1976. 6. 19Pa. ISBN 0-8104-5071-2.

SHAUGHNESSY, MARY ROSE. Women and Success in American Society in the Works of Edna Ferber. Gordon Pr., NY. 1976. 34. 95Hdbd. ISBN 0-87968-454-2. LC 76-16530.

SHAW, HARRY. Concise Dictionary of Literary Terms. McGraw-Hill, NY. 1972(1976). 2. 95Pa. ISBN 0-07-056483-3. LC 76-15974.

SHAW, HARRY. 20 Steps to Better Writing. Littlefield, Adams, Totowa, NJ. 1975. 140p. 1. 95Pa. ISBN 0-8226-0389-X. LC 75-1499.

SHAW, SAMUEL. Ernest Hemingway. Ungar, NY. 1973. 136p.

SHEEHY, EUGENE P., and Kenneth A. Lohf, Comp. Sherwood Anderson. Talisman Pr., Los Gatos, CA. 1960. 8. 00Hdbd. ISBN 0-527-82100-4. LC 73-10001.

SHEPHERD, HENRY ELLIOT. The Representative Authors of Maryland; From the Earliest Time to the Present Day with Biographical Notes and Comments Upon Their Work.

Gale, Detroit, MI. 1911(1976). 11.50Hdbd. ISBN 0-8103-4281-2. LC 75-43960.

SHERMAN, PAUL, Ed. Thoreau;A Collection of Critical Essays. Prentice Hall, Englewood Cliffs, NJ. 1962. 188p. 1.95Pa.

SHERMAN, STUART P. The Significance of Sinclair Lewis. Books for Libraries Pr., Freeport, NY. 1972. 20p.

SHINE, MURIEL G. The Fictional Children of Henry James. Univ. of North Carolina Pr., Chapel Hill, NC. 1969. 192p.

SHOCKLEY, ANN ALLEN. Living Black American Authors;A Biographical Directory. R. R. Bowker, NY. 1973. 220p. 12.95Hdbd. ISBN 0-8352-0662-9. LC 73-17005.

SHULENBERGER, ARVID. Cooper's Theory of Fiction;His Prefaces and Their Relation to His Novels. Octagon, NY. 1972.

SHUMAKER, WAYNE. Elements of Critical Theory. Greenwood Pr., Westport, CT. 1952(1975). 131p. 9.75 Hdbd. ISBN 0-8371-7663-8. LC 74-9398.

SIMMONDS, ROY S. Steinbeck's Literary Achievement. Ball State Univ. Pr., Muncie, IN. 1976. 40p. 1.50Pa. LC 76-7672.

SIMON, LINDA. The Biography of Alice B. Toklas. Doubleday, NY. 10.00 Hdbd. ISBN 0-385-08140-5.

SIMON, LINDA, Ed. Gertrude Stein; A Composite Portrait. Avon, NY. 1974. 192p. 1.65Pa. ISBN 0-380-00169-1.

SIMPSON, LEWIS P. The Dispossessed Garden;Pastoral and History in Southern Literature. Univ. of Georgia Pr., Athens, GA. 1975. 109p. 6.00Hdbd. ISBN 0-8203-0355-0. LC 74-80942.

SINCLAIR, UPTON. My Lifetime in Letters. Univ. of Missouri Pr., Columbia, MO. 1960. 412p. LC 59-14141.

SINGER, GODFREY FRANK. The Epistolary Novel;Its Origin, Development, Decline and Residuary Influence. Russell and Russell, NY. 1933(1963). 266p. LC 63-9508.

SKAGGS, MERRILL MAGUIRE. The Fold of Southern Fiction. Univ. of Georgia Pr., Athens, GA. 1972. 280p. ISBN 0-8203-0294-5. LC 76-190050.

SKLAR, ROBERT. F. Scott Fitzgerald;The Last Laocoon. Oxford Univ. Pr., NY. 1967. 376p.

SLADE, JOSEPH W. Thomas Pynchon. Warner, NY. 1974. 256p. 1.50Pa. ISBN 0-446-78523-7. LC 74-196000.

SLATER, JOSEPH, Ed. The Correspondence of Emerson and Carlyle. Columbia Univ. Pr., NY. 1965. 622p. 12.50Hdbd. LC 63-17539.

SLATOFF, WALTER J. Quest for Failure;A Study of William Faulkner. Cornell Univ. Pr., Ithaca, NY. 1960. 273p.

SLATOFF, WALTER J. With Respect to Readers;Dimensions of Literary Response. Cornell Univ. Pr., Ithaca, NY. 1970. 212p. ISBN 0-8014-0580-7. LC 77-123995.

SLOTE, BERNICE, and Virginia Faulkner, Eds. The Art of Willa Cather.

Univ. of Nebraska, Lincoln, NB. 1974. 8.50Hdbd. ISBN 0-8032-0841-3. LC 74-78479.

SLOTKIN, RICHARD. Regeneration Through Violence;The Mythology of the American Frontier;1600-1860. Wesleyan Univ. Pr., Middletown, CT. 1973. 670p. ISBN 0-8195-4055-2. LC 72-3725.

SLUSSER, GEORGE EDGAR. The Bradbury Chronicles. Borgo Pr., San Bernadino, CA. 1977. 1.95Pa. LC 77-774.

SLUSSER, GEORGE EDGAR. The Farthest Shores of Ursula K. LeGuin. Borgo Pr., San Bernardino, CA. 1976. 1.95Pa. ISBN 0-87877-205-7. LC 76-41929.

SLUSSER, GEORGE EDGAR. Harlan Ellison;Unrepentant Harlequin. Borgo Pr., San Bernadino, CA. 1977. 1.95 Pa. ISBN 0-89370-209-9. LC 77-768.

SMARIDGE, NORAH. Famous Literary Teams for Young People. Dodd, Mead, NY. 1977. 5.50Hdbd. ISBN 396-07407-3. LC 76-53636.

SMART, GEORGE K. Religious Elements in Faulkner's Early Novels; A Selective Concordance. Univ. of Miami Pr., Coral Gables, FL. 1965. 144p.

SMITH, CLARK ASHTON. Planets and Dimensions. Mirage Pr., Baltimore, MD. 1973. 87p. LC 73-175550.

SMITH, DAVID NICHOL. The Functions of Criticism. Norwood Editions, Norwood, PA. 1976. 6.00Hdbd. ISBN 0-8482-2475-2. LC 76-45086.

SMITH, HELEN REAGAN. Basic Story Techniques. Univ. of Oklahoma Pr., Norman, OK. 1964(1967). 253p. LC 64-13590.

SMITH, HENRY NASH, Ed. Mark Twain;A Collection of Critical Essays. Prentice-Hall, Englewood Cliffs, NJ. 1963. 179p. 5.95Hdbd. 1.95Pa.

SMITH, HENRY NASH. Mark Twain; The Development of a Writer. Harvard Univ. Pr. 1962. 4.75Hdbd.

SMITH, HENRY NASH, and William M. Gibson, Eds. Mark Twain-Howells Letters;The Correspondence of Samuel L. Clemens and William D. Howells;1872-1910. Harvard Univ. Pr., Cambridge, MA. 1960. 454p. LC 60-5397.

SMITH, MYRON J., JR. Cloak-and-Dagger Bibliography;An Annotated Guide to Spy Fiction;1937-1975. Scarecrow Pr., Metuchen, NJ. 1976. 225p. 9.50Hdbd. ISBN 0-8108-0897-8. LC 75-44319.

SMITH, SAMUEL STEPHENSON. The Craft of the Critic. Books for Libraries Pr., Freeport, NY. 1931(1969). 401p. ISBN 8369-1180-6. LC 76-90681.

SMITH, VIVIAN BRIAN. Vance and Nettie Palmer. Twayne, NY. 1975. 154p. 6.95Hdbd. ISBN 0-8057-2667-5. LC 74-9791.

SMYTH, ALBERT H. Bayard Taylor. Gale, Detroit, MI. 1896(1971). 12.50Hdbd. LC 75-99057.

SNELL, EDWIN MARION. The Modern Fables of Henry James. Russell and Russell, NY. 1967.

SNELL, GEORGE. The Shapers of

American Fiction;1798-1947. Cooper Square, NY. 1961. 316p. LC 61-13269.

SNYDER, GERALD S. The Right to be Informed;Censorship in the United States. Messner, NY. 1976. 191p. 7.29Hdbd. ISBN 0-671-32809-3. LC 76-16191.

SNYDER, ROBERT. This is Henry Miller;Henry Miller from Brooklyn; Conversations with this Author from the Henry Miller Odyssey. Nash, Los Angeles, CA. 1974. 125p. 12.50Hdbd. ISBN 0-8402-1076-0. LC 73-92969.

SOKOLOFF, B. A., and David E. Arnason. John Updike;A Comprehensive Bibliography. Norwood Editions, Norwood, PA. 1973. 12.50Hdbd. LC 73-174165.

SOKOLOFF, B. A., and Mark E. Posner. Saul Bellow;A Comprehensive Bibliography. Norwood Editions, Norwood, PA. 1973. 12.50Hdbd. LC 73-6681.

SOLOMON, ERIC. Stephen Crane;From Parody to Realism. Harvard Univ. Pr., Cambridge, MA. 1966. 8.95Hdbd. ISBN 0-674-83806-8.

SOLOMON, ERIC. Stephen Crane in England;A Portrait of the Artist. Ohio State Univ. Pr. 1965. 4.50Hdbd. ISBN 0-8142-0115-6.

SOLOMON, PEARL CHESTER. Dickens and Melville in their Time. Columbia Univ. Pr., NY. 1974(1975). 9.00 Hdbd. ISBN 0-231-03889-5. LC 74-13307.

SOLOTAROFF, THEODORE. The Red Hot Vacuum and Other Pieces on the Writing of the Sixties. Antheneum, NY. 1961(1970). 336p. LC 70-124982.

SOMERLOTT, ROBERT. The Writing of Modern Fiction. The Writer, Boston, MA. 1972. 147p. ISBN 0-87116-068-4. LC 71-188590.

SONNENSCHEIN, WILLIAM SWAN. The Best Books;A Reader's Guide and Literary Reference Book. Gale, Detroit, MI. 1969. 2759p. 165.00Set Hdbd. LC 68-58760.

SORELL, WALTER. Facets of Comedy. Grosset and Dunlap, NY. 1973. 340p. 2.95Pa. ISBN 0-448-00016-4. LC 79-145726.

SOUTHALL, IVAN. A Journey of Discovery;On Writing for Children. Macmillan, NY. 1975(1976). 101p. 6.95 Hdbd. ISBN 0-02-786150-3. LC 75-31547.

SPACKS, PATRICIA MEYER, Ed. Contemporary Women Novelists;A Collection of Critical Essays. Prentice-Hall, Englewood Cliffs, NJ. 1977. 7.95Hdbd. ISBN 0-13-171330-2. LC 77-4503. 2.95Pa. ISBN 0-13-171322-1.

SPACKS, PATRICIA MEYER. The Female Imagination. Random House, NY. 1975. 10.00Hdbd. ISBN 0-394-49184-X. LC 74-21320.

SPANNUTH, JACOB B., Comp. Doings of Gotham by Edgar Allan Poe, as described in a Series of Letters to the Editors of the Columbia spy, together with various editorial comments and criticisms by Poe;also a Poem entitled "New Year's Address of the Carriers of the Columbia Spy". Folcroft, Folcroft, PA. 1974. 25.00Hdbd. ISBN 0-8414-6707-2. LC 74-26950.

SPATZ, JONAS. Hollywood in Fiction;Some Versions of the American

Myth. Mouton, The Hague, Paris. 1969. 148p. LC 75-75887.

SPENCER, HERBERT. Literary Style and Music. Kennikat, Port Washington, NY. 1951(1970). 6.00Hdbd. ISBN 0-8046-0667-6. LC 78-91057.

SPENCER, SHARON. Space, Time and Structure in the Modern Novel. Swallow Pr. 1971(1974). 251p. 3.95Hdbd. ISBN 0-8147-7751-1. LC 74-195202.

SPENDER, STEPHEN. Love-Hate Relations; English and American Sensibilities. Random House, NY. 1974. 318p. 8.95Hdbd. ISBN 0-394-49062-2. LC 73-20138.

SPENDER, STEPHEN. New Realism; A Discussion. Folcroft, Folcroft, PA. 1939. 7.50Hdbd.

SPENGEMANN, WILLIAM C. The Adventurous Muse; The Poetics of American Fiction; 1789-1900. Yale Univ. Pr., New Haven, CT. 1977. 15.00Hdbd. ISBN 0-300-02042-2. LC 76-26936.

SPENGEMANN, WILLIAM C. Mark Twain and the Backwoods Angel; The Matter of Innocence in the Works of Samuel L. Clemens. Kent State Univ. Pr. 1966. 141p.

SPIEGEL, ALAN. Fiction and the Camera Eye; Visual Consciousness in Film and the Modern Novel. Univ. Pr. of Virginia, Charlottesville, VA. 1975(1976). 9.75Hdbd. ISBN 0-8139-0598-2. LC 75-22353.

SPILLER, ROBERT E., Ed. The American Literary Revolution; 1783-1837. Doubleday, Garden City, NY. 1967. 500p.

SPILLER, ROBERT E. The Cyle of American Literature; An Essay in Historical Criticism. Free Pr., NY. 1967. 243p. LC 55-3833.

SPILLER, ROBERT E., and Philip C. Blackburn. A Descriptive Bibliography of the Writings of James Fenimore Cooper. Burt Franklin, NY. 1903(1968). 259p. LC 68-58431.

SPILLER, ROBERT E.. Fenimore Cooper; Critic of His Times. Russell and Russell, NY. 1963. 9.00Hdbd.

SPILLER, ROBERT E. Four Makers of the American Mind; Emerson, Thoreau, Whitman, and Melville. Duke Univ. Pr., Durham, NC. 1976. 82p. 6.75Hdbd. ISBN 0-8223-0372-8. LC 76-24188.

SPILLER, ROBERT E., and Willard Thorp, Thomas H. Johnson, Henry Seidel Canby, Richard M. Ludwig, William M. Gibson. Macmillian Pub. NY., Fourth Ed. 1974. 1,556p. LC 73-14014.

SPILLER, ROBERT E. The Oblique Light; Studies in Literary History and Biography. Macmillian, NY. 1948 (1968). 279p. LC 68-20748.

SPILLER, ROBERT E. The Third Dimension; Studies in Literary History. Macmillan, NY. 1965. 245p. LC 65-13122.

SPILLER, ROBERT E. Milestones in American Literary History. Greenwood Pr., Westport, CT. 1977. 11.95 Hdbd. ISBN 0-8371-9403-2. LC 76-47170.

SPRADLEY, JAMES P., and George E. McDonough. Anthropology Through Literature; Cross Cultural Perspectives. Little, 1973. 6.95Pa. ISBN 0-316-80760-5.

SPRINGER, HASKELL S. Comp. The Merrill Studies in Billy Budd. Merrill Pub., Columbus, OH. 1970. 142p.

SPRINGER, HASKELL S. Washington Irving;A Reference Guide. G.K. Hall, Boston, MA. 1976. 20.00Hdbd. ISBN 0-8161-1101-4. LC 76-2489.

SPRINGER, MARLENE. Edith Wharton and Kate Chopin;A Reference Guide. G.K. Hall, Boston, MA. 1976. 24.00Hdbd. ISBN 0-8161-1099-9. LC 76-1831.

STAAL, ARIE. Hawthorne's Narrative Art. Revisionist Pr., NY. 1976. 34.95Hdbd. ISBN 0-87700-250-9. LC 76-47634.

STAEHELIN-WACKERNAGEL ADELHEID. Edited by H. Ludeke. The Cooper Monographs on English and American Language and Literature. Verlag Bern, Switzerland. 1961. 165p.

STAFFORD, WILLIAM T., Ed. Melville's Billy Budd and the Critics; Second Edition. Wadsworth, Belmont, CA. 1968. 272p.

STAFFORD, WILLIAM T. A Name, Title, and Place Index to the Critical Writings of Henry James. Microcard Editions, Englewood, CO. 1975. 270p. 19.95Hdbd. ISBN 0-910972-47-8. LC 75-8093.

STAFFORD, WILLIAM T., Ed. Perspectives on James's The Portrait of a Lady. New York Univ. Pr., NY. 1967. 303p.

STAINES, DAVID, Ed. The Canadian Imagination;Dimensions of a Literary Culture. Harvard Univ. Pr., Cambridge, MA. 1977. 265p. Hdbd. ISBN 0-674-09355-0. LC 77-9587.

STALLMAN, R.W. Stephen Crane;A Biography. Braziller, NY. 1968. 664p. LC 68-16110.

STALLMAN, R.W. Stephen Crane;A Critical Bibliography. Iowa State Univ. Pr., Ames, IA. 1972. 750p. 25.00 Hdbd. ISBN 0-8138-0357-8.

STALLMAN, R.W., and Lillian Gilkes, Eds. Stephen Crane;Letters. New York Univ. Pr., NY. 1960. 366p. LC 59-15192.

STALLMAN, R.W., Ed. The Critic's Notebook. Greenwood Pr., Westport, CT. 1950(1977). 18.00Hdbd. ISBN 0-8371-9324-9. LC 76-48931.

STALLMAN, R.W., Comp. Critiques and Essays in Criticism;1920-1948; Representing the Achievement of Modern British and American Critics. Ronald Pr., NY. 1949. 571p. LC 49-7475.

STANZEL, FRANZ. Transl. by James P. Pusack. Narrative Situations in the Novel;Tom Jones, Moby-Dick, The Ambassordors, Ulysses. Indiana Univ. Pr., Bloomington, IN. 1971. 186p. ISBN 253-33970-7. LC 70-138411.

STARK, JOHN O. The Literature of Exhaustion;Borges, Nabokov, and Barth. Duke Univ. Pr., Durham, NC. 1974. 196p. 7.95Hdbd. ISBN 0-8223-0316-7. LC 73-92536.

STARRETT, VINCENT. Born in a Bookshop;Chapters from the Chicago Renascence. Univ. of Oklahoma Pr., Norman, OK. 1965. 325p. LC 65-24204.

STEELE, RICHARD LOWELL. Thomas Wolfe;A Study in Psychoanalytic Literary Criticism. Dorrance, Philadelphia, PA. 1976. 7.95Hdbd. ISBN 0-8059-2334-9. LC 77-357018.

STEGNER, WALLACE, Ed. The American Novel from James Fenimore Cooper to William Faulkner. Basic, NY. 1965. 236p. LC 65-14125.

STEIN, GERTRUDE. How to Write. Dover, NY. 1975. 395p. 3.50Pa. LC 74-17880.

STEIN, GERTRUDE. Lectures in America. Beacon Pr., Boston, MA. 1935 (1967). 246p.

STEINBECK, ELAINE, and Robert Wallsten, Eds. Steinbeck;A Life in Letters. Penguin, NY. 1976. 5.95Pa. ISBN 0-14-004288-1. LC 76-18821.

STEINBECK, JOHN. Journal of a Novel;The East of Eden Letters. Viking Pr., NY. 1969. 182p.

STEINBRUNNER, CHRIS, and Otto Penzler, Eds. Encyclopedia of Mystery and Detection. McGraw-Hill, NY. 1976. 436p. 19.95Hdbd. ISBN 0-07-061121-1. LC 75-31645.

STEINER, GEORGE. Language and Silence;Essays on Language, Literature, and the Inhuman. Atheneum, NY. 1958(1967). 426p. LC 67-14332.

STENERSON, DOUGLAS C. H. L. Mencken;Iconoclast from Baltimore. University of Chicago Pr., Chicago, IL. 1971. 287p. ISBN 0-226-77249-7. LC 78-158683.

STEPHENS, MARTHA. The Question of Flannery O'Connor. Louisiana State Univ. Pr., Baton Rouge, LA. 1973. 205p. 8.50Hdbd. ISBN 0-8071-0000-5. LC 73-77656.

STEPHEN, ROBERT O., Ed. Ernest Hemingway;The Critical Reception. B. Franklin, NY. 1976. 19.95Hdbd. ISBN 0-89102-052-7. LC 76-48711.

STERN, J. P. On Realism. Routledge and Kegan. 1973. 8.25Hdbd. ISBN 0-7100-7379-8.

STERN, MADELEINE B. The Life of Margaret Fuller. Haskell House, NY. 1942(1968). 549p. LC 68-29738.

STERN, MILTON R., Ed. American Literature Survey;The American Romantics;1800-1860. Viking, NY. 1975. 3.50Pa. LC 74-3690.

STERN, MILTON R., Ed. Discussions of Moby-Dick. D. C. Heath, Boston, MA. 1960. 134p.

STERN, MILTON R. The Fine Hammered Steel of Herman Melville. Univ. of Illinois Pr., Chicago, IL. 1968. 255p.

STERN, MILTON R. The Golden Moment;The Novels of F. Scott Fitzgerald. Univ. of Illinois Pr., Chicago, IL. 1970. 462p.

STEVENS, MICHAEL. V. Sackville-West;A Critical Biography. Scribner's, NY. 1974. 7.95Hdbd. ISBN 0-684-13677-5. LC 73-19357.

STEVENS, PETER. Modern Canadian Prose;A Guide to Information Sources. Gale, Detroit, MI. 18.00Hdbd. ISBN 0-8103-1245-X. LC 73-16996.

STEVENSON, ELIZABETH. The Crooked Corridor;A Study of Henry James. Macmillan, NY. 1949. 172p.

STEVENSON, LIONEL. Appraisals of Canadian Literature. Folcroft, Folcroft, PA. 1926. 15.00Hdbd.

STEVENSON, ROBERT LOUIS. George Scott-Moncrieff, Ed. RLS;Selected Essays. Regnery, Chicago, IL. 1959. 300p.

STEVICK, PHILIP. The Chapter in Fiction;Theories of Narrative Division. Syracuse Univ. Pr., Syracuse, NY. 1970. 188p. ISBN 8156-0070-4. LC 75-125079.

STEWART, DOUGLAS. The Flesh and the Spirit. Folcroft, Folcroft, PA. 1948. 15.00Hdbd.

STEWART, GEORGE R. Bret Harte, Argonaut and Exile. Kennikat Pr., Port Washington, NY. 1931. 10.00Hdbd.

STEWART, JOHN L. The Burden of Time;The Fugitives and Agrarians. Princeton Univ. Pr., Princeton, NJ. 1965(1966). 551p. LC 65-12994.

STEWART, LAWRENCE DELBERT. Paul Bowles;The Illumination of North Africa. Southern Illinois Univ. Pr., Carbondale, IL. 1974. 175p. 6.95 Hdbd. ISBN 0-8093-0651-4. LC 74-2273.

STEWART, RANDALL. Nathaniel Hawthorne;A Biography. Archon Books. 1970. 279p. ISBN 0-208-00829-2. LC 74-114425.

STEWART, RANDALL. Edited by George Core. Regionalism and Beyond;Essays of Randall Stewart. Vanderbilt Univ. Pr., Nashville, TN. 1968. 286p. LC 67-20426.

STIEG, LEWIS F., Comp. Irving Stone;A Bibliography. Friends of the Libraries of the Univ. of Southern California, Los Angeles, CA. 1973. 56p.

STINE, JANE. Investigating;Gathering Information. Houghton Mifflin, Boston, MA. 1975. 118p. 2.76Pa. ISBN 0-395-19760-0. LC 74-12601.

STINEBACK, DAVID C. Shifting World;Social Change and Nostalgia in the American Novel. Bucknell Univ. Pr., Lewisburg, PA. 1975. 12.00Hdbd. ISBN 0-8387-1686-5. LC 74-31510.

STONE, ALBERT E., JR., Ed. Twentieth Century Interpretations of The Ambassadors. Prentice-Hall, Englewood Cliffs, NJ. 1969. 121p.

STONE, DONALD DAVID. Novelists in a Changing World;Meredith, James, and the Transformation of English Fiction in the 1880's. Harvard Univ. Pr., Cambridge, MA. 1972. 381 p. ISBN 674-62830-6. LC 75-169861.

STONE, EDWARD. The Battle and the Books;Some Aspects of Henry James. Ohio Univ. Pr., Athens, OH. 1964. 234p.

STONE, EDWARD. A Certain Morbidness;A View of American Literature. Southern Illinois Univ. Pr., Carbondale, IL. 1969. 183p. ISBN 8093-0385-X. LC 69-11507.

STONE, EDWARD. Voices of Despair;Four Motifs in American Literature. Ohio Univ. Pr. 1966. 240p. LC 65-24646.

STORY, NORAH. Oxford Companion to Canadian History and Literature. Oxford Univ. Pr. 1967. 24.95Hdbd.

STOUCK, DAVID. Willa Cather's Imagination. Univ. of Nebraska Pr., Lincoln, NB. 1975. 253p. 9.50Hdbd. ISBN 0-8032-0848-0. LC 74-81363.

STOUT, JANIS P. Sodoms in Eden; The City in American Fiction before 1860. Greenwood Pr., Westport, CT. 1976. 12.50Hdbd. ISBN 0-8371-8585-8. LC 75-35356.

STOVALL, FLOYD, Ed. The Development of American Literary Criticism. College and Univ. Pr., New Haven, CT. 262p.

STOWE, CHARLES EDWARD, Comp. Life of Harriet Beecher Stowe; Her Letters and Journals. Houghton, Mifflin, Boston, MA. 530p. LC 67-23881.

STOWE, HARRIET BEECHER. The Key to Uncle Tom's Cabin. Arno Pr., NY. 1968. 508p.

STRAUMANN, HEINRICH. American Literature in the Twentieth Century. Harper and Row, NY. 1968. 224p. LC 65-13202.

STRELKA, JOSEPH P., Ed. Anagogic Qualities of Literature. Pennsylvania State Univ. Pr., University Park, PA. 1971. 335p. 9.50Hdbd. ISBN 0-271-01145-9. LC 79-136962.

STRELKA, JOSEPH P., Ed. Literary Criticism and Sociology. Pennsylvania State Univ. Pr. 1973. 12.95Hdbd. ISBN 0-271-01152-1. LC 73-136963.

STRELKA, JOSEPH P., Ed. Perspectives in Literary Symbolism. Pennsylvania State Univ. Pr. 12.00Hdbd. ISBN 0-271-73137-0. LC 67-27116.

STROUD, PARRY. Stephen Vincent Benet. Twayne. 1962. 6.95Hdbd. ISBN 0-8057-0052-8.

STROUT, CUSHING, Ed. Hawthorne in England; Selections from Our Old Home and The English Note-Books. Cornell Univ. Pr., Ithaca, NY. 1965. 274p. LC 65-15775.

STUBBS, JOHN CALDWELL. The Pursuit of Form; A Study of Hawthorne and the Romance. Univ. of Illinois Pr., Chicago, IL. 1970.

STUCKEY, W. J. The Pulitzer Prize Novels; A Critical Backward Look. Univ. of Oklahoma Pr., Norman, OK. 1966. 224p. LC 66-10295.

STUHLMANN, GUNTHER, Ed. Henry Miller Letters to Anais Nin. Putnam's Sons, NY. 1965. 356p. LC 65-10859.

SULLIVAN, WALTER. Death by Melancholy; Essays on Modern Southern Fiction. Louisiana State Univ. Pr., Baton Rouge, LA. 1972. 133p. ISBN 0-8071-0236-9. LC 72-79339.

SULLIVAN, WALTER. A Requiem for the Renascence; The State of Fiction in the Modern South. Univ. of Georgia Pr., Athens, GA. 1976. 81p. 6.00Hdbd. ISBN 0-8203-0390-9. LC 75-21176.

SUMMERS, MONTAGUE. Gothic Quest; A History of the Gothic Novel. Russell and Russell, NY. 1938(1964). 15.00Hdbd. ISBN 0-8462-0522-X. LC 64-8919.

SURMELIAN, LEON. Techniques of Fiction Writing; Measure and Madness. Doubleday, Garden City, NY. 1968. 255p. LC 66-24323.

SUTHERLAND, ZENA, and May Hill

Arbuthnot. Children and Books. Scott, Foresman, Glenview, IL. 1977. 14.-95Hdbd. ISBN 0-673-15037-2. LC 76-26136.

SUTTON, WILLIAM A. The Road to Winesburg;A Mosaic of the Imaginative Life of Sherwood Anderson. Scarecrow Pr., Metuchen, NJ. 1972. 17.-00Hdbd. ISBN 0-8108-0312-7.

SUTTON, WILLIAM A. Black Like It Is/Was;Erskine Caldwell's Treatment of Racial Themes. Scarecrow Pr., Metuchen, NJ. 1974. 164p. 6.00 Hdbd. ISBN 0-8108-0723-8. LC 74-5389.

SWAN, H. Who's Who in Fiction?;A Dictionary of Noted Names in Novels, Tales, Romances, Poetry, and Drama. E. P. Dutton, NY. 1906(1975). ISBN 0-8103-4114-X. LC 73-167218.

SWANBERG, W. A. Dreiser;A Biography. Scribner's, NY. 1965. 7.50Hdbd. Bantam, NY. 1.25Pa.

SWEENEY, GERARD M. Melville's Use of Classical Mythology. Rodopi, Amsterdam. 1975. 169p. 10.00Pa. ISBN 9-06-203258-3. LC 75-328900.

SWIGART, LESLIE KAY, Comp. Harlan Ellison;A Bibliographical Checklist. Williams Pub., Dallas, TX. 1973. 117p.

SWIGG, RICHARD. Lawrence, Hardy, and American Literature. Oxford Univ. Pr., NY;London;Toronto. 1972. 368p. ISBN 0-19-212552-4.

SWIGGART, PETER. The Art of Faulkner's Novels. Univ. of Texas Pr., Austin, TX. 1962. 230p.

SWINGEWOOD, ALAN. The Novel and Revolution. Barnes and Noble, NY. 1975. 288p. 22.50Hdbd. ISBN 0-06-496682-8. LC 75-21103.

SYMONS, ARTHUR. Symbolist Movement in Literature. Dutton. 1.95Pa. ISBN 0-525-47021-2.

SYMONS, ARTHUR. Studies in Comparative Literature No. 35. Haskell. 1971. 18.95Hdbd. ISBN 0-8383-1316-7. LC 79-166209.

SYMONS, JULIAN. Mortal Consequences;A History from the Detective Story to the Crime Novel. Harper, NY. 1972. 6.95Hdbd. ISBN 0-06-014187-5. LC 72-138767.

T

TAKAKI, RONALD T. Violence in the Black Imagination;Essays and Documents. Putnam's Sons, NY. 1972. 458 p. ISBN 399-10943-9. LC 70-181408.

TANNER, TONY. City of Words;American Fiction;1950-1970. Harper-Row, NY. 1971. 10.00Hdbd. ISBN 0-06-0142170-0. LC 70-156554.

TONNER, TONY. The Reign of Wonder;Naivety and Reality in American Literature. Cambridge Univ. Pr., Cambridge, MA. 1965. 388p. LC 65-15304.

TARRANT, DESMOND. James Branch Cabell;The Dream and the Reality. University of Oklahoma Pr. 1967. 8.95Hdbd. ISBN 0-8061-0755-3.

TAVUCHIS NICHOLAS, and William Goode. The Family Through Literature. McGraw-Hill, NY. 1975. 6.95Pa. ISBN 0-07-023756-5. LC 74-8935.

TAYLOR, C. CLARKE. John Updike; A Bibliography. Kent State Univ. Pr., Kent, OH. 1968. 82p. LC 67-65584.

TAYLOR, GORDON O. The Passages of Thought;Psychological Representation in the American Novel;1870-1900. Oxford Univ. Pr., NY. 1969. 172 p. LC 74-75608.

TAYLOR, LLOYD C. Margaret Ayer Barnes. Twayne, NY. 1973. 5.50Hdbd. ISBN 0-8057-0037-4. LC 73-15837.

TAYLOR, WALTER FULLER. The Economic Novel in America. Octagon, NY. 1969. 378p. LC 64-24845.

TEDLOCK, E. W., JR., and C. V. Wicker, Eds. Steinbeck and His Critics; A Record of Twenty-Five Years. Univ. of New Mexico Pr., Albuquerque, NM. 1957. 310p.

TEMPLE, RUTH Z. The Critic's Alchemy. College and Univ. Pr. 1953. 3.45Pa.

TENNENHOUSE, LEONARD, Ed. The Practice of Psychoanalytic Criticism. Wayne State Univ. Pr., Detroit, MI. 1976. 279p. 13.50Hdbd. ISBN 0-8143-1562-3. LC 76-26079. 5.95Pa.

TENNEY, THOMAS. Mark Twain;A Reference Guide. G. K. Hall, Boston, MA. 1977. 45.00Hdbd. ISBN 0-8161-79662-2. LC 76-41752.

TERRY, JOHN SKALLY, Ed. Thomas Wolfe's Letters to His Mother, Julia Elizabeth Wolfe. Scribner's, NY. 1943. 368p.

THARPE, JAC. John Barth;The Comic Sublimity of Paradox. Southern Illinois Univ. Pr., Carbondale, IL. 1974. 133p. 6.95Hdbd. ISBN 0-8093-0702-2. LC 74-12263.

THARPE, JAC. Nathaniel Hawthorne; Identity and Knowledge. Southern Illinois Univ. Pr., Carbondale, IL. 1967.

THOMAS, ALFRED K. The Epic of Evolution; Its Etiology and Art; A Study of Vardis Fisher's Testament of Man. Revisionist Pr., NY. 1973. 443p. 34.95Hdbd. ISBN 0-87700-199-5. LC 73-8571.

THOMAS, CLARA. Canadian Novelists; 1920-1945. Folcroft, Folcroft, PA. 1946. 15.00Hdbd.

THOMAS, PAYNE EDWARD LLOYD. A Guide for Authors; Manuscript, Proof and Illustration. Thomas, Springfield, IL. 1975. 83p. 3.00Pa. ISBN 0-398-03443-5. LC 75-319945.

THOMPSON, G. R. Poe's Fiction; Romantic Irony in the Gothic Tales. Univ. of Wisconsin Pr. 1973. 12.50Hdbd. ISBN 0-299-06380-1.

THOMPSON, GARY RICHARD, Ed. The Gothic Imagination; Essays in Dark Romanticism. Washington State Univ. Pr. 1974. 176p. 6.00Hdbd. LC 74-186329.

THOMPSON, LAWRANCE. Melville's Quarrel with God. Princeton Univ. Pr., Princeton, NJ. 1952. 474p.

THOMPSON, LAWRANCE. William Faulkner; An Introduction and Interpretation; Second Edition. Holt, Rinehart, NY. 1967. 209p.

THORBURN, DAVID, and Geoffrey Hartman. Romanticism; Vistas, Instances, Continuities. Cornell Univ. Pr., Ithaca, NY. 1973. 284p. 13.50Hdbd. ISBN 0-8014-0791-5. LC 73-8405. 3.95Pa. ISBN 0-8014-9144-4.

THORP, WILLARD. American Writing in the Twentieth Century. Harvard Univ. Pr., Cambridge, MA. 1960. 353p. LC 59-14739.

THWAITE, MARY F. From Primer to Pleasure in Reading; An Introduction to the History of Children's Books in England from the Invention of Printing to 1914 with an Outline of Some Developments in other Countries. Horn Book, Boston, MA. 1973. 340p. 12.50Hdbd.

TICKNOR, CAROLINE. Hawthorne and His Publisher. Kennikat Press, Port Washington, NY. 339p. LC 68-8240.

TILLEY, W. H. The Background of the Princess Casamassima. Univ. of Florida Pr., Gainesville, FL. 1960. 61p.

TINDALL, WILLIAM Y. Literary Symbol. Peter Smith. 5.00Hdbd. ISBN 0-8446-3076-4.

TISCHLER, NANCY M. Black Masks; Negro Characters in Modern Southern Fiction. Pennsylvania State Univ. Pr., University Park, PA. 1969. 223p. ISBN 271-00082-1. LC 68-8187.

TITUS, WILLIAM A. Wisconsin Writers; Sketches and Studies. Gale, Detroit, MI. 1974. 433p. 16.50Hdbd. ISBN 0-8103-3658-8. LC 74-4303.

TJADER, MARGUERITE. Theodore Dreiser; A New Dimension. Silvermine Publishers, Norwalk, CT. 1965.

244p.5.95Hdbd.LC 65-20596.

TOBIN,RICHARD L.,Ed.The Golden Age;The Saturday Review 50th Anniversary Reader.Bantam,NY.1974. 376p.1.95Pa.

TOKLAS,ALICE B.Staying on Alone. Liveright,NY.1973.426p.11.95Hdbd. ISBN 0-87140-569-5.LC 73-82424.

TOMINAGA,THOMAS T.Iris Murdoch and Muriel Spark;A Bibliography.Scarecrow Pr.,Metuchen,NJ. 1976.237p.10.00Hdbd.ISBN 0-8108-0907-9.LC 76-909.

TOMKINS,MARY E.Ida M.Tarbell. Twayne,NY.1974.7.50Hdbd.ISBN 0-8057-0714-X.LC 73-22293.

TOMPKINS,JANE P.,Ed.Twentieth Century Interpretations of The Turn of the Screw and Other Tales.Prentice-Hall,Englewood Cliffs,NJ.1970. 114p.

TOOKER,DAN,and Roger Hofheins. Fiction!Interviews with Northern California Novelists.Harcourt,NY. 1976.7.95Hdbd.ISBN 0-15-130650-8. LC 76-28347.3.95Pa.

TOYE,WILLIAM,Ed.Supplement to the Oxford Companion to Canadian History and Literature.Oxford Univ. Pr.,NY.1974.11.50Hdbd.ISBN 0-19-540205-7.

TRACHTENBERG,ALAN,Ed.Memoirs of Waldo Frank.Univ.of Massachusetts Pr.,Amherst,MA.1973.268 p.15.00Hdbd.LC 73-123541.

TREAT,LAWRENCE,Ed.The Mystery Writer's Handbook;by the Mystery Writers of America.Writer's Digest,Cincinnati,OH.1975.7.95Hdbd.ISBN 9-11654-41-0.LC 75-33828.

TREMAINE,MARIE.Bibliography of Canadian Imprints;1751-1800.Univ.of Toronto Pr.1952.45.00Hdbd. ISBN 0-8020-7024-8.LC 52-2955.

TRILLING,LIONEL.Beyond Culture; Essays on Literature and Learning. Viking,NY.1965.233p.LC 65-24276.

TRILLING,DIANA.Claremont Essays.Harcourt,NY.1964.243p.LC 64-11530.

TRILLING,LIONEL.A Gathering of Fugitives.Beacon Pr.,Boston,MA. 1956.167p.

TRILLING,LIONEL.The Liberal Imagination;Essays on Literature and Society.Anchor/Doubleday,Garden City,NY.293p.

TRIMBLE,JOHN R.Writing with Style;Conversations on the Art of Writing.Prentice-Hall,Englewood Cliffs,NJ.1975.5.95Hdbd.ISBN 0-13-970376-4.LC 74-23088.2.50Pa. ISBN 0-13-970368-3.

TROYKA,LYNN QUITMAN,Ed.Guide to Writing.Harper's College Pr., NY.1974(1975).197p.3.95Hdbd.ISBN 0-06-160400-3.LC 74-6586.

TUCK,DOROTHY.Crowell's Handbook of Faulkner.Crowell,NY.1964. 259p.

TUCKER,FERRIS.Modern Commonwealth Literature.Ungar,NY.1977. Hdbd.LC 75-35425.

TURNBULL,ANDREW,Ed.The Letters of F.Scott Fitzgerald.Scribner's.NY.1963.615p. LC 63-16755.

TURNBULL, ANDREW. Thomas Wolfe. Scribner's, NY. 1967. 374p. LC 68-10727.

TURNER, ARLIN. George W. Cable; A Biography. Louisiana State Univ. Pr., Baton Rouge, LA. 1966. 391p. LC 56-9165.

TURNER, ARLIN. The Record of a Literary Friendship;Mark Twain, G.W.Cable. Michigan State Univ. Pr. 1960(1965). 141p. LC 59-15221.

TURNER, ARLIN. Nathaniel Hawthorne;An Introduction and Interpretation. Barnes and Noble, NY. 1961.

TURNER, DARWIN T. In a Minor Chord;Three Afro-American Writers and Their Search for Identity. Southern Illinois Univ. Pr., Carbondale, IL. 1971. 153p. ISBN 0-8093-0481-3. LC 72-132491.

TURNER, DOROTHEA. Jane Mander. Twayne, NY. 1972. 164p. 5.50Hdbd. LC 76-120493.

TURNER, ERNEST SACKVILLE. Boys will be Boys;The Story of Sweeney Todd, Deadwood Dick, Sexton Blake, Billy Bunter, Dick Barton, et al. Gale, Detroit, MI. 1974(1975). 14.00 Hdbd. ISBN 0-8103-4091-7. LC 76-175338.

TURNER, GEORGE. Stylistics. Penguin. 1974. 2.25Pa. ISBN 0-14-021643-X.

TUTTLETON, JAMES W. The Novels of Manners in America. Univ. of North Carolina Pr., Chapel Hill, NC. 304p. ISBN 0-8078-1188-2. LC 70-174787.

TWAIN, MARK. Mark Twain's Burlesque Autobiography. Norwood Editions, Norwood, PA. 1975. 4.50Hdbd. ISBN 0-88305-664-X. LC 75-14383.

TYTELL, JOHN. Naked Angels;The Lives and Literature of the Beat Generation. McGraw-Hill, NY. 4.50Hdbd.

U

ULLYETTE, JEAN M. Guidelines for Creative Writing. Owen Pub., Dansville, NY. 1968. 49p. 1.35Pa.

UMPHLETT, WILEY LEE. The Sporting Myth and the American Experience; Studies in Contemporary Fiction. Bucknell Univ. Pr., Lewisburg, PA. 1974. 8.50Hdbd. LC 73-8306.

UNDERWOOD, JOHN C. Literature and Insurgency. Biblo. 1914. 15.00Hdbd. ISBN 0-8196-0160-8.

UPDIKE, JOHN. Assorted Prose. Knopf, NY. 1965. 326p. LC 65-13460.

V

VAID, KRISHNA BALDEV. Technique in the Tales of Henry James. Harvard Univ. Pr., Cambridge, MA. 1964. 285p.

VANDERBILT, KERMIT. The Achievement of William Dean Howells; A Reinterpretation by Kermit Vanderbilt. Princeton Univ. Pr., Princeton, NJ. 1968. 226p.

VAN DOREN, CARL. The American Novel;1789-1939. Macmillan, NY. 1921(1968). 406p.

VAN DOREN, CARL. Sinclair Lewis; A Biographical Sketch. Kennikat Pr., Port Washington, NY. 1933. 205p.

VAN NOSTRAND, ALBERT D., Ed. Literary Criticism in America. Books for Libraries Pr., Freeport, NY. 1957(1970). 333p. ISBN 0-8369-1632-8. LC 74-111868.

VAN NOSTRAND, ALBERT D. Everyman His Own Poet;Romantic Gospels in American Literature. McGraw-Hill, NY. 1968. 272p. LC 68-18578.

VANNATTA, DENNIS P. Nathanael West;An Annotated Bibliography of the Scholarship and Works. Garland Pub. NY. 1976. 15.00Hdbd. ISBN 0-8240-9987-7. LC 75-24093.

VAN WHY, JOSEPH S. Nook Farm. Stowe-Day Foundation, Hartford, CT. 1975. 72p. 2.75Pa. LC 75-20778.

VARGO, EDWARD P. Rainstorms and Fire;Ritual in the Novels of John Updike. Kennikat Pr., Port Washington, NY. 1973. 229p. 9.95Hdbd. ISBN 0-8046-9053-7. LC 73-83271.

VEEDER, WILLIAM R. Henry James; The Lessons of the Master. Univ. of Chicago Pr., Chicago, IL. 16.00Hdbd. ISBN 0-226-85223-7. LC 75-8957.

VERLAND, ORM. James Fenimore Cooper's The Prairie;The Making and Meaning of an American Classic. Universitetsforlaget, Oslo. Humanities Pr., NY. 1973. 205p. ISBN 8-200-04613-3. LC 74-324641.

VERNON, JOHN. The Garden and the Map;Schizophrenia in Twentieth-Century Literature and Culture. Univ. of Illinois Pr. 1973. 8.95Hdbd. ISBN 0-252-00256-3. LC 72-85612.

VICKERY, JOHN B. The Literary Impact of the Golden Bough. Princeton Univ. Pr. 1976. 6.95Pa.

VICKERY, JOHN B., Ed. Myth and Literature; Contemporary Theory and Practice. Univ. of Nebraska Pr., Lincoln, NB. 1966(1973). 391p. 4.50Pa. LC 65-11563.

VICKERY, OLGA W., Interpretation. The Novels of William Faulkner. Louisiana State Univ. Pr. 1959. 270p.

VIDAL, GORE. Matters of Fact and of Fiction; Essays 1973-1976. Random House, NY. 1977. 10.00Hdbd. ISBN 0-394-41128-5. LC 76-53459.

VINCENT, HOWARD P., Ed. Bartleby The Scrivener. Kent State Univ. Pr., Kent, OH. 1966. 199p.

VINCENT, HOWARD P., Ed. Melville and Hawthorne in the Berkshires. Kent State Univ. Pr., 1968. 168p. LC 68-18936.

VINCENT, HOWARD P., Comp. The Merrill Studies in Moby-Dick. Merrill Pub., Columbus, OH. 1969. 163p.

VINCENT, HOWARD P. The Trying-Out of Moby-Dick. Southern Illinois Univ. Pr., Carbondale, IL. 1949. 400p.

VINCENT, HOWARD P., Ed. Twentieth Century Interpretations of Billy Budd; A Collection of Critical Essays. Prentice-Hall, Englewood Cliffs, NJ. 1971. 112p.

VINSON, JAMES, and D. L. Kirkpatrick. Contemporary Novelists. St. Martin's Pr., NY. St. James Pr., London. 1976. 163p. 35.00Hdbd. ISBN 0-900997-28-1. LC 75-189694.

VINSON, JAMES, Ed. Contemporary Writers Series. 1976.

VIOLETTE, AUGUSTA GENEVIEVE. Economic Feminism in American Literature Prior to 1848. Univ. Pr., Orono, ME. 1925(1971). 11.50Hdbd. ISBN 0-8337-4714-2. LC 79-165410.

VITELLI, JAMES R. Van Wyck Brooks; A Reference Guide. G. K. Hall, Boston, MA. 1976(1977). 12.00Hdbd. ISBN 0-8161-7978-6. LC 76-21335.

VOGEL, DAN. The Three Masks of American Tragedy. Louisiana State Univ. Pr., Baton Rouge, LA. 1972. 180p. LC 73-90865.

VOLPE, EDMOND LORIS. A Reader's Guide to William Faulkner. Octagon Books, NY. 1964(1974). 427p. 14.50Hdbd. ISBN 0-374-98086-1. LC 73-21109.

WADLINGTON, WARWICK. The Confidence Game in American Literature. Princeton Univ. Pr., Princeton, NJ. 1975. 331p. 13.50Hdbd. ISBN 0-691-06294-3. LC 75-3480.

WAELTI-WALTERS, JENNIFER. Michel Butor. Sono Nis Pr. 1977. 10.00 Hdbd. ISBN 0-919462-33-2.

WAGENKNECHT, EDWARD. Cavalcade of the American Novel;From the Birth of the Nation to the Middle of the Twentieth Century. Henry Holt, NY. 1952. 575p. LC 52-7022.

WAGENKNECHT, EDWARD. Edgar Allan Poe;The Man Behind the Legend. Oxford, NY. 1963. 6.00Hdbd.

WAGENKNECHT, EDWARD. Harriet Beecher Stowe;The Known and the Unknown. Oxford, NY. 1965. 6.00Hdbd.

WAGENKNECHT, EDWARD. The Letters of James Branch Cabell. Univ. of Oklahoma Pr., Norman, OK. 1974. 15.00Hdbd. LC 74-5963.

WAGENKNECHT, EDWARD. Mark Twain;The Man and His Work. Univ. of Oklahoma Pr., Norman, OK. 1935 (1967). 4.95Hdbd.

WAGENKNECHT, EDWARD. Nathaniel Hawthorne;Man and Writer. Oxford Univ. Pr., NY. 1961(1966). 233p. LC 61-6301.

WAGENKNECHT, EDWARD. Ralph Waldo Emerson;Portrait of a Balanced Soul. Oxford Univ. Pr., NY. 1974. 307p. LC 73-87615.

WAGENKNECHT, EDWARD. Washington Irving;Moderation Displayed. Oxford Univ. Pr., NY. 1962. 223p.

WAGER, WILLIS. American Literature;A World View. New York Univ. Pr., NY. 1968. 291p. LC 68-29434.

WAGGONER, HYATT H. Hawthorne; A Critical Study. Harvard Univ. Pr., Cambridge, MA. 1963.

WAGGONER, HYATT H. William Faulkner;From Jefferson to the World. Univ. of Kentucky Pr., Lexington, KY. 1966. 279p.

WAGNER, GEOFFREY. The Novel and the Cinema. Fairleigh Dickinson Univ. Pr., Rutherford, NJ. 1975. 394p. 15.00Hdbd. ISBN 0-8386-1618-6. LC 74-20939.

WAGNER, LINDA W. Ernest Hemingway;A Reference Guide. Hall, Boston, MA. 1977. 363p. 22.00. LC 76-21821.

WAGNER, LINDA WELSHIMER, Comp. Ernest Hemingway;Five Decades of Criticism. Michigan State Univ. Pr., East Lansing, MI. 1974. 328p. 10.00Hdbd. ISBN 0-87013-182-6. LC 73-91870.

WAGNER, LINDA WELSHIMER. Hemingway and Faulkner;Inventors/Masters. Scarecrow Pr., Metuchen, NJ. 1975. 297p. 11.00Hdbd. ISBN 0-8108-0862-5. LC 75-23367.

WAGNER, LINDA WELSHIMER, Ed. William Faulkner;Four Decades of Criticism. Michigan State Univ. Pr. 1973. 374p.

WAHR, F. B. Emerson and Goethe. Gordon Pr. 35.00Hdbd. ISBN 0-8490-0104-8.

WAKEMAN, JOHN, Ed. World Authors;1950-1970;A Companion Volume to Twentieth Century Authors. Wilson, NY. 1975. 1594p. 60.00Hdbd. ISBN 0-8242-0419-0. LC 75-172140.

WALCUTT, CHARLES C. American Literary Naturalism. Greenwood Pr. 1973. 15.50Hdbd. ISBN 0-8371-7017-6. LC 73-10584. 5.95Pa. ISBN 0-8371-8989-6.

WALCUTT, CHARLES CHILD. American Literary Naturalism;A Divided Stream. Univ. of Minnesota Pr., MinneapolisMMN. 1956. 332p. LC 56-12465.

WALCUTT, CHARLES CHILD, Ed. Seven Novelists in the American Naturalist Tradition;An Introduction. Univ. of Minnesota Pr., Minneapolis, MN. 1974. 331p. 10.50Hdbd. ISBN 0-8166-0730-3. LC 74-14209.

WALDEN, DANIEL, Ed. On Being Jewish;American Jewish Writers from Cahan to Bellow. Fawcett, NY. 1974. 480p. 1.75Pa. LC 74-80850.

WALDHORN, ARTHUR. A Reader's Guide to Ernest Hemingway. Octagon, NY. 1972(1975). 284p. 11.50Hdbd. ISBN 0-374-98146-9. LC 75-21603.

WALDMAN, M. The Propaganda Novel. Gordon Pr. 35.00Hdbd. ISBN 0-8490-0900-6.

WALDMEIR, JOSEPH J. American Novels of the Second World War. Mouton, The Hague, Paris. 1971. 180p. LC 68-23202.

WALDMEIR, JOSEPH J., Ed. Recent American Fiction;Some Critical Views. Houghton Mifflin, Boston, MA. 1963. 292p.

WALDRIP, LOUISE, and Shirley Ann Bauer. A Bibliography of the Works of Katherine Anne Porter and A Bibliography of the Criticism of the Works of Katherine Anne Porter. Scarecrow Pr., Metuchen, NJ. 1969. 219p. ISBN 8108-0275-9.

WALKER, DALE, Comp. The Fiction of Jack London;A Chronological Bibliography. Texas Western Pr., El Paso, TX. 1972. 40p. ISBN 87404-0442. LC 70-190574.

WALKER, DOROTHEA. Alice Brown. Twayne, NY. 1974. 7.95Hdbd. ISBN 0-8057-0099-4. LC 73-17019.

WALKER, FRANKLIN DICKERSON. Irreverent Pilgrims;Melville, Browne, and Mark Twain in the Holy Land. Univ. of Washington Pr., Seattle, WA. 1974. 234p. 9.95Hdbd. ISBN 0-295-95344-6. LC 74-10644.

WALKER, FRANKLIN. Jack London and the Klondike;The Genesis of an American Writer. Huntington Library;San Marino, CA. 1966. 288p.

WALKER, FRANKLIN. San Francisco's Literary Frontier. Univ. of Washington Pr., Seattle, WA. 1939(1969). 400p. LC 39-20996.

WALKER, WARREN S. James Fenimore Cooper;An Introduction and Interpretation. Barnes and Noble, NY. 1962.

WALKER, WARREN S. Twentieth-Century Short Story Explication;Interpretation, 1970-72. Shoe String Pr., Hamden, CT. LC 67-24192.

WALKER, WILLIAM E., and Robert L. Welker, Eds. Reality and Myth;Essays in American Literature in Memory of Richmond Croom Beatty. Vanderbilt Univ. Pr., Nashville, TN. 1964. 312p. LC 63-14647.

WALLACE, RONALD. Henry James and the Comic Form. Univ. of Michigan Pr., Ann Arbor, MI. 1975. 202p. 9.50Hdbd. ISBN 0-472-08954-4. LC 74-78990.

WALLACE, WILLIAM S. Dictionary of North American Authors Deceased Before 1950. Gale, Detroit, MI. 1951(1968). 12.50Hdbd. ISBN 0-8103-3153-5.

WALLACH, MARK I., and Christopher Morley. Twayne, Boston, MA. 1976. 6.95Hdbd. ISBN 0-8057-7178-6. LC 76-17922.

WALPOLE, HUGH, SIR. The Art of James Branch Cabell. Folcroft Library Editions, Folcroft, PA. 1974. 4.95Hdbd. LC 74-19401.

WALSER, RICHARD. Thomas Wolfe; An Introduction and Interpretation. Barnes and Noble, NY. 1961. 152p. 1.00Pa.

WAPLES, DOROTHY. The Whig Myth of James Fenimore Cooper. Archon Books, Hamden, CT. 1968.

WARD, ALFRED CHARLES. American Literature;1880-1930. Cooper Square, NY. 1975. 273p. 8.00Hdbd. ISBN 0-8154-0506-5. LC 74-14490.

WARD, ALFRED CHARLES. Longman Companion to Twentieth Century Literature. Longman, London. 1975. 597p. 16.50Hdbd. ISBN 0-582-36205-9. LC 76-351801.

WARD, J. A. The Imagination of Disaster;Evil in the Fiction of Henry James. Univ. of Nebraska Pr., Lincoln, NB. 1961. 185p.

WARD, J. A. The Search for Form; Studies in the Structure of James's Fiction. Univ. of North Carolina Pr., Chapel Hill, NC. 1967. 228p.

WARFEL, HARRY REDCAY. Charles Brockden Brown;American Gothic Novelist. Octagon, NY. 1949(1974). 11.00Hdbd. ISBN 0-374-98244-9. LC 73-19931.

WARFEL, HARRY REDCAY. Noah Webster;Schoolmaster to America. Octagon, NY. 1936(1966). 460p. LC 66-28378.

WARNER, CHARLES DUDLEY, and William Cullen Bryant and George Palmer Putnam. Studies of Irving. Folcroft Library Editions, Folcroft, PA. 1973. 25.00Hdbd. LC 73-9634.

WARNER, CHARLES DUDLEY. Washington Irving. Kennikat Pr., Port Washington, NY. 1968. 304p. LC 67-27660.

WARNER, HARRY, JR. All Our Yesterdays;An Informal History of Science Fiction Fandom in the Forties. Advent, Chicago, IL. 1969(1971). 336p. ISBN 911682-00-7. LC 69-17980.

WARREN, BARBARA. Feminine Image in Literature. Hayden, Rochelle Park, NJ. 4.60.

WARREN, ROBERT PENN, Ed. Faulkner;A Collection of Critical Essays. Prentice-Hall, Englewood Cliffs, NJ. 1966. 311p.

WASSERSTROM, WILLIAM. Heiress of all the Ages;Sex and Sentiment in the Genteel Tradition. Univ. of Minnesota Pr., Minneapolis, MN. 157p. LC 59-7949.

WATKINS, FLOYD C. The Flesh and the Word; Eliot, Hemingway, Faulkner. Venderbilt Univ. Pr., Nashville, TN. 1971. 282p. LC 75-157740.

WATKINS, FLOYD C. Thomas Wolfe's Characters;Portraits from Life. Univ. of Oklahoma Pr., Norman, OK. 1957. 194p.

WATT, WILLIAM W. Shilling Shockers of The Gothic School;A Study of Chapbook Gothic Romances. Russell and Russell, NY. 1932(1967). 53p. LC 66-27175.

WATTERS, REGINALD E. Checklist of Canadian Literature and Background Materials;1628-1960. Univ. of Toronto Pr. 1972. 30.00Hdbd. ISBN 0-8020-1866-1. LC 72-0713.

WATTERS, REGINALD E., and Inglis F. Bell. On Canadian Literature;1806-1960. A Check List of Articles, Books and Theses on English-Canadian Literature;Its Authors and Languages. Univ. of Toronto Pr. 1966. 8.50 Hdbd. ISBN 0-8020-5166-9. LC 66-1582.

WATTS, EMILY STIPES. Ernest Hemingway and the Arts. Univ. of Illinois Pr., Chicago, IL. 1971. 241p.

WEATHERBY, WILLIAM J. Squaring off;Mailer versus Baldwin. Mason/Charter, NY. 1977. 8.95hdbd. ISBN 0-88405-449-7. LC 76-53559.

WEATHERFORD, RICHARD M., Ed. Stephen Crane;The Critical Heritage. Routledge and Kegan Paul, London;Boston, MA. 1973. 343p. 17.00Hdbd. ISBN 0-7100-7636-3. LC 73-77042.

WEAVER, RAYMOND M. Herman Melville;Mariner and Mystic. Cooper Square, NY. 1968. 399p. LC 59-13250.

WEBB, CONSTANCE. Richard Wright. Putnam, NY. 1968. 7.95Hdbd.

WEBB, EUGENE. The Dark Dove;the Sacred and Secular in Modern Literature. Univ. of Washington Pr., Seattle, WA. 1975. 280p. 8.95Hdbd. ISBN 0-295-95377-2. LC 74-28210.

WEBB, JAMES W., and A. Wigfall Green. William Faulkner of Oxford. Louisiana State Univ. Pr. 1965. 229p. LC 65-23763.

WEBER, CARL J. Hardy in America; A Study of Thomas Hardy and His American Readers. Russell and Russell, NY. 1946(1966). 10.00Hdbd. ISBN 0-8462-0757-5.

WEBER, PAUL C. America in Imaginative German Literature in the First Half of the 19th Century. AMS Pr., NY. 1926. 15.00Hdbd. ISBN 0-404-50429-9.

WEBSTER, SAMUEL CHARLES, Ed. Mark Twain, Business Man. Little, Brown, Boston, MA. 1946. 409p.

WECTER, DIXON, Ed. Mark Twain to Mrs. Fairbanks. Huntington, San Marino, CA. 1949. 286p.

WEEKS, ROBERT P., Ed. Hemingway; A Collection of Critical Essays. Prentice-Hall, Englewood Cliffs, NJ. 1962. 180p.

WEGELIN, CHRISTOF. The Image of Europe in Henry James. Southern Methodist Univ. Pr., Dallas, TX. 1958. 200p.

WEGELIN, OSCAR. Early American Fiction; 1774-1830; A Compilation of the Titles of Works of Fiction, by Writers Born or Residing in North America, North of the Mexican Border and Printed Previous to 1831. Peter Smith, Gloucester, MA. 1963. 37p.

WEIL, DOROTHY. In Defense of Women; Susanna Rowson; (1762-1824). Pennsylvania State Univ. Pr., University Park, PA. 1976. 204p. 12.50Hdbd. ISBN 0-271-01205-6. LC 75-26963.

WEINBERG, HELEN. The New Novel in America; The Kafkan Mode in Contemporary Fiction. Cornell Univ. Pr., Ithaca, NY. 1970. 248p.

WEINSTEIN, PHILIP M. Henry James and the Requirements of the Imagination. Harvard Univ. Pr.

WEINTRAUB, STANLEY, Ed. Biography and Truth; The Bobbs-Merrill Series in Composition and Rhetoric. Bobbs-Merrill, Indianapolis, IN. 1967. 64p. 1.00Pa.

WEISS, SUSAN ARCHER. The Home Life of Poe. Folcroft Library Editions, Folcroft, PA. 1907(1974). 229p. 30.00Hdbd. LC 74-3361.

WEIXLMANN, JOSEPH. John Barth; A Descriptive Primary and Annotated Secondary Bibliography, Including a Descriptive Catalog of Manuscript Holdings in United States Libraries. Garland Pub., NY. 1976. 23.-00Hdbd. ISBN 0-8240-9987-7. LC 75-24076.

WELLS, GEOFFREY HARRY. Deucalion; Or, The Future of Literary Criticism. Norwood, Norwood, PA. 1974. 8.50Hdbd. ISBN 0-88305-785-9. LC 74-31088.

WELLS, WALTER. Tycoons and Locusts; A Regional Look at Hollywood Fiction of the 1930s. Southern Illinois Univ. Pr., Carbondale, IL. 1973. 139p. ISBN 0-8093-0606-9. LC 73-4266.

WEST, REBECCA. Henry James. Haskell House, NY. 1974. 9.95Hdbd. ISBN 0-8383-1833-9. LC 73-21774.

WEST, THOMAS R. Flesh of Steel; Literature and the Machine in American Culture. Vanderbilt Univ. Pr. 1967. 5.00Hdbd. ISBN 0-8265-1092-2. LC 67-13997.

WEST, VICTOR ROYCE. Folklore in the Works of Mark Twain. Folcroft, Folcroft, PA. 1974. 10.00Hdbd. ISBN 0-8414-9589-0. LC 74-31097.

WEST, THOMAS REED. Nature, Community, and Will;A Study in Literary and Social Thought. Univ. of Missouri Pr., Columbia, MO. 1976. 138p. 8.00Hdbd. ISBN 0-8262-0196-2. LC 75-44076.

WESTBROOK, MAX, Ed. The Modern American Novel;Essays in Criticism. Random House, NY. 1966. 243p. LC 66-12537.

WESTON, HAROLD. Form in Literature;A Theory of Technique. Folcroft, Folcroft, PA. 1974. 15.00Hdbd. ISBN 0-8414-9580-7. LC 74-31015.

WHARTON, EDITH. A Backward Glance. Scribner's, NY. 385p.

WHARTON, EDITH. The Writing of Fiction. Octagon, NY. 1966. 178p. LC 66-28379.

WHICHER, STEPHEN E. Freedom and Fate;An Inner Life of Ralph Waldo Emerson. A.S. Barnes, NY. 1953 (1961). 203p. LC 53-9552.

WHISSEN, THOMAS R. Components of Composition. Allyn and Bacon, Boston, MA. 1975. 122p. 3.95Pa. LC 74-20547.

WHITBREAD, THOMAS B., Ed. Seven Contemporary Authors. Univ. of Texas Pr., Auston, TX. 1966(1968). 175p. LC 66-15706.

WHITCOMB, SELDEN L. Chronological Outlines of American Literature. Macmillan, NY. and London. 1894. LC 68-30590.

WHITE, GLENN, Comp. Connecticut Handbook. Connecticut Council of Teachers of English, Danbury, CT. 1976. 70p. 2.00Pa. LC 76-371300.

WHITE, JOHN J. Mythology in the Modern Novel;A Study of Prefigurative Techniques. Princeton Univ. Pr. Princeton, NJ. 1972. 8.50Hdbd. LC 71-155004.

WHITE, MARY LOU. Children's Literature;Criticism and Response. C.E. Merrill Pub., Columbus, OH. 1976. 252p. 5.95Pa. ISBN 0-675-08621-3. LC 75-39319.

WHITE, RAY L., Ed. Achievement of Sherwood Anderson;Essays in Critisim. Univ. of North Carolina Pr. 1966. 8.25Hdbd. ISBN 0-8078-0997-7. 2.95Pa. ISBN 0-8078-4026-2.

WHITE, WILLIAM, Comp. The Merrill Studies in The Sun Also Rises. Merrill Pub., Columbus, OH. 1969. 106p. ISBN 675-09447-X. LC 72-93997.

WHITELOCK. The Great Tradition. Univ. of Queensland Pr. 18.25Hdbd. ISBN 0-7022-0871-X.

WHITEMAN, MAXWELL. A Century of Fiction by American Negroes; 1853-1952;A Descriptive Bibliography. Saifer, Philadelphia, PA. 1955(1968). 64p. LC 55-10876.

WHITLOW, ROGER. Black American Literature;A Critical History, with a 1,520-title Bibliography of Works Written by and About Black Americans. Littlefield, Adams, Totowa, NJ. 1973(1974). 3.95Pa. LC 74-10582.

WHITTEN, MARY E. Creative Pattern Practice;A New Approach to Writing. Harcourt, NY. 1975. 349p. 5.95Pa. ISBN 0-15-515808-2. LC 74-28821.

WICKER, BRIAN. The Story-Shaped

World;Fiction and Metaphysics;Some Variations on a Theme. Athlone Pr., London. 1975. 230p. 12.95Hdbd. ISBN 0-485-11152-7. LC 75-332969.

WICKES, GEORGE, Ed. Henry Miller and The Critics. Southern Illinois Univ. Pr., Carbondale, IL. 1963(1967). 194p. LC 63-14289.

WICKES, GEORGE, Ed. Lawrence Durrell, Henry Miller;A Private Correspondence. E.P. Dutton, NY. 1962(1963). 400p. LC 62-14726.

WIDMER, ELEANOR, and Kingsley Widmer, Eds. Freedom and Culture; Literary Censorship in the Seventies. Wadsworth Pub. 1970. 4.95Pa.

WIDMER, KINGSLEY. Henry Miller. Twayne, NY. 1963. 192p. LC 63-17372.

WIDMER, KINGSLEY. The Ways of Nihilism;A Study of Herman Melville's Short Novels. California State Colleges. 1970. 149p.

WIESENFARTH, JOSEPH. Henry James and the Dramatic Analogy;A Study of the Major Novels of the Middle Period. Fordham Univ. Pr., NY. 1963. 139p.

WIGGINS, JAMES B., Ed. Religion as Story. Harper and Row, NY. 1975. 4.50Pa. ISBN 0-06-069353-3. LC 75-9339.

WIGGINS, ROBERT A. Mark Twain; Jackleg Novelist. Univ. of Washington Pr., Seattle, WA. 1964. 130p. LC 64-18428.

WILCOX, EARL J., and David L. Rankin. Fundamentals of Fiction. Allyn and Bacon, Boston, MA. 1975(1976). 4.95Pa. ISBN 0-205-04818-8.

WILDE, WILLIAM HENRY. Henry Kendall. Twayne, Boston, MA. 1976. 7.95Hdbd. ISBN 0-8057-6229-9. LC 75-41479.

WILEY, MARGARET LENORE. Studies in American Literature;Creative Scepticism in Emerson, Melville and Henry James. Folcroft Library Editions, Folcroft, PA. 1974(1975). 6.50Hdbd. ISBN 0-8414-5986-X. LC 74-32433.

WILKES, G.A., and J.C. Reid. Literature of Australia and New Zealand. Pennsylvania State Univ. Pr. 1971. 10.95Hdbd. LC 71-121856.

WILLEN, GERALD, Ed. A Casebook on Henry James's "The Turn of the Screw". Crowell, NY. 1960. 325p.

WILLEY, BASIL. Eighteenth Century Background;Studies on the Idea of Nature in the Thought of the Period. Columbia Univ. Pr., NY. 1941. 12.50 Hdbd. ISBN 0-231-01234-9. LC 40-31307.

WILLIAMS, AMES W., and Vincent Starrett. Stephen Crane;A Bibliography. Burt Franklin, NY. 1948. 161p. LC 79-102856.

WILLIAMS, BLANCHE COLTON. Our Short Story Writers. Books for Libraries Pr., Freeport, NY. 1922 (1969). 384p. ISBN 8369-1164-4. LC 74-90694.

WILLIAMS, C.B. Style and Vocabulary Numerical Studies. Hafner. 1970. 6.95Hdbd.

WILLIAMS, DAVID. Faulkner's Women;The Myth and the Muse. 1977. 288p. 16.00Hdbd. ISBN 0-7735-0257-2.

WILLIAMS, JOAN, Ed. Novel and Romance;1700-1800;A Documentary Record. Barnes and Noble, NY. 1970. 8.00Hdbd. ISBN 0-389-01063-4.

WILLIAMS, NAN SCHRAM. Confess for Profit;Writing and Selling the Personal Story;A Comprehensive Gui de. Douglas-West, Los Angeles, CA. 1973. 225p. 6.95Hdbd. ISBN 0-913264-09-1. LC 72-92133.

WILLIAMS, STANLEY T., and Mary Allen Edge, Comp. By. A Bibliography of the Writings of Washington Irving;A Check List. Burt Franklin, NY. 1936(1970). 200p. LC 79-123513.

WILLIAMSON, DANIEL RAYMOND. Feature Writing for Newspapers. Hastings House, NY. 1975. 12.50Hdbd. ISBN 0-8038-2312-6. LC 75-17898. 7.50Pa. ISBN 0-8038-2313-4.

WILSON, EDMUND. Axel's Castle. Scribner, NY. 1931. 6.95Hdbd. ISBN 0-684-71938-X. 3.95Pa. ISBN 0-684-71938-X.

WILSON, EDMUND. The Bit Between My Teeth;A Literary Chronicle of 1950-1965. Farrar, Straus, NY. 1939 (1967). 694p. LC 65-23978.

WILSON, EDMUND. Classics and Commercials;A Literary Chronicle of the Forties. Farrar, Straus, NY. 1950. 534p. LC 50-10620.

WILSON, EDMUND. Ed. by Elena Wilson. Letters on Literature and Politics;1912-1972. Farrar, Straus, NY. 1977. 20.00Hdbd. ISBN 0-374-18508-5. LC 76-54860.

WILSON, EDMUND. O Canada;An American's Notes on Canadian Culture. Octagon, NY. 1976. 12.50Hdbd. ISBN 0-374-98650-9. LC 76-44392.

WILSON, EDMUND, Ed. The Shock of Recognition;The Development of Literature in the United States Recorded by the Men Who Made it. Octagon, NY. 1955(1974). 36.00Hdbd. ISBN 0-574-98668-1. LC 74-6363.

WILSON, EDMUND. The Triple Thinkers;Twelve Essays on Literary Subjects. Oxford Univ. Pr., NY. 1938 (1948). 270p.

WILSON, EDMUND. Edited by Leon Edel. The Twenties;From Notebooks and Diaries of the Period. Farrar, Straus, NY. 1975. 557p. 10.00Hdbd. ISBN 0-374-27963-2. LC 74-34339.

WILSON, EDMUND. The Wound and the Bow;Seven Studies in Literature. Oxford Univ. Pr., NY. 1947(1965). 242p.

WILSON, G. F. A Bibliography of the Writings of W. H. Hudson. Kennikat Pr., Port Washington, NY. 79p. LC 67-27665.

WILSON, PHILLIP. William Satchell. Twayne, NY. 1968. 168p. 4.50. LC 67-25198.

WILSON, ROBERT A., Comp. Gertrude Stein;A Bibliography. Phoenix Bookshop, NY. 1974. 227p. 15.00Hdbd. LC 73-85937.

WINEGARTEN, RENEE. Writers and Revolution;The Fatal Lure of Action. Watts. 1974. 9.95Hdbd. ISBN 0-531-06368-2. 4.95Pa. ISBN 0-531-06500-6.

WINTLE, JUSTIN, and Emma Fisher. The Pied Pipers;Interviews with the Influential Creators of Children's Literature. Paddington Pr., NY.

1975. 320p. 10.95Hdbd. ISBN 0-8467-0038-7. LC 74-15918.

WINWAR, FRANCES. Haunted Palace; A Life of Edgar Allan Poe. Harper. 1959. 6.50Hdbd.

WIRT, SHERWOOD ELIOT, and Ruth McKinney. You Can Tell the World; New Directions for Christian Writers. Augsburg Pub., Minneapolis, MN. 1975. 127p. 3.50Pa. ISBN 0-8066-1479-X. LC 75-2834.

WISE, WINIFRED E. Harriet Beecher Stowe; Woman with a Cause. Putnam, NY. 1965. 190p. LC 65-13309.

WITHAM, W. TASKER. The Adolescent in the American Novel; 1920-1960. Ungar, NY. 1964. 345p. LC 63-8849.

WITTIG, SUSAN. Steps to Structure; An Introduction to Composition and Rhetoric. Winthrop, Cambridge, MA. 1975. 177p. 4.95Hdbd. ISBN 0-87626-853-X. LC 74-34038.

WOLF, WILLIAM J. Thoreau; Mystic, Prophet, Ecologist. United Church Pr., Philadelphia, PA. 1974. 223p. 5.95Hdbd. ISBN 0-8298-0269-X. LC 73-22368.

WOLFE, GEORGE H., Ed. Faulkner; 50 Years After; The Marble Faun. Univ. of Alabama Pr. 1976. 8.00Hdbd. ISBN 0-8173-7609-7. LC 75-40380.

WOLFE, THOMAS. The Story of a Novel. Scribner's, NY. 1936. 3.50.93p.

WOODBERRY, GEORGE E. The Life of Edgar Allan Poe; Personal and Literary, with his Chief Correspondence with Men of Letters. Biblo and Tannen, NY. 1909(1965). Vol. 1-383p., Vol. 2-481p. LC 65-23484.

WOODBERRY, GEORGE E. Nathaniel Hawthorne. Houghton, Mifflin, Boston, MA. 1902. Republished Gale, Detroit, MI. 1967. 302p. LC 67-23888.

WOODBERRY, GEORGE E. Ralph Waldo Emerson. Haskell House, NY. 1968. 205p. LC 68-24947.

WOODBRIDGE, HENSLEY C., and John London and George H. Tweney, Comp. Talisman Pr., Georgetown, CA. 1966. 422p. LC 66-27365.

WOODBURY, CHARLES J. Talks with Emerson. Horizon Pr., NY. 1970. 177p.

WOODCOCK, GEORGE, Ed. A Choice of Critics; Selections from Canadian Literature. Oxford Univ. Pr., Toronto, Canada. 1966. 247p. 5.00Hdbd.

WOODRESS, JAMES. Booth Tarkington; Gentleman from Indiana. Greenwood Pr., NY. 1954(1969). 350p. LC 69-14155.

WOODRESS, JAMES, Ed. Eight American Authors; A Review of Research and Criticism. W. W. Norton, NY. 1963(1971). 392p.

WOODRESS, JAMES. Willa Cather; Her Life and Art. University of Nebraska Pr., Lincoln, NB. 1970(1975). 288p. 3.50Pa. ISBN 0-8032-5815-1. LC 75-301308.

WOODRUFF, STUART C. Short Stories of Ambrose Bierce; A Study in Polarity. Univ. of Pittsburgh Pr., Pittsburgh, PA. 1964. 2.95Pa. ISBN 0-8229-5087-1. LC 64-22147.

WOODSON, THOMAS, Ed. Twentieth

Century Interpretations of the Fall of the House of Usher. Prentice-Hall, Englewood Cliffs, NJ. 1969. 4.95 Hdbd. ISBN 0-13-301739-7. 1.25 Pa. ISBN 0-13-301721-4.

WOOLF, VIRGINIA. Granite and Rainbow. Harcourt, Brace, NY. 1958. 239p. LC 58-10898.

WRIGHT, LYLE H. American Fiction;1774-1850;A Contribution Toward A Bibliography. Huntington Library, San Marino, CA. 1969. 411p. LC 68-29777.

WRIGHT, LYLE H. American Fiction;1851-1875;A Contribution Toward A Bibliography. Huntington Library, San Marino, CA. 1965. 438p. LC 65-20870.

WRIGHT, LYLE H. American Fiction;1876-1900;A Contribution Toward A Bibliography. Huntington Library, San Marino, CA. 1966. 683p. LC 66-24112.

WRIGHT, NATHALIA. American Novelists in Italy;The Discoverers;Allston to James. Univ. of Pennsylvania Pr., Philadelphia, PA. 1965. 288p. LC 63-7858.

WRIGHT, WALTER F. The Madness of Art;A Study of Henry James. Univ. of Nebraska Pr., Lincoln, NB. 1962. 269p.

Y

YATES, NORRIS W. The American Humorist. Iowa State Univ. Pr., Ames, IA. 1964. 410p. 10.00Hdbd. ISBN 0-8138-2205-0.

YELLIN, JEAN FAGAN. The Intricate Knot; Black Figures in American Literature; 1776-1863. New York Univ. Pr., NY. 1972. Hdbd. ISBN 8147-9650-8. LC 72-76556. Pa. ISBN 8147-9650-6.

YODER, JON A. Upton Sinclair. Ungar, NY. 1975. 112p. 7.00Hdbd. ISBN 0-8044-2989-8. LC 74-78450.

YOUNG, ALAN. Ernest Buckler. McClelland and Stewart, Toronto. 1976. 64p. 1.95. ISBN 0-7710-9622-4. LC 77-351078.

YOUNG, JAMES O. Black Writers of the Thirties. Louisiana State Univ. Pr., Baton Rouge, LA. 1973. 257p. 10.00Hdbd. ISBN 0-8071-0060-9. LC 72-96402.

YOUNG, PHILIP. Ernest Hemingway; A Reconsideration. Pennsylvania State Univ. Pr., University Park, PA. 1966. 297p.

YOUNG, PHILIP, and Charles W. Mann. The Hemingway Manuscripts; An Inventory. Pennsylvania State Univ. Pr., University Park, PA. 1969. 138p. ISBN 271-00080-5. LC 68-8189.

YOUNG, PHILIP. Three Bags Full; Essays in American Fiction. Harcourt Brace, NY. 1952(1972). 231p. ISBN 0-15-190174-0. LC 73-174517.

Z

ZAVARZADEH, MAS'UD. The Mythopoeic Reality; The Postwar American Nonfiction Novel. Univ. of Illinois Pr., Urbana, IL. 1976. 10.00Hdbd. ISBN 0-252-00523-6. LC 76-49509.

ZINSSER, WILLIAM. On Writing Well; An Informal Guide to Writing Nonfiction. Harper and Row, NY. 1976. 6.95Hdbd. ISBN 0-06-014798-9. LC 75-6364.

ZIOLKOWSKI, THEODORE. Disenchanted Images; A Literary Iconology. Princeton Univ. Pr., Princeton, NJ. 1977. 12.50Hdbd. ISBN 0-691-06334-6. LC 76-45917.

ZOELLNER, ROBERT. The Salt-Sea Mastodon; A Reading of Moby-Dick. Univ. of California Pr., Berkeley, CA. 1973. 288p.

ZYLA, WOLODYMYR T., and Wendell M. Aycock. Texas Tech. Univ. 1973. 166p. 5.00Hdbd. LC 74-157882.

Author Criticism
Arranged by author of work criticized.

HENRY ADAMS

Biographies

Adams, Maurianne. Autobiography.
Cooley, Thomas. Educated Lives;The Rise of Modern Autobiography in America.

Criticism-General

Berthoff, Warner. Fictions and Events.
Blackmur.R.P.The Lion and the Honeycomb.
Bloomfield, Morton W., Ed. The Interpretation of Narrative.
More, Paul Elmer. Shelburne Essays on American Literature.
Rahv, Philip. Literature in America.
Rees, Robert A., and Earl N. Harbeert, Eds. Fifteen American Authors Before 1900.
Smith, Henry Nash, Ed. Mark Twain.
Spiller, Robert E. The Cycle of American Literature.
Spiller, Robert E. The Oblique Light.
Straumann, Heinrich. American Literature in the Twentieth Century.

ANTONIO AGAPIDA

See Washington Irving.

JAMES AGEE

Biographies

Madden, David, Ed. Remembering James Agee.

Criticism By

Coles, Robert. Irony in the Mind's Life.

Criticism-General

Barson, Alfred T. A Way of Seeing.
Cohen, Hennig, Ed. Landmarks of American Writing.
French, Warren, Ed. The Fifties;Fiction, Poetry, Drama.
Frohock, W.M. The Novel of Violence in America.
Kramer, Victor A. James Agee.
Larsen, Erling. James Agee.
Moreau, Genevieve. The Restless Journey of James Agee.
Ohlin, Peter. Agee.
Seib, Kenneth. James Agee.
Updike, John. Assorted Prose.

CONRAD POTTER AIKEN

Criticism-General

Updike, John. Assorted Prose.

LOUISA MAY ALCOTT

Criticism-General

Christy, A.E. The Orient in American Transcendentalism.

Reference Works

Bibliographies

Gulliver, Lucile. Louisa May Alcott.

THOMAS BAILEY ALDRICH

Criticism-General

Cowie, Alexander. The Rise of the American Novel.

NELSON ALGREN

Biographies

Cox, Martha Heasley. Nelson Algren.

Criticism-General

Gelfant, Blanche Housman. The American City Novel.

JAMES LANE ALLEN

Criticism-General

Wagenknecht, Edward. Cavalcade of the American Novel.

WASHINGTON ALLSTON

Criticism-General

Wright, Nathalia. American Novelists in Italy.

SHERWOOD ANDERSON

Criticism By

Anderson, Sherwood. The "Writer's Book".

Criticism-General

Anderson, David D., Ed. Sherwood Anderson;Dimensions of His Literary Art.
Angoff, Allan, Ed. American Writing Today.
Appel, Paul P., Ed. Homage to Sherwood Anderson.
Bowden, Edwin T. The Dungeon of th the Heart.
Brown, John Russell, and Bernard Harris. The American Novel and the Nineteen Twenties.
Bryer, Jackson R., Ed. Fifteen Modern American Authors.
Burbank, Rex. Sherwood Anderson.
Campbell, Hilbert H., and Charles E. Modlin, Eds. Sherwood Anderson;Centennial Studies.
Churchill, Allen. The Literary Decade.
Cooley, Thomas. Educated Lives.
Cowley, Malcolm, Ed. After the Genteel Tradition.
Fanning, Michael. France and Sherwood Anderson.
Geismar, Maxwell. The Last of the Provincials.
Gelfant, Blanche Housman. The American City Novel.
Heiney, Donald. Recent American Literature.
Heiney, Donald. Recent American Literature To 1930.
Hilfer, Anthony Channell. The Revolt from the Village.
Howe, Irving. Sherwood Anderson.
Kazin, Alfred. On Native Grounds.
Michaud, Regis. The American Novel Today.
Millgate, Michael. American Social Fiction.
Nolte, William H., Ed. H. L. Mencken's Smart Set Criticism.
Rideout, Walter B., Ed. Sherwood Anderson.

Schorer, Mark. The World We Imagine.
Seward, William W., Jr. Contrasts In Modern Writers.
Shapiro, Charles, Ed. Twelve Original Essays on American Novels.
Stegner, Wallace, Ed. The American Novel from James Fenimore Cooper to William Faulkner.
Sutton, William A. The Road to Winesburg.
Tanner, Tony. The Reign of Wonder.
Trilling, Lionel. The Liberal Imagination.
Wagenknecht, Edward. Cavalcade of the American Novel.
Walcutt, Charles Child. American Literary Naturalism, A Divided Stream.
Westbrook, Max, Ed. The Modern American Novel.
White, Ray L., Ed. Achievement of Sherwood Anderson.

Criticism - Specific Works

Winesburg Ohio

Bowden, Edwin T. The Dugeon of the Heart.
Stegner, Wallace, Ed. The American Novel from James Fenimore Cooper to William Faulkner.

Reference Works

Bibliographies

Rogers, Douglas G. Sherwood Anderson.
Sheehy, Eugene. Sherwood Anderson.

HARRIETTE ARNOW

Biographies

Eckley, Wilton. Harriette Arnow.

TIMOTHY SHAY ARTHUR

Criticism-General

Cowie, Alexander. The Rise of the American Novel.

ISAAC ASIMOV

Criticism-General

Goble, Neil. Asimov Analyzed.
Knight, Damon. In Search of Wonder.
Orlander, Joseph D., and Martin Harry Greenberg, Eds. Isaac Asimov.
Patrouch, Joseph F. The Science Fiction of Isaac Asimov.

Reference Works

Bibliographies

Miller, Marjorie M. Isaac Asimov.

GERTRUDE ATHERTON

Criticism-General

Heiney, Donald. Recent American Literature.
Heiney, Donald. Recent American Literature to 1930.
Underwood, John Curtis. Literature and Insurgency.

MARGARET ATWOOD

Criticism-General

Northey, Margot. The Haunted Wilderness.

LOUIS STANTON AUCHINCLOSS

Criticism-General

Hicks, Granville. Literary Horizons.
McCormack, Thomas, Ed. Afterwords; Novelists on Their Novels.

Criticism - Specific Works

Rector of Justin

McCormack, Thomas, Ed. Afterwords; Novelists on Their Novels.

MARY AUSTIN

Criticism-General

Wagenknecht, Edward. Cavalcade of the American Novel.

JAMES BALDWIN

Biographies

Eckman, Fern Marja. The Furious Passage of James Baldwin.

Criticism-General

Adams, Maurianne, Ed. Autobiography.
Baker, Houston A., Jr. Black Literature in America.
Balakian, Nona, and Charles Simmons, Eds. The Creative Present.
Bigsby, C.W.E., The Black American Writer.
Cooke, M.G., Ed. Modern Black Novelists.
Gayle, Addison, Jr. The Way of the New World.
Gross, Seymour L., and John Edward Hardy, Eds. Images of the Negro in American Literature.
Harper, Howard M., Jr. Desperate Faith.
Hicks, Granville. Literary Horizons.
McCarthy, Harold T. The Expatriate Perspective.
Margolies, Edward. Native Sons.
May, John R. Toward a New Earth.
Noble, David W. The Eternal Adam and the New World Garden.
O'Daniel, Therman B., Ed. James Baldwin.
Podhoretz, Norman. Doings and Undoings.
Straumann, Heinrich. American Literature in the Twentieth Century.
Weatherby, William J. Squaring Off; Mailer versus Baldwin.

AMIRI BARAKA

Criticism-General

Hudson, Theodore R. From LeRoi Jones to Amiri Baraka.

DJUNA BARNES

Biographies

Scott, James B. Djuna Barnes.

MARGARET AYER BARNES

Biographies

Taylor, Lloyd C. Margaret Ayer Barnes.

R.H. BARLOW

Criticism-General

Warner, Harry, Jr. All Our Yesterdays.

JOHN BARTH

Criticism-General

Gado, Frank, Comp. First Person.
Harris, Charles B. Contemporary American Novelists of the Absurd.
Hassan, Ihab. Contemporary American Literature.
Hauck, Richard Boyd. A Cheerful Nihilism
Hicks, Granville. Literary Horizons.
Lehan, Richard. A Dangerous Crossing.
May, John R. Toward a New Earth.
Morrell, David. John Barth
Olderman, Raymond M. Beyond the Wasteland.
Parker, Dorothy. The Portable Dorothy Parker.
Rubin, Louis D., Jr., Ed. The Comic Imagination in American Literature.
Schulz, Max F. Black Humor Fiction of the Sixties.
Stark, John O. The Literature of Exhaustion.
Tharpe, Jac. John Barth.

Criticism - Specific Works

The End of the Road

Parker, Dorothy. The Portable Dorothy Parker.

Reference Works

Bibliographies

Weixlmann, Joseph. John Barth.

PETER S. BEAGLE

Criticism-General

Tooker, Dan. Fiction! Interviews with Northern Carlifornia Novelists.

RICHMOND CROOM BEATTY

Criticism-General

Walker, William E., Ed. Reality and Myth.

THOMAS BEER

Criticism-General

Angoff, Charles. The Tone of the Twenties and Other Essays.

EDWARD BELLAMY

Criticism-General

Franklin, H. Bruce. Future Perfect.
Martin, Jay. Harvest of Change.
Taylor, Walter Fuller. The Economic Novel in America.

SAUL BELLOW

Criticism-General

Balakian, Nona, and Charles Simmons, Eds. The Creative Present.
Baumbach, Jonathan. The Landscape of Nightmare.
Fiedler, Leslie. The Collected Essays of Leslie Fiedle; Vol. II.
French, Warren, Ed. The Fifties; Fiction, Poetry, Drama.
Gindin, James. Harvest of a Quiet Eye.
Hall, James. The Lunatic Giant in the Drawing Room.
Handy, William J. Modern Fiction.
Harper, Howard M., Jr. Desperate Faith.
Hassan, Ihab. Contemporary American Literature.
Hassan, Ihab. Radical Innocence.
Hicks, Granville. Literary Horizons.
Howe, Irving. The Critical Point on Literature and Culture.
Kazin, Alfred. Bright Book of Life.
Kegan, Robert. The Sweeter Welcome.
Lehan, Richard. A Dangerous Crossing.
Lutwack, Leonard. Heroic Fiction.
Malin, Irving, Ed. Contemporary American-Jewish Literature.
Noble, David W. The Eternal Adam and the New World Garden.
Podhoretz, Norman. Doings and Undoings.
Proffer, Carl R., Ed. Soviet Criticism of American Literature in the Sixties.
Rahv, Philip. Literature and the Sixth Sense.
Schulz, Max F. Radical Sophistication.
Scott, Nathan A., Jr., Ed. Adversity and Grace.
Solotaroff, Theodore. The Red Hot Vacuum.
Walden, Daniel, Ed. On Being Jewish.
Waldmeir, Joseph J., Ed. Recent American Fiction.
Weinberg, Helen. The New Novel in America.
Westbrook, Max, Ed. The Modern American Novel.

Criticism - Specific Works

The Adventures of Angie March

French, Warren, Ed. The Fifties; Fiction, Poetry, Drama.

Henderson and The Rain King

Westbrook, Max, Ed. The Modern American Novel.

Seize The Day

Handy, William J. Modern Fiction; A Formalist Approach.

Reference Works

Bibliographies

Sokoloff, B. A., and Mark E. Posner. Saul Bellow.

ROBERT BENCHLY

Criticism-General

Churchill, Allen. The Literary Decade.
Hassan, Ihab. Radical Innocence.

STEPHEN VINCENT BENET

Criticism-General

Abbe, George, Ed. Stephen Vincent

on Writing.
Stroud, Parry. Stephen Vincent Benet.

THOMAS BERGER

Criticism-General

Schulz, Max F. Black Humor Fiction of the Sixties.

AMBROSE BIERCE

Biographies

O'Connor, Richard. Ambrose Bierce.

Criticism-General

Grenander, M. E. Ambrose Bierce.
Franklin, H. Bruce. Future Perfect.
Martin, Jay. Harvests of Change.
Rubin, Louis D., Jr., Ed. The Comic Imagination in American Literature.
Snell, George. The Shapers of American Fiction.
Woodruff, Stuart C. Short Stories of Ambrose Bierce.

JOSH BILLINGS

Biographies

Kesterson, David B. Josh Billings.

LEONARD BISHOP

Criticism-General

Gelfant, Blanche. The American City Novel.

ROBERT BLOCH

Criticism-General

Warner, Harry, Jr. All Our Yesterdays.

ROLF BOLDREWOOD

Criticism - Specific Works

Robbery under Arms

Argyle, Barry. An Introduction to the Australian Novel.

PAUL BOWLES

Criticism-General

Stewart, Lawrence Delbert. Paul Bowles; The Illumination of North Africa.
Waldmeir, Joseph J., Ed. Recent American Fiction.

JAMES BOYD

Criticism-General

Cooperman, Stanley. World War I and the American Novel.

KAY BOYLE

Criticism-General

Tooker, Dan. Fiction! Interviews with Northern California Novelists.

RAY BRADBURY

Criticism-General

Hillegas, Mark R. The Future as Nightmare.
Knight, Damon. In Search of Wonder.
Slusser, George Edgar. The Bradbury Chronicles.

WILLIAM BRADFORD

Criticism-General

Gallagher, Edward Joseph. Early Puritan Writers.

Criticism - Specific Works

Of Plymouth Plantation

Bowden, Edwin T. The Dungeon of the Heart.

NAN BRITTON

Criticism - Specific Works

The President's Daughter

Parker, Dorothy. The Portable Dorothy Parker.

LOUIS BROMFIELD

Criticism-General

Churchill, Allen. The Literary Decade.

VAN WYCK BROOKS

Criticism By

Brooks, Van Wyck. The Malady of the Ideal.
Brooks, Van Wyck. The World of Washington Irving.

Criticism-General

Berthoff, Warner. Fictions and Events.
Cowley, Malcolm, Ed. After the Genteel Tradition.
Piper, Henry Dan. Think Back on Us.
Wilson, Edmund. Classics and Commercials.

Reference Works

Bibliographies

Vitelli, James R. Van Wyck Brooks.

ALICE BROWN

Biographies

Walker, Dorothea. Alice Brown.

CHARLES BROCKDEN BROWN

Criticism-General

Bank, Stanley, Ed. American Romanticism.
Chase, Richard. The American Novel and Its Tradition.
Hoyt, Charles Alva, Ed. Minor American Novelists.

Patter, Fred Lewis. The First Century of American Literature.
Snell, George. The Shapers of American Fiction.
Warfel, Harry Redcay. Charles Brockden Brown.

JOHN ROSS BROWNE

Criticism-General

Walker, Franklin Dickerson. Irreverent Pilgrims.

PEARL S. BUCK

Biographies

Harris, Theodore F. Pearl S. Buck.

Criticism-General

Buck, Pearl S., and Theodore F. Harris. For Spacious Skies.
French, Warren G., and Walter E. Kidd. American Winners of the Nobel Literary Prize.
Heiney, Donald. Recent American Literature.

ERNEST BUCKLER

Criticism-General

Chambers, Robert D. Sinclair Ross and Ernest Buckler.
Young, Al. Ernest Buckler.

ANTHONY BURGESS

Criticism - Specific Works

Nothing Like The Sun

McCormack, Thomas, Ed. Novelists on Their Novels.

KENNETH DUVA BURKE

Criticism-General

Piper, Henry Dan, Ed. Think Back On Us.

EDGAR RICE BURROUGHS

Criticism-General

Porges, Irwin. Edgar Rice Burroughs; The Man and His Works.

WILLIAM S. BURROUGHS

Criticism-General

Odier, Daniel. The Job; Interviews with William S. Burroughs.
Solotaroff, Theodore. The Red Hot Vacuum.
Tanner, Tony. City of Words.
Tytell, John. Naked Angels.

Criticism - Specific Works

Naked Lunch

Tytell, John. Naked Angels.

MICHAEL BUTOR

Criticism-General

Waelti-Walters, Jennifer. Michel Butor.

JAMES BRANCH CABELL

Letters

Colum, Padraic, and Margaret Freeman Cabell. Between Friends.
Wagenknecht, Edward. The Letters of James Branch Cabell.

Criticism-General

Churchill, Allen. The Literary Decade.
Cowley, Malcolm, Ed. After the Genteel Tradition.
Godshalk, William Leigh. In Quest of Cabell.
Heiney, Donald. Recent American Literature.
Heiney, Donald. Recent American Literature To 1930.
Hoyt, Charles Alva, Ed. Minor American Novelists.
Nolte, William H., Ed. H. L. Mencken's Smart Set Criticism.
Michaud, Regis. The American Novel Today.
Rubin, Louis D., Jr. Death of the Novel.
Rubin, Louis D., Jr., and Robert D. Jacobs, Eds. Southern Renascence.
Straumann, Heinrich. American Literature in the Twentieth Century.
Tarrant, Desmond. James Branch Cabell.
Walpole, Hugh, Sir. The Art of James Branch Cabell.

Wilson, Edmund. The Bit Between My Teeth.

Reference Works

Bibliographies

Holt, Guy. A Bibliography of the Writings of James Branch Cabell.

GEORGE WASHINGTON CABLE

Biographies

Bikle, Lucy L. George W. Cable; His Life and Letters.
Butcher, Philip. George W. Cable; The Northampton Years.
Turner, Arlin. George W. Cable.

Letters

Bikle, Lucy L. Cable. George W. Cable; His Life and Letters.

Criticism-General

Cowie, Alexander. The Rise of the American Novel.
Martin, Jay. Harvests of Change.
Turner, Arlin. The Record of a Literary Friendship.

ABRAHAM CAHAN

Criticism-General

Walden, Daniel. On Being Jewish.

JAMES M. CAIN

Criticism-General

Madden, David, Ed. Tough Guy Writers of the Thirties.

ERSKINE CALDWELL

Criticism By

Caldwell, Erskine. Call It Experience.

Criticism-General

Beach, Joseph Warren. American Fiction.
Heiney, Donald. Recent American Literature.
Rubin, Louis D., Jr., and Robert D. Jacobs, Eds. Southern Renascence.
Straumann, Heinrich. American Literature in the Twentieth Century.
Sutton, William Alfred. Black Like It Is/Was.

Criticism - Specific Works

Tobacco Road

Beach, Joseph Warren. American Fiction;1920-1940.

GEORGE HENRY CALVERT

Biographies

Everson, Ida Gertrude. George Henry Calvert.

TRUMAN CAPOTE

Criticism-General

Aldridge, John W., Ed. After the Lost Generation.
Austen, Roger. Playing the Game.
Balakian, Nona, and Charles Simmons, Eds. The Creative Present.
French, Warren, Ed. The Forties; Fiction, Poetry, Drama.
Gossett, Louise Y. Violence in Recent Southern Fiction.
Hassan, Ihab. Contemporary American Literature;1945-1972.
Hassan, Ihab. Radical Innocence;Studies in the Contemporary American Novel.
Kazin, Alfred. Bright Book of Life.
McCormack, Thomas, Ed. Afterwords;Novelists on Their Novels.
Nin, Anais. The Novel of the Future.
Parker, Dorothy. The Portable Dorothy Parker.
Schorer, Mark. The World We Imagine.
Waldmeir, Joseph J., Ed. Recent American Fiction.

Criticism - Specific Works

Breakfast at Tiffany's

Parker, Dorothy. The Portable Dorothy Parker.

DON CARPENTER

Criticism-General

Tooker, Dan. Fiction!Interviews with Northern California Novelists.

JOHN DICKSON CARR

Criticism-General

Hoyt, Charles Alva, Ed. Minor American Novelists.

WILLA CATHER

Biographies

Cather, Willa. (Autobiography). Willa Cather in Europe.
Edel, Leon, and Edward K. Brown. Willa Cather; A Critical Biography.
Lewis, Edith. Willa Cather Living.
Woodress, James Leslie. Willa Cather; Her Life and Art.

Criticism-General

Auchincloss, Louis. Pioneers and Caretakers.
Bennett, Mildred R. The World of Willa Cather.
Berthoff, Warner. The Ferment of Realism.
Bowden, Edwin T. The Dungeon of the Heart.
Bryer, Jackson R., Ed. Fifteen Modern American Authors.
Churchill, Allen. The Literary Decade.
Cooperman, Stanley. World War I and the American Novel.
Cowley, Malcolm, Ed. After the Genteel Tradition.
Crothers, George D., Ed. Invitation to Learning; English and American Novels.
Gerber, Philip L. Willa Cather.
Geismar, Maxwell. The Last of the Provincials.
Heiney, Donald. Recent American Literature.
Heiney, Donald. Recent American Literature to 1930.
Hilfer, Anthony Channell. The Revolt from the Village.
Hoffman, Frederick J. The Twenties.
Kazin, Alfred. On Native Grounds.
Lee, Robert Edson. From West to East.
Michaud, Regis. The American Novel Today.
Murphy, John J., Ed. Five Essays on Willa Cather.
Porter, Katherine Anne. The Collected Essays and Occasional Writings of Katherine Anne Porter.
Rahv, Philip. Literature in America.
Slote, Bernice and Virginia Faulkner, Eds. The Art of Willa Cather.
Snell, George. The Shapers of American Fiction.
Stegner, Wallace, Ed. The American Novel.
Stouck, David. Willa Cather's Imagination.
Straumann, Heinrich. American Literature in the Twentieth Century.

Criticism - Specific Works

My Antonia

Bowden, Edwin T. The Dungeon of the Heart.
Stegner, Wallace, Ed. The American Novel.

Professor's House

Crothers, George D, Ed. Invitation to Learning; English and American Novels.

RAYMOND CHANDLER

Biographies

Macshane, Frank. Raymond Chandler.

Criticism-General

Madden, David, Ed. Tough Guy Writers of the Thirties.
Pendo, Stephen. Raymond Chandler on Screen.

JOHN CHEEVER

Criticism-General

Hassan, Ihab. Radical Innocence.
Proffer, Carl R., Ed./Transl. Soviet Criticism of American Literature in the Sixties.
Straumann, Heinrich. American Literature in the Twentieth Century.

Criticism - Specific Works

The Brigadier and the Golf Widow

Proffer, Carl R., Ed./Transl. Soviet Criticism of American Literature in the Sixties.

CHARLES WADDELL CHESNUTT

Biographies

Chesnutt, Helen M. Charles Waddell Chesnutt; Pioneer of the Color Line.

Criticism-General

Hoyt, Charles Alva, Ed. Minor American Novelists.
Margolies, Edward. Native Sons.

KATE CHOPIN

Biographies

Seyersted, Per. Kate Chopin; A Critical Biography.

Criticism-General

Berthoff, Warner. The Ferment of Realism.

Reference Works

Bibliographies

Springer, Marlene. Edith Wharton and Kate Chopin.

ARTHUR C. CLARKE

Criticism-General

Olander, Joseph D., and Martin Harry Greenberg, Eds. Arthur C. Clarke.

MARCUS CLARKE

Criticism-General

Argyle, Barry. An Introduction to the Australian Novel; 1830-1930.

SAMUEL LANGHORNE CLEMENS

See Mark Twain.

LEONARD COHEN

Criticism-General

Gnarowski, Michael. Leonard Cohen; The Artist and His Critics.
Northey, Margot. The Haunted Wilderness.

Criticism - Specific Works

Beautiful Losers

Northey, Margot. The Haunted Wilderness.

EVAN S. CONNELL

Criticism-General

Tooker, Dan. Fiction!Interviews with Northern California Novelists.

W. PAUL COOK

Criticism-General

Warner, Harry, Jr. All Our Yesterdays.

JOHN ESTEN COOKE

Criticism-General

Cowie, Alexander. The Rise of the American Novel.
Martin, Jay. Harvests of Change.

ALFRED COOPEL

See Alfred Coppel.

JAMES FENIMORE COOPER

Biographies

Dekker, George. James Fenimore Cooper; The American Scott.
Phillips, Mary. James Fenimore Cooper.

Letters

Beard, James Franklin, Ed. The Letters and Journals of James Fenimore Cooper, Vol. I, II, III, IV, V and VI.

Criticism By

Rahv, Philip. Literature in America.

Criticism-General

Bank, Stanley, Ed. American Romanticism.
Berbrich, Joan D. Three Voices from Paumanok.
Bowden, Edwin T. The Dungeon of the Heart.
Bewley, Marius. The Eccentric Design.
Bewley, Marius. Masks and Mirrors.
Chase, Richard. The American Novel and Its Tradition.
Dekker, George, and John P. McWilliams, Eds. Fenimore Cooper; The Critical Heritage.
Erskine, John, Ph.D. Leading American Novelists.
Foster, Richard, Ed. Six American Novelists of the Nineteenth Century.
Griffith, Malcolm A., and Donald M. Kartiganer. Theories of American Literature.

House, Kay Seymour. Cooper's Americans.
Howard, David, et al. Tradition and Tolerance in Nineteenth-Century Fiction.
Kaul, A.N. The American Vision.
Kuhlmann, Susan. Knave, Fool and Genius.
Lawrence, D.H. Studies in Classic American Literature.
Loshe, Lillie Deming. The Early American Novel; 1789-1830.
McCarthy, Harold T. The Expatriate Perspective.
McWilliams, John P., Jr. Political Justice in a Republic.
Miller, Wayne Charles. An Armed America; Its Face in Fiction.
Mills, Nicolaus. American and English Fiction in the Nineteen Century.
Mizener, Arthur. Twelve Great American Novels.
Noble, David W. The Eternal Adam and the New World Garden.
Pattee, Fred Lewis. The First Century of American Literature.
Peck, H. Daniel. A World by Itself.
Philbrick, Thomas. James Fenimore Cooper and the Development of American Sea Fiction.
Porte, Joel. The Romance In America.
Rahv, Philip. Literature in America.
Rees, Robert A., and Earl N. Harbert. Fifteen American Authors Before 1900.
Ringe, Donald A. James Fenimore Cooper.
Shapiro, Charles, Ed. Twelve Original Essays.
Shulenberger, Arvid. Cooper's Theory of Fiction.
Snell, George. The Shapers of American Fiction.
Spiller, Robert E. The Cycle of American Literature.
Spiller, Robert E. Fenimore Cooper; Critic of His Times.
Spiller, Robert E., et al. Literary History of the United States.
Spiller, Robert E. The Oblique Light.
Stegner, Wallace, Ed. The American Novel.
Tuttleton, James W. The Novel of Manners in America.
Twain, Mark. The Portable Mark Twain.
Verland, Orm. James Fenimore Cooper's The Prairie.
Wager, Willis. American Literature; A World View.
Walker, Warren S. James Fenimore Cooper.
Waples, Dorothy. The Whig Myth of James Fenimore Cooper.
Wright, Nathalia. American Novelists in Italy.

Criticism - Specific Works

The Deerslayer

Bowden, Edwin T. The Dungeon of the Heart.
Mizener, Arthur. Twelve Great American Novels.
Shapiro, Charles, Ed. Twelve Original Essays on Great American Novels.

Leather Stocking Tales

Howard, David, et al. Tradition and Tolerance in Nineteenth-Century Fiction.

The Pioneers

Stegner, Wallace, Ed. The American Novel.

Reference Works

Bibliographies

Spiller, Robert E., and Philip C. Blackburn. A Descriptive Bibliography of the Writings of James Fenimore Cooper.

ROBERT COOVER

Criticism-General

Gado, Frank. First Person.
Schulz, Max F. Black Humor Fiction of the Sixties.

ALFRED COPPEL

Criticism-General

Tooker, Dan. Fiction! Interviews with Northern California Novelists.

JOHN COTTON

Criticism-General

Gallagher, Edward Joseph. Early Puritan Writers.

JOHN COULTER

Biographies

Anthony, Geraldine. John Coulter.

MALCOM COWLEY

Criticism-General

Aldridge, John W. In Search of Heresy.
Piper, Henry Dan, Ed. Think Back On Us.

JAMES GOULD COZZENS

Criticism-General

Frohock, W. M. Strangers to this Ground.
Kazin, Alfred. Bright Book of Life.
Langford, Richard E. Essays in Modern American Literature.
Michel, Pierre. James Gould Cozzens.
Miller, Wayne Charles. An Armed America; Its Face in Fiction.
Millgate, Michael. American Social Fiction.
Mizener, Arthur. The Sense of Life in the Modern Novel.
Mizener, Arthur. Twelve Great American Novels.
Noble, David W. The Eternal Adam and the New World Garden.
Seward, William W., Jr. Contrasts in Modern Writers.
Straumann, Heinrich. American Literature in the Twentieth Century.
Whitbread, Thomas B., Ed. Seven Contemporary Authors.

Reference Works

Bibliographies

Michel, Pierre. James Gould Cozzens.

STEPHEN CRANE

Biographies

Cady, Edwin H., Ed. My Stephen Crane.
Gilkes, Lillian. Cora Crane; A Biography of Mrs. Stephen Crane.
Stallman, R. W. Stephen Crane.

Letters

Cady, Edwin H., and Lester G. Wells, Eds. Stephen Crane's Love Letters to Nellie Crouse.
Stallman, R. W., and Lillian Gilkes. Stephen Crane; Letters.

Criticism-General

Ahnebrink, Lars. The Beginnings of Naturalism in American Fiction.
Bassan, Maurice, Ed. Stephen Crane; A Collection of Critical Essays.
Bergon, Frank. Stephen Crane's Artistry.
Berthoff, Warner. The Ferment of Realism.
Berthoff, Warner. Fictions and Events.
Berryman, John. Stephen Crane.
Bradley, Sculley, et al., Ed. The Red Badge of Courage.
Bryer, Jackson R., Ed. Fifteen Modern American Authors.
Cady, Edwin H. The Light of Common Day.
Cady, Edwin H. Stephen Crane.
Cowley, Malcolm. Exile's Return.
Cowley, Malcolm. Edited by Henry Dan Piper. Think Back On Us.
Crothers, George D., Ed. Invitation to Learning.
Franchere, Ruth. Stephen Crane; The Story of an American Writer.
Geismar, Maxwell. Rebels and Ancestors.
Gibson, Donald B. The Fiction of Stephen Crane.
Gullason, Thomas A. Stephen Crane's Career.
Heiney, Donald. Recent American Literature.
Heiney, Donald. Recent American Literature To 1930.
Hoffman, Michael J. The Subversive Vision.
Holton, Milne. Cylinder of Vision.
Keet, Alfred E. Stephen Crane; In Memoriam.
LaFrance, Marston, Ed. Patterns of Commitment in American Literature.
LaFrance, Marston. Reading of Stephen Crane.
Langford, Richard E., Ed. Essays in Modern American Literature.
MacMillan, Dougald. Transition; The Story of a Literary Era.
Martin, Jay. Harvests of Change.
O'Donnell, Bernard. Analysis of Prose Style to Determine Authorship of the O'Ruddy.
Pizer, Donald, Ed. The Literary Criticism of Frank Norris.
Pizer, Donald. Realism and Naturalism.
Rahv, Philip. Literature in America.
Rees, Robert A., and Earl N. Harbert, Eds. Fifteen American Authors Before 1900.
Schneider, Robert W. Five Novelists of the Progressive Era.
Shapiro, Charles, Ed. Twelve Original Essays.
Snell, George. The Shapers of American Fiction.
Solomon, Eric. Stephen Crane; From Parody to Realism.
Solomon, Eric. Stephen Crane in England.
Stegner, Wallace, Ed. The American Novel.

Stone, Edward. A Certain Morbidness.
Taylor, Gordon O. The Passages of Thought.
Vickery, John B., Ed. Myth and Literature.
Wagenknecht, Edward. Cavalcade of the American Novel.
Walcutt, Charles Child. American Literary Naturalism, A Divided Stream.
Weatherford, Richard M. Stephen Crane; The Critical Heritage.

Criticism - Specific Works

George's Mother

Pizer, Donald, Ed. The Literary Criticism of Frank Norris.

Halfway House

Geismar, Maxwell. Rebels and Ancestors.

Maggie

Pizer, Donald, Ed. The Literary Criticism of Frank Norris.

The Monster

Langford, Richard E., Ed. Essays in Modern American Literature.

O'Ruddy

O'Donnell, Bernard. Analysis of Prose Style to Determine Authorship of the O'Ruddy.

Red Badge of Courage

Bradley, Sculley, et al., Ed. The Red Badge of Courage.
Crothers, George D. Invitation to Learning; English and American Novels.
Hoffman, Michael J. The Subsersive Vision.
Shapiro, Charles, Ed. Twelve Original Essays on Great American Novels.
Stegner, Wallace, Ed. The American Novel.

Reference Works

Bibliographies

Gross, Theodore L., and Stanley Wertheim. Hawthorne, Melville, Stephen Crane.
Stallman, R. W. Stephen Crane.
Williams, Ames W., and Vincent Starrett. Stephen Crane.

MARY CAROLINE CRAWFORD

Criticism-General

Wagenknecht, Edward. Cavalcade of the American Novel.

GEOFFREY CRAYON

See Washington Irving.

J. HECTOR ST. JOHN de CREVECOEUR

Criticism-General

Lawrence, D. H. Studies in Classic American Literature.

ROBERT CRICHTON

Criticism - Specific Works

The Secret of Santa Vittoria

McCormack, Thomas, Ed. Afterwords; Novelists on Their Novels.

COUNTEE CULLEN

Criticism-General

Margolies, Edward. Native Sons.

MARIA SUSAN CUMMINS

Criticism-General

Cowie, Alexander. The Rise of the American Novel.

GEORGE WILLIAM CURTIS

Criticism-General

Cowie, Alexander. The Rise of the American Novel.

RICHARD HENRY DANA

Criticism - Specific Works

Two Years Before the Mast

Lawrence. D.H. Studies in Classic American Literature.

ELEANOR DARK

Biographies

Day, A. Grove. Eleanor Dark.

DONALD GRADY DAVIDSON

Criticism-General

Hubbell, Jay B. Who Are the Major American Writers?
Walker, William E., and Robert L. Welker, Eds. Reality and Myth.

JOHN W. DE FOREST

Criticism-General

Cowie, Alexander. The Rise of the American Novel.
Falk, Robert. The Victorian Mode in American Fiction.
Hoyt, Charles Alva, Ed. Minor American Novelists.
Lee, Robert Edson. From West to East.
Milne, Gordon. The American Political Novel.
Stegner, Wallace, Ed. The American Novel.

Criticism-Specific Works

Miss Ravenel's Conversion

Stegner, Wallace, Ed. The American Novel.

MAZO DE LA ROCHE - see p. 229

BERNARD DE VOTO

Criticism-General

Forsythe, Robert S. Bernard DeVoto.

JOHN DEWEY

Criticism-General

Straumann, Heinrich. American Literature in the Twentieth Century.

JAMES DICKEY

Criticism-General

Calhoun, Richard J., Ed. James Dickey; The Expansive Imagination.

JAMES PATRICK DONLEAVY

Criticism-General

Masinton, Charles G. J.P. Donleavy; His Sadness and Humor.

JOHN DOS PASSOS

Biographies

Becker, George Joseph. John Dos Passos.
Landsberg, Melvin. Dos Passos' Path to U.S.A.; A Political Biography.

Letters

Ludington, Townsend, Ed. The Fourteenth Chronicle.

Criticism-General

Aldridge, John W., Ed. After the Lost Generation.
Belkind, Allen, Ed. Dos Passos; the Critics, and the Writer's Intention.
Blake, Nelson Manfred. Novelists' America.
Brantley, John D. The Fiction of John Dos Passos.
Brown, John Russell. The American Novel and the Nineteen Twenties.
Churchill, Allen. The Literary Decade.
Cowley, Malcolm. Exile's Return.
Cowley, Malcolm. Think Back on Us.
Feied, Frederick. No Pie in the Sky.
Frohock, W.M. The Novel of Violence in America.
Gado, Frank, Ed. First Person.
Gelfant, Blanche Housman. The American City Novel.
Geismar, Maxwell. Writers in Crisis.
Hassan, Ihab. Radical Innocence.
Heiney, Donald. Recent American Literature.
Heiney, Donald. Recent American Literature To 1930.
Hook, Andrew, Ed. Dos Passos; A Collection of Critical Essays.
Lehan, Richard. A Dangerous Crossing.
Magny, Edmonde. The Age of the American Novel.
Martin, Jay. Harvests of Change.
Millgate, Michael. American Social Fiction.
Mizener, Arthur. Twelve Great American Novels.
Mizener, Sharon Fusselman. Manhattan Transients.
Straumann, Heinrich. American Literature in the Twentieth Century.

THEODORE DREISER

Biographies

Kennell, Ruth Epperson. Theodore Dreiser and the Soviet Union.

Lundquist, James. Theodore Dreiser.
Matthiessen, F.O. Theodore Dreiser.
Moers, Ellen. Two Dreisers.
Shapiro, Charles. Theodore Dreiser; Our Bitter Patriot.
Swanberg, W.A. Dreiser; A Biography.

Letters

Campbell, Louise, Ed. Letters to Louise.
Elias, Robert H., Ed. Letters of Theodore Dreiser, Volumes One, Two and Three.

Criticism-General

Berthoff, Warner. The Ferment of Realism.
Block, Haskell M. Naturalistic Triptych.
Bourne, Randolph. History of a Literary Radical and Other Essays.
Bryer, Jackson R., Ed. Fifteen Modern American Authors.
Churchill, Allen. The Literary Decade.
Cowley, Malcolm, Ed. After the Genteel Tradition.
Crothers, George D., Ed. Invitation to Learning; English and American Novels.
Elias, Robert H. Theodore Dreiser; Apostle of Nature.
French, Warren, Ed. The Forties; Fiction, Poetry, Drama.
Geismar, Maxwell. Rebels and Ancestors.
Gelfant, Blanche Housman. The American City Novel.
Gerber, Philip L. Plots and Characters in the Fiction of Theodore Dreiser.
Gerber, Philip L. Theodore Dreiser.
Handy, William J. Modern Fiction.
Heiney, Donald. Recent American Literature.
Heiney, Donald. Recent American Literature To 1930.
Kazin, Alfred. On Native Grounds.
Kazin, Alfred, and Charles Shapiro, Eds. The Stature of Theodore Dreiser.
Knight, Grant C. The Strenous Age in American Literature.
Lehan, Richard. Theodore Dreiser; His World and His Novels.
Lydenberg, John, Ed. Dreiser; A Collection of Critical Essays.
McAleer, John J. Theodore Dreiser; An Introduction and Interpretation.
Martin, Jay. Harvests of Change.
Michaud, Regis. The American Novel.
Millgate, Michael. American Social Fiction.
Morgan, H. Wayne. American Writers in Rebellion.
Noble, David W. The Eternal Adam and the New World Garden.
Nolte, William H., Ed. H.L. Mencken's Smart Set Criticism.
Parker, Dorothy. The Portable Dorothy Parker.
Pizer, Donald. The Novels of Theodore Dreiser.
Rahv, Philip. Literature in America.
Salzman, Jack, Ed. Theodore Dreiser; The Critical Reception.
Schneider, Robert W. Five Novelists of the Progressive Era.
Seward, William W., Jr. Contrasts
i in Modern Writers.
Shapiro, Charled, Ed. Twelve Original Essays.
Spiller, Robert E. The Cycle of American Literature.
Stegner, Wallace, Ed. The American Novel.
Straumann, Heinrich. American Literature in the Twentieth Century.
Taylor, Gordon O. The Passages of Thought.
Tjader, Marguerite. Theodore Dreiser.

DREISER

Walcutt, Charles Child. American Literary Naturalism;A Divided Stream.

Westbrook, Max, Ed. The Modern American Novel.

Criticism - Specific Works

An American Tragedy

Crothers, George D., Ed. Invitation to Learning;English and American Novels.

Westbrook, Max. The Modern American Novel.

Bulwark

French, Warren, Ed. The Forties;Fiction, Poetry, Drama.

Dawn

Parker, Dorothy. The Portable Dorothy Parker.

The Double Soul

Geismar, Maxwell. Rebels and Ancestors.

Sister Carrie

Crothers, George D., Ed. Invitation to Learning;English and American Novels.

Stegner, Wallace, Ed. The American Novel.

Reference Works

Bibliographies

McDonald, Edward David. A Bibliography of the Writings of Theodore Dreiser.

Orton, Vrest. Dreiserana;A Book About his Books.

ISADORA DUNCAN

Criticism - Specific Works

My Life

Parker, Dorothy. The Portable Dorothy Parker.

LAWRENCE DURELL

Criticism-General

Nin, Anais. The Novel of the Future.

H.S. EDE

Criticism - Specific Works

Savage Messiah

Parker, Dorothy. The Portable Dorothy Parker.

MRS. E.D.E.N.

Criticism-General

Cowie, Alexander. The Rise of the American Novel.

MARIA EDGEWORTH

Criticism-General

Oliver, Grace A. A Study of Maria Edgeworth.

JONATHAN EDWARDS

Criticism-General

Hauck, Richard Boyd. A Cheerful Nihilism.

EDWARD EGGLESTON

Criticism-General

Cowie, Alexander. The Rise of the American Novel.
Martin, Jay. Harvests of Change.

HARLAN ELLISON

Criticism-General

Slusser, George Edgar. Harlan Ellison; Unrepentant Harlequin.

Reference Works

Bibliographies

Swigart, Leslie Kay. Harlan Ellison; A Bibliographical Checklist.

RALPH ELLISON

Criticism-General

Baker, Houston A., Jr. Black Literature in America.
Baumbach, Jonathan. The Landscape of Nightmare.
Bigsby, C.W.E., Ed. The Black American Writer.
Cooke, M.G., Ed. Modern Black Novelists; A Collection of Critical Essays.
Covo, Jacqueline. The Blinking Eye.
Gross, Seymour L., Ed. Images of the Negro in American Literature.
Hassan, Ihab. Radical Innocence.
Hersey, John Richard. Ralph Ellison.
Kartiganer, Donald M., and Malcolm A. Griffith. Theories of American Literature.
Kazin, Alfred. Bright Book of Life.
Lehan, Richard. A Dangerous Crossing.
Lutwack, Leonard. Heroic Fiction.
May, John R. Toward a New Earth; Apocalypse in the American Novel.
Ruotolo, Lucio P. Six Essential Heroes.
Waldmeir, Joseph J., Ed. Recent American Fiction.

Criticism - Specific Works

The Invisible Man

Lutwack, Leonard. Heroic Fiction.

RALPH WALDO EMERSON

Biographies

Bode, Carl, Ed. Ralph Waldo Emerson; A Profile.
Choate, Joseph H. Ralph Waldo Emerson.
Holmes, Oliver Wendell. Ralph Waldo Emerson.
Michaud, Regis. Emerson; The Enraptured Yankee.
Pommer, Henry F. Emerson's First Marriage.
Rusk, Ralph L. The Life of Ralph Waldo Emerson.
Whicher, Stephen E. Freedom and Fate.

Woodberry, George Edward. Ralph Waldo Emerson.
Woodbury, Charles J. Talks with Emerson.

Letters

Holmes, Oliver Wendell. Ralph Waldo Emerson.
Slater, Joseph, Ed. The Correspondence of Emerson and Carlyle.

Criticism By

Rahv, Philip, Comp. Literature in America.

Criticism-General

Berthoff, Warner. Fictions and Events.
Bewley, Marius. Masks and Mirrors.
Burroughs, John. Literary Values and Other Papers.
Cameron, Kenneth Walter. Ralph Waldo Emerson's Reading.
Carpenter, Frederic Ives. Emerson Handbook.
Christy, A. E. The Orient in American Transcendentalism.
Cooke, George Willis. Ralph Waldo Emerson;His Life, Writings and Philosophy.
Duncan, Jeffrey L. The Power and Form of Emerson's Thought.
Green, Martin. Re-Appraisals.
Gregg, Edith W., Ed. One First Love.
Konvitz, Milton R., Ed. The Recognition of Ralph Waldo Emerson.
Levin, David. Emerson;Prophecy, Metamorphosis and Influence.
McNeir, Waldo, and Leo B. Levy, Eds. Studies in American Literature.
Mead, Edwin D. The Influence of Emerson.
Metzger, Charles R. Emerson and Greenough.
Mignon, Charles W. Emerson's Essays;Notes.
Miles, Josephine. Ralph Waldo Emerson.
Neufeldt, Nick, Ed. Ralph Waldo Emerson.
Pattee, Fred Lewis. The First Century of American Literature.
Paul, Sherman, Ed. Six Classic American Writers.
Rahv, Philip. Literature in America.
Ramakrishna, Rao. Emerson;His Muse and Message.
Reaver, J. Russell. Emerson as Mythmaker.
Spiller, Robert E., et al. Four Makers of the American Mind.
Spiller, Robert E. The Oblique Light.
Tanner, Tony. The Reign of Wonder.
Violette, Augusta Genevieve. Feminism in American Literature Prior to 1848.
Wahr, F. B. Emerson and Goethe.
Wiley, Margaret Lenore. Studies in American Literature.
Woodress, James, Ed. Eight American Authors.

Reference Works

Bibliographies

Cameron, Kenneth Walter. Ralph Waldo Emerson's Reading.

JAMES T. FARRELL

Criticism By

Robbins, Jack Alan, Ed. Literary Essays, 1954-1974/James T. Farrell.

Criticism-General

Aldridge, John W. In Search of Heresy.
Beach, Joseph Warren. American Fiction;1920-1940.
Blake, Nelson Manfred. Novelists' America.
Frohock, W.M. The Novel of Violence in America.
Heiney, Donald. Recent American Literature.
Leary, Lewis, Ed. American Literary Essays.
Seward, William W., Jr. Contrasts in Modern Writers.
Straumann, Heinrich. American Literature in the Twentieth Century.
Walcutt, Charles Child. American Literary Naturalism, A Divided Stream.

Criticism - Specific Works

Studs Lonigan

Beach, Joseph Warren. American Fiction;1920-1940.

Reference Works

Bibliographies

Branch, Edgar. A Bibliography of James T. Farrell's Writings;1921-1957.

JESSIE FAUCET-see p.182

WILLIAM FAULKNER

Biographies

Coughlan, Robert. The Private World of William Faulkner.
Cullen, John B. Old Times in the Faulkner Country.
Faulkner, John. My Brother Bill.
Falkner, Murry C. The Falkners of Mississippi.
Leary, Lewis Gaston. William Faulkner of Yoknapatawpha County.
Seyppel, Joachim. William Faulkner.
Webb, James W., and A. Wigfall Green, Eds. William Faulkner of Oxford.

Criticism-General

Adams, Richard P. Faulkner;Myth and Motion.
Backman, Melvin. Faulkner;The Major Years.
Barth, J. Robert, Ed. Religious Perspectives in Faulkner's Fiction.
Bassett, John, Ed. William Faulkner; The Critical Heritage.
Beach, Joseph Warren. American Fiction;1920-1940.
Beck, Warren. Man in Motion.
Beja, Morris. Epiphany in the Modern Novel.
Blake, Nelson Manfred. Novelists' America.
Bleikasten, Andre. The Most Splendid Failure;Faulkner's The Sound and the Fury.
Bowden, Edwin T. The Dungeon of the Heart.
Brooks, Cleanth. The Hidden God.
Brooks, Cleanth. William Faulkner; The Yoknapatawpha Country.
Broughton, Panthea Reid. William Faulkner;The Abstract and the Actual.
Brown, John Russel. The American Novel and the Nineteen Twenties.
Bryer, Jackson R., Ed. Fifteen Modern American Authors.
Brylowski, Walter. Faulkner's Olympian Laugh.
Churchill, Allen. The Literary Decade.

Cohen, Hennig, Ed. Landmarks of American Writing.
Coindreau, Maurice Edgar. The Time of William Faulkner;A French View of Modern American Fiction.
Cooperman, Stanley. World War I and the American Novel.
Cowan, Michael H., Ed. Twentieth Century Interpretations of The Sound and the Fury.
Cowley, Malcolm. Think Back On Us.
Crothers, George D., Ed. Invitation to Learning;English and American Novels.
Cullen, John B. Old Times in the Faulkner Country.
Dabney, Lewis M. The Indians of Yoknapatawpha.
Early, James. The Making of Go Down, Moses.
Edel, Leon. The Modern Psychological Novel
Fadiman, Regina K. Faulkner's Light in August.
French, Warren G., and Walter E. Kidd, Ed. American Winners of the Nobel Literary Prize.
French, Warren, Ed. The Fifties;Fiction, Poetry, Drama.
Frohock, W. M. The Novel of Violence in America.
Geismar, Maxwell. Writers in Crisis.
Gold, Joseph. William Faulkner;A Study in Humanism From Metaphor to Discourse.
Goldman, Arnold, Ed. Twentieth Century Interpretations of Absalom, Absalom!
Green, Martin. Re-Appraisals.
Gross, Seymour L., and John Edward Hardy. Images of the Negro in American Literature.
Guerard, Albert Joseph. The Triumph of the Novel.
Guetti, James. The Limits of Metaphor.
Hall, James. The Lunatic Giant in the Drawing Room;The British and American Novel.
Handy, William J. Modern Fiction; A Formalist Approach.
Hardy, John Edward. Man in the Modern Novel.
Hauck, Richard Boyd. A Cheerful Nihilism.
Heiney, Donald. Recent American Literature.
Hoffman, Frederick J. William Faulkner.
Hoffman, Frederick J., and Olga W. Vickery, Eds. William Faulkner; Three Decades of Criticism.
Holman, C. Hugh. Three Modes of Modern Southern Fiction.
Howe, Irving. William Faulkner.
Humphrey, Robert. Stream of Consciousness in the Modern Novel.
Hunt, John Wesley. William Faulkner;Art in Theological Tension.
Irwin, John T. Doubling and Incest/Repitition and Revenge.
Jehlen, Myra. Class and Character in Faulkner's South.
Kazin, Alfred. Bright Book of Life.
Kellogg, Jean Defrees. Dark Prophets of Hope.
LaFrance, Marston, Ed. Patterns of Commitment in American Literature.
Langford, Richard E. et al. Essays in Modern American Literature.
Leary, Lewis Gaston. William Faulkner of Yoknapatawpha County.
Lehan, Richard. A Dangerous Crossing.
Levins, Lynn Gartrell. Faulkner's Heroic Design.
Lewis, Wyndham. Men Without Art.
Longley, John Lewis, Jr. The Tragic Mask.
McHaney, Thomas L. William Faulkner's The Wild Palms;A Study.
McNeir, Waldo, and Leo B. Levy, Eds. Studies in American Literature.
Magny, Claude-Edmonde. The Age of

the American Novel.
May, John R. Toward a New Earth.
Meriwether, James B., Ed. A Faulkner Miscellany.
Meriwether, James B., Ed. The Merrill Studies in The Sound and the Fury.
Miller, James E., Jr. Quests Surd and Absurd.
Millgate, Michael. The Achievement of William Faulkner.
Miner, Ward L. The World of William Faulkner.
Minter, David L., Ed. Twentieth Century Interpretations of Light in August.
Mizener, Arthur. Twelve Great American Novels.
Morris, Wright. The Territory Ahead.
Noble, David W. The Eternal Adan and the New World Garden.
O'Connor, William Van. The Grotesque; An American Genre and Other Essays.
O'Connor, William Van. Seven Modern American Novelists.
O'Connor, William Van. The Tangled Fire of William Faulkner.
O'Faolain, Sean. The Vanishing Hero.
Page, Sally R. Faulkner's Women.
Proffer, Carl R., Ed./Translator. Soviet Criticism of American Literature in the Sixties.
Rahv, Philip. Literature in America.
Reed, Joseph W., Jr. Faulkner's Narrative.
Richardson, Kenneth. Force and Faith in the Novels of William Faulkner.
Robb, Mary Cooper. William Faulkner.
Rubin, Louis D., Jr., Ed. The Comic Imagination in American Literature.
Rubin, Louis D., Jr. Essays in American Literature.
Rubin, Louis D., Jr., and Robert D. Jacobs. Southern Renascence.
Ruotolo, Lucio P. Six Existential Heroes.
Seward, William W., Jr. Contrasts in Modern Writers.
Shapiro, Charles, Ed. Twelve Original Essays.
Slatoff, Walter J. Quest for Failure.
Snell, George. The Shapers of American Fiction.
Spiller, Robert E. The Cycle of American Literature.
Stegner, Wallace, Ed. The American Novel.
Stewart, Randall. Regionalism and Beyond.
Stone, Edward. A Certain Morbidness.
Sullivan, Walter. Death by Melancholy.
Swiggart, Peter. The Art of Faulkner's Novels.
Thompson, Lawrance. William Faulkner.
Tuck, Dorothy. Crowell's Handbook of Faulkner.
Van Nostrand, A. D. Everyman His Own Poet.
Vickery, John B., Ed. Myth and Literature.
Vickery, Olga W. The Novels of William Faulkner.
Volpe, Edmond Loris. A Reader's Guide to William Faulkner.
Wager, Willis. American Literature; A World View.
Waggoner, Hyatt H. William Faulkner; From Jefferson to the World.
Wagner, Linda Welshimer. Hemingway and Faulkner.
Wagner, Linda Welshimer, Ed. William Faulkner, Four Decades of Criticism.
Warren, Robert Penn, Ed. Faulkner; A Collection of Critical Essays.
Watkins, Floyd C. The Flesh and the Word.
Weisgerber, Jean. Faulkner and

FAULKNER

Dostoevsky; Influence and Confluence.
Westbrook, Max, Ed. The Modern American Novel.
Williams, David. Faulkner's Women; The Myth and the Muse.
Wolfe, George H. Faulkner; 50 Years After The Marble Faun.
Zyla, Wolodymyr T., and Wendell M. Aycock, Eds. William Faulkner; Prevailing Verities and World Literature.

Criticism - Specific Works

Absalom, Absalom

Beach, Joseph Warren. American Fiction; 1920-1940.
Goldman, Arnold, Ed. Twentieth Century Interpretations of Absalom, Absalom!
Guetti, James. The Limits of Metaphor.

As I Lay Dying

Beach, Joseph Warren. American Fiction; 1920-1940.
Cullen, John B. Old Times in the Faulkner Country.
Handy, William J. Modern Fiction; A Formalist Approach.
Westbrook, Max, Ed. The Modern American Novel.
Williams, David. Faulkner's Women; The Myth and the Muse.

The Bear

Dabney, Lewis M. The Indians of Yoknapatawpha.
Early, James. The Making of Go Down, Moses.

A Courtship

Dabney, Lewis M. The Indians of Yoknapatawpha.

Delta Autumn

Early, James. The Making of Go Down, Moses.

The Fire and the Hearth

Early, James. The Making of Go Down, Moses.

Go Down Moses

Dabney, Lewis M. The Indians of Yoknapatawpha.
Early, James. The Making of Go Down, Moses.

A Justice

Dabney, Lewis M. The Indiana of Yoknapatawpha.

Light in August

Beach, Joseph Warren. American Fiction; 1920-1940.
Bowden, Edwin T. The Dungeon of the Heart.
Coindreau, Maurice Edgar. Reeves, George McMillan, Ed./Translator. The Time of William Faulkner; A French View of Modern American Fiction.
Fadiman, Regina K. Faulkner's Light in August.
McNeir, Waldo, and Leo B. Levy, Eds. Studies in American Literature.
Minter, David L., Ed. Twentieth Century Interpretations of Light in August.
Shapiro, Charles, Ed. Twelve Original Essays on Great American Novels.
Williams, David. Faulkner's Women; The Myth and the Muse.

Lo!

Dabney, Lewis M. The Indians of

Yoknapatawpha.

The Mansion

Cullen, John, and Floyd C. Watkins. Old Times in the Faulkner Country.

The Old People

Dabney, Lewis M. The Indians of Yoknapatawpha.
Early, James. The Making of Go Down, Moses.

Red Leaves

Dabney, Lewis M. The Indians of Yoknapatawpha.

Sanctuary

Cullen, John B., and Floyd C. Watkins. Old Times in the Faulkner Country.
Williams, David. Faulkner's Women; The Myth and the Muse.

The Sound and The Fury

Beach, Joseph Warren. American Fiction;1920-1940.
Bleikasten, Andre. The Most Splendid Failure;Faulkner's The Sound and the Fury.
Coindreau, Maurice Edgar. Reeves, George McMillan, Ed./Translator. The Time of William Faulkner;A French View of Modern American Fiction.
Cowan, Michael H., Ed. Twentieth Century Interpretations of The Sound and the Fury.
Crothers, George D., Ed. Invitation to Learning;English and American Novels.
Cullen, John B., and Floyd C. Watkins. Old Times in the Faulkner Country.

Edel, Leon. The Modern Psychological Novel.
Langford, Richard E., et al., Eds. Essays in Modern American Literature.
Meriwether, James B., Comp. The Merrill Studies in The Sound and the Fury.
Mizener, Arthur. Twelve Great American Novels.
Stegner, Wallace, Ed. The American Novel;From James Fenimore Cooper to William Faulkner.
Westbrook, Max, Ed. The Modern American Novel.
Williams, David. Faulkner's Women; The Myth and the Muse.

The Town

Cullen, John B., and Floyd C. Watkins. Old Times in the Faulkner Country.

Was

Early, James. The Making of Go Down, Moses.

The Wild Palms

Beach, Joseph Warren. American Fiction;1920-1940.
Coindreau, Maurice Edgar. George McMillan Reeves, Ed./Translator. The Time of William Faulkner;A French View of Modern American Fiction.

Reference Works

Bibliographies

Basset, John. William Faulkner;An Annotated Checklist of Criticism.
McHaney, Thomas L. William Faulkner;A Reference Guide.

Massey, Linton R., Comp. Man Working, 1919-1962; William Faulkner.
Meriwether, James B. The Literary Career of William Faulkner.

Dictionaries

Ford, Margaret Patricia and Suzanne Kincaid. Who's Who in Faulkner.
Runyan, Harry. A Faulkner Glossary.
Smart, George K. Religious Elements in Faulkner's Early Novels; A Selective Concordance.

JESSIE FAUCET

Criticism-General

Gloster, Hugh M. Negro Voices in American Fiction.

THEODORE SEDGWICK FAY

Criticism-General

Wright, Nathalia. American Novelists in Italy.

EDNA FERBER

Criticism-General

Churchill, Allen. The Literary Decade.
Shaughnessy, Mary Rose. Women and Success in American Society in the Works of Edna Ferber.

Criticism - Specific Works

The Ice Palace

Parker, Dorothy. The Portable Dorothy Parker.

DOROTHY CANFIELD FISHER

Criticism-General

Wagenknecht, Edward. Cavalcade of the American Novel.

VARDIS FISHER

Criticism-General

Grover, Dorys C. A Solitary Voice.
Grover, Dorys C. Vardis Fisher; The Novelist as Poet.
Thomas, Alfred K. The Epic of Evolution; Its Etiology and Art.

F. SCOTT FITZGERALD

Biographies

Graham, Sheilah. The Real F. Scott Fitzgerald.
Latham, Aaron. Crazy Sundays; F. Scott Fitzgerald in Hollywood.
Mayfield, Sara. Exiles from Paradise; Zelda and Scott Fitzgerald.
Mizener, Arthur. The Far Side of Paradise.
Mizener, Arthur. Scott Fitzgerald and his world.
Sklar, Robert. F. Scott Fitzgerald; The Last Laocoon.
Turnbull, Andrew. Scott Fitzgerald.

Letters

Kuehl, John, and Jackson R. Bryer, Eds. Dear Scott/Dear Max;The Fitzgerald-Perkins Correspondence.
Turnbull, Andrew, Ed. The Letters of F. Scott Fitzgerald.

Criticism-General

Aldridge, John W. After the Lost Generation.
Angoff, Allan, Ed. American Writing Today.
Bewley, Marius. The Eccentric Design.
Bewley, Marius. Masks and Mirrors.
Blake, Nelson Manfred. Novelists' America.
Brown, John Russell, and Bernard Harris. The American Novel and the Nineteen Twenties.
Bruccoli, Matthew J. Apparatus for F. Scott Fitzgerald's The Great Gatsby.
Bruccoli, Matthew J. The Composition of Tender is the Night.
Bryer, Jackson R., Ed. Fifteen Modern American Authors.
Callahan, John F. The Illusions of a Nation;Myth and History in the Novels of F. Scott Fitzgerald.
Churchill, Allen. The Literary Decade.
Cowley, Malcolm. Exile's Return.
Cowley, Malcolm.Henry Dan Piper, Ed. Think Back on Us.
Crosland, Andrew T. A Concordance to The Great Gatsby.
Crothers, George D., Ed. Invitation to Learning;English and American Novels.
Eble, Kenneth E., Ed. F. Scott Fitzgerald;A Collection of Criticism.
Frohock, W. M. Strangers to this Ground.
Geismar, Maxwell. The Last of the Provincials;The American Novel; 1915-1925.
Gindin, James. Harvest of a Quiet Eye.
Hardy, John Edward. Man in the Modern Novel.
Heiney, Donald. Recent American Literature.
Heiney, Donald. Recent American Literture to 1930.
Higgins, John A. F. Scott Fitzgerald; A Study of the Stories.
Hindus, Milton. F. Scott Fitzgerald; An Introduction and Interpretation.
Hoffman, Frederick, Ed. The Great Gatsby;A Study.
Hoffman, Frederick. The Twenties; American Writing in the Postwar Decade.
Kazin, Alfred, Ed. F. Scott Fitzgerald; The Man and His Work.
LaHood, Marvin J., Ed. Tender is the Night;Essays in Criticism.
Langford, Richard E., et al., Eds. Essays in Modern American Literature.
Lehan, Richard D. F. Scott Fitzgerald and the Craft of Fiction.
Lockridge. Ernest, Ed. Twentieth Century Interpretations of The Great Gatsby.
Mencken, H. L. William H. Nolte, Ed. H. L. Mencken's Smart Set Criticism.
Miller, James E., Jr. F. Scott Fitzgerald;His Art and His Technique.
Millgate, Michael. American Social Fiction;James to Cozzens.
Mizener, Arthur, Ed. F. Scott Fitzgerald;A Collection of Critical Essays.
Mizener, Arthur. The Sense of Live In The Modern Novel.
Mizener, Arthur. Twelve Great American Novels.
Morris, Wright. The Territory Ahead.

FITZGERALD

Nelson, Gerald B. Ten Versions of America.
Noble, David W. The Eternal Adam and the New World Garden.
O'Connor, William Van, Ed. Seven Modern American Novelists.
Perosa, Sergio. The Art of F. Scott Fitzgerald.
Piper, Henry Dan. F. Scott Fitzgerald;A Critical Portrait.
Porter, Bernard H. The First Publications of F. Scott Fitzgerald.
Rahv, Philip. Literature in America.
Raleigh, John Henry. Time, Place, and Idea;Essays on the Novel.
Schorer, Mark. The World We Imagine.
Schulberg, Budd. The Four Seasons of Success.
Shapiro, Charles, Ed. Twelve Original Essays on Great American Novels.
Stegner, Wallace, Ed. The American Novel;from James Fenimore Cooper to William Faulkner.
Stern, Milton R. The Golden Moment;The Novels of F. Scott Fitzgerald.
Trilling, Lionel. The Liberal Imagination.
Tuttleton, James W. The Novels of Manners in America.
Westbrook, Max, Ed. The Modern American Novel;Essays in Criticism.
Wilson, Edmund. The Bit Between My Teeth.

Criticism - Specific Works

The Beautiful and the Damned

Eble, Kenneth E., Ed. F. Scott Fitzgerald;A Collection of Criticism.
Higgins, John A. F. Scott Fitzgerald;A Study of the Stories.

The Great Gatsby

Angoff, Allan, Ed. American Writing Today;Its Independence and Vigor.
Bruccoli, Matthew J. Apparatus for F. Scott Fitzgerald's The Great Gatsby.
Crosland, Andrew T. A Concordance to The Great Gatsby.
Crothers, George D., Ed. Invitation to Learning;English and American Novels.
Eble, Kenneth E., Ed. F. Scott Fitzgerald;A Collection of Criticism.
Higgins, John A. F. Scott Fitzgerald;A Study of the Stories.
Hoffman, Frederick J. The Great Gatsby;A Study.
Hoffman, Frederick J. The Twenties;American Writing in the Postwar Decade.
Kazin, Alfred, Ed. F. Scott Fitzgerald;The Man and His Work.
Langford, Richard E., et al, Eds. Essays in Modern American Literature.
Lockridge, Ernest, Ed. Twentieth Century Interpretations of The Great Gatsby.
Mizener, Arthur, Ed. F. Scott Fitzgerald;A Collection of Critical Essays.
Raleigh, John Henry. Time, Place, and Idea;Essays on the Novel.
Shapiro, Charles, Ed. Twelve Original Essays on Great American Novels.
Stegner, Wallace, Ed. The American Novel from James Fenimore Cooper to William Faulkner.
Westbrook, Max, Ed. The Modern American Novel;Essays in Criticism.

The Last Tycoon

Higgins, John A. F. Scott Fitzgerald;A Study of the Stories.
Kazin, Alfred, Ed. F. Scott Fitzgerald;The Man and His Work.

Ode to a Nightingale

Eble, Kenneth E., Ed. F. Scott Fitzgerald; A Collection of Criticism.

Tender Is The Night

Bruccoli, Matthew J. The Composition of Tender is the Night; A Study of the Manuscripts.
Eble, Kenneth E., Ed. F. Scott Fitzgerald; A Collection of Criticism.
Higgins, John A. F. Scott Fitzgerald; A Study of the Stories.
Kazin, Alfred, Ed. F. Scott Fitzgerald; The Man and His Work.
LaHood, Marvin J., Ed. Tender Is The Night; Essays in Criticism.
Mizener, Arthur. Twelve Great American Novels.

This Side of Paradise

Eble, Kenneth E., Ed. F. Scott Fitzgerald; A Collection of Criticism.
Kazin, Alfred, Ed. F. Scott Fitzgerald; The Man and His Work.

Reference Works

Bibliographies

Bruccoli, Matthew J. F. Scott Fitzgerald; A Descriptive Bibliography.
Bryer, Jackson R. The Critical Reputation of F. Scott Fitzgerald; A Bibliographical Study.

SARAH LEE FLEMING

Criticism-General

Gloster, Hugh M. Negro Voices in American Fiction.

TIMOTHY FLINT

Criticism-General

Lee, Robert Edson. From West to East; Studies in the Literature of The American West.

FORD MADOX FORD

Biographies

Ford, Madox Ford. It Was the Nightingale.
Ford, Madox Ford. Michael Killigrew, Ed. Your Mirror to My Times.
Mizener, Arthur. The Saddest Story.

Criticism-General

Andreach, Robert F. The Slain and Resurrected God.
Schorer, Mark. The World We Imagine.

Criticism - Specific Works

The Last Post

Parker, Dorothy. The Portable Dorothy Parker.

WALDO FRANK

Biographies

Trachtenberg, Alan, Ed. Memoirs of Waldo Frank.

Criticism-General

Michaud, Regis. The American Novel Today.
Munson, Gorham Bert. Waldo Frank; A Study.

BENJAMIN FRANKLIN

Criticism-General

Cowley, Malcolm. Think Back On Us.
Hauck, Richard Boyd. A Cheerful Nihilism.
Lawrence, D.H. Studies in Classic American Literature.
More, Paul Elmer. Shelburne Essays on American Literature.
Paul, Sherman, Ed. Six Classic American Writers.
Rees, Robert A., and Earl N. Harbert, Eds. Fifteen American Authors Before 1900.
Rubin, Louis D., Jr., Ed. The Comic Imagination in American Literature.
Spiller, Robert E. The Cycle of American Literature.
Spiller, Robert E. The Oblique Light.
Wager, Willis. American Literature.

AUSTIN FREEMAN

Criticism-General

Donaldson, Norman. In Search of Dr. Thorndyke.

PHILLIP FRENEAU

Criticism-General

Pattee, Fred Lewis. The First Century of American Literature; 1770-1870.

BRUCE J. FRIEDMAN

Criticism-General

Schulz, Max F. Black Humor Fiction of the Sixties.
Schulz, Max F. Bruce Jay Friedman.

MARGARET FULLER

Biographies

Brown, Arthur W. Margaret Fuller.
Higginson, Thomas Wentworth. Margaret Fuller Ossoli.
Howe, Julia Ward. Margaret Fuller; Marchesa Ossoli.
Stern, Madeleine B. The Life of Margaret Fuller.

Letters

Howe, Julia Ward. Love-Letters of Margaret Fuller; 1845-1846.

Criticism By

McMaster, Helen Neill. Margaret Fuller as a Literary Critic.

Criticism-General

Chevigny, Bell Gale. The Woman and the Myth.
Douglas, Ann. The Feminization of American Culture.
Hubbell, Jay B. Who Are the Major American Writers?

Violette, Augusta Genevieve. Economic Feminism in American Literature Prior to 1848.

JOSEPH FURPHY

Criticism - Specific Works

Such Is Life

Argyle, Barry. An Introduction to the Australian Novel;1830-1930.
Kiernan, Brian. Images of Society and Nature.

ERNEST J. GAINES

Criticism-General

Tooker, Dan. Fiction! Interviews with Northern California Novelists.

ZONA GALE

Criticism-General

Michaud, Regis. The American Novel Today.

EARL STANLEY GARDNER

Criticism-General

Johnston, Alva. The Case of Erle Stanley Gardner.

LEONARD GARDNER

Criticism-General

Tooker, Dan. Fiction! Interviews with Northern California Novelists.

HAMLIN GARLAND

Biographies

Holloway, Jean. Hamlin Garland.

Criticism-General

Ahnebrink, Lars. The Beginnings of Naturalism in American Fiction.
Cowie, Alexander. The Rise of the American Novel.
Heiney, Donald. Recent American Literature.
Heiney, Donald. Recent American Literature to 1930.
Martin, Jay. Harvests of Change.
Morgan, H. Wayne. American Writers in Rebellion.
Pizer, Donald. Realism and Naturalism in Nineteenth-Century American Literature.
Schorer, Mark. The World We Imagine.
Taylor, Walter Fuller. The Economic Novel in America.
Walcutt, Charles Child. American Literary Naturalism, A Divided Stream.

Reference Works

Bibliographies

Bryer, Jackson R., and Eugene Harding. Hamlin Garland and the Critics.

WASHINGTON GLADDEN

Criticism-General

Knudten, Richard D. Systematic

Thought of Washington Gladden.

ELLEN GLASGOW

Biographies

Field, Louise Maunsell. Ellen Glasgow.

Criticism By

Geismar, Maxwell. Rebels and Ancestors; The American Novel; 1890-1915.

Criticism-General

Auchincloss, Louis. Pioneers and Caretakers.
Geismar, Maxwell. Rebels and Ancestors; The American Novel; 1890-1915.
Heiney, Donald. Recent American Literature.
Heiney, Donald. Recent American Literature To 1930.
Holman, C. Hugh. Three Modes of Modern Southern Fiction.
Inge, M. Thomas, Ed. Ellen Glasgow; Centennial Essays.
Jessup, Josephine Lurie. Faith of Our Feminists.
Kazin, Alfred. On Native Grounds.
Rahv, Philip. Literature in America.
Rubin, Louis D., Jr. Death of the Novel; Essays in American Literature.
Rubin, Louis, D., Jr., and Robert D. Jacobs, Eds. Southern Renascence.
Walter, William E., and Robert L. Welker, Eds. Reality and Myth; Essays in American Literature in Memory of Richmond Croom Beatty.

Reference Works

Bibliographies

Kelly, William W. Ellen Glasgow.

HERBERT GOLD

Criticism-General

Balakian, Nona, and Charles Simmons, Eds. The Creative Present.
Hassan, Ihab. Radical Innocence.
Hicks, Granville, and Jack Alan Robbins. Literary Horizons.
Tooker, Dan. Fiction! Interviews with Northern California Novelists.

WILLIAM GOLDING

Criticism-General

Ruotolo, Lucio P. Six Existential Heroes.
Whitbread, Thomas B., Ed. Seven Contemporary Authors.

H. B. GOODWIN

Criticism-General

Cowie, Alexander. The Rise of the American Novel.

CAROLINE GORDON

Criticism-General

Rubin, Louis D., Jr., and Robert D. Jacobs, Eds. Southern Renascence.

DOROTHY GREES

See Henry Handel Richardson.

ZANE GREY

Biographies

Gruber, Frank. Zane Grey.
Ronald, Ann. Zane Grey.

SARAH GRIMKE

Criticism-General

Violette, Augusta Genevieve. Economic Feminism in American Literature Prior to 1848.

FREDERICK P. GROVE

Letters

Pacey, Desmond, Ed. The Letters of Frederick Philip Grove.

JAMES NORMAN HALL

Criticism-General

Johnson, R. L. The American Heritage of James Norman Hall.
Lee, Robert Edson. From West to East.

DASHIELL HAMMETT

Criticism-General

Madden, David, Ed. Tough Guy Writers of the Thirties.

Criticism - Specific Works

The Glass Key

Parker, Dorothy. The Portable Dorothy Parker.

HENRY HANDEL

Criticism - Specific Works

The Fortunes of Richard Mahony

Argyle, Barry. An Introduction to the Australian Novel; 1830-1930.

REBECCA HARDING

Criticism-General

Rideout, Walter B. The Radical Novel in the United States 1900-1954.

MARION HARLAND

Criticism-General

Cowie, Alexander. The Rise of the American Novel.

FRANCES E. WATKINS HARPER

Criticism-General

Gloster, Hugh M. Negro Voices in American Fiction.

FRANK HARRIS

Biographies

Pullar, Philippa. Frank Harris.

GEORGE WASHINGTON HARRIS

Criticism-General

Rickels, Milton. George Washington Harris.

JOEL CHANALER HARRIS

Criticism-General

Green, Elizabeth Lay. The Negro in Contemporary American Literature.
Martin, Jay. Harvests of Change.

BRET HARTE

Biographies

Merwin, Henry Childs. The Life of Bret Harte.
O'Connor, Richard. Bret Harte; A Biography.
Stewart, George R. Bret Harte; Argonaut and Exile.

Criticism-General

Duckett, Margaret. Mark Twain and Bret Harte.
Erskine, John. Leading American Novelists.
Leary, Lewis, Ed. American Literary Essays.
Patee, Fred Lewis. The Development of the American Short Story.
Patee, Fred Lewis. A History of American Literature Since 1870.

Reference Works

Bibliographies

Gaer, Joseph, Ed. Bret Harte.

JOHN HAWKES

Criticism-General

Greiner, Donald J. Comic Terror; The Novels of John Hawkes.
Hassan, Ihab. Contemporary American Literature; 1945-1972.
Kuehl, John Richard. John Hawkes and the Craft of Conflict.
Nin, Anais. The Novel of the Future.

Reference Works

Bibliographies

Scotto, Robert M. Three Contemporary American Novelists.

NATHANIEL HAWTHORNE

Biographies

Arvin, Newton. Nathaniel Hawthorne.
Cantwell, Robert. Nathaniel Hawthorne; The American Years.
Gorman, Herbert. Hawthorne; A Study in Solitude.
Hall, Lawrence Sargent. Hawthorne; Critic of Society.
Hawthorne, Julian. Nathaniel Hawthorne and His Wife.

Hawthorne, Julian. Hawthorne and His Circle.
Hoeltje, Hubert H. Inward Sky;The Mind and Heart of Nathaniel Hawthorne.
O'Connor, Evangeline Maria. An Analytical Index to the Works of Nathaniel Hawthorne with a Sketch of His Life.
Stewart, Randall. Nathaniel Hawthorne.
Strout, Cushing, Ed. Hawthorne in England.
Woodberry, George E. Nathaniel Hawthorne.

Letters

Woodberry, George E. Nathaniel Hawthorne.

Criticism-General

Asselineau, Roger, Comp. The Merrill Studies in The House of Seven Gables.
Bank, Stanley, Ed. American Romanticism.
Baym, Nina. The Shape of Hawthorne's Careet.
Becker, John E. Hawthorne's Historical Allegory.
Bell, Michael Davitt. Hawthorne and the Historical Romance of New England.
Bell, Millicent. Hawthorne's View of the Artist.
Bewley, Marius. The Eccentric Design;Form in the Classic American Novel.
Bowden, Edwin T. The Dungeon of the Heart.
Brodhead, Richard H. Hawthorne, Melville, and the Novel.
Chandler, Elizabeth Lathrop. A Study of the Sources of the Tales and Romances Written by Nathaniel Hawthorne Before 1853.
Chase, Richard. The American Novel and Its Tradition.
Cohen, Hennig, Ed. Landmarks of American Writing.
Cowie, Alexander. The Rise of the American Novel.
Crews, Frederick C. The Sins of the Fathers.
Crothers, George D., Ed. Invitation to Learning;English and American Novels.
Crowley, J. Donald, Ed. Hawthorne; the Critical Heritage.
Crowley, J. Donald, Ed. Nathaniel Hawthorne;A Collection of Criticism.
Dauber, Kenneth. Rediscovering Hawthorne.
Davidson, Edward Hutchins. Hawthorne's Last Phase.
Donohue, Agnes McNeill, Ed. A Casebook on the Hawthorne Question.
Dryden, Edgar A. Nathaniel Hawthorne;The Poetics of Enchantment.
Eakin, Paul John. The New England Girl.
Elder, Marjorie J. Nathaniel Hawthorne;Transcendental Symbolist.
Erskine, John. Leading American Novelists.
Faust, Bertha. Hawthorne's Contemporaneous Reputation.
Fick, Leonard J. The Light Beyond.
Fogle, Richard Harter. Hawthorne's Fiction;The Light and The Dark.
Folsom, James K. Man's Accidents and God's Purposes.
Fossum, Robert H. Hawthorne's Inviolable Circle;The Problem of Time.
Foster, Richard, Ed. Six American Novelists of the Nineteenth Century.
Frank, Neal. Hawthorne's Early Tales;A Critical Study.
Franklin, H. Bruce. Future Perfect.
Gale, Robert L. Plots and Characters

in the Fiction and Sketches of Nathaniel Hawthorne.
Gerber, John C., Ed. Twentieth Century Interpretations of The Scarlet Letter.
Green, Martin. Re-Appraisals.
Gross, Seymour L., Ed. Nathaniel Hawthorne;The House of the Seven Gables.
Gross, Seymour L., Ed. A Scarlet Letter Handbook.
Hartley, L.P. The Novelist's Responsibility.
Hoffman, Daniel. Form and Fable in American Fiction.
Howard, David, et al., Eds. Tradition and Tolerance in Nineteenth-Century Fiction.
James, Henry. Hawthorne.
Kaul, A.N. The American Vision.
Kaul, A.N., Ed. Hawthorne;A Collection of Critical Essays.
Kesselring, Marion Louise. Hawthorne's Reading;1828-1850.
LaFrance, Marston. Patterns of Commitment in American Literature.
Lathrop, George Parsons. Study of Hawthorne.
Lawrence, D.H. Studies in Classic American Literature.
Levin, Harry. The Power of Blackness.
Lewis, R.W.B. Trials of the Word.
Lundblad, Jane. Nathaniel Hawthorne and European Literary Tradition.
McCarthy, Harold T. The Expatriate Perspective.
McPherson, Hugo. Hawthorne as Myth-Maker.
Male, Roy R. Hawthorne's Tragic Vision.
Martin, Terence. Nathaniel Hawthorne.
May, John R. Toward a New Earth.
Michaud, Regis. The American Novel Today.
Mills, Nicolaus. American and English Fiction in the Nineteenth Century.
More, Paul Elmer. Shelburne Essays on American Literature.
Noble, David W. The Eternal Adam and the New World Garden
Normand, Jean. Nathaniel Hawthorne; An Approach to an Analysis of Artistic Creation.
O'Connor, William Van. The Grotesque;An American Genre and Other Essays.
Pattee, Fred Lewis. The Development of the American Short Story.
Pattee, Fred Lewis. The First Century of American Literature;1770-1870.
Pearce, Roy Harvey. Historicism Once More.
Poirier, Richard. A World Elsewhere;The Place of Style in American Literature.
Porte, Joel. The Romance in America.
Rahv, Philip. Literature and The Sixth Sense.
Rahv, Philip. Literature in America.
Rubin, Louis D., Jr., Ed. The Comic Imagination in American Literature.
Schubert, Leland. Hawthorne, the Artist.
Scott, William Thompson. Chesterton and Other Essays.
Shapiro, Charles, Ed. Twelve Original Essays on Great American Novels.
Snell, George. The Shapers of American Fiction;1798-1947.
Spiller, Robert E. The Cycle of American Literature.
Spiller, Robert E. The Oblique Light.
Staal, Arie. Hawthorne's Narrative Art.
Stegner, Wallace, Ed. The American Novel from James Fenimore Cooper to William Faulkner.
Stewart, Randall. George Core, Ed. Regionalism and Beyond;Essays of Randall Stewart.

Stubbs, John Caldwell. The Pursuit of Form;A Study of Hawthorne and the Romance.
Swigg, Richard. Lawrence, Hardy, and American Literature.
Tharpe, Jac. Nathaniel Hawthorne; Identity and Knowledge.
Trilling, Lionel. Beyond Culture;Essays on Literature and Learning.
Turner, Arlin. Nathaniel Hawthorne.
Vincent, Howard P., Ed. Melville and Hawthorne in the Berkshires.
Wagenknecht, Edward. Nathaniel Hawthorne;Man and Writer.
Waggoner, Hyatt H. Hawthorne;A Critical Study.
Woodress, James, Ed. Eight American Authors.
Wright, Nathalia. American Novelists in Italy.
Young, Philip. Three Bags Full.

Criticism - Specific Works

Blithdale Romance

Chase, Richard. The American Novel and Its Tradition.
Hoffman, Daniel. Form and Fable in American Fiction.
Howard, David, et al., Eds. Tradition and Tolerance in Nineteenth-Century Fiction.
Lawrence, D.H. Studies in Classic American Literature.

The House of the Seven Gables

Gross, Seymour L., Ed. The House of the Seven Gables;An Authoritative Text Backgrounds and Sources;Essays in Criticism.

The Scarlett Letter

Bowden, Edwin T. The Dungeon of the Heart.

Chase, Richard. The American Novel and its Tradition.
Crothers, George D., Ed. Invitation to Learning;English and American Novels.
Gerber, John C., Ed. Twentieth Century Interpretations of The Scarlet Letter.
Gross, Seymour L., Ed. A Scarlet Letter Handbook.
Hoffman, Daniel. Form and Fable in American Fiction.
Lawrence, D.H. Studies in Classic American Literature.
Mizener, Arthur. Twelve Great American Novels.
Shapiro, Charles, Ed. Twelve Original Essays on Great American Novels.
Stegner, Wallace, Ed. The American Novel from James Fenimore Cooper to William Faulkner.
Vincent, Howard P., Ed. Melville and Hawthorne in the Berkshires.

Reference Works

Bibliographies

Browne, Nina E. A Bibliography of Nathaniel Hawthorne.
Clark, C.E. Frazer. Hawthorne at Auction;1894-1971.
Gross, Theodore L., and Stanley Wertheim. Hawthorne, Melville, Stephen Crane;A Critical Bibliography.

WILLIAM HAY

Criticism-General

Argyle, Barry. An Introduction to the Australian Novel;1830-1930.

Criticism - Specific Works

The Escape of The Notorious Sir William Means

Argyle, Barry. An Introduction to the Australian Novel;1830-1930.

BEN HECHT

Criticism-General

Fetherling, Doug. The Five Lives of Ben Hecht.
Mersand, Joseph. Traditions in American Literature.
Michaud, Regis. The American Novel Today.

THOMAS HEGGEN

Criticism-General

Leggett, John. Ross and Tom;Two American Tragedies.
Schulberg, Budd. The Four Seasons of Success.

JOSEPH HELLER

Criticism-General

Harris, Charles B. Contemporary American Novelists of the Absurd.
Hicks, Granville, and Jack Alan Robbins. Literary Horizons.
Lehan, Richard. A Dangerous Crossing.
Miller, Wayne Charles. An Armed America;Its Face in Fiction.
Nagel, James. Critical Essays on Catch-22.
Nelson, Gerald B. Ten Versions of America.
Olderman, Raymond M. Beyond the Waste Land;A Study of the American Novel in the Nineteen-Sixties.
Whitbread, Thomas B. Seven Contemporary Authors.

Reference Works

Bibliographies

Scotto, Robert M. Three Contemporary American Novelists;An Annotated Bibliography.

ERNEST HEMINGWAY

Biographies

Barger, James. Ernest Hemingway.
Donaldson, Scott. By Force of Will; the Life and Art of Ernest Hemingway.
Fenton, Charles A. The Apprenticeship of Ernest Hemingway.
Hemingway, Leicester. My Brother, Ernest Hemingway.
Hotchner, A. E. Papa Hemingway;A Personal Memoir.
Hovey, Richard B. Hemingway;The Inward Terrain.
Klimo, Vernon. Hemingway and Jake; An Extraordinary Friendship.
Montgomery, Constance Cappel. Hemingway in Michigan.
Sanford, Marcelline Hemingway. At the Hemingways.
Seward, William. My Friend Ernest Hemingway.
Shaw, Samuel. Ernest Hemingway.
Ticknor, Caroline. Hawthorne and His Publisher.

Criticism-General

Aldridge, John W., Ed. After the Lost Generation.
Aldridge, John W. In Search of Heresy.
Angoff, Allan, Ed. American Writing Today.
Arnold, Lloyd R. High on the Wild with Hemingway.
Asselineau, Roger. The Literary Reputation of Hemingway in Europe.
Astro, Richard, and Jackson J. Benson, Eds. Hemingway in Our Time.
Baker, Carlos, Ed. Ernest Hemingway; Critiques of Four Major Novels.
Baker, Carlos. Hemingway; The Writer as Artist.
Baker, Carlos, Ed. Hemingway and His Critics.
Beach, Joseph Warren. American Fiction; 1920-1940.
Benson, Jackson J., Ed. The Short Stories of Ernest Hemingway.
Brooks, Cleanth. The Hidden God.
Bryer, Jackson R., Ed. Fifteen Modern American Authors.
Cohen, Hennig, Ed. Landmarks of American Writing.
Cowley, Malcolm. Exile's Return; A Literary Odyssey of the 1920s.
Cowley, Malcolm. Think Back on Us.
Crothers, George D., Ed. Invitation to Learning; English and American Novels.
DeFalco, Joseph. The Hero in Hemingway's Short Stories.
French, Warren G., and Walter E. Kidd, Eds. American Winners of the Nobel Literary Prize.
French, Warren G. The Fifties; Fiction, Poetry, Drama.
Frohock, W.M. The Novel of Violence in America.
Geismar, Maxwell. Writers in Crisis; The American Novel, 1925-1940.
Gellens, Jay, Ed. Twentieth Century Interpretations of A Farewell to Arms.
Graham, John, Comp. The Merrill Studies in A Farewell to Arms.
Gurko, Leo. Ernest Hemingway and the Pursuit of Heroism.
Handy, William J. Modern Fiction; A Formalist Approach.
Hardy, John Edward. Man in the Modern Novel.
Heiney, Donald. Recent American Literature.
Hoffman, Frederick J. The Twenties.
Jobes, Katharine T., Ed. Twentieth Century Interpretations of The Old Man and the Sea.
Kazin, Alfred. Bright Book of Life.
Killinger, John. Hemingway and the Dead Gods.
Kvam, Wayne E. Hemingway in Germany.
Lehan, Richard. A Dangerous Crossing.
Lewis, Robert W., Jr. Hemingway on Love.
Lewis, Wyndham. Men Without Art.
Lutwack, Leonard. Heroic Fiction.
McCarthy, Harold T. The Expatriate Perspective.
MacMillan, Dougald. Transition; The Story of a Literary Era; 1927-1938.
Madden, David, Ed. Tough Guy Writers of the Thirties.
Magny, Claude-Edmonde. The Age of the American Novel.
Mizener, Arthur. The Sense of Life in the Modern Novel.
Mizener, Arthur. Twelve Great American Novels.
Morris, Wright. The Territory Ahead.
Nahal, Chaman. The Narrative Pattern in Ernest Hemingway's Fiction.
Nelson, Gerald B. Ten Versions of America.
Noble, David W. The Eternal Adam and the New World Garden.
O'Connor, William Van. The Grotesque; An American Genre and Other Essays.
O'Connor, William Van. Seven Modern American Novelists.

O'Faolain, Sean. The Vanishing Hero.
Parker, Dorothy. The Portable Dorothy Parker.
Proffer, Carl R., Ed./Translator. Soviet Criticism of American Literature in the Sixties.
Rahv, Philip. Literature and the Sixthe Sense.
Rahv, Philip. Literature in America.
Reynolds, Michael S. Hemingway's First War; The Making of A Farewell to Arms.
Rovit, Earl. Ernest Hemingway.
Sarason, Bertram D. Hemingway and The Sun Set.
Seward, William W., Jr. Contrasts in Modern Writers.
Shapiro, Charles, Ed. Twelve Original Essays on Great American Novels.
Spiller, Robert E. The Cycle of American Literature.
Stegner, Wallace, Ed. The American Novel from James Fenimore Cooper to William Faulkner.
Stephens, Robert O. Ernest Hemingway; The Critical Reception.
Tanner, Tony. The Reign of Wonder.
Wagner, Linda W. Ernest Hemingway; A Reference Guide.
Wagner, Linda W., Comp. Ernest Hemingway; Five Decades of Criticism.
Waldhorn, Arthur. A Reader's Guide to Ernest Hemingway.
Watkins, Floyd C. The Flesh and the Word.
Watts, Emily Stipes. Ernest Hemingway and the Arts.
Weeks, Robert P., Ed. Hemingway; A Collection of Critical Essays.
Westbrook, Max, Ed. The Modern American Novel.
White, William, Comp. The Merrill Studies in The Sun Also Rises.
Wilson, Edmund. The Wound and the Bow.
Young, Philip. Ernest Hemingway; A Reconsideration.
Young, Philip. Three Bags Full; Essays in American Fiction.

Criticism - Specific Works

Across the River and Into The Trees

Kvam, Wayne E. Hemingway in Germany.

Death in the Afternoon

Beach, Joseph Warren. American Fiction; 1920-1940.

Green Hills of Africa

Beach, Joseph Warren. American Fiction; 1920-1940.

A Farewell To Arms

Angoff, Allan, Ed. American Writing Today.
Beach, Joseph Warren. American Fiction; 1920-1940.
Crothers, George D., Ed. Invitation to Learning; English and American Novels.
Gellens, Jay, Ed. Twentieth Century Interpretations of A Farewell To Arms.
Graham, John, Comp. The Merrill Studies in A Farewell to Arms.
Reynolds, Michael S. Hemingway's First War; The Making of A Farewell To Arms.
Stegner, Wallace, Ed. The American Novel from James Fenimore Cooper to William Faulkner.
Westbrook, Max, Ed. The Modern American Novel.

For Whom the Bells Toll

Beach, Joseph Warren. American Fiction; 1920-1940.

Kvam, Wayne E. Hemingway in Germany.
Lutwack, Leonard. Heroic Fiction.
Proffer, Carl R., Ed./Translator. Soviet Criticism of American Literature in the Sixties.

Men Without Women

Parker, Dorothy. The Portable Dorothy Parker.

The Old Man and The Sea

French, Warren, Ed. The Fifties; Fiction, Poetry, Drama.
Handy, William J. Modern Fiction; A Formalist Approach.
Jobes, Katharine T., Ed. Twentieth Century Interpretations of The Old Man and the Sea.
Kvam, Wayne E. Hemingway in Germany.
Seward, William W., Jr. Contrasts in Modern Writers.
Westbrook, Max, Ed. The Moderm American Novel.

The Sun Also Rises

Beach, Joseph Warren; American Fiction; 1920-1940.
Hoffman, Frederick J. The Twenties.
Kvam, Wayne E. Hemingway in Germany.
Mizener, Arthur. Twelve Great American Novels.
Sarason, Bertram D. Hemingway and The Sun Set.
Shapiro, Charles, Ed. Twelve Original Essays on Great American Novels.
Westbrook, Max, Ed. The Modern American Novel.
White, William, Comp. The Merrill Studies in The Sun Also Rises.

To Have and Have Not

Madden, David, Ed. Tough Guy Writers of the Thirties.

Reference Works

Bibliographies

Bruccoli, Matthew J. Hemingway at Auction; 1930-1973.
Cohn, Louis Henry. A Bibliography of the Works of Ernest Hemingway.
Hanneman, Audre. Ernest Hemingway; A Comprehensive Bibliography.
Samuels, Lee. A Hemingway Check List.
Young, Philip, and Charles W. Mann. The Hemingway Manuscripts.

CAROLINE LEE HENLY

Criticism-General

Cowie, Alexander. The Rise of the American Novel.

O. HENRY

Criticism-General

Davis, Robert H., and Arthur B. Maurice. The Caliph of Bagdad.
Heiney, Donald. Recent American Literature.
Heiney, Donald. Recent American Literature to 1930.
Long, E. Hudson. O. Henry; The Man and His Work.
Nolte, William H., Ed. H. L. Mencken's Smart Set Criticism.

Pattee, Fred Lewis. The Development of the American Short Story.

Letters

Davis, Robert H., and Arthur B. Maurice. The Caliph of Bagdad.

XAVIER HERBERT

Criticism-General

Heseltine, Harry P. Xavier Herbert.
Kiernan, Brian. Images of Society and Nature.

Criticism - Specific Works

Capricornia

Kiernan, Brian. Images of Society and Nature.

JOSEPH HERGESHEIMER

Criticism-General

Michaud, Regis. The American Novel Today.

ROBERT HERRICK

Criticism-General

Knight, Grant C. The Strenous Age in American Literature.
Nevins, Blake. Robert Herrick; The Development of a Novelist.
Wagenknecht, Edward. Cavalcade of the American Novel.

GRANVILLE HICKS

Criticism-General

Robbins, Jack Alan, Ed. Granville Hicks in the New Masses.

THOMAS WENTWORTH HIGGINSON

Criticism-General

Franklin, H. Bruce. Future Perfect; American Science Fiction of the Nineteenth Century.

CHESTER HIMES

Criticism-General

Gayle, Addison, Jr. The Way of the New World.
Lundquist, James. Chester Himes.

JOSIA GILBERT HOLLAND

Criticism-General

Cowie, Alexander. The Rise of the American Novel.

OLIVER WENDELL HOLMES

Criticism-General

Cowie, Alexander. The Rise of the American Novel.
Leary, Lewis, Ed. American Literary Essays.
Rubin, Louis D., Jr., Ed. The Comic

Imagination in American Literature.

HUGH HOOD

Criticism-General

Morley, Patricia A. The Comedians.

THOMAS HOOKER

Criticism-General

Gallagher, Edward Joseph. Early Puritan Writers.

PAULINE E. HOPKINS

Criticism-General

Gloster, Hugh M. Negro Voices in American Fiction.

FRANCIS HOPKINSON

Criticism-General

Hastings, George Everett. The Life and Works of Francis Hopkinson.

E. W. HOWE

Criticism-General

Martin, Jay. Harvests of Change; American Literature; 1865-1914.

I. HOWE

Criticism-General

Solotaroff, Theodore. The Red Hot Vacuum.

W. D. HOWELLS

Biographies

Brooks, Van Wyck. Howells; His Life and World.
Cady, Edwin H. William Dean Howells, Dean of American Letters.
Nordloh, David J., Ed. Years of My Youth, and Three Essays.
Kirk, Clara Marburg. W. D. Howells; Traveler from Altruria; 1889-1894.

Letters

Smith, Henry Nash, and William M. Gibson, Eds. Mark Twain-Howells Letters.

Criticism-General

Berthoff, Warner. The Ferment of Realism; American Literature; 1884-1919.
Bloomfield, Morton W., Ed. The Interpretation of Narrative; Theory and Practice.
Bowden, Edwin T. The Dungeon of the Heart.
Cady, Edwin H. The Light of Common Day.
Carter, Everett. Howells and the Age of Realism.
Cooley, Thomas. Educated Lives.

Cowie, Alexander. The Rise of the American Novel.
Crothers, George D., Ed. Invitation to Learning; English and American Novels.
Eakin, Paul John. The New England Girl.
Eble, Kenneth E., Ed. Howells; A Century of Criticism.
Falk, Robert. The Victorian Mode in American Fiction; 1865-1885.
Firkins, Oscar W. William Dean Howells; A Study.
Foster, Richard, Ed. Six American Novelists of the Nineteenth Century.
Gindin, James. Harvest of a Quiet Eye.
Harvey, Alexander. William Dean Howells.
Heiney, Donald. Recent American Literature.
Heiney, Donald. Recent American Literature to 1930.
Hough, Robert L. The Quiet Rebel.
Howells, W. D. Literary Friends and Acquaintance.
Howells, W. D. My Mark Twain; Reminiscences and Criticisms.
Hubbell, Jay B. Who Are the Major American Writers?
Hubbell, Jay B. Southern Life in Fiction.
Jones, Howard Mumford, and Richard M. Ludwig.
Martin, Jay. Harvests of Change.
Nolte, William H., Ed. H. L. Mencken's Smart Set Criticism.
Michaud, Regis. The American Novel Today.
Millgate, Michael. American Social Fiction.
Morgan, H. Wayne. American Writers in Rebellion.
Noble, David W. The Eternal Adam and the New World Garden.
Pizer, Donald. Realism and Naturalism in Nineteenth-Century American Literature.
Rahv, Philip. Literature in America.
Rees, Robert A., and Earl N. Harbert, Ed. Fifteen American Authors Before 1900.
Schneider, Robert W. Five Novelists of the Progressive Era.
Snell, George. The Shapers of American Fiction; 1798-1947.
Spiller, Robert E. The Cycle of American Literature.
Stegner, Wallace, Ed. The American Novel.
Taylor, Gordon O. The Passages of Thought.
Taylor, Walter Fuller. The Economic Novel in America.
Tuttleton, James W. The Novel of Manners in America.
Underwood, John Curtis. Literature and Insurgency.
Vanderbilt, Kermit. The Achievement of William Dean Howells.
Wright, Nathalia. American Novelists in Italy.

Criticism - Specific Works

The Rise of Silas Lapham

Bowden, Edwin T. The Dungeon of the Heart.
Crothers, George D., Ed. Invitation to Learning; English and American Novels.
Stegner, Wallace, Ed. The American Novel from James Fenimore Cooper to William Faulkner.

Reference Works

Bibliographies

Brenni, Vito J., Comp. William Dean Howells.
Eichelberger, Clayton L. Published Comment on William Dean Howells through 1920.

LANGSTON HUGHES

Biographies

Dickinson, Donald C. A Bio-Bibliography of Langston Hughes.

Criticism-General

Emanual, James A. Langston Hughes.
Gross, Seymour L., and John Edward Hardy, Eds. Images of the Negro in American Literature.
Littlejohn, David. Black on White; A Critical Survey of Writing By American Negroes.
O'Daniel, Therman B., Ed. Langston Hughes;Black Genius.

ZORA NEALE HURSTON

Criticism-General

Gloster, Hugh M. Negro Voices in American Fiction.

WASHINGTON IRVING

Biographies

Hellman, George S. Washington Irving Esquire.
Irving, Pierre Monroe. The Life and Letters of Washington Irving.
Johnston, Johanna. The Heart That Would Not Hold.
Myers, Andrew B. The Worlds of Washington Irving;1783-1859.
Sanderlin, George. Washington Irving as Others Saw Him.
Warner, Charles Dudley. Washington Irving.

Letters

Irving, Pierre M. The Life and Letters of Washington Irving. Volumes I, II, III, and IV.

Criticism-General

Bank, Stanley, Ed. American Romanticism;A Shape for Fiction.
Brooks, Van Wyck. The World of Washington Irving.
Hedges, William L. Washington Irving;An American Study;1802-1832.
Hoffman, Daniel. Form and Fable in American Fiction.
Leary, Lewis, Ed. American Literary Essays.
Lee, Robert Edson. From West to East.
Pattee, Fred Lewis. The Development of the American Short Story.
Paul, Sherman, Ed. Six Classic American Writers.
Rees, Robert A., and Earl N. Harbert, Ed. Fifteen American Authors Before 1900.
Rubin, Louis D., Jr. Ed. The Comic Imagination in American Literature.
Snell, George. The Shapers of American Fiction;1798-1947.
Spiller, Robert E. The Cycle of American Literature.
Spiller, Robert E., et al., Eds. Literary History of the United States.
Wagenknecht, Edward. Washington Irving;Moderation Displayed.
Warner, Charles Dudley, et al. Studies of Washington Irving.
Wright, Nathalia. American Novelists in Italy.
Young, Philip. Three Bags Full;Essays in American Fiction.

ISHERWOOD

Criticism - Specific Works

Legend of Sleepy Hollow

Hoffman, Daniel. Form and Fable in American Fiction.

Reference Works

Bibliographies

Langfeld, William R., and Philip C. Blackburn. Washington Irving.
Springer, Haskell S. Washington Irving; A Reference Guide.
Williams, Stanley T., and Mary Allen Edge, Eds. A Bibliography of the Writings of Washington Irving.

CHRISTOPHER ISHERWOOD

Criticism-General

Austen, Roger. Playing the Game; The Homosexual Novel in America.

SHIRLEY JACKSON

Criticism-General

Friedman, Lenemaja. Shirley Jackson.

Criticism - Specific Works

We Have Always Lived in the Castle

Parker, Dorothy. The Portable Dorothy Parker.

HENRY JAMES

Biographies

Anderson, Quentin. The American Henry James.
Canby, Henry Seidel. Turn West, Turn East; Mark Twain and Henry James.
Dupee, Frederick W. Henry James.
Edel, Leon. Henry James; The Conquest of London.
Edel, Leon. Henry James; The Master.
Edel, Leon. Henry James; The Middle Years.
Edel, Leon. Henry James; The Treacherous Years.
Edel, Leon. Henry James; The Untried Years.
Hyde, H. Montgomery. Henry James At Home.
James, Henry. The Middle Years.
James, Henry. Notes of a Son and Brother.
Kelley, Cornelia Pulsifer. The Early Development of Henry James.
LeClair, Robert C. Young Henry James; 1843-1870.
McCarthy, Harold T. Henry James; The Creative Process.
Matthiessen, F.O. Henry James; The Major Phase.
Moore, Harry T. Henry James.
West, Rebecca. Henry James.

Letters

Edel, Leon, Ed. Letters/Henry James.
James, Henry. Theatre and Friendship; Some Henry James Letters.

Criticism By

James, Henry. The Question of Our Speech; The Lesson of Balzac. Two Lectures.

Rahv, Philip, Ed. Literature in America.

Criticism-General

Andreas, Osborn. Henry James and the Expanding Horizon.
Auchincloss, Louis. Reading Henry James.
Banta, Martha. Henry James and the Occult.
Beach, Joseph Warren. The Method of Henry James.
Bell, Millicent. Edith Wharton and Henry James.
Berthoff, Warner. The Ferment of Realism.
Bewley, Marius. The Eccentric Design; Form in the Classic American Novel.
Bewley, Marius. Masks and Mirrors.
Blackmur, R. P. The Lion and the Honeycomb.
Bowden, Edwin T. The Dungeon of the Heart.
Bowden, Edwin T. The Themes of Henry James.
Briggs, Julia. Night Visitors.
Brooks, Peter. The Melodramatic Imagination.
Buitenhuis, Peter. The Grasping Imagination.
Buitenhuis, Peter, Ed. Twentieth Century Interpretations of The Portrait of a Lady.
Chase, Richard. The American Novel and Its Tradition.
Clair, John A. The Ironic Dimension in the Fiction of Henry James.
Cooley, Thomas. Educated Lives; The Rise of Modern Autobiography in America.
Cornwell, Ethel F. The Still Point.
Cowie, Alexander. The Rise of the American Novel.
Cox, C. B. The Free Spirit.
Cranfill, Thomas Mabry, and Robert Lanier Clark, Jr. An Anatomy of The Turn of the Screw.
Crews, Frederick C. The Tragedy of Manners.
Crothers, George D., Ed. Invitation to Learning; English and American Novels.
Eakin, Paul John. The New England Girl.
Edel, Leon, Ed. Henry James; A Collection of Critical Essays.
Edel, Leon, Ed. Henry James; The Future of the Novel.
Edgar, Pelham. Henry James; Man and Author.
Egan, Michael. Henry James; The Ibsen Years.
Falk, Robert. The Victorian Mode in American Fiction; 1865-1885.
Foster, Richard, Ed. Six American Novelists of the Nineteenth Century.
Gale, Robert L. The Caught Image.
Gale, Robert L. Plots and Characters in the Fiction of Henry James.
Gard, Roger, Ed. Henry James; The Critical Heritage.
Geismar, Maxwell. Henry James and the Jacobites.
Gindin, James. Harvest of a Quiet Eye.
Goode, John, Ed. The Air of Reality.
Graham, George Kenneth. Henry James; The Drama of Fulfillment; An Approach to the Novels.
Green, Martin. Re-Appraisals.
Grover, Philip. Henry James and the French Novel.
Halperin, John, Ed. The Theory of the the Novel; New Essays.
Hardy, Barbara. The Appropriate Form; An Essay on the Novel.
Hartley, L. P. The Novelist's Responsibility.
Heiney, Donald. Recent American Literature.
Heiney, Donald. Recent American Literature To 1930.

Hocks, Richard A. Henry James and Pragmatistic Thought.
Hoffmann, Charles G. The Short Novels of Henry James.
Hoffman, Michael J. The Subversive Vision; American Romanticism in Literature.
Holder, Alan. Three Voyagers in Search of Europe.
Holder-Barell, Alexander. The Development of Imagery and its Functional Significance in Henry James's Novels.
Holland, Laurence Bedwell. The Expense of Vision.
Howard, David, et al., Eds. Tradition and Tolerance in Nineteenth-Century Fiction.
Hubbell, Jay B. Southern Life in Fiction.
Hunking, Elizabeth Morse Walsh, Comp. The Picturesque English of Henry James.
Isle, Walter. Experiments in Form.
Jefferson, D. W. Henry James and the Modern Reader.
Jones, Granville M. Henry James's Psychology of Experience.
Knight, Grant C. The Strenuous Age in American Literature.
Kraft, James. The Early Tales of Henry James.
Krook, Dorothea. The Ordeal of Consciousness in Henry James.
Kuhlmann, Susan. Knave, Fool and Genius.
LaFrance, Marston, Ed. Patterns of Commitment in American Literature.
Langford, Richard E., et al., Eds. Essays in Modern American Literature.
Leary, Lewis, Ed. American Literary Essays.
Leavis, F. R. The Great Tradition.
Lebowitz, Naomi. The Imagination of Loving.
Lewis, Wyndham. Men Without Art.
Leyburn, Ellen Douglass. Strange Alloy.
McCarthy, Harold T. The Expatriate Perspective.
McElderry, Bruce R., Jr. Henry James.
Markow-Totevy, Georges. Henry James.
Maves, Carl. Sensuous Pessimism.
Michaud, Regis. The American Novel Today.
Millgate, Michael. American Social Fiction.
Mizener, Arthur. Twelve Great American Novels.
Moseley, James G. A Complex Inheritance.
Nettels, Elsa. James and Conrad.
Noble, David W. The Eternal Adam and the New World Garden.
O'Faolain, Sean. The Vanishing Hero.
O'Neill, John P. Workable Design.
Paterson, John. The Novel as Faith.
Pearce, Roy Harvey. Historicism Once More.
Peterson, Dale L. The Clement Vision.
Pirie, Gordon. Henry James.
Pizer, Donald. Realism and Naturalism in Nineteenth-Century American Literature.
Poirier, Richard. The Comic Sense of Henry James.
Poirier, Richard. A World Elsewhere.
Porte, Joel. The Romance in America.
Powers, Lyall H. Henry James and the Naturalist Movement.
Powers, Lyall H., Ed. Henry James's Major Novels; Essays in Criticism.
Putt, S. Gorley. Henry James; A Reader's Guide.
Rahv, Philip. Literature and the Sixth Sense.
Rahv, Philip. Literature in America.
Raleigh, John Henry. Time, Place, and Idea.

Rubin, Louis D., Jr., Ed. The Comic Imagination in American Literature.

Rubin, Louis D., Jr. Essays in American Literature.

Samuels, Charles Thomas. The Ambiguity of Henry James.

Schneider, Daniel J. Symbolism;The Manichean Vision.

Sears, Sallie. The Negative Imagination.

Segal, Ora. The Lucid Reflector.

Seward, William W., Jr. Contrasts in Modern Writers.

Shapiro, Charles, Ed. Twelve Original Essays on Great American Novels.

Sharp, Sister M. Corona. The Confidante in Henry James.

Shine, Muriel G. The Fictional Children of Henry James.

Snell, Edwin Marion. The Modern Fables of Henry James.

Snell, George. The Shapers of American Fiction;1798-1947.

Spender, Stephen. Love-Hate Relations;English and American Sensibilities.

Spiller, Robert E. The Cycle of American Literature.

Spiller, Robert E., et al., Eds. Literary History of the United States.

Stafford, William T. A Name, Title, and Place Index to the Critical Writings of Henry James.

Stafford, William T., Ed. Perspectives on James's The Portrait of a Lady.

Stallman, R. W. The Houses that James Built and Other Literary Studies.

Stanzel, Franz. Narrative Situations in the Novel.

Stegner, Wallace, Ed. The American Novel from James Fenimore Cooper to William Faulkner.

Stevenson, Elizabeth. The Crooked Corridor.

Stewart, Randall. George Core, Ed. Regionalism and Beyond;Essays of Randall Stewart.

Stone, Donald David. Novelists in a Changing World.

Stone, Edward. A Certain Morbidness;A View of American Literature.

Stone, Edward. The Battle and the Books;Some Aspects of Henry James.

Straumann, Heinrich. American Literature in the Twentieth Century.

Tanner, Tony. The Reign of Wonder.

Taylor, Gordon O. The Passages of Thought.

Tilley, W. H. The Background of The Princess Casamassima.

Tompkins, Jane P., Ed. Twentieth Century Interpretations of The Turn of the Screw and Other Tales.

Trilling, Lionel. The Liberal Imagination;Essays on Literature and Society.

Tuttleton, James W. The Novel of Manners in America.

Underwood, John Curtis. Literature and Insurgency.

Vaid, Krishna Baldev. Technique in the Tales of Henry James.

Van Nostrand, A. D. Everyman His Own Poet.

Veeder, William R. Henry James;The Lessons of the Master.

Wagenknecht, Edward. Cavalcade of the American Novel.

Wager, Willis. American Literature; A World View.

Wallace, Ronald. Henry James and the Comic Form.

Ward, J. A. The Imagination of Disaster.

Ward, J. A. The Search for Form.

Wegelin, Christof. The Image of Europe in Henry James.

Weinstein, Philip M. Henry James and the Requirements of the Imagination.

Wiesenfarth, Joseph. Henry James and the Dramatic Analogy.

Wiley, Margaret Lenore. Studies in American Literature.
Willen, Gerald, Ed. A Casebook on Henry James's The Turn of the Screw.
Wilson, Edmund. The Triple Thinkers.
Woodress, James, Ed. Eight American Authors.
Woolf, Virginia. Granite and Rainbow; Essays by Virginia Woolf.
Wright, Nathalia. American Novelists in Italy.
Wright, Walter F. The Madness of Art.

Criticism - Specific Works

The Ambassadors

Crothers, George D., Ed. Invitation to Learning; English and American Novels.
Mizener, Arthur. Twelve Great American Novels.
Shapiro, Charles, Ed. Twelve Original Essays on Great American Novels.
Stanzel, Franz. Translated by James P. Pusack. Narrative Situations in the Novel.
Stone, Albert E., Jr., Ed. Twentieth Century Interpretations of The Ambassadors.

Daisy Miller

Hoffman, Michael J. The Subversive Vision.

House of Mirth

Shapiro, Charles, Ed. Twelve Original Essays on Great American Novels.

The Portrait of a Lady

Bowden, Edwin T. The Dungeon of the Heart.
Buitenhuis, Peter, Ed. Twentieth Century Interpretations of The Portrait of a Lady.
Chase, Richard. The American Novel and Its Tradition.
Langford, Richard E., et al., Eds. Essays in Modern American Literature.
Leavis, F. R. The Great Tradition.
Stafford, William T., Ed. Perspectives on James's The Portrait of a Lady.
Stegner, Wallace, Ed. The American Novel.

The Princess Casamassima

Tilley, W. H. The Background of The Princess Casamassima.
Trilling, Lionel. The Liberal Imagination.

The Turn of the Screw

Briggs, Julia. Night Visitors; The Rise and Fall of the English Ghost Story.
Cranfill, Thomas Mabry, and Robert Lanier Clark, Jr. An Anatomy of The Turn of the Screw.
Halperin, John, Ed. The Theory of the Novel.
Tompkins, Jane P., Ed. Twentieth Century Interpretations of The Turn of the Screw and Other Tales.
Willen, Gerald, Ed. A Casebook on Henry James's The Turn of the Screw.

Reference Works

Bibliographies

Phillips, Le Roy. A Bibliography of

the Writings of Henry James.
Stafford, William T. A Name, Title, and Place Index to the Critical Writings of Henry James.

Dictionaries

Leeming, Glenda. Who's who in Henry James.

Quotations

Hunking, Elizabeth Morse Walsh, Comp. The Picturesque English of Henry James; A Collection of Quotations.

ROBINSON JEFFERS

Criticism-General

Heiney, Donald. Recent American Literature.

SARAH ORNE JEWETT

Criticism-General

Auchincloss, Louis. Pioneers and Caretakers.
Martin, Jay. Harvests of Change; American Literature; 1865-1914.
Wagenknecht, Edward. Cavalcade of the American Novel.

MARY JOHNSTON

Criticism-General

Wagenknecht, Edward. Cavalcade of the American Novel.

LE ROI JONES

Criticism-General

Baker, Houston A., Jr. Black Literature in America.
Hudson, Theodore R. From LeRoi Jones to Amiri Baraka; The Literary Works.
Margolies, Edward. Native Sons; A Critical Study of Twentieth-Century Negro American Authors.

HENRY KENDALL

Criticism-General

Wilde, William Henry. Henry Kendall.

JACK KEROUAC

Criticism-General

Cassady, Carolyn. Heart Beat; My Life with Jack and Neal.
Charters, Ann. Kerouac.
Feied, Frederick. No Pie in the Sky.
Frohock, W. M. Strangers to this Ground.
Hipkiss, Robert A. Jack Kerouac; Prophet of the New Romanticism.
Krim, Seymour. Shake it for the World, Smartass.
Langford, Richard E., et al., Eds. Essays in Modern American Literature.
Parker, Dorothy. The Portable Dorothy Parker.
Tytell, John. Naked Angels; The Lives and Literature of the Beat Generation.

Waldmeir, Joseph J., Ed. Recent American Fiction.

Criticism - Specific Works

On The Road

Tytell, John. Naked Angels; The Lives and Literature of the Beat Generation.

The Subterraneans

Parker, Dorothy. The Portable Dorothy Parker.

KEN KESEY

Criticism-General

Hipkiss, Robert A. Jack Kerouac; Prophet of the New Romanticism.

HENRY KINGSLEY

Criticism - Specific Works

The Recollections

Argyle, Barry. An Introduction to the Australian Novel; 1830-1930.

JOHN KNOWLES

Criticism-General

Hipkiss, Robert A. Jack Kerouac; Prophet of the New Romanticism.

RING LARDNER

Criticism-General

Geismar, Maxwell. Writers in Crisis.
Parker, Dorothy. The Portable Dorothy Parker.
Rahv, Philip. Literature in America.

Criticism - Specific Works

Round Up

Parker, Dorothy. The Portable Dorothy Parker.

NELLA LARSEN

Criticism-General

Gloster, Hugh M. Negro Voices in American Fiction.

T. E. LAWRENCE

Criticism-General

Blackmur, R.P. The Lion and the Honeycomb.

STEPHEN LEACOCK

Criticism-General

Bowker, Alan, Ed. The Social Criticism of Stephen Leacock.

JAMES LEIGH

Criticism-General

Tooker, Dan. Fiction!Interviews with Northern California Novelists.

DORIS LESSING

Criticism-General

Rose, Ellen Cronan. The Tree Outside the Window.

JANET LEWIS

Criticism-General

Tooker, Dan. Fiction!Interviews with Northern California Novelists.

SINCLAIR LEWIS

Biographies

Lundquist, James. Sinclair Lewis.
Van Doren, Carl. Sinclair Lewis.

Criticism-General

Bewley, Marius. Masks and Mirrors.
Blake, Nelson Manfred. Novelists' America.
Brown, John Russell. The American Novel and the Nineteen Twenties.
Churchill, Allen. The Literary Decade.
Cohen, Hennig, Ed. Landmarks of American Writing.
Cowley, Malcolm, Ed. After the Genteel Tradition.
Crothers, George D., Ed. Invitation to Learning;English and American Novels.
French, Warren G., and Walter E. Kidd, Eds. American Winners of the Nobel Literary Prize.
Geismar, Maxwell. The Last of the Provincials.
Grebstein, Sheldon Norman. Sinclair Lewis.
Griffin, Robert J., Ed. Twentieth Century Interpretations of Arrowsmith.
Heiney, Donald. Recent American Literature.
Heiney, Donald. Recent American Literature To 1930.
Hilfer, Anthony Channell. The Revolt from the Village;1915-1930.
Kazin, Alfred. On Native Grounds.
Ketterer, David. New Worlds for Old.
Light, Martin, Comp. The Merrill Studies in Babbitt.
Light, Martin. The Quixotic Vision of Sinclair Lewis.
Michaud, Regis. The American Novel Today.
Millgate, Michael. American Social Fiction.
Nolte, William H., Ed. H. L. Mencken's Smart Set Criticism.
O'Connor, William Van, Ed. Seven Modern American Novelists.
Parker, Dorothy. The Portable Dorothy Parker.
Schorer, Mark. Sinclair Lewis;An American Life.
Schorer, Mark, Ed. Sinclair Lewis; A Collection of Critical Essays.
Schulberg, Budd. The Four Seasons of Success.
Seward, William W., Jr. Contrasts in Modern Writers.
Sherman, Stuart P. The Significance of Sinclair Lewis.
Slosser, George Edgar. The Farthest Shores of Ursula K. LeGuin.
Stegner, Wallace, Ed. The American Novel.

LOCKRIDGE

Straumann, Heinrich. American Literature in the Twentieth Century.

Tuttleton, James W. The Novel of Manners in America.

Westbrook, Max, Ed. The Modern American Novel.

Criticism - Specific Works

Arrowsmith

Griffin, Robert J., Ed. Twentieth Century Interpretations of Arrowsmith.

Babbitt

Light, Martin, Comp. The Merrill Studies in Babbitt.

Schorer, Mark, Ed. Sinclair Lewis.

Main Street

Crothers, George D., Ed. Invitation to Learning; English and American Novels.

Schorer, Mark, Ed. Sinclair Lewis.

Stegner, Wallace, Ed. The American Novel from James Fenimore Cooper to William Faulkner.

The Man Who Knew Coolidge

Parker, Dorothy. The Portable Dorothy Parker.

ROSS LOCKRIDGE

Criticism-General

Leggett, John. Ross and Tom; Two American Tragedies.

JACK LONDON

Biographies

Hendricks, King, and Irving Shepard, Eds. Letters from Jack London.

London, Joan. Jack London and His Times.

Criticism-General

Berthoff, Warner. The Ferment of Realism.

Feied, Frederick. No Pie in the Sky.

Franchere, Ruth. Jack London; The Pursuit of a Dream.

Geismar, Maxwell. Rebels and Ancestore; The American Novel; 1890-1915.

Heiney, Donald. Recent American Literature To 1930.

Knight, Grant C. The Strenuous Age in American Literature.

Labor, Earle. Jack London.

McClintock, James I. White Logic.

Martin, Jay. Harvests of Change; American Literature; 1865-1914.

Stegner, Wallace, Ed. The American Novel from James Fenimore Cooper to William Faulkner.

Wagenknecht, Edward. Cavalcade of the American Novel.

Walcutt, Charles Child. American Literary Naturalism; A Divided Stream.

Walker, Franklin. Jack London and The Klondike.

Criticism - Specific Works

Martin Eden

Stegner, Wallace, Ed. The American Novel from James Fenimore Cooper to William Faulkner.

The Short Cut

Geismar, Maxwell. Rebels and Ancestors.

Reference Works

Bibliographies

Walker, Dale L., Comp. The Fiction of Jack London;A Chronological Bibliography.
Woodbridge, Hensley C., and John London, George H. Tweney, Comp. Jack London;A Bibliography.

HOWARD P. LOVECRAFT

Biographies

DeCamp, Lyon Sprague. Lovecraft; A Biography.
Derleth, August William. Some Notes on H.P. Lovecraft.
Long, Frank Belknap. Howard Philips Lovecraft;Dreamer on the Nightside.

Letters

Derleth, August, and Donald Wandrei, Eds. H.P. Lovecraft;Selected Letters;1929-1931.

Reference Works

Bibliographies

Owings, Mark. The Revised H.P. Lovecraft Bibliography.

JAMES RUSSELL LOWELL

Criticism-General

Howells, W.D. Literary Friends and Acquaintance.
Pattee, Fred Lewis. The Development of the American Short Story.
Rahv, Philip. Literature in America.

MALCOLM LOWRY

Criticism - Specific Works

Under The Volcano

French, Warren, Ed. The Forties; Fiction, Poetry, Drama.

ROBERT MCALMON

Criticism-General

Austen, Roger. Playing the Game.
Michaud, Regis. The American Novel Today.

MARY MCCARTHY

Biographies

Grumbach, Doris. The Company She Kept.
McCarthy, Mary. Memories of a Catholic Girlhood.

Criticism-General

Auchincloss, Louis. Pioneers and Caretakers.

Balakian, Nona, and Charles Simmons, Eds. The Creative Present.
French, Warren, Ed. The Fifties; Fiction, Poetry, Drama.
Podhoretz, Norman. Doings and Undoings.
Proffer, Carl R., Ed./Translator. Soviet Criticism of American Literature in the Sixties.
Seward, William W., Jr. Contrasts in Modern Writers.

Reference Works

Bibliographies

Goldman, Sherli Evens. Mary McCarthy; A Bibliography.

CARSON MCCULLERS

Biographies

Cook, Richard M. Carson McCullers.

Criticism-General

Auchincloss, Louis. Pioneers and Caretakers; A Study of 9 American Women Novelists.
Balakian, Nona, and Charles Simmons, Eds. The Creative Present.
Gossett, Louise Y. Violence in Recent Southern Fiction.
Hassan, Ihab. Radical Innocence; Studies in the Contemporary American Novel.
McNeir, Waldo, and Leo B. Levy, Eds. Studies in American Literature.
Proffer, Carl R., Ed./Translator. Soviet Criticism of American Literature in the Sixties.
Schorer, Mark. The World We Imagine.

Waldmeir, Joseph J., Ed. Recent American Fiction; Some Critical Views.

Criticism - Specific Works

The Heart is a Lonely Hunter

McNeir, Waldo, and Leo B. Levy, Eds. Studies in American Literature.

Reference Works

Bibliographies

Kiernan, Robert F. Katherine Anne Porter and Carson McCullers; A Reference Guide.

JOHN D. MACDONALD

Criticism-General

Campbell, Frank D. John D. MacDonald and the Colorful World of Travic McGee.

CLAUDE MCKAY

Criticism-General

Margolies, Edward. Native Sons; A Critical Study of Twentieth-Century Negro American Authors.

NORMAN MAILER

Biographies

Lucid, Robert F. Norman Mailer; The Man and His Work.

Criticism By

Mailer, Norman. Existential Errands.

Criticism-General

Aldridge, John W., Ed. After the Lost Generation.
Balakian, Nona, and Charles Simmons, Ed. The Creative Present.
Braudy, Leo, Ed. Norman Mailer; A Collection of Critical Essays.
Fiedler, Leslie. The Collected Essays of Leslie Fiedler.
French, Warren, Ed. The Fifties; Fiction, Poetry, Drama.
Gayle, Addison, Jr. The Way of the New World; The Black Novel in America.
Gilman, Richard. The Confusion of Realms.
Harper, Howard M., Jr. Desperate Faith.
Hassan, Ihab. Contemporary American Literature; 1945-1972.
Hassan, Ihab. Radical Innocence.
Heiney, Donald. Recent American Literature.
Hicks, Granville, and Jack Alan Robbins. Literary Horizons; A Quarter of American Fiction.
Kartiganer, Donald M., and Malcolm A. Griffith. Theories of American Literature.
Kaufmann, Donald L. Normal Mailer; The Countdown.
Kazin, Alfred. Bright Book of Life.
Krim, Seymour. Shake it for the World, Smartass.
Leeds, Barry H. The Structured Vision of Norman Mailer.
Lehan, Richard. A Dangerous Crossing.
Lucid, Robert F. Norman Mailer; The Man and His Work.
McCormack, Thomas, Ed. Afterwords Novelists on Their Novels.
Millett, Kate. Sexual Politics.
Noble, David W. The Eternal Adam and the New World Garden.
Podhoretz, Norman. Doings and Undoings.
Proffer, Carl R., Ed./Translator; Soviet Criticism of American Literature.
Rahv, Philip. Literature and the Sixth Sense.
Schulz, Max F. Radical Sophistication.
Scott, Nathan A., Jr., Ed. Adversity and Grace.
Solotaroff, Robert. Down Mailer's Way.
Trilling, Diana. Claremont Essays.
Waldmeir, Joseph, Ed. Recent American Fiction; Some Critical Views.
Weatherby, William J. Squaring Off; Mailer versus Baldwin.
Weinberg, Helen. The New Novel in America.

Criticism - Specific Works

Advertisements for Myself

French, Warren, Ed. The Fifties; Fiction, Poetry, Drama.

Reference Works

Bibliographies

Adams, Laura, Comp. Norman Mailer; A Comprehensive Bibliography.

BERNARD MALAMUD

Biographies

Richman, Sidney. Bernard Malamud.

Criticism-General

Astro, Richard, Ed. The Fiction of Bernard Malamud.
Balakian, Nona, and Charles Simmons, Eds. The Creative Present.
Baumbach, Jonathan. The Landscape of Nightmare; Studies in the Contemporary American Novel.
Field, Leslie A., and Joyce W. Field. Bernard Malamud and the Critics.
Field, Leslie A., Comp. Bernard Malamud; A Collection of Critical Essays.
French, Warren, Ed. The Fifties; Fiction, Poetry, Drama.
Handy, William J. Modern Fiction; A Formalist Approach.
Hassan, Ihab. Contemporary American Literature; 1945-1972.
Hassan, Ihab. Radical Innocence.
Hicks, Granville, and Jack Alan Robbins. Literary Horizons; A Quarter Century of American Fiction.
Kegan, Robert. The Sweeter Welcome; Voices for a Vision of Affirmation.
Malin, Irving, Ed. Contemporary American-Jewish Literature.
Rahv, Philip. Literature and the Sixth Sense.
Ruotolo, Lucio P. Six Existential Heroes; The Politics of Faith.
Schulz, Max F. Radical Sophistication; Studies in Contemporary Jewish-American Novelists.
Solotaroff, Theodore. The Red Hot Vacuum.
Waldmeir, Joseph J., Ed. Recent American Fiction; Some Critical Views.

Criticism - Specific Works

The Fixer

Handy, William J. Modern Fiction; A Formalist Approach.

JANE MANDER

Criticism-General

Turner, Dorothea. Jane Mander.

JOHN P. MARQUAND

Criticism-General

Beach, Joseph Warren. American Fiction; 1920-1940.
Heiney, Donald. Recent American Literature.
Miller, Wayne Charles. An Armed America; Its Face in Fiction.

Criticism - Specific Works

The Late George Apply

Beach, Joseph Warren. American Fiction; 1920-1940.

Wickfor Point

Beach, Joseph Warren. American Fiction; 1920-1940.

EDGAR LEE MASTERS

Biographies

Masters, Edgar Lee. Across Spoon River.

RICHARD MATHER

Criticism-General

Gallagher, Edward Joseph. Early Puritan Writers.

BRANDER MATHEWS

Criticism-General

Hubbell, Jay B. Who Are the Major American Writers?

HERMAN MELVILLE

Biographies

Allen, Gay Wilson. Melville and His World.
Anderson, Charles R. Melville in the South Seas.
Arvin, Newton. Herman Melville; A Critical Biography.
Howard, Leon. Herman Melville.
Humphreys, A. R. Herman Melville.
Leyda, Jay. The Melville Log; Vol. One.
Leyda, Jay. The Melville Log; Vol. Two.
Miller, Edwin Haviland. Melville.
Sealts, Merton M., Jr. Melville as Lecturer.
Sealts, Merton M., Comp. The Early Lives of Melville.
Weaver, Raymond M. Herman Melville; Mariner and Mystic.
Vincent, Howard P., Ed. Melville and Hawthorne in the Berkshires.

Letters

Davis, Merrell R., and William H. Gilman, Eds. The Letters of Herman Melville.
Minnigerode, Meade. Some Personal Letters of Herman Melville.

Criticism-General

Anderson, Charles R. Melville in the South Seas.

Bank, Stanley, Ed. American Romanticism.
Bernstein, John. Pacifism and Rebellion in the Writings of Herman Melville.
Berthoff, Warner. Fictions and Events.
Berthoff, Warner. The Example of Melville.
Bewley, Marius. The Eccentric Design.
Bickley, Robert Bruce. The Method of Melville's Short Fiction.
Blackmur, R. P. The Lion and the Honeycomb.
Bowden, Edwin T. The Dungeon of the Heart.
Bowen, Merlin. The Long Encounter.
Branch, Watson Galley, Comp. Melville, the Critical Heritage.
Braswell, William. Melville's Religious Thought.
Brodhead, Richard H. Hawthorne, Melville and the Novel.
Brodtkorb, Paul, Jr. Ishmael's White World.
Browne, Ray B. Melville's Drive to Humanism.
Chase, Richard. The American Novel and Its Tradition.
Chase, Richard, Ed. Melville; A Collection of Critical Essays.
Chase, Richard. Herman Melville; A Critical Study.
Cohen, Hennig, Ed. Landmarks of American Writing.
Cowie, Alexander. The Rise of the American Novel.
Crothers, George D., Ed. Invitation to Learning; English and American Novels.
Davis, Merrell R. Melville's Mardi.
Dillingham, William B. An Artist in the Rigging.
Douglas, Ann. The Feminization of American Culture.

Flibbert, Joseph. Melville and the Art of Burlesque.
Fogle, Richard Harter. Melville's Shorter Tales.
Foster, Richard, Ed. Six American Novelists of the Nineteenth Century.
Franklin, H. Bruce. Future Perfect.
Franklin, H. Bruce. The Wake of the Gods.
Freeman, John. Herman Melville.
Friedman, Maurice. Problematic Rebel; Melville, Dostoievsky, Kafka, Camus.
Geist, Stanley. Herman Melville.
Gleim, William S. The Meaning of Moby Dick.
Green, Martin. Re-Appraisals; Some Commonsense Readings in American Literature.
Grejda, Edward S. The Joy of the Snow.
Grejda, Edward S. The Common Continent of Men.
Gross, Theodore L. Hawthorne, Melville, Stephen Crane.
Gross, Seymour L. Images of the Negro in American Literature.
Guetti, James. The Limits of Metaphor.
Hauck, Richard Boyd. A Cheerful Nihilism.
Hayford, Harrison, and Hershel Parker, Eds. Herman Melville; Moby-Dick.
Herbert, Thomas Walter. Moby Dick and Calvinism.
Hetherington, Hugh W. Melville's Reviewers; British and American.
Hillway, Tyrus. Herman Melville.
Hillway, Tyrus, and Luther S. Mansfield. Moby-Dick; Centennial Essays.
Hoffman, Daniel. Form and Fable in American Fiction.
Kaul, A. N. The American Vision.
Kazin, Alfred, Ed. The Open Form.
LaFrance, Marston, Ed. Patterns of
Langford, Richard E., et al., Eds. Essays in Modern American Literature.
Lawrence, D. H. Studies in Classic American Literature.
Lebowitz, Alan. Progress Into Silence; A Study of Melville's Heroes.
Levin, Harry. The Power of Blackness.
Lewis, R. W. B. Trials of the Word.
McCarthy, Harold T. The Expatriate Perspective.
McNeir, Waldo, and Leo B. Levy, Eds. Studies in American Literature.
Mason, Ronald. The Spirit Above the Dust.
Maxwell, D. E. S. Herman Melville.
May, John R. Toward a New Earth; Apocalypse in the American Novel.
Miller, James E., Jr. A Reader's Guide to Herman Melville.
Miller, Wayne Charles. An Armed America; Its Face in Fiction.
Mills, Nicolaus. American and English Fiction in the Nineteenth Century.
Mizener, Arthur. Twelve Great American Novels.
Moore, Maxine. The Lonely Game.
Morris, Wright. The Territory Ahead.
Nnolim, Charles E. Melville's Benito Cereno.
Noble, David W. The Eternal Adam and the New World Garden.
Parker, Hershell, Ed. The Recognition of Herman Melville.
Percival. M. O. A Reading of Moby Dick.
Pops, Martin Leonard. The Melville Archetype.
Porte, Joel. The Romance in America.
Rubin, Louis D., Jr., Ed. The Comic Imagination in American Literature.
Ricks, Beatrice. Herman Melville.

Sedgwick, William Ellery. Herman Melville; The Tragedy of Mind.
Seelye, John. Melville; The Ironic Diagram.
Seltzer, Leon F. The Vision of Melville and Conrad.
Shapiro, Charles, Ed. Twelve Original Essays.
Snell, George. The Shapers of American Fiction; 1798-1947.
Solomon, Pearl Chester. Dickens and Melville in Their Time.
Spiller, Robert E. The Cycle of American Literature.
Spiller, Robert E., et al. Four Makers of the American Mind; Emerson, Thoreau, Whitman, and Melville.
Spiller, Robert E., et al., Eds. Literary History of the United States.
Springer, Haskell S., Comp. The Merrill Studies in Billy Budd.
Stafford, William T., Ed. Melville's Billy Budd and the Critics.
Stanzel, Franz. Narrative Situations in the Novel.
Stegner, Wallace, Ed. The American Novel from James Fenimore Cooper to William Faulkner.
Stern, Milton R., Ed. Discussions of Moby-Dick.
Stern, Milton R. The Fine Hammered Steel of Herman Melville.
Stewart, Randall. George Core, Ed. Regionalism and Beyond; Essays of Randall Stewart.
Stone, Edward. A Certain Morbidness; A View of American Literature.
Sweeney, Gerard M. Melville's Use of Classical Mythology.
Swigg, Richard. Lawrence, Hardy, and American Literature.
Thompson, Lawrance. Melville's Quarrel with God.
Van Nostrand, A. D. Everyman His Own Poet.
Vickery, John B., Ed. Myth and Literature.
Vincent, Howard P., Ed. Bartleby the Scrivener.
Vincent, Howard P., Ed. Melville and Hawthorne in the Berkshires.
Vincent, Howard P., Comp. The Merrill Studies in Moby-Dick.
Vincent, Howard P. The Trying-Out of Moby-Dick.
Vincent, Howard P., Ed. Twentieth Century Interpretations of Billy Budd.
Walker, Franklin Dickerson. Irreverent Pilgrims.
Walker, William E., and Robert L. Welker, Eds. Reality and Myth.
Widmer, Kingsley. The Ways of Nihilism.
Wiley, Margaret Lenore. Studies in American Literature.
Woodress, James, Ed. Eight American Authors.
Young, Philip. Three Bags Full.
Zoellner, Robert. The Salt-Sea Mastodon.

Criticism-Specific Works

Billy Budd

Chase, Richard. The American Novel and its Tradition.
Chase, Richard, Ed. Melville; A Collection of Critical Essays.
Hauck, Richard Boyd. A Cheerful Nihilism.
Springer, Haskell S., Comp. The Merrill Studies in Billy Budd.
Stafford, William T., Ed. Melville's Billy Budd and the Critics.
Vincent, Howard P., Ed. Twentieth Century Interpretations of Billy Budd.

The Confidence Man

Berthoff, Warner. Fictions and Events.
Hoffman, Daniel. Form and Fable in American Fiction.

Lewis, R.W.B. Trials of the Word.
Parker, Hershel, Ed. The Confidence Man; His Masquerade.

Israel Potter

Rampersad, Arnold. Melville's Israel Potter; A Pilgrimage and Progress.

Mardi

Davis, Merrell R. Melville's Mardi.

Moby Dick

Bowden, Edwin T. The Dungeon of the Heart.
Brodtkorb, Paul, Jr. Ishmael's White World.
Chase, Richard. The American Novel and its Tradition.
Chase, Richard, Ed. Melville; A Collection of Critical Essays.
Crothers, George D., Ed. Invitation to Learning; English and American Novels.
Gleim, William S. The Meaning of Moby Dick.
Guetti, James. The Limits of Metaphor.
Hayford, Harrison. Moby Dick; An Authoritative Text.
Herbert, Thomas Walter. Moby Dick and Calvinism.
Hillway, Tyrus, and Luther S. Mansfield, Ed. Moby-Dick; Centennial Essays.
Hoffman, Daniel. Form and Fable in American Fiction.
Kazin, Alfred, Ed. The Open Form.
Lawrence, D.H. Studies in Classic American Literature.
Percival, M.O. A Reading of Moby-Dick.
Shapiro, Charles, Ed. Twelve Original Essays on Great American Novels.
Stanzel, Franz. Narrative Situations in the Novel.
Stegner, Wallace, Ed. The American Novel from James Fenimore Cooper to William Faulkner.
Stern, Milton R., Ed. Discussions of Moby-Dick.
Swigg, Richard. Lawrence, Hardy and American Literature.
Van Nostrand, A.D. Everyman His Own Poet.
Vincent, Howard P., Ed. Melville and Hawthorne in the Berkshires.
Vincent, Howard P., Comp. The Merrill Studies in Moby-Dick.
Vincent, Howard P. The Trying-Out of Moby-Dick.
Zoellner, Robert. The Salt-Sea Mastodon.

Omoo

Lawrence, D.H. Studies in Classic American Literature.

Typee

Lawrence, D.H. Studies in Classic American Literature.

Reference Works

Bibliographies

Minnigerode, Meade. Some Personal Letters of Herman Melville and a Bibliography.
Myerson, Joel, and Arthur H. Miller, Jr. Melville Dissertations.
Parker, Hershel, Ed. Herman Melville; The Confidence-Man; His Masquerade.
Sealts, Merton M., Jr. Melville's Reading; A Check-List of Books Owned and Borrowed.

H. L. MENCKEN

Biographies

Goldberg, Isaac. The Man Mencken.
Mayfield, Sara. The Constant Circle.
Stenerson, Douglas C. H. L. Mencken; Iconoclast From Baltimore.

Letters

Bode, Carl, Ed. The New Mencken Letters.

Criticism-General

Angoff, Charles. The Tone of the Twenties and Other Essays.
Churchill, Allen. The Literary Decade.
Cohen, Hennig, Ed. Landmarks of American Writing.
Cowley, Malcolm, Ed. After the Genteel Tradition.
Cowley, Malcolm. Henry Dan Piper, Ed. Think Back On Us;A Contemporary Chronicle of the 1930's by Malcolm Cowley.
Geismar, Maxwell. The Last of the Provincials.
Hilfer, Anthony Channell. The Revolt from the Village;1915-1930.
Hobson, Fred C. The Serpent in Eden;H.L.Mencken and the South.
Hubbell, Jay B. Who Are the Major American Writers?
Rahv, Philip. Literature in America.
Rubin, Louis D., Jr., Ed. The Comic Imagination in American Literature.
Rubin, Louis D., Jr. Essays in American Literature.
Straumann, Heinrich. American Literature in the Twentieth Century.

HENRY MILLER

Biographies

Belmont, Georges. Henry Miller in Conversation.
Snyder, Robert. This is Henry, Henry Miller from Brooklyn.

Letters

Fowlie, Wallace, and Henry Miller. Letters of Henry Miller and Wallace Fowlie;1943-1972.
Gordon, William A., Writer and Critic.
Stuhlmann, Gunther, Ed. Henry Miller Letters to Anais Nin.
Wickes, George, Ed. Lawrence Durrell/Henry Miller;A Private Correspondence.

Criticism By

Miller, Henry. The Books in My Life.
Miller, Henry. Henry Miller on Writing.
Miller, Henry. Reflections on the Death of Mishima.
Miller, Henry. Sunday After the War.
Miller, Henry. The Wisdom of the Heart.

Criticism-General

Gordon, William A. The Mind and Art of Henry Miller.
Hassan,Ihab. The Literature of Silence;Henry Miller and Samuel Beckett.
Heiney, Donald. Recent American Literature.
McCarthy, Harold T. The Expatriate Perspective.

Mailer, Norman. Existential Errands.
Millett, Kate. Sexual Politics.
Mitchell, Edward, Ed. Henry Miller; Three Decades of Criticism.
Pattee, Fred Lewis. A History of American Literature Since 1870.
Proffer, Carl R., Ed./Translator. Soviet Criticism of American Literature in the Sixties.
Rahv, Philip. Literature and the Sixth Sense.
Scward, William W., Jr. Contrasts in Modern Writers.
Solotaroff, Theodore. The Red Hot Vacuum.
Straumann, Heinrich. American Literature in the Twentieth Century.
Wickes, George, Ed. Henry Miller and the Critics.
Widmer, Kingsley. Henry Miller.
Whitbread, Thomas B., Ed. Seven Contemporary Authors.

MARGARET MITCHELL

Biographies

Farr, Finis. Margaret Mitchell of Atlanta.

Letters

Harwell, Richard, Ed. Margaret Mitchell's Gone with the Wind Letters.

Criticism-General

Straumann, Heinrich. American Literature in the Twentieth Century.
Wagenknecht, Edward. Cavalcade of the American Novel.

CHRISTOPHER MORLEY

Biographies

Wallach, Mark I., and Jon Bracker. Christopher Morley.

Criticism-General

Churchill, Allen. The Literary Decade.

Reference Works

Bibliographies

Lee, Alfred Pyle. A Bibliography of Christopher Morley.

WRIGHT MORRIS

Criticism-General

Baumbach, Jonathan. The Landscape of Nightmare.
Hassan, Ihab. Contemporary American Literature; 1945-1972.
Hicks, Granville. Literary Horizons.
McCormack, Thomas, Ed. Afterwords; Novelists on Their Novels.
Wager, Willis. American Literature; A World View.

Criticism - Specific Works

One Day

McCormack, Thomas, Ed. Afterwords; Novelists on Their Novels.

IRIS MURDOCH

Criticism-General

Berthoff, Warner. Fictions and Events.
Hall, James. The Lunatic Giant in the Drawing Room;The British and American Novel.

Reference Works

Bibliographies

Tominaga, Thomas T. Iris Murdoch and Muriel Spark;A Bibliography.

VLADIMIR NABOKOV

Biographies

Bruss, Elizabeth W. Autobiographical Acts.

Criticism By

Nabokov, Vladimir. Strong Opinions.

Criticism-General

Adams, Maurianne, Ed. Autobiography. The Bobbs-Merrill Series in Composition and Rhetoric.
Appell, Alfred. Nabokov's Dark Cinema.
Evans, J. Martin. America;The View from Europe.
Fowler, Douglas. Reading Nabokov.
Hicks, Granville, and Jack Alan Robbins.
Hunter, James. B. F. Skinner and Contemporary Literature.
Lee, Lawrence L. Vladimir Nabokov.
Mason, Bobbie Ann. Nabokov's Garden;a Guide to Ada.
Nelson, Gerald B. Ten Versions of America.
Norton, Donald E. Vladimir Nabokov.
Seward, William W., Jr. Contrasts in Modern Writers.
Stark, John O. The Literature of Exhaustion.
Updike, John. Assorted Prose.
Wilson, Edmund. Classics and Commercials.

Criticism - Specific Works

Ada

Mason, Bobbie A. Nabokov's Garden;A Study of Ada.

Lolita

Hunter, James. B. F. Skinner and Contemporary Literature;An Analysis of Lolita.

Reference Works

Bibliographies

Field, Andrew. Nabokov;A Bibliography.

BLAKE NEVIUS

Reference Works

Bibliographies

Nevius, Blake. The American Novel; Sinclair Lewis to the Present.

REINHOLD NIEBUHR

Criticism-General

Straumann, Heinrich. American Literature in the Twentieth Century.

ANAIS NIN

Letters

Stuhlmann, Gunther, Ed. Henry Miller Letters to Anais Nin.

Criticism By

Nin, Anais. The Novel of the Future.

Reference Works

Bibliographies

Franklin, Benjamin. Anais Nin; A Bibliography.

BENJAMIN FRANKLIN NORRIS

See Frank Norris.

FRANK NORRIS

Biographies

Gaer, Joseph. Frank Norris.

Criticism By

Norris, Frank. The Responsibilities of the Novelist and Other Literary Essays.
Pizer, Donald, Ed. The Literary Criticism of Frank Norris.

Criticism-General

Ahnebrink, Lars. The Beginnings of Naturalism in American Fiction.
Berthoff, Warner. The Ferment of Realism.
Geismar, Maxwell. Rebels and Ancestors.
Heiney, Donald. Recent American Literature.
Heiney, Donald. Recent American Literature To 1930.
Knight, Grant C. The Strenuous Age in American Literature.
Leary, Lewis, Ed. American Literary Essays.
Lutwack, Leonard. Heroic Fiction.
Martin, Jay. Harvests of Change; American Literature; 1865-1914.
Millgate, Michael. American Social Fiction.
Morgan, H. Wayne. American Writers in Rebellion.
Noble, David W. The Eternal Adam and the New World Garden.
Pizer, Donald. Realism and Naturalism; in Nineteenth-Century American Literature.
Rees, Robert A., and Earl N. Harbert, Eds. Fifteen American Authors Before 1900.
Schneider, Robert W. Five Novelists of the Progressive Era.
Snell, George. The Shapers of American Fiction; 1798-1947.
Stegner, Wallace, Ed. The American Novel from James Fenimore Cooper to William Faulkner.
Taylor, Gordon O. The Passages of Thought.
Taylor, Walter Fuller. The Economic Novel in America.

Underwood, John Curtis. Literature and Insurgency;Ten Studies in Racial Evolution.
Walcutt, Charles Child. American Literary Naturalis;a Divided Stream.

Criticism - Specific Works

And The Brute

Geismar, Maxwell. Rebels and Ancestors.

McTeague:A Story of San Francisco

Stegner, Wallace, Ed. The American Novel from James Fenimore Cooper to William Faulkner.

The Octupus

Lutwack, Leonard. Heroic Fiction.

Reference Works

Bibliographies

Crisler, Jesse E., and Joseph R. McElrath, Jr. Frank Norris;A Reference Guide.

JOYCE CAROL OATES

Criticism By

Oates, Joyce Carol. New Heaven;New Earth;The Visionary Experience in Literature.

Criticism-General

Kazin, Alfred. Bright Book of Life.

FLANNERY O'CONNOR

Criticism-General

Baumbach, Jonathan. The Landscape of Nightmare.
French, Warren, Ed. The Fifties;Fiction, Poetry, Drama.
Friedman, Melvin J., and Lewis A. Lawson. The Added Dimension.
Gossett, Louise Y. Violence in Recent Southern Fiction.
Hicks, Granville, and Jack Alan Robbins. Literary Horizons
Hoyt, Charles Alva. Minor American Novelists.
McFarland, Dorothy Tuck. Flannery O'Connor.
May, John R. Toward a New Earth.
Rubin, Louis D., Jr., Ed. The Comic Imagination in American Literature.
Rubin, Louis D., Jr. Essays in American Literature.
Scott, Nathan A., Jr., Ed. Adversity and Grace.
Stephens, Martha. The Question of Flannery O'Connor.
Sullivan, Walter. Death by Melancholy.
Waldmeir, Joseph J., Ed. Recent American Fiction.

Criticism - Specific Works

Everything That Rises

Sullivan, Walter. Death by Melancholy.

FRANK O'CONNOR

Criticism-General

O'Donovan, Michael. Towards an Appreciation of Literature.

JOHN O'HARA

Criticism-General

Heiney, Donald. Recent American Literature.
Podhoretz, Norman. Doings and Undoings.
Tuttleton, James W. The Novel of Manners in America.

Reference Works

Bibliographies

Bruccoli, Matthew J. John O'Hara; A Checklist.
Wilson, Edmund. Classics and Commercials.

JONATHAN OLDSTYLE

See Washington Irving.

EUGENE O'NEILL

Criticism-General

Cowley, Malcolm, Ed. After the Genteel Tradition.

SARAH MARGARET FULLER MARCHISA D'OSSOLI

See Margaret Fuller.

THOMAS PAINE

Criticism-General

Violette, Augusta Genevieve. Economic Feminism in American Literature Prior to 1848.
Wager, Willis. American Literature.

NETTIE PALMER

Criticism-General

Smith, Vivian Brian. Vance and Nettie Palmer.

VANCE PALMER

Criticism-General

Smith, Vivian Brian. Vance and Nettie Palmer.

DOROTHY PARKER

Criticism By

Parker, Dorothy. The Portable Dorothy Parker.

Criticism-General

Wilson, Edmund. Classics and Commercials.

CARDINE H. PEMBERTON

Criticism-General

Rideout, Walter B. The Radical Novel in the United States; 1900-1954.

WALKER PERCY

Criticism-General

Kazin, Alfred. Bright Book of Life.
Lehan, Richard. A Dangerous Crossing.
Rubin, Louis D., Jr., Ed. The Comic Imagination in American Literature.

WILLIAM LYON PHELPS

Churchill, Allen. The Literary Decade.
Parker, Dorothy. The Portable Dorothy Parker.

EDGAR ALLAN POE

Biographies

Jacobs, William Jay. Edgar Allan Poe.
Porges, Irwin. Edgard Allan Poe.
Shanks, Edward. Edgar Allan Poe.
Wagenknecht, Edward. Edgar Allan Poe; The Man Behind the Legend.
Weiss, Susan Archer. The Home Life of Poe.
Winwar, Frances. Haunted Palace; A Life of Edgar Allan Poe.
Woodberry, George E. The Life of Edgar Allan Poe; Personal and Literary.

Letters

Ostrom, John Ward, Ed. The Letters of Edgar Allan Poe, 2 Volumes.
Harrison, James A., Ed. The Last Letters of Edgar Allan Poe.
Quinn, Arthur H., and Richard H. Hart, Eds. Letters and Documents in the Enoch Pratt Free Library.

Criticism-General

Alterton, Margaret. Origins of Poe's Critical Theory.
Anderson, Carl L. Poe in Northlight; The Scandinavian Response to His Life and Work.
Asselineau, Roger, Comp. The Merrill Studies in The House of the Seven Gables.
Bank, Stanley, Ed. American Romanticism; A Shape for Fiction.
Baudelaire, Charles P. Baudelaire on Poe.
Bonaparte, Marie. Life and Works of Edgar Allan Poe.
Carlson, Eric W. Introduction to Poe; A Thematic Reader.
Chiari, Joseph. Symbolisme from Poe to Mallarme.
Davidson, Edward H. Poe; A Critical Study.
Dillon, John Milton. Edgar Allan Poe; His Genius and Character.
Fletcher, Richard M. The Stylistic Development of Edgar Allan Poe.
Gregory, Horace. Spirit of Time and Place.
Haines, Charles. Edgar A. Poe; His Writings and Influence.
Howarth, William L., Ed. Twentieth Century Interpretations of Poe's Tales.
Hubbell, Jay B. Who Are the Major American Writers?
Keiley, Jarvis. Edgar Allan Poe; A Probe.
Ketterer, David. New Worlds for Old.
Krutch, Joseph Wood. Edgar Allan Poe; A Study in Genius.
Lawrence, D. H. Studies in Classic American Literature.
Leary, Lewis, Ed. American Literary Essays.

Levin, Harry. The Power of Blackness.
More, Paul Elmer. Shelburne Essays on American Literature.
Moss, Sidney P. Poe's Literary Battles.
Nevins, Francis M., Jr., Ed. The Mystery Writer's Art.
Ostrom, John Ward, Ed. The Letters of Edgar Allan Poe; 2 Volumes.
Parks, Edd W. Edgar Allan Poe as Literary Critic.
Pattee, Fred Lewis. The Development of the American Short Story.
Porte, Joel. The Romance in America.
Quinn, Arthur H. Edgar Allan Poe; A Critical Biography.
Rahv, Philip. Literature in America.
Ransome, Arthur. Edgar Allan Poe; A Critical Study.
Rubin, Louis D., Jr., and Robert D. Jacobs, Eds. Southern Renascence.
Rubin, Louis D., Jr. Essays in American Literature.
Rubin, Louis D., Jr., Ed. The Comic Imagination in American Literature.
Snell, George. The Shapers of American Fiction; 1798-1947.
Spiller, Robert E. The Cycle of American Literature.
Spiller, Robert E., et al., Eds. Literary History of the United States.
Swigg, Richard. Lawrence, Hardy, and American Literature.
Thompson, G. R. Poe's Fiction; Romantic Irony in the Gothic Tales.
Van Nostrand, A. D. Everyman His Own Poet.
Wager, Willis. American Literature; A World View.
Woodress, James, Ed. Eight American Authors.
Woodson, Thomas, Ed. Twentieth Century Interpretations of the Fall of the House of Usher.

Criticism - Specific Works

The Fall of the House of Usher

Woodson, Thomas, Ed. Twentieth Century Interpretations of the Fall of the House of Usher.

Reference Works

Bibliographies

Heartman, Charles Frederick. A Bibliography of First Printings of the Writings of Edgar Allan Poe.
Hyneman, Esther F. Edgar Allan Poe; An Annotated Bibliography.

KATHERINE ANNE PORTER

Biographies

Hardy, John Edward. Katherine Anne Porter.
Hendrick, George. Katherine Anne Porter.
Kiernan, Robert F. Katherine Anne Porter and Carson McCullers.

Criticism By

Porter, Katherine Anne. The Collected Essays and Occasional Writings of Katherine Anne Porter.

Criticism-General

Heiney, Donald. Recent American Literature to 1930.
Heiney, Donald. Recent American Literature.
Kazin, Alfred. Bright Book of Life.

Mooney, Harry J., Jr. The Fiction and Criticism of Katherine Anne Porter.
Nance, William L. Katherine Anne Porter and the Art of Rejection.
Parker, Dorothy. The Portable Dorothy Parker.
Rubin, Louis D., Jr., and Robert D. Jacobs, Eds. Southern Renascence.
Schorer, Mark. The World We Imagine.
Solotaroff, Theodore. The Red Hot Vacuum.
Straumann, Heinrich. American Literature in the Twentieth Century.
Sullivan, Walter. Death by Melancholy.
Wilson, Edmund. Classics and Commercials.

Criticism - Specific Works

Ship of Fools

Mooney, Harry J., Jr. The Fiction and Criticism of Katherine Anne Porter.
Parker, Dorothy. The Portable Dorothy Parker.
Solotaroff, Theodore. The Red Hot Vacuum.

Reference Works

Bibliographies

Waldrip, Louise, and Shirley Ann Bauer. A Bibliography of the Works of Katherine Anne Porter.

WILLIAM SYDNEY PORTER

See O. Henry.

MELVILLE DAVISSON POST

Criticism-General

Norton, Charles A. Melville Davisson Post; Man of Many Mysteries.

JAMES PURDY

Criticism-General

Adams, Stephen D. James Purdy.
Chupack, Henry. James Purdy.
French, Warren, Ed. The Fifties; Fiction, Poetry, Drama.
Hassan, Ihab. Contemporary American Literature; 1945-1972.
Hipkiss, Robert A. Jack Kerouac, Prophet of the New Romanticism.
Langford, Richard E., et al., Eds. Essays in Modern American Literature.
Schwarzschild, Bettina. Not-Right House; Essays on James Purdy.
Solotaroff, Theodore. The Red Hot Vacuum.
Waldmeir, Joseph J., Ed. Recent American Fiction.

THOMAS PYNCHON

Criticism-General

Harris, Charles B. Contemporary American Novelists of the Absurd.
Kazin, Alfred. Bright Book of Life.
Lehan, Richard. A Dangerous Crossing.
Levine, George and David Leverenz, Eds. Mindful Pleasures.
May, John R. Toward a New Earth.
Schulz, Max F. Black Humor Fiction of the Sixties.
Slade, Joseph W. Thomas Pynchon.

QUEEN

Reference Works

Bibliographies

Scotto, Robert M. Three Contemporary American Novelists.

ELLERY QUEEN

Criticism-General

Parker, Dorothy. The Portable Dorothy Parker.

Criticism - Specific Works

The New York Murders

Parker, Dorothy. The Portable Dorothy Parker.

Reference Works

Bibliographies

Nevins, Francis M. Royal Bloodline; Ellery Queen, Author and Detective.

AYN RAND

Biographies

Branden, Nathaniel, and Barbara Franden. Who is Ayn Rand?

Criticism By

Rand, Ayn. The Romantic Manifesto.

Criticism-General

Seward, William W., Jr. Contrasts in Modern Writers.

JOHN CROWE RANSOM

Criticism-General

Stewart, John L. The Burden of Time.

RALPH RASHLEIGH

Criticism-General

Argyle, Barry. An Introduction to the Australian Novel; 1830-1930.

MARJORIE K. RAWLINGS

Biographies

Bellman, Samuel Irving. Marjorie Kinnan Rawlings.

HENRY HANDEL RICHARDSON

Criticism-General

Argyle, Barry. An Introduction to the Australian Novel; 1830-1930.
Green, Dorothy. Ulysses Bound; Henry Handel Richardson and Her Fiction.
Kiernan, Brian. Images of Society and Nature.
Singer, Godfrey Frank. The Epistolary Novel.

MORDECAI RICHLER

Criticism-General

Mandel, Eli, Ed. Contexts of Canadian Criticism.

228   CHICOREL INDEX SERIES

Staines, David, Ed. The Canadian Imagination.
Tucker, Ferris. Modern Commonwealth Literature.
Woodcock, George, Ed. A Choice of Critics.

CONRAD RICHTER

Biographies

Gaston, Edwin W., Jr. Conrad Richter.

Criticism-General

Edwards, Clifford D. Conrad Richter's Ohio Trilogy.
Seward, William W., Jr. Contrasts in Modern Writers.

Criticism - Specific Works

Ohio Trilogy

Edwards, Clifford D. Conrad Richter's Ohio Trilogy.

EDWARD F. RICKETTS

Criticism-General

Astro, Richard. John Steinbeck and Edward F. Ricketts; The Shaping of a Novelist.

ELIZABETH MADOX ROBERTS

Biographies

Campbell, Harry Modean and Ruel E. Foster. Elizabeth Madox Roberts.

McDowell, Frederick P.W. Elizabeth Madox Roberts.

Criticism-General

Auchincloss, Louis. Pioneers and Caretakers.

KENNETH ROBERTS

Criticism-General

Harris, Janet. A Century of American History in Fiction.

EDWIN ARLINGTON ROBINSON

Criticism-General

Bryer, Jackson R., Ed. Fifteen Modern American Authors.
Cowley, Malcolm, Ed. After the Genteel Tradition.
Martin, Jay. Harvests of Change.
Spiller, Robert E. The Cycle of American Literature.

ROWLAND E. ROBINSON

Criticism-General

Baker, Ronald L. Folklore in the Writings of Rowland E. Robinson.

MAZO DE LA ROCHE

Biographies

Hambleton, Ronald. Mazo de la Roche of Jalna.

E. P. ROE

Criticism-General

Cowie, Alexander. The Rise of the American Novel.

OLE EDVART ROLVAAG

Criticism-General

Heiney, Donald. Recent American Literature.
Heiney, Donald. Recent American Literature To 1930.

SINCLAIR ROSS

Criticism-General

Chambers, Robert D. Sinclair Ross and Ernest Buckler.

PHILIP ROTH

Criticism-General

Detweiler, Robert. Four Spiritual Crises in Mid-Century American Fiction.
Fiedler, Leslie. The Collected Essays of Leslie Fiedler.
Hicks, Granville, and Jack Alan Robbins. Literary Horizons.
Howe, Irving. The Critical Point on Literature and Culture.
Hunter, James. B. F. Skinner and Contemporary Literature.
McDaniel, John N. The Fiction of Philip Roth.
Malin, Irving, Ed. Contemporary American Jewish Literature; Critical Essays.
Nelson, Gerald B. Ten Versions of America.
Pinsker, Sanford. The Comedy that "hoits"; An Essay on the Fiction of Philip Roth.
Podhoretz, Norman. Doings and Undoings.
Solotaroff, Theodore. The Red Hot Vacuum.

Criticism-Specific Works

Portnoy's Complaint

Hunter, James. B. F. Skinner and Cotemporary Literature.

Reference Works

Plots and Characters

Nelson, Gerald B. Ten Versions of America.

Bibliographies

Rodgers, Bernard F., Jr. Philip Roth; A Bibliography.

CHARLES ROWECRAFT

Criticism-General

Argyle, Barry. An Introduction to the Australian Novel; 1830-1930.

DAMON RUNYON

Biographies

Hoyt, Edwin. A Gentleman of Broadway.

V. SACKVILLE-WEST

Biographies

Stevens, Michael. V. Sackville-West; A Critical Biography.

J.D. SALINGER

Criticism-General

Balakian, Nona, and Charles Simmons, Eds. The Creative Present.
Baumbach, Jonathan. The Landscape of Nightmare.
Bowden, Edwin T. The Dungeon of the Heart.
Detweiler, Robert. Four Spiritual Crises in Mid-Century American Fiction.
French, Warren G. J.D. Salinger.
French, Warren, Ed. The Fifties; Fiction, Poetry, Drama.
Green, Martin. Re-Appraisals; Some Commonsense Readings in American Literature.
Grunwald, Henry A., Ed. Salinger; A Critical and Personal Portrait.
Hall, James. The Lunatic Giant in the Drawing Room.
Harper, Howard M., Jr. Desperate Faith.
Hassan, Ihab. Radical Innocence.
Hassan, Ihab. Contemporary American Literature; 1945-1972.
Heiney, Donald. Recent American Literature.
Hipkiss, Robert A. Jack Kerouac; Prophet of the New Romanticism.
Laser, Marvin, and Norman Fruman, Eds. Studies in J.D. Salinger.
McCarthy, Mary. The Writing on the Wall and Other Literary Essays.
Miller, James E., Jr. Quests Surd and Absurd.
Mizener, Arthur. The Sense of Life in the Modern Novel.
Nist, John, Ed. Style in English.
Proffer, Carl R., Ed./Translator. Soviet Criticism of American Literature in the Sixties.
Saito, George, and Philip Williams. Soseki and Salinger; American Students on Japanese Fiction.
Scott, Nathan A., Jr., Ed. Adversity and Grace.
Stone, Edward. A Certain Morbidness; A View of American Literature.
Updike, John. Assorted Prose.
Waldmeir, Joseph J., Ed. Recent American Fiction; Some Critical Views.
Weinberg, Helen. The New Novel in America.
Westbrook, Max, Ed. The Modern American Novel; Essays in Criticism.

Criticism - Specific Works

Catcher in the Rye

Bowden, Edwin T. The Dungeon of the Heart.
Nist, John, Ed. Style in English.
Westbrook, Max, Ed. The Modern American Novel.

Fanny and Zooey

Green, Martin. Re-Appraisals.

WILLIAM SAROYAN

Criticism By

Saroyan, William. Places Where I've Done Time.

Criticism-General

Angoff, Charles. The Tone of the Twenties and Other Essays.
Heiney, Donald. Recent American Literature.
Schulberg, Budd. The Four Seasons of Success.
Straumann, Heinrich. American Literature in the Twentieth Century.
Wilson, Edmund. Classics and Commercials.

WILLIAM SATCHELL

Biographies

Wilson, Phillip. William Satchell.

Criticism-General

Wilson, Phillip. William Satchell.

JACK SCHAEFER

Criticism-General

Haslam, Gerald W. Jack Schaefer.

HOWARD SCOTT

Criticism-General

Warner, Harry, Jr. All Our Yesterdays.

CATHARINE MARIA SEDGWICK

Criticism-General

Foster, Edward Halsey. Catherine Maria Sedgwick.

THOM. SERGANT

Criticism-General

Pizer, Donald. Realism and Naturalism; in Nineteenth-Century American Literature.

QUINTUS SERVINTUS

Criticism-General

Argyle, Barry. An Introduction to the Australian Novel; 1830-1930.

HENRY WHEELER SHAW

See Josh Billings.

IRWIN SHAW

Criticism-General

Heiney, Donald. Recent American Literature.
Mersand, Joseph. Traditions in American Literature.

THOMAS SHEPARD

Criticism-General

Gallagher, Edward Joseph. Early Puritan Writers.

WILLIAM GILMORE SIMMS

Criticism-General

Bank, Stanley. American Romanticism.

Erskine, John, Ph.D. Leading American Novelists.

UPTON SINCLAIR

Biographies

Gaer, Joseph. Upton Sinclair.
Harris, Leon. Upton Sinclair; American Rebel.
Yoder, Jon A. Upton Sinclair.

Letters

Sinclair, Upton. My Lifetime in Letters.

Criticism-General

Cowley, Malcolm, Ed. After the Genteel Tradition.
Heiney, Donald. Recent American Literature To 1930.
Heiney, Donald. Recent American Literature.
Parker, Dorothy. The Portable Dorothy Parker.
Seward, William W., Jr. Contrasts in Modern Writers.
Straumann, Heinrich. American Literature in the Twentieth Century.
Updike, John. Assorted Prose.

Criticism - Specific Works

Money Writes

Parker, Dorothy. The Portable Dorothy Parker.

Reference Works

Bibliographies

Gottesman, Ronald. Upton Sinclair; An Annotated Checklist.
Gottesman, Ronald. The Literary Manuscripts of Upton Sinclair.

BETTY SMITH

Criticism-General

Gelfant, Blanche Housman. The American City Novel.

C.A. SMITH

Criticism-General

Warner, Harry, Jr. All Our Yesterdays.

MURIEL SPARK

Criticism-General

Berthoff, Warner. Fictions and Events; Essays in Criticism and Literary History.
Kemp, Peter. Muriel Spark.
Tominaga, Thomas T. Iris Murdoch and Muriel Spark.
Updike, John. Assorted Prose.

E. SPENCER

Criticism - Specific Works

The Voice at the Back Door

French, Warren. The Fifties.

JEAN STAFFORD

Criticism-General

Auchincloss, Louis. Pioneers and Caretakers.

LAURENCE STALLINGS

Biographies

Bregenzer, Don Marshall. A Round-Table in Poictesme.

STEAD

Criticism - Specific Works

Seven Poor Men of Sydney

Kiernan, Brian. Images of Society and Nature.

For Love Alone

Kiernan, Brian. Images of Society and Nature.

LINCOLN STEFFENS

Criticism-General

Cooley, Thomas. Educated Lives.
Straumann, Heinrich. American Literature in the Twentieth Century.

WALLACE STEGNER

Biographies

Robinson, Forrest. Wallace Stegner.

Tooker, Dan. Fiction! Interviews with Northern California Novelists.

GERTRUDE STEIN

Biographies

Brinnin, John Malcolm. The Third Rose; Gertrude Stein and Her World.
Hoffman, Michael J. Gertrude Stein.
Toklas, Alice B. Staying on Alone.

Criticism By

Stein, Gertrude. Lectures in America.
Stein, Gertrude. How to Write.

Criticism-General

Angoff, Allan, Ed. American Writing Today.
Berthoff, Warner. The Ferment of Realism.
Cooley, Thomas. Educated Lives.
Copeland, Carolyn Faunce. Language and Time and Gertrude Stein.
Heiney, Donald. Recent American Literature.
Lewis, Wyndham. Time and Western Man.
Lisca, Peter. The Wide World of John Steinbeck.
Mellow, James R. Charmed Circle.
Russell, Francis. Three Studies in Twentieth Century Obscurity.
Schorer, Mark. The World We Imagine.
Simmonds, Roy S. Steinbeck's Literary Achievement.
Simon, Linda, Ed. Gertrued Stein; A Composite Portrait.

Strauman, Heinrich. American Literature in the Twentieth Century.
Tanner, Tony. The Reign of Wonder.

Reference Works

Bibliographies

Firmage, George James. A Check-list of the Published Writings of Gertrude Stein.
Haas, Robert Bartlett, Comp. A Catalogue of the Published and Unpublished Writings of Gertrude Stein.
Wilson, Robert A. Gertrude Stein; a Bibliography.

JOHN STEINBECK

Biographies

Astro, Richard, Ed. Steinbeck; The Man and His Work.
Astro, Richard. John Steinbeck and Edward F. Ricketts; The Shaping of a Novelist.
French, Warren. John Steinbeck.
Lisca, Peter. The Wide World of John Steinbeck.

Letters

Steinbeck, Elaine, and Robert Wallsten, Eds. Steinbeck; A Life in Letters.
Steinbeck, John. Journal of a Novel; The East of Eden Letters.

Criticism-General

Angoff, Allan, Ed. American Writing Today.
Beach, Joseph Warren. American Fiction; 1920-1940.
Blake, Nelson Manfred. Novelists' America.
Bowden, Edwin T. The Dungeon of the Heart.
Bryer, Jackson R., Ed. Fifteen Modern American Authors.
Davis, Robert Murray, Ed. Steinbeck; A Collection of Critical Essays.
French, Warren, Ed. A Companion to The Grapes of Wrath.
French, Warren, Ed. The Fifties; Fiction, Poetry, Drama.
French, Warren, and Walter E. Kidd, Eds. American Winners of the Nobel Literary Prize.
Frohock, W. M. The Novel of Violence in America.
Geismar, Maxwell. Writers in Crisis.
Krim, Seymour. Shake it for the World, Smartass.
Langford, Richard E., et al., Eds. Essays in Modern American Literature.
Levant, Howard. The Novels of John Steinbeck.
Lutwack, Leonard. Heroic Fiction.
Magny, Claude-Edmonde. Translated by Eleanor Hochman. The Age of the American Novel.
Marks, Lester Jay. Thematic Design in the Novels of John Steinbeck.
Schulberg, Budd. The Four Seasons of Success.
Seward, William W., Jr. Contrasts in Modern Writers.
Simmonds, Roy S. Steinbeck's Literary Achievement.
Snell, George. The Shapers of American Fiction; 1798-1947.
Straumann, Heinrich. American Literature in the Twentieth Century.
Tedlock, E. W., and C. U. Wicker, Eds, Steinbeck and His Critics.
Westbrook, Max, Ed. The Modern American Novel.
Wilson, Edmund. Classics and Commercials.

Criticism - Specific Works

The Grapes of Wrath

Beach, Joseph Warren. American Fiction;1920-1940.
Bowden, Edwin T. The Dungeon of the Heart.
Langford, Richard E., et al., Eds. Essays in Modern American Literature.
Lutwack, Leonard. Heroic Fiction.
Westbrook, Max, Ed. The Modern American Novel.

In Dubious Battle

Beach, Joseph Warren. American Fiction;1920-1940.

The Long Valley

Beach, Joseph Warren. American Fiction;1920-1940.

Of Mice and Men

Beach, Joseph Warren. American Fiction;1920-1940.

To a God Unknown

Beach, Joseph Warren. American Fiction;1920-1940.

Tortilla Flat

Beach, Joseph Warren. American Fiction;1920-1940.

Reference Works

Bibliographies

Goldstone, Adrian H., and John R. Payne. John Steinbeck.
Hayashi, Tetsumaro. John Steinbeck.
Hayashi, Tetsumaro. A New Steinbeck.

Dictionaries

Hayashi, Tetsumaro, Ed. John Steinbeck;A Dictionary of his Fictional Characters.

Study Guides

Hayashi, Tetsumaro, Ed. A Study Guide to Steinbeck;A Handbook to His Major Works.
Hayashi, Tetsumaro, Ed. Steinbeck's Literary Dimension;A Guide to Comparative Studies.

ANN SOPHIA STEPHENS

Criticism-General

Cowie, Alexander. The Rise of the American Novel.

WALLACE STEVENS

Criticism-General

Berthoff, Warner. Fictions and Events.
Bewley, Marius. Masks and Mirrors.
Bryer, Jackson R., Ed. Fifteen Modern American Authors.
Cooperman, Stanley. World War I and the American Novel.
French, Warren, Ed. The Forties;Fiction, Poetry, Drama.
LaFrance, Marston, Ed. Patterns of Commitment in American Literature.

Criticism - Specific Works

   Notes Toward a Supreme Fiction

French, Warren, Ed. The Forties; Fiction, Poetry, Drama.

FRANK R. STOCKTON

Biographies

Griffin, Martin I. J. Frank R. Stockton; A Critical Biography.

HARRIET BEECHER STOWE

Biographies

Gilbertson, Catherine. Harriet Beecher Stowe.
Johnston, Johanna. Runaway to Heaven.
Stowe, Charles Edward. Life of Harriet Beecher Stowe; Comp. from Her Letters and Journals.
Wagenknecht, Edward. Harriet Beecher Stowe.

Criticism By

Stowe, Harriet Beecher. The Key to Uncle Tom's Cabin.

Criticism-General

Cowie, Alexander. The Rise of the American Novel.
Crothers, George D., Ed. Invitation to Learning; English and American Novels.
Eakin, Paul John. The New England Girl.

Erskine, John, Ph. D. Leading American Novelists.
Gross, Seymour L., and John Edward Hardy, Eds. Images of the Negro in American Literature.
Wagenknecht, Edward. Cavalcade of the American Novel.
Wright, Nathalia. American Novelists in Italy.

Criticism - Specific Works

   Uncle Tom's Cabin

Crothers, George D., Ed. Invitation to Learning; English and American Novels.
Stowe, Harriet Beecher. The Key to Uncle Tom's Cabin.

Reference Works

   Bibliographies

Hildreth, Margaret Holbrook. Harriet Beecher Stowe.

JESSE STUART

Biographies

Blair, Everetta Love. Jesse Stuart; His Life and Works.

Criticism By

Perry, Dick. Reflections of Jesse Stuart on a Land of Many Moods.

WILLIAM STYRON

Biographies

Friedman, Melvin J. William Styron.

Ratner, Marc L. William Styron.

Criticism-General

Balakian, Nona, and Charles Simmons, Eds. The Creative Present.
Baumbach, Jonathan. The Landscape of Nightmare.
Clarke, John Henrik, Ed. William Styron's Nat Turner.
Detweiler, Robert. Four Spiritual Crises in Mid-Century American Fiction.
Gayle, Addison, Jr. The Way of the New World.
Gossett, Louise Y. Violence in Recent Southern Fiction.
Hassan, Ihab. Contemporary American Literature;1945-1972.
Hassan, Ihab. Radical Innocence.
Morris, Robert K., and Irving Malin, Eds. The Achievement of William Styron.
Proffer, Carl R., Ed./Translator. Soviet Criticism of American Literature in the Sixties.
Scott, Nathan A., Jr., Ed. Adversity and Grace.
Waldmeir, Joseph J., Ed. Recent American Fiction.

Criticism - Specific Works

Confessions of Nat Turner

Clarke, John Henrik, Ed. William Styron's Nat Turner;Ten Black Writers Respond.

IDA MINERVA TARBELL

Biographies

Tomkins, Mary E. Ida M. Tarbell.

BOOTH TARKINGTON

Biographies

Woodress, James. Booth Tarkington; Gentleman from Indiana.

Criticism-General

Fennimore, Keith J. Booth Tarkington.
Heiney, Donald. Recent American Literature.
Heiney, Donald. Recent American Literature to 1930.
Parker, Dorothy. The Portable Dorothy Parker.
Wagenknecht, Edward. Cavalcade of the American Novel.

Criticism - Specific Works

Ambler

Parker, Dorothy. The Portable Dorothy Parker.

ALLEN TATE

Criticism-General

Stewart, John L. The Burden of Time.
Sullivan, Walter. Death by Melancholy.

BAYARD TAYLOR

Criticism-General

Cowie, Alexander. The Rise of the American Novel.
Smyth, Albert H. Bayard Taylor.

HENRY DAVID THOREAU

Biographies

Krutch, Joseph Wood. Henry David Thoreau.
Thoreau, Henry David. Intro. by Leo Marx. Excursions.
Torrey, Bradford, and Francis H. Allen, Eds. The Journal of Henry D. Thoreau.

Criticism-General

Burroughs, John. Literary Values and Other Papers.
Cavell, Stanley. The Senses of Walden.
Christy, A. E. The Orient in American Transcendentalism.
Cohen, Hennig, Ed. Landmarks of American Writing.
Dickens, Robert. Thoreau; The Complete Individualist.
Foerster, Norman. The Intellectual Heritage of Thoreau.
Glick, Wendell, Ed. The Recognition of Henry David Thoreau.
Hicks, John H., Ed. Thoreau in Our Season.
Hoffman, Michael J. The Subversive Vision.
McIntosh, James. Thoreau as Romantic Naturalist.
Miller, Henry. Stand Still Like the Hummingbird.
More, Paul Elmer. Shelburne Essays on American Literature.
Morris, Wright. The Territory Ahead.
Paul, Sherman, Ed. Six Classic American Writers.
Shanley, J. Lyndon. The Making of Walden with the Text of the First Version.
Sherman, Paul, Ed. Thoreau.
Spiller, Robert E. The Cycle of American Literature.
Spiller, Robert E. Four Makers of the American Mind.
Spiller, Robert E., et al., Eds. Literary History of the United States.
Stevenson, Robert Louis. RLS; Selected Essays.
Tanner, Tony. The Reign of Wonder.
Van Nostrand, A. D. Everyman His Own Poet.
Woodress, James, Ed. Eight American Authors.

Criticism - Specific Works

Walden

Cavell, Stanley. The Senses of Walden.
Shanley, J. Lyndon. The Making of Walden with the Text of the First Version.

THOMAS BANGS THORPE

Biographies

Rickels, Milton. Thomas Bangs Thorpe; Humorist of the Old Southwest.

JAMES THURBER

Criticism-General

Parker, Dorothy. The Portable Dorothy Parker.
Updike, John. Assorted Prose.

Criticism - Specific Works

The Years with Ross

Parker, Dorothy. The Portable Dorothy Parker.

Reference Works

Bibliographies

Bowden, Edwin T. James Thurber; A Bibliography.

JEAN TOOMER

Criticism-General

Margolies, Edward. Native Sons; A Critical Study of Twentieth-Century Negro American Authors.
Turner, Darwin T. In a Minor Chord.

B. TRAVEN

Criticism-General

Baumann, Michael L. B. Traven; An Introduction.
Chankin, Donald O. Anonymity and Death.

LIONEL TRILLING

Criticism By

Trilling, Lionel. The Liberal Imagination.
Trilling, Lionel. A Gathering of Fugitives.

Criticism-General

French, Warren, Ed. The Forties; Fiction, Poetry, Drama.
Frohock, W. M. Strangers to This Ground.
Kartiganer, Donald M., and Malcolm A. Griffith. Theories of American Literature.
Kazin, Alfred, Ed. The Open Form.
Malin, Irving, Ed. Contemporary American-Jewish Literature.
Proffer, Carl R., Ed./Translator. Soviet Criticism of American Literature in the Sixties.
Rahv, Philip. Literature in America.

Criticism - Specific Works

The Middle of the Journey

French, Warren, Ed. The Forties; Fiction, Poetry, Drama.

JAMES TUCKER

Criticism-General

Argyle, Barry. An Introduction to the Australian Novel; 1830-1930.

MARK TWAIN

Biographies

Canby, Henry Seidel. Turn West; Turn East; Mark Twain and Henry James.
Ferguson, John DeLancey. Mark Twain; Man and Legend.
Geismar, Maxwell. Mark Twain; An American Prophet.
Harnsberger, Caroline Thomas. Mark Twain; Family Man.
Henderson, Archibald. Mark Twain.
Kaplan, Justin. Mr. Clemens and Mark Twain.
Kaplan, Justin. Mark Twain and His World.
Masters, Edgar Lee. Mark Twain; A Portrait.

Quick, Dorothy. Enchantment.
Turner, Arlin. The Record of a Literary Friendship.
Twain, Mark. (Clemens, Samuel Langhorne). Mark Twain's Burlesque Autobiography.
Wagenknecht, Edward. Mark Twain; The Man and His Work.

Letters

Leary, Lewis, Ed. Mark Twain's Letters to Mary.
Smith, Henry Nash, and William M. Gibson. Mark Twain-Howells Letters.
Wecter, Dixon, Ed. Mark Twain to Mrs. Fairbanks.

Criticism By

DeVoto, Bernard. The Portable Mark Twain.

Criticism-General

Anderson, Frederick, Ed. Mark Twain The Critical Heritage.
Andrews, Kenneth R. Nook Farm; Mark Twain's Hartford Circle.
Baetzhold, Howard G. Mark Twain and John Bull.
Baldanza, Frank. Mark Twain.
Bellamy, Gladys Carmen. Mark Twain As a Literary Artist.
Berthoff, Warner. The Ferment of Realism.
Bewley, Marius. The Eccentric Design.
Bewley, Marius. Masks and Mirrors.
Blues, Thomas. Mark Twain and the Community.
Bowden, Edwin T. The Dungeon of the Heart.
Branch, Edgar Marquess. The Literary Apprenticeship of Mark Twain.
Brashear, Minnie M., and Robert M. Rodney. The Art Humor and Humanity of Mark Twain.
Cady, Edwin H. The Light of Common Day.
Cardwell, Guy A., Ed. Discussions of Mark Twain.
Carrington, George C. The Dramatic Unity of Huckleberry Finn.
Chase, Richard. The American Novel and Its Tradition.
Cohen, Hennig, Ed. Landmarks of American Writing.
Cooley, Thomas. Educated Lives.
Covici, Pascal, Jr. Mark Twain's Humor.
Cowie, Alexander. The Rise of the American Novel.
Cox, James M. Mark Twain; The Fate of Humor.
Crothers, George D., Ed. Invitation to Learning; English and American Novels.
Duckett, Margaret. Mark Twain and Bret Harte.
Ensor, Allison. Mark Twain and The Bible.
Falk, Robert. The Victorian Mode in American Fiction; 1865-1885.
Fatout, Paul. Mark Twain on the Lecture Circuit.
Foster, Richard, Ed. Six American Novelists of the Nineteenth Century.
Franklin, H. Bruce. Future Perfect.
Ganzel, Dewey. Mark Twain Abroad.
Geismar, Maxwell, Ed. Mark Twain and the three R's: Race, Religion, Revolution-and Related Matters.
Green, Martin. Re-Appraisals.
Gross, Seymour L., and John Edward Hardy, Eds. Images of the Negro in American Literature.
Hassler, Kenneth Wayne. Mark Twain; Dean of American Humorists.
Hauck, Richard Boyd. A Cheerful Nihilism.
Hemminghaus, Edgar H. Mark Twain in Germany.

Hilfer, Anthony Channell. The Revolt from the Village;1915-1930.
Hill, Hamlin. Mark Twain and Elisha Bliss.
Hill, Hamlin Lewis. Mark Twain; God's Fool.
Hoffman, Daniel. Form and Fable in American Fiction.
Howells, William Dean. My Mark Twain.
Howells, William Dean. Literary Friends and Acquaintance.
Hubbell, Jay B. Southern Life in Fiction.
Kaul, A. N. The American Vision.
Kazin, Alfred, Ed. The Open Form; Essays for Our Time.
Kuhlmann, Susan. Knave, Fool, and Genius.
LaFrance, Marston, Ed. Patterns of Commitment in American Literature.
Leary, Lewis, Ed. American Literary Essays.
Leavis, F. R. Anna Karenina and Other Essays.
Lee, Robert Edson. From West to East.
Liljegren, Sten B. Revolt Against Romanticism in American Literature;As Evidenced in the Works of S. L. Clemens.
Long, E. Hudson. Mark Twain Handbook.
Lorch, Fred W. The Trouble Begins at Eight;Mark Twain's Lecture Tours.
Lynn, Kenneth S. Mark Twain and Southwestern Humor.
McCarthy, Harold T. The Expatriate Perspective.
Marks, Barry A., Ed. Mark Twain's Huckleberry Finn.
Martin, Jay. Harvests of Change.
May, John R. Toward a New Earth; Apocalypse in the American Novel.
Mencken, H. L. Edited by William H. Nolte. H. L. Mencken's Smart Set Criticism.
Mills, Nicolaus. American and English Fiction in the Nineteenth Century.
Milne, Gordon. The American Political Novel.
Mizener, Arthur. Twelve Great American Novels.
Morgan, H. Wayne. American Writers in Rebellion.
Morris, Wright. The Territory Ahead.
Noble, David W. The Eternal Adam and the New World Garden.
O'Connor, William Van. The Grotesque;An American Genre and Other Essays.
Pattee, Fred Lewis. A History of American Literature Since 1870.
Petit, Arthur G. Mark Twain and the South.
Pizer, Donald. Realism and Naturalism in Nineteenth-Century American Literature.
Poirier, Richard. A World Elsewhere.
Rahv, Philip. Literature in America.
Rogers, Franklin R. Mark Twain's Burlesque Patterns.
Rubin, Louis D., Jr., Ed. The Comic Imagination in American Literature.
Rubin, Louis D., Jr. Essays in American Literature.
Schmitter, Dean Morgan, Comp. Mark Twain;A Collection of Criticism.
Scott, Arthur L. Mark Twain At Large.
Searle, William. The Saint and The Skeptics.
Serrano-Plaja, Arturo. Magic Realism in Cervantes.
Seward, William W., Jr. Contrasts in Modern Writers.
Shapiro, Charles, Ed. Twelve Original Essays on Great American Novels.
Smith, Henry Nash, Ed. Mark Twain.

Smith, Henry Nash. Mark Twain;The Development of a Writer.
Snell, George. The Shapers of American Fiction;1798-1947.
Spender, Stephen. Love-Hate Relations;English and American Sensibilities.
Spengemann, William C. Mark Twain and the Backwoods Angel.
Spiller, Robert E. The Cycle of American Literature.
Spiller, Robert E., et al., Eds. Literary History of the United States.
Stegner, Wallace, Ed. The American Novel from James Fenimore Cooper to William Faulkner.
Tanner, Tony. The Reign of Wonder.
Taylor, Walter Fuller. The Economic Novel in America.
Trilling, Diana. Claremont Essays.
Trilling, Lionel. The Liberal Imagination.
Underwood, John Curtis. Literature and Insurgency.
Vickery, John B., Ed. Myth and Literature.
Wagenknecht, Edward. Cavalcade of the American Novel.
Wager, Willis. American Literature; A World View.
Walker, Franklin Dickerson. Irreverent Pilgrims.
Webster, Samuel Charles, Ed. Mark Twain;Business Man.
West, Victor Royce. Folklore in the works of Mark Twain.
Wiggins, Robert A. Mark Twain;Jackleg Novelist.
Woodress, James, Ed. Eight American Authors.
Young, Philip. Three Bags Full.

Criticism - Specific Works

Connecticut Yankee

Howells, William Dean. My Mark Twain;Reminiscences and Criticisms.

Schmitter, Dean Morgan, Ed. Mark Twain;A Collection of Criticism.
Smith, Henry Nash, Ed. Mark Twain; A Collection of Critical Essays.

Gilded Age

Howells, William Dean. My Mark Twain;Reminiscences and Criticisms.

Huckleberry Finn

Bowden, Edwin T. The Dungeon of the Heart.
Cady, Edwin H. The Light of Common Day.
Carrington, George C. The Dramatic Unity of Huckleberry Finn.
Chase, Richard. The American Novel and its Tradition.
Crothers, George D., Ed. Invitation to Learning;English and American Novels.
Hoffman, Daniel. Form and Fable in American Fiction.
Kaul, A.N. The American Vision.
Kazin, Alfred, Ed. The Open Form.
Marks, Barry A., Ed. Mark Twain's Huckleberry Finn.
Mizener, Arthur. Twelve Great American Novels.
O'Connor, William Van. The Grotesque;An American Genre and Other Essays.
Schmitter, Dean Morgan. Mark Twain;A Collection of Criticism.
Shapiro, Charles, Ed. Twelve Original Essays on Great American Novels.
Smith, Henry Nash, Ed. Mark Twain; A Collection of Critical Essays.
Stegner, Wallace, Ed. The American Novel from James Fenimore Cooper to William Faulkner.
Trilling, Lionel. The Liberal Imagination;Essays on Literature and Society.

Innocence Abroad

Schmitter, Dean Morgan, Ed. Mark Twain; A Collection of Criticism.

Pilgrim's Progress

Leavis, F.R. Anna Karenina and other Essays.
McCarthy, Harold T. The Expatriate Perspective.

Roughing It

Howells, William Dean. My Mark Twain; Reminiscences and Criticisms.

Tom Sawyer

Howells, William Dean. My Mark Twain; Reminiscences and Criticisms.
Rubin, Louis D., Jr. Death of the Novel; Essays in American Literatuure.
Schmitter, Dean Morgan, Ed. Mark Twain; A Collection of Criticism.
Smith, Henry Nash, Ed. Mark Twain; A Collection of Critical Essays.
Trilling, Diana. Claremont Essays.

Tramp Abroad

Howells, William Dean. My Mark Twain; Reminiscences and Criticisms.

Reference Works

Bibliographies

Johnson, Merle DeVore. A Bibliography of the Works of Mark Twain; Samuel Langhorne Clemens.
Tenney, Thomas. Mark Twain; A Reference Guide.

Dictionaries

Ramsay, Robert L., Ph.D., and Frances G. Emberson, Ph.D. A Mark Twain Lexicon.

JOHN UPDIKE

Criticism By

Updike, John. Assorted Prose.

Criticism-General

Detweiler, Robert. Four Spiritual Crises in Mid-Century American Fiction.
Gado, Frank, Comp. First Person.
Harper, Howard M., Jr. Desperate Faith.
Hassan, Ihab. Contemporary American Literature; 1945-1972.
Hicks, Granville, and Jack Alan Robbins. Literary Horizons.
Kazin, Alfred. Bright Book of Life.
Markle, Joyce B. Fighters and Lovers.
Parker, Dorothy. The Portable Dorothy Parker.
Proffer, Carl R., Ed./Translator. Soviet Criticism of American Literature in the Sixties.
Straumann, Heinrich. American Literature in the Twentieth Century.
Vargo, Edward P. Rainstorms and Fire.

Criticism - Specific Works

The Poorhouse Fair

Parker, Dorothy. The Portable Dorothy Parker.

Reference Works

Bibliographies

Sokoloff, B. A. John Updike.
Taylor, C. Clarke. John Updike.

BROOKS VAN WYCK

Criticism-General

Hubbell, Jay B. Who Are the Major American Writers?

GORE VIDAL

Criticism By

Vidal, Gore. Homage to Daniel Shays. Collected Essays 1952-1972.
Vidal, Gore. Matters of Fact and of Fiction: Essays 1973-1976.

Criticism-General

Aldridge, John W., Ed. After the Lost Generation.
Austen, Roger. Playing the Game; The Homosexual Novel in America.
Dick, Bernard F. The Apostate Angel; A Critical Study of Gore Vidal.

KURT VONNEGUT

Goldsmith, David H. Kurt Vonnegut; Fantasist of Fire and Ice.
Harris, Charles B. Contemporary American Novelists of the Absurd.
Hassan, Ihab. Contemporary American Literature; 1945-1972.
Hicks, Granville, and Jack Alan Robbins. Literary Horizons.
Hillegas, Mark R. The Future as Nightmare; H. G. Wells and the Anti-utopians.
Kazin, Alfred. Bright Book of Life.
Klinkowitz, Jerome, and John Somer; Eds. The Vonnegut Statement.
May, John R. Toward a New Earth.
Nelson, Gerald B. Ten Versions of America.
Olderman, Raymond M. Beyond the Waste Land.
Reed, Peter J. Kurt Vonnegut, Jr.
Schatt, Stanley. Kurt Vonnegut, Jr.
Schulz, Max F. Black Humor Fiction of the Sixties.

Criticism - Specific Works

Cat's Cradle

Klinkowitz, Jerome, and John Somer, Eds. The Vonnegut Statement.
Reed, Peter J. Kurt Vonnegut, Jr.

God Bless You Mr. Rosewater

Reed, Peter J. Kurt Vonnegut, Jr.

Gutenberg Galaxy

Klinkowitz, Jerome and John Somer, Eds. The Vonnegut Statement.

Mechanical Bride

Klinkowitz, Jerome, and John Somer, Eds. The Vonnegut Statement.

Mother Night

Klinkowitz, Jerome, and John Somer, Eds. The Vonnegut Statement.
Reed, Peter J. Kurt Vonnegut, Jr.

Player Piano

Klinkowitz, Jerome, and John Somer, Eds. The Vonnegut Statement.

Reed, Peter J. Kurt Vonnegut, Jr.

Sirens of Titan

Klinkowitz, Jerome, and John Somer, Eds. The Vonnegut Statement.
Reed, Peter J. Kurt Vonnegut, Jr.

Slaughterhouse Five

Klinkowitz, Jerome, and John Somer, Eds. The Vonnegut Statement.
Reed, Peter J. Kurt Vonnegut, Jr.

LAUNCELOT WAGSTAFFE

See Washington Irving.

EDWARD LEWIS WALLANT

Criticism-General

Baumbach, Jonathan. The Landscape of Nightmare.
Hoyt, Charles Alva, Ed. Minor American Novelists.

SUSAN WARNER

Criticism-General

Cowie, Alexander. The Rise of the American Novel.

ROBERT PENN WARREN

Criticism-General

Baumbach, Jonathan. The Landscape of Nightmare.
Brooks, Cleanth. American Literature; The Makers and the Making.
Brooks, Cleanth. The Hidden God.
French, Warren, Ed. The Forties; Fiction, Poetry, Drama.
Frohock, W. M. The Novel of Violence in America.
Gado, Frank, Comp. First Person.
Gossett, Louise Y. Violence in Recent Southern Fiction.
Guttenberg, Barnett. Web of Being.
Hall, James. The Lunatic Giant in the Drawing Room.
Heiney, Donald. Recent American Literature.
Mizener, Arthur. Twelve Great American Novels.
Noble, David W. The Eternal Adam and the New World Garden.
Rahv, Philip. Literature in America.
Rubin, Louis D., Jr., and Robert D. Jacobs, Eds. Southern Renascence.
Seward, William W., Jr. Contrasts. in Modern Writers.
Stewart, John L. The Burden of Time.
Straumann, Heinrich. American Literature in the Twentieth Century.
Sullivan, Walter. Death by Melancholy.
Westbrook, Max, Ed. The Modern American Novel.

Criticism - Specific Works

All The King's Men

French, Warren, Ed. The Forties; Fiction, Poetry, Drama.
Mizener, Arthur. Twelve Great American Novels.
Westbrook, Max, Ed. The Modern American Novel.

Band Of Angels

Sullivan, Walter. Death by Melancholy.

Reference Works

Bibliographies

Huff, Mary Nance, Comp. Robert Penn Warren;A Bibliography.

FRANK WATERS

Criticism-General

Lyon, Thomas J. Frank Waters.

NOAH WEBSTER

Biographies

Warfel, Harry R. Noah Webster;Schoolmaster to America.

NATHANIEL WALLENSTEIN WEINSTEIN

See Nathanael West.

EUDORA WELTY

Criticism-General

Balakian, Nona, and Charles Simmons, Eds. The Creative Present.
French, Warren, Ed. The Forties; Fiction, Poetry, Drama.
Gossett, Louise Y. Violence in Recent Southern Fiction.
Gross, Seymour L., and John Edward Hardy, Eds. Images of the Negro in American Literature.
Hardy, John Edward. Man in the Modern Novel.

Heiney, Donald. Recent American Literature.
Nelson, Gerald B. Ten Versions of America.
Nin, Anais. The Novel of the Future.
Rubin, Louis D., Jr., Ed. The Comic Imagination in American Literature.
Rubin, Louis D., Jr., and Robert D. Jacobs. Southern Renascence.

Criticism - Specific Works

A Curtain of Green

French, Warren, Ed. The Forties; Fiction, Poetry, Drama.

GLENWAY WESCOTT

Criticism-General

Gado, Frank, Ed. First Person.
Straumann, Heinrich. American Literature in the Twentieth Century.

NATHANAEL WEST

Criticism-General

Brown, John Russen. The American Novel and the Nineteen Twenties.
Comerchero, Victor. Nathanael West;The Ironic Prophet.
Hoyt, Charles Alva, Ed. Minor American Novelists.
Jackson, Thomas H., Ed. Twentieth Century Interpretations of Miss Lonelyhearts.
Madden, David, Ed. Nathanael West; The Cheaters and the Cheated.
Malin, Irving. Nathanael West's Novels.

Martin, Jay, Ed. Nathanael West; A Collection of Critical Essays.
Nelson, Gerald B. Ten Versions of America.
O'Connor, William Van. Seven Modern American Novelists.
Podhoretz, Norman. Doings and Undoings.
Reid, Randall. The Fiction of Nathanael West; No Redeemer, No Promised Land.
Schulberg, Budd. The Four Seasons of Success.
Schulz, Max F. Radical Sophistication.
Whitbread, Thomas B., Ed. Seven Contemporary Authors.

Reference Works

Bibliographies

Vannatta, Dennis P. Nathanael West.

EDITH WHARTON

Biographies

Auchincloss, Louis. Edith Wharton; A Woman in Her Time.
Bell, Millicent. Edith Wharton and Henry James.

Criticism By

Wharton, Edith. A Backward Glance.
Wharton, Edith. The Writing of Fiction.

Criticism-General

Auchincloss, Louis. Pioneers and Caretakers.
Bewley, Marius. Masks and Mirrors.
Gelfant, Blanche Housman. The American City Novel.
Heiney, Donald. Recent American Literature.
Heiney, Donald. Recent American Literature to 1930.
Howe, Irving, Ed. Edith Wharton.
Jackson, Thomas H., Ed. Twentieth Century Interpretations of Miss Lonelyhearts.
Kazin, Alfred. On Native Grounds.
Kellogg, Grace. The Two Lives of Edith Wharton.
Lawson, Richard H. Edith Wharton.
Lewis, Richard Warrington Baldwin. Edith Wharton.
Lindberg, Gary H. Edith Wharton and the Novel of Manners.
Lubbock, Percy. Portrait of Edith Wharton.
Martin, Jay. Harvests of Change.
Michaud, Regis. The American Novel Today.
Miller, James E., Jr. Quests Surd and Absurd.
Millgate, Michael. American Social Fiction.
Mizener, Arthur. Twelve Great American Novels.
Nevius, Blake. Edith Wharton; A Study of Her Fiction.
O'Connor, William Van, Ed. Seven Modern American Novelists.
Pattee, Fred Lewis. The First Century of American Literature.
Shapiro, Charles, Ed. Twelve Original Essays on Great American Novels.
Snell, George. The Shapers of American Fiction.
Stegner, Wallace, Ed. The American Novel from James Fenimore Cooper to William Faulkner.
Straumann, Heinrich. American Literature in the Twentieth Century.
Trilling, Diana. Claremont Essays.
Tuttleton, James W. The Novel of Manners in America.

Underwood, John Curtis. Literature and Insurgency.
Wagenknecht, Edward. Cavalcade of the American Novel.
Wilson, Edmund. Classics and Commercials.
Wilson, Edmund. The Wound and the Bow.

Criticism - Specific Works

The Age of Innocence

Mizener, Arthur. Twelve Great American Novels.

The House of Mirth

Stegner, Wallace, Ed. The American Novel from James Fenimore Cooper to William Faulkner.

E. B. WHITE

Letters

Guth, Dorothy Lobrano. Letters of E.B. White.

PATRICK WHITE

Biographies

Lawson, Alan. Patrick White.

Criticism-General

Argyle, Barry. Patrick White.
Beatson, Peter. The Eye in the Mandala.
Brissenden, R. F. Patrick White.
Dutton, Geoffrey. Patrick White.

Dyce, J.R. Patrick White as Playwright.
Kiernan, Brian. Images of Society and Nature.
Morley, Patricia. The Mystery of Unity; Theme and Technique in the Novels of Patrick White.

WILLIAM HALE WHITE

See Mark Rutherford.

STEWART EDWARD WHITE

Criticism-General

Underwood, John Curtis. Literature and Insurgency.

RUDY WIEBE

Morley, Patricia A. The Comedians.

ELIE WIESEL

Reference Works

Bibliographies

Abramowitz, Molly. Elie Wiesel; A Bibliography.

THORNTON WILDER

Criticism-General

Churchill, Allen. The Literary Decade.

Heiney, Donald. Recent American Literature.
Straumann, Heinrich. American Literature in the Twentieth Century.

MARY E. WILKINS

Criticism-General

Martin, Jay. Harvests of Change.

JOHN WILLIAMS

Criticism-General

Gayle, Addison, Jr. The Way of the New World.

EDMUND WILSON

Criticism By

Wilson, Edmund. Axel's Castle.
Wilson, Edmund. The Bit Between My Teeth.
Wilson, Edmund. Classics and Commercials; A Literary Chronicle of the Forties.
Wilson, Edmund. Letters on Literature and Politics.
Wilson, Edmund. The Triple Thinkers.
Wilson, Edmund. The Wound and the Bow.

Criticism-General

Berthoff, Warner. Fictions and Events.
Cowley, Malcolm. Think Back on Us.
Parker, Dorothy. The Portable Dorothy Parker.
Rubin, Louis D., Jr. Death of the Novel; Essays in American Literature.
Spiller, Robert E. The Oblique Light.

THEODORE WINTHROP

Criticism-General

Cowie, Alexander. The Rise of the American Novel.

THOMAS WOLFE

Biographies

Raynolds, Robert. Thomas Wolfe; Memoir of a Friendship.
Turnbull, Andrew. Thomas Wolfe.

Letters

Holman, C. Hugh, and Sue Fields Ross. The Letters of Thomas Wolfe to his Mother.
Nowell, Elizabeth. The Letters of Thomas Wolfe.
Terry, John Skally, Ed. Thomas Wolfe's Letters to His Mother.

Criticism By

Wolfe, Thomas. The Story of a Novel.

Criticism-General

Angoff, Allan, Ed. American Writing Today.
Angoff, Charles. The Tone of the Twenties and Other Essays.

Beach, Joseph Warren. American Fiction;1920-1940.
Beja, Morris. Epiphany in the Modern Novel.
Blake, Nelson Manfred. Novelists' America.
Bowden, Edwin T. The Dungeon of the Heart.
Bryer, Jackson R., Ed. Fifteen Modern American Authors.
Churchill, Allen. The Literary Decade.
Cowley, Malcolm. Think Back On Us.
Field, Leslie A., Ed. Thomas Wolfe; Three Decades of Criticism.
Frohock, W. M. The Novel of Violence in America.
Geismar, Maxwell. Writers in Crisis; The American Novel;1925-1940.
Gelfant, Blanche Housman. The American City Novel.
Gurko, Leo. Thomas Wolfe;Beyond the Romantic Ego.
Heiney, Donald. Recent American Literature.
Hilfer, Anthony Channell. The Revolt from the Village;1915-1930.
Holman, Clarence Hugh. The Loneliness at the Core.
Holman, C. Hugh. Three Modes of Modern Southern Fiction.
Holman, C. Hugh. The World of Thomas Wolfe.
Johnson, Pamela Hansford. The Art of Thomas Wolfe.
McElderry, B. R., Jr. Thomas Wolfe.
Morris, Wright. The Territory Ahead.
Muller, Herbert J. Thomas Wolfe.
O'Connor, William Van, Ed. Seven Modern American Novelists.
Rahv, Philip. Literature in America.
Reeves, Paschal, Ed. Thomas Wolfe and the Glass of Time.
Rubin, Louis D., Jr., and Robert D. Jacobs, Eds. Southern Renascence.
Rubin, Louis D., Jr., Ed. Thomas Wolfe;A Collection of Critical Essays.
Rubin, Louis D., Jr. Thomas Wolfe; The Weather of His Youth.
Ryssel, Fritz Heinrich. Transl. by Helen Sebba. Thomas Wolfe.
Snell, George. The Shapers of American Fiction;1798-1947.
Steele, Richard Lowell. Thomas Wolfe.
Stegner, Wallace, Ed. The American Novel from James Fenimore Cooper to William Faulkner.
Straumann, Heinrich. American Literature in the Twentieth Century.
Walser, Richard. Thomas Wolfe;An Introduction and Interpretation.
Watkins, Floyd C. Thomas Wolfe's Characters.
Westbrook, Max, Ed. The Modern American Novel.

Criticism - Specific Works

Can't Go Home Again

Beach, Joseph Warren. American Fiction;1920-1940.
Walser, Richard. Thomas Wolfe;An Introduction and Interpretation.

Look Homeward Angel

Angoff, Allan, Ed. American Writing Today.
Beach, Joseph Warren. American Fiction;1920-1940.
Bowden, Edwin T., The Dungeon of the Heart.
Steele, Richard Lowell. Thomas Wolfe;A Study in Psychoanalytic Literary Criticism.
Stegner, Wallace, Ed. The American Novel from James Fenimore Cooper to William Faulkner.
Walser, Richard. Thomas Wolfe;An Introduction and Interpretation.

Of Time and the River

Beach, Joseph Warren. American Fiction;1920-1940.
Walser, Richard. Thomas Wolfe.

The Web and the Rock

Beach, Joseph Warren. American Fiction;1920-1940.
Walser, Richard. Thomas Wolfe.

CONSTANCE FENIMORE WOOLSON

Criticism-General

Cowie, Alexander. The Rise of the American Novel.
Wagenknecht, Edward. Cavalcade of the American Novel.

RICHARD WRIGHT

Biographies

Webb, Constance. Richard Wright.

Criticism-General

Cooke, M.G., Ed. Modern Black Novelists.
Cowley, Malcolm. Edited by Henry Dan Piper. Think Back On Us;A Contemporary Chronicle of the 1930's by Malcolm Cowley.
Fabre, Michel. The Unfinished Quest of Richard Wright.
Gross, Seymour L., and John Edward Hardy, Eds. Images of the Negro in American Literature.
Howe, Irving. The Critical Point on Literature and Culture.
Lehan, Richard. A Dangerous Crossing.
McCarthy, Harold T. The Expatriate Perspective.
Margolies, Edward. Native Sons;A Critical Study of Twentieth-Century Negro American Authors.
Ray, David, Ed. Richard Wright;Impressions and Perspectives.
Schulz, Max F. Black Humor Fiction of the Sixties.

ELLA YOUNG

Criticism-General

Nin, Anais. The Novel of the Future.

Geographical Index

U.S.A. - GENERAL

Abbe, George, Ed. Stephen Vincent Benet on Writing.
Abrams, M.H. Natural Supernaturalism; Tradition and Revolution in Romantic Literature.
Abrams, Meyer H. Mirror and the Lamp.
Aldiss, Brian Wilson. Billion Year Spree; the true history of science fiction.
Allibone, Samuel Austin. A Critical Dictionary of English Literature and British and American Authors, Living and Deceased.
Altick, Richard D., and Andrew Wright. Selective Bibliography for the Study of English and American Literature.
American Library Association. Freedom of Inquiry.
Amis, Kingsley. New Maps of Hell.
Aquino, John. Science Fiction as Literature.
Armstrong, John. Paradise Myth.
Ash, Brian. Faces of the Future.
Astro, Richard. John Steinbeck and Edward F. Ricketts; The Shaping of a Novelist.
Barnes, Myra Edwards. Linquistics and Languages in Science Fiction-Fantasy.
Barns, Florence Elberta. Texas Writers of Today.
Beck, Warren A., and Myles L. Clowers, Eds. Understanding American History through Fiction.
Baker, Houston A. Singers of Daybreak.
Baker, Houston A. Black Literature in America.
Bateson, Frederick Wilse. A Guide to English and American Literature.
Benson, Frederick R. Writers in Arms.
Berger, Monroe. Real and Imagined Worlds.
Black, Michael H. The Literature of Fidelity.
Blair, Walter. American Literature; A Brief History.
Blasing, Mutlu Konuk. The Art of Life.
Bone, Robert. The Negro Novel in America.
Bradley, Edward Sculley, Ed. The American Tradition in Literature.
Brasch, Ila Wales, and Walter Milton Brasch. A Comprehensive Annotated Bibliography of American Black English.
Brooks, Cleanth, Comp. American Literature; The Makers and the Making.
Brown, L.K. Completed by Leon Edel. Willa Cather; A Critical Biography.
Bruccoli, Matthew J., et al., Eds. First Printings of American Authors.
Burgess, Anthony. The Novel Now.
Callow, James T. Guide to American Literature from its Beginnings through Walt Whitman.
Cary, Norman Reed. Christian Criticism in the Twentieth Century.
Cazamian, Louis Francois. Criticism in the Making.
Chapman, Abraham. Jewish-American Literature.
Chevigny, Bell Gale. The Woman and the Myth.
Clack, Doris H. Black Literature Resources; Analysis and Organization.
Coan, Otis W., and Richard G. Lillard. America In Fiction.
Cockcroft, Thomas G.L. Index to the Weird Fiction Magazines.
Clifford, Gay. The Transformation of Allegory.
Cook, Sylvia Jenkins. From Tobacco Road to Route 66.

GEOGRAPHICS-U.S.A.-GENERAL

Cornillon, Susan Koppelman, Ed. Images of Women in Fiction Feminist Perspectives.

Craig, David. The Real Foundation; Literature and Social Change.

Davis, David Brion. Homicide in American Fiction;1798-1860.

Day, Martin Steele. A Handbook of American Literature.

DeCamp, Lyon Sprague. Literary Swordsmen and Sorcerers.

Deegan, Dorothy Yost. The Stereotype of the Single Woman in American novels.

DeJovine, F. Anthony. The Young Hero in American Fiction.

DeMott, Robert, and Sanford E. Marovitz, Eds. Artful Thunder.

Deodene, Frank, and William P. French. Black American Fiction Since 1952.

Denny, Margaret, and William H. Gilman, Eds. The American Writer and the European Tradition.

DeVoto, Bernard. The World of Fiction.

Diamond, Arlyn, and Lee R. Edwards, Eds. The Authority of Experience.

Dickinson, A.T., Jr. American Historical Fiction.

Donoghue, Denis. Thieves of Fire.

Doyle, Paul A. Guide to Basic Information Sources in English Literature.

Downs, Robert B, Ed. First Freedom; Liberty and Justice in the World of Books and Reading.

Dudley, Edward and Maxmillian E. Novak, Eds. The Wild Man Within.

Etulain, Richard W. Western American Literature.

Etulain, Richard W., Comp. The Popular Western.

Feidelson, Charles, Jr., and Paul Brodtkorb, Jr. Interpretations of American Literature.

Ferguson, John DeLancey, Ph.D. American Literature in Spain.

Folsom, James K. The American Western Novel.

Forst, Lilian R. Romanticism in Perspective.

Foster, Jeannette H. Sex Variant Women in Literature.

Friedman, Norman. Form and Meaning in Fiction.

Gayle, Addison. The Way of the New World.

Glicksberg, Charles Irving. The Literature of Commitment.

Gohdes, Clarence. Bibliographical Guide to the Study of the Literature of the U.S.A.

Gohdes, Clarence. Literature and Theater of the States and Regions of the U.S.A.

Gordon, David J. Literary Art and the Unconscious.

Green, Rose Basile. The Italian-American Novel.

Grismer, Raymond Leonard. A Reference Index to Twelve Thousand Spanish American Authors.

Hardwick, Elizabeth. Seduction and Betrayal;Women and Literature.

Hart, James David. The Popular Book;A History of America's Literary Taste.

Haslam, Gerald W., Comp. Western Writing.

Haviland, Virginia. Children and Literature;Views and Reviews.

Havlice, Patricia Pate. Index to Literary Biography.

Henderson, Harry B. Versions of the Past.

Henry, Jeannette, Ed. American Indian Reader;Literature.

Hirschfelder, Arlene B. American Indian and Eskimo Authors.

Holliday, Carl. A History of Southern Literature.

Hotchkiss, Jeanette. American Historical Fiction and Biography for Children and Young People.

Howard, Leon. Literature and the American Tradition.

Hoyt, Olga G. and Edwin P. Hoyt. Censorship in America.

Hsu, Kai-yu, Comp. Asian-American Authors.

Hubbell, Jay B. South and Southwest; Literary Essays and Reminiscences.

Hubbell, Jay B. Who Are the Major American Writers?

Ifkovic, Edward, Comp. American Letter; Immigrant and Ethnic Writing.

Jackson, Blyden. The Waiting Years.

Jan, Isabelle. On Children's Literature.

Jones, Howard Mumford. The Theory of American Literature.

Jones, Howard Mumford. Jeffersonianism and the American Novel.

Jones, Joseph Jay. Radical Cousins; Nineteenth Century American and Australian Writers.

Jordan, Alice Mabel. From Rollo to Tom Sawyer and other Papers.

Kamman, William Frederic. Socialism in German American Literature.

Kennedy, Arthur G., and Donald B. Sands. A Concise Bibliography for Students of English.

Kingston, Carolyn T. The Tragic Mode in Children's Literature.

Kirk, John Foster. A Supplement to Allibone's Critical Dictionary of English Literature and British and American Authors.

Klein, Holger, Ed. The First World War in Fiction.

Kolodny, Annette. The Lay of the Land.

Laurenson, Diana T., and Alan Swingewood. The Sociology of Literature.

Leary, Lewis, Ed. American Literary Essays.

Leavis, Frank Raymond. For Continuity.

Lewis, Wyndham. The Writer and the Absolute.

Lewis, Wyndham. Time and Western Man.

Lieber, Todd M. Endless Experiments; Essays on the Heroic Experience in American Romanticism.

Lieberman, Elias, Ph. D. The American Short Story.

Lucock, Halford E. American Mirror.

Lynn, Kenneth S. Visions of America; Eleven Literary Historical Essays.

MacCann, Donnarae, and Olga Richard. The Child's First Books.

McClellan, Grant S. Censorship in the United States.

McNulty, John Bard. Modes of Literature.

Major, Clarence. The Dark and Feeling; Black American Writers and their Work.

Marcus, Steven. Representations; Essays on Literature and Society.

Masinton, Charles G. J. P. Donleavy; The Style of His Sadness and Humor.

Massey, Irving J. Uncreating Word.

Mays, Benjamin E. The Negro's God as Reflected in His Literature.

Meeker, Joseph W. The Comedy of Survival.

Miner, Earl Roy. The Japanese Tradition in British and American Literature.

Moers, Ellen. Literary Women.

Moon, Eric, Ed. Book Selection and Censorship in the Sixties.

Morse, J. Mitchell. Prejudice and Literature.

Mumford, Lewis. The Golden Day.

Murry, John Middleton. Unprofessional Essays.

New York(City) Public Library. No Crystal Stair; A Bibliography.

O'Brien, Edward Joseph Harrington. The Advance of the American Short Story.

Olson, Elder. Aristotle's Poetics and English Literature.

GEOGRAPHICS-U.S.A.-GENERAL

Pattee, Fred Lewis. A History of American Literature.
Pearson, Carol, and Katherine Pope. Who Am I This Time?
Peden, William. The American Short Story.
Peet, Louis Harman. Handy Book of American Authors.
Penzoldt, Peter, Ph.D. The Supernatural in Fiction.
Pfeiffer, John R. Fantasy and Science Fiction.
Pilkington, William T. My Blood's Country.
Powell, Lawrence Clark. Southwest Classics.
Pritchard, John Paul. Return to the Fountains.
Quinn, Arthur Hobson. American Fiction.
Reigelman, Milton M. The Midland; A Venture in Literary Regionalism.
Righter, William. Myth and Literature.
Rose, Alan Henry. Demonic Vision.
Rose, Mark. Science Fiction; A Collection of Critical Essays.
Rosenblatt, Roger. Black Fiction.
Ross, Ralph Gilbert, Ed. Makers of American Thought.
Rubin, Louis D., Jr., and C. Hugh Holman. Southern Literary Study.
Rubin, Louis D., Jr. Death of the Novel; Essays in American Literature.
Rudich, Norman, Ed. Weapons of Criticism; Marxism in America and the Literary Tradition.
Ruland, Richard. America in Modern European Literature.
Ruland, Richard, Ed. The Native Muse; Theories of American Literature.
Ruland, Vernon. Horizons of Criticism.
Rule, Jane. Lesbian Images.
Sachs, Viola. The Myth of America.
Sevigg, Richard. Lawrence Hardy and American Literature.
Simpson, Lewis P. The Dispossessed Garden.
Singer, Godfrey Frank. The Epistolary Novel; Its Origin, Development, Decline and Residuary Influence.
Smith, Clark Ashton. Planets and Dimensions.
Snyder, Gerald S. The Right to be Informed; Censorship in the United States.
Spacks, Patricia Ann Meyer. The Female Imagination.
Spiller, Robert E., et al., Eds. Literary History of the United States.
Spiller, Robert E. Milestones in American Literary History.
Stallman, Robert Wooster. The Critic's Notebook.
Stineback, David C. Shifting World.
Stone, Edward. Voices of Despair.
Stovall, Floyd, Ed. The Development of American Literary Criticism.
Strelka, Joseph P., Ed. Anagogic Qualities of Literature.
Stuckey, W.J. The Pulitzer Prize Novels.
Symons, Julian. Mortal Consequences; A History From the Detective Story to the Crime Novel.
Takaki, Ronald T. Violence in the Black Imagination.
Tavuchis, Nicholas, Comp. The Family through Literature.
Thwaite, Mary F. From Primer to Pleasure in Reading.
Trilling, Lionel. Beyond Culture.
Trilling, Lionel. A Gathering of Fugitives.
Trilling, Lionel. The Liberal Imagination.
Turner, Ernest Sackville. Boys will be Boys.
Van Nostrand, Albert D., Ed. Literary Criticism in America.
Vickery, John B. The Literary Impact of the Golden Bough.
Wadlington, Warwick. The Confidence Game in American Literature.

Walcutt, Charles C. American Literary Naturalism.
Walden, Daniel. On Being Jewish; American Jewish Writers from Cahan to Bellow.
West, Thomas Reed. Nature, Community and Will.
Whitcomb, Selden L. Chronological Outlines of American Literature.
White, Mary Lou. Children's Literature; Criticism and Response.
Wilson, Edmond. O Canada; An American's Notes on Canadian Culture.
Wilson, Edmund. The Shock of Recognition; the Development of Literature in the U.S.

U.S.A. -17th CENTURY

Bowden, Edwin T. The Dungeon of the Heart.
Foerster, Norman, Ed. The Reinterpretation of American Literature.
Foerster, Norman. Image of America; Our Literature from Puritanism to the Space Age.
Gallasher, Edward Joseph. Early Puritan Writers.
Hubbell, Jay B. The South in American Literature; 1607-1900.
Kartiganer, Donald M., and Malcolm A. Griffith. Theories of American Literature.
McNeir, Waldo, and Leo B. Levy, Eds. Studies in American Literature.
Miller, Wayne Charles. An Armed America; Its Face in Fiction.
Parrington, Vernon Louis. Main Currents in American Thought.
Slotkin, Richard. Regeneration through Violence.
Staehelin-Wackernagel, Adelheid. The Cooper Monographs.
Wagenknecht, Edward. Cavalcade of the American Novel.

U.S.A. -18th CENTURY

Birkhead, Edith. The Tale of Terror.
Blake, Fay M. The Strike in the American Novel.
Blanck, Jacob, Comp. Bibliography of American Literature. Vol. 1. Henry Adams to Donn Byrne.
Blanck, Jacob, Comp. Bibliography of American Literature. Vol. 2. George W. Cable to Timothy Dwight.
Blanck, Jacob, Comp. Bibliography of American Literature. Vol. 3. Edward Eggleston to Bret Harte.
Blanck, Jacob, Comp. Bibliography of American Literature. Vol. 4.
Blanck, Jacob, Comp. Bibliography of American Literature. Vol. 5. Washington Irving to Henry Wadsworth Longfellow.
Blanck, Jacob, Comp. Bibliography of American Literature. Vol. 6. Augustus Baldwin Longstreet to Thomas William Parsons.
Brown, Clarence Arthur. The Achievement of American Criticism.
Brown, Herbert Ross. The Sentimental Novel in America 1789-1860.
Davis, David Brion. Homicide in American Fiction; 1798-1860.
Dickinson, H. T., Ed. Politics and Literature in the Eighteenth Century.
Dunlap, George Arthur. The City in the American Novel; 1789-1900.
Emerson, Everett, Ed. American Literature; 1764-1789.
Flory, Claude Reherd. Economic Criticism in American Fiction; 1792-1900.
Foerster, Norman, Ed. The Reinterpretation of American Literature.
Foerster, Norman. Image of America.
Foster, Edward Halsey. The Civilized Wilderness.

GEOGRAPHICS-U.S.A.-18th CENTURY

Gerstenberger, Donna, and George Hendrick. The American Novel 1789-1959.

Gross, Seymour L., and John Edward Hardy, Eds. Images of the Negro in American Literature.

Gunn, Drewey Wayne. American And British Writers in Mexico;1556-1973.

Harap, Louis. The Image of the Jew in American Literature.

Hastings, George Everett. The Life and Works of Francis Hopkinson.

Hauck, Richard Boyd. A Cheerful Nihilism.

Heilman, Robert Bechtold. American in English Fiction;1760-1800.

Holman, C. Hugh, Comp. The American Novel through Henry James.

Hubbell, Jay B. The South in American Literature;1607-1900.

Johnson, James Gibson. Southern Fiction prior to 1860.

Kirby, David K. American Fiction to 1900.

Lawrence, D. H. Studies in Classic American Literature.

Leary, Lewis Gaston. Soundings;Some Early American Writers.

Leisy, Ernest E. The American Historical Novel.

Loshe, Lillie Deming. The Early American Novel;1789-1830.

Major, Mabel, and T. M. Pearce. Southwest Heritage.

Mantz, Harold Elmer. French Criticism of American Literature Before 1850.

Miller, Wayne Charles. An Armed America;Its Face in Fiction.

Milne, Gordon. The American Political Novel.

More, Paul Elmer. Essays on American Literature.

Noel, Thomas. Theories of the Fable in the Eighteenth Century.

Parks, Edd Winfield. Ante-Bellum Southern Literary Critics.

Parrington, Vernon Louis. Main Currents in American Thought.

Pattee, Fred Lewis. The First Century of American Literature;1770-1870.

Paul, Sherman, Ed. Six Classic American Writers.

Petter, Henri. The Early American Novel.

Pritchard, John Paul. Criticism in America.

Rahv, Philip. Literature in America.

Rees, Robert A., and Earl N. Harbert, Eds. Fifteen American Authors Before 1900.

Rubin, Louis D., Jr., Ed. A Bibliographical Guide to the Study of Southern Literature.

Rubin, Louis D., Jr., Ed. The Comic Imagination in American Literature.

Slotkin, Richard. Regeneration through Violence.

Snell, George. The Shapers of American Fiction;1798-1947.

Spengemann, William C. The Adventurous Muse.

Spiller, Robert E. The Cycle of American Literature.

Spiller, Robert E. The Third Dimension.

Spiller, Robert E., Ed. The American Literary Revolution;1783-1837.

Spiller, Robert E. The Cycle of American Literature.

Staehelin-Wackernagel, Adelheid. The Cooper Monographs.

Van Doren, Carl. The American Novel;1789-1939.

Violette, Augusta Genevieve. Economic Feminism in American Literature Prior to 1848.

Wagenknecht, Edward. Cavalcade of the American Novel.

Wager, Willis. American Literature; A World View.

Warfel, Harry Redcay. Charles Brockden Brown;American Gothic Novelist.

Warfel, Harry R. Noah Webster; Schoolmaster to America.

Wegelin, Oscar. Early American Fiction; 1774-1830.

Weil, Dorothy. In Defense of Women; Susanna Rowson.

Willey, Basil. Eighteenth Century Background; Studies on the Idea of Nature in the Thought of the Period.

Williams, Joan, Ed. Novel and Romance; 1700-1800; A Documentary Record.

Wright, Lyle A. American Fiction; 1774-1850.

Yellin, Jean Fagan. The Intricate Knot; Black Figures in American Literature; 1776-1863.

Young, Philip. Three Bags Full.

U.S.A. -19th CENTURY

Ahnebrink, Lars. The Beginnings of Naturalism in American Fiction.

Aichinger, Peter. The American Soldier in Fiction; 1880-1963.

Anderson, Carl L. Poe in Northlight.

Anderson, Frederick, Ed. Mark Twain; The Critical Heritage.

Auchincloss, Louis. Pioneers and Caretakers.

Austen, Roger. Playing the Game.

Babbitt, Irving. Spanish Character and other Essays.

Baetzhold, Howard G. Mark Twain and John Bull.

Baker, Houston, A., Jr. Black Literature in America.

Baker, Ronald L. Folklore in the Writings of Rowland B. Robinson.

Baldanza, Frank. Mark Twain; An Introduction and Interpretation.

Bank, Stanley, Ed. American Romanticism; A Shape for Fiction.

Barnett, James Harwood. Divorce and the American Divorce Novel; 18558-1937.

Barnett, Louise K. The Ignoble Savage.

Becker, John E. Hawthorne's Historical Allegory.

Berbrich, Joan D. Three Voices from Paumanok.

Berthoff, Warner. The Ferment of Realism.

Berthoff, Warner. Fictions and Events; Essays in Criticism and Literary History.

Bewley, Marius. The Eccentric Design.

Bewley, Marius. Masks and Mirrors.

Birkhead, Edith. The Tale of Terror.

Blackmur, R. P. The Lion and the Honeycomb.

Blake, Fay M. The Strike in the American Novel.

Blanck, Jacob, Comp. Bibliography of American Literature; Vol. 1; Henry Adams to Donn Byrne.

Blanck, Jacob, Comp. Bibliography of American Literature; Vol. 2; George W. Cable to Timothy Dwight.

Blanck, Jacob, Comp. Bibliography of American Literature; Vol. 3; Edward Eggleston to Bret Harte.

Blanck, Jacob, Comp. Bibliography of American Literature; Vol. 4; Nathaniel Hawthorne to Joseph Holt Ingraham.

Blanck, Jacob, Comp. Bibliography of American Literature; Vol. 5; Washington to Henry Wadsworth Longfellow.

Blanck, Jacob, Comp. Bibliography of American Literature; Vol. 6; Augustus Baldwin Longstreet to Thomas William Parsons.

Bloomfield, Morton W., Ed. The Interpretation of Narrative; Theory and Practice.

Bluestein, Gene. The Voice of the Folk; Folklore and American Literary Theory.

Boas, George, Ed. Romanticism in America.

GEOGRAPHICS-U.S.A.-19th CENTURY

Bolger, Stephen Garrett. The Irish Character in American Fiction; 1830-1860.
Bornstein, George, Ed. Romantic and Modern;Revaluations of Literary Tradition.
Bowden, Edwin T. The Dungeon of the Heart.
Brignano, Russell Carl. Black Americans in Autobiography.
Brodhead, Richard H. Hawthorne, Melville and the Novel.
Broderick, Dorothy M. Image in the Black in Children's Fiction.
Brooks, Van Wyck. The World of Washington Irving.
Brown, Arthur W. Margaret Fuller.
Brown, Clarence Arthur. The Achievement of American Criticism.
Brown, Herbert Ross. The Sentimental Novel in America 1789-1860.
Bryer, Jackson R., and Eugene Harding. Hamlin Garland the the Critics.
Buell, Lawrence. Literary Transcendentalism;Style and Vision in the American Renaissance.
Burroughs, John. Literary Values and Other Papers.
Cady, Edwin H. The Light of Common Day.
Callow, James T. Guide to American Literature from Emily Dickinson to the Present.
Cargill, Oscar. Toward a Pluralistic Criticism.
Carter, Everett. The American Idea.
Carter, Everett. Howells and the Age of Realism.
Cavell, Stanley. The Senses of Walden.
Charvat, William. The Origins of American Critical Thought;1810-1835.
Chase, Richard. The American Novel and its Tradition.
Chevigny, Bell Gale. The Woman and the Myth.
Christy, A. E. The Orient in American Transcendentalism.
Cockshut, A. O. J. Truth to Life.
Cohen, Hennig, Ed. Humor of the Old Southwest.
Cohen, Hennig, Ed. Landmarks of American Writing.
Cooley, Thomas. Educated Lives;The Rise of Modern Autobiography in America.
Crisler, Jesse E., and Joseph R. McElrath, Jr. Frank Norris;A Reference Guide.
Crothers, George D., Ed. Invitation to Learning;English and American Novels.
Davis, David Brion. Homicide in American Fiction, 1798-1860.
Davis, Robert H., and Arthur B. Maurice. The Caliph of Bagdad.
Dickens, Robert. Thoreau;the Complete Individualist.
Dolan, Paul J. Of War and War's Alarms.
Doubleday, Neal Frank. Variety of Attempt.
Douglas, Ann. The Feminization of American Culture.
Duckett, Margaret. Mark Twain and Bret Harte.
Duffey, Bernard. The Chicago Renaissance in American Letters.
Dunlap, George Arthur. The City in the American Novel;1789-1900.
Eakin, Paul John. The New England Girl.
Edel, Leon. Henry James;The Conquest of London.
Edmiston, Susan, and Linda D. Cinno. Literary New York;A History and Guide.
Ellmann, Mary. Thinking About Women.
Erskine, John, Ph. D. Leading American Novelists.
Everson, Ida Gertrude. George Henry Calvert;American Literary Pioneer.
Falk, Robert. The Victorian Mode in American Fiction;1865-1885.

GEOGRAPHICS-U.S.A.-19th CENTURY

Fasse, Barbara. Le Belle Dame Sans Merci and The Aesthetics of Romanticism.
Faust, Bertha. Hawthorne's Contemporaneous Reputation.
Feidelson, Charles, Jr. Symbolism and American Literature.
Fiedler, Leslie A. Love and Death in the American Novel.
Fletcher, Richard M. The Stylistic Development of Edgar Allan Poe.
Flory, Claude Reherd. Economic Criticism in American Fiction;1792 to 1900.
Foerster, Norman. The Intellectual Heritage of Thoreau.
Foerster, Norman. Image of America.
Fogle, Richard Harter. The Permanent Pleasure;Essays on Classics of Romanticism.
Fogle, Richard Harter, Comp. Romantic Poets and Prose Writers.
Foster, Edward Halsey. Catharine Maria Sedgwick.
Foster, Edward Halsey. The Civilized Wilderness.
Foster, Richard, Ed. Six American Novelists of the Nineteenth Century.
Fraiberg, Louis. Psychoanalysis and American Literary Criticism.
Friedman, Maurice. Problematic Rebel;Melville, Dostoievsky, Kafka, Camus.
Gaer, Joseph. Frank Norris.
Gaston, Edwin W., Jr. The Early Novel of the Southwest.
Gayle, Addison, Jr. The Way of the New World.
Geismar, Maxwell. Rebels and Ancestors;The American Novel, 1890-1915.
Gerstenberger, Donna, and George Hendrick. The American Novel; 1789-1959.
Gilbertson, Catherine. Harriet Beecher Stowe.
Gindin, James. Harvest of a Quiet Eye.
Glick, Wendell, Ed. The Recognition of Henry David Thoreau.
Gloster, Hugh M. Negro Voices in American Fiction.
Gohdes, Clarence. American Literature in Nineteenth Century England.
Green, Martin. Re-Appraisals;Some commonsense Readings in American Literature.
Green, Rose Basile. The Italian-American Novel.
Gregory, Horace. Spirit of Time and Place.
Grejda, Edward S. The Common Continent of Men.
Grenander, M. E. Ambrose Bierce.
Griffin, Martin I. J. Frank R. Stockton; A Critical Biography.
Gross, Seymour L., and John Edward Hardy, Eds. Images of the Negro in American Literature.
Gross, Theodore L., and S. Wertheim. Hawthorne, Melville, Stephan Crane;A Critical Bibliography.
Guetti, James. The Limits of Metaphor.
Gulliver, Lucile. Louisa May Alcott.
Gunn, Drewey Wayne. American and British Writers in Mexico;1556-1973.
Gurian, Jay. Western American Writing;Tradition and Promise.
Hackett, Alice Payne, and James Henry Burke. 80 Years of Best Sellers;1895-1975.
Halperin, John, Ed. The Theory of the Novel;New Essays.
Harap, Louis. The Image of the Jew in American Literature.
Hartley, L. P. The Novelist's Responsibility.
Harris, Janet. A Century of American History in Fiction.
Hauck, Richard Boyd. A Cheerful Nihilism.

GEOGRAPHICS-U.S.A.-19th CENTURY

Hedges, William L. Washington Irving; An American Study, 1802-1832.
Hicks, John H., Ed. Thoreau in Our Season.
Hildreth, Margaret Holbrook. Harriet Beecher Stowe.
Hoffman, Daniel. Form and Fable in American Fiction.
Hoffman, Michael J. The Subversive Vision.
Holman, C. Hugh, Comp. The American Novel through Henry James.
Holman, C. Hugh. The Roots of Southern Writing.
Hough, Robert L. The Quiet Rebel.
Howard, David, et al., Eds. Tradition and Tolerance in Nineteenth-Century Fiction.
Howe, Irving. Sherwood Anderson.
Howells, W. D. Literary Friends and Acquaintance.
Hubbell, Jay B. Southern Life in Fiction.
Inge, M. Thomas, Ed. The Frontier Humorists; Critical Views.
Johnson, James Gibson. Southern Fiction Prior to 1860; An Attempt at a First-Hand Bibliography.
Jones, Howard Mumford. Guide to American Literature and its Backgrounds Since 1890.
Kallsen, Loren J., Ed. Kentucky Tragedy.
Kartiganer, Donald M., and Malcolm A Griffith. Theories of American Literature.
Kaul, A. N. The American Vision.
Kazin, Alfred. On Native Grounds.
Kazin, Alfred, Ed. The Open Form; Essays for our Time.
Kellogg, Jean Defrees. Dark Prophets of Hope; Dostoevsky, Sartre, Camus, Faulkner.
Kesterson, David B. Josh Billings; (Henry Wheeler Shaw).
Killinger, John. Hemingway and the Dead Gods.
Kirby, David K. American Fiction to 1900.
Kolb, Harold H., Jr. Illusion of Life; American Realism As a Literary Form.
Kostelanetz, Richard. The End of Intelligent Writing.
Krutch, Joseph Wood. Henry David Thoreau.
Kuhlmann, Susan. Knave, Fool, and Genius.
LaFrance, Marston. Patterns of Commitment in American Literature.
Langford, Richard E., et al., Eds. Essays in Modern American Literature.
Lawrence, D. H. Studies in Classic American Literature.
Leary, Lewis, Ed. American Literary Essays.
Leary, Lewis. Soundings; Some Early American Writers.
Leavis, F. R. Anna Karenina and other Essays.
Leavis, F. R. The Great Tradition.
Lee, Robert Edson. From West to East.
Leisy, Ernest E. The American Historical Novel.
Levin, Harry. The Power of Blackness.
Lewis, R. W. B. Trials of the Word.
Lewis, Wyndham. Men Without Art.
Liljegren, Sten B. Revolt Against Romanticism in American Literature.
Lively, Robert A. Fiction Fights the Civil War.
Long, E. Hudson. O. Henry; The Man and His Work.
Loshe, Lillie Deming. The Early American Novel; 1789-1830.
Lynn, Kenneth S. Mark Twain and Southwestern Humor.
Macleod, Anne. A Moral Tale; Children's Fiction and American Culture.
McCarthy, Harold T. The Expatriate Perspective.

McCracken, Elizabeth. The Feminine in Fiction.
McIntosh, James. Thoreau as Romantic Naturalist.
McMaster, Helen Neill. Margaret Fuller as a Literary Critic.
McMichael, George. Journey to Obscurity; The Life of Octave Thanet.
McNeir, Waldo, and Leo B. Levy, Eds. Studies in American Literature.
Major, Mabel, and T. M. Pearce. Southwest Heritage; A Literary History with Bibliographies.
Mantz, Harold Elmer. French Criticism of American Literature Before 1850.
Martin, Jay. Harvests of Change.
Maurice, Arthur Bartlett. New York in Fiction.
May, John R. Toward a New Earth.
Mencken, H. L. Edited by William H. Nolte. H. L. Mencken's Smart Set Criticism.
Mersand, Joseph. Traditions in American Literature.
Michaud, Regis. The American Novel Today.
Miller, Henry. Stand Still Like the Hummingbird.
Miller, Wayne Charles. An Armed America; Its Face in Fiction.
Millgate, Michael. American Social Fiction; James to Cozzens.
Mills, Nicolaus. American and English Fiction in the Nineteenth Century.
Milne, Gordon. The American Political Novel.
Milne, Gordon. The Sense of Society.
Milton, John R., Comp. The Literature of South Dakota.
Mizener, Arthur. The Sense of Life in the Modern Novel.
Mizener, Arthur. Twelve Great American Novels.
More, Paul Elmer. Edited by Daniel Aaron. Shelburne Essays on American Literature.
Morgan, H. Wayne. American Writers in Rebellion.
Morris, Wright. The Territory Ahead.
Nettels, Elsa. James and Conrad.
Nevins, Francis M., Jr., Ed. The Mystery Writer's Art.
Noble, David W. The Eternal Adam and the New World Garden.
Norris, Frank. The Responsibilities of the Novelist.
Nye, Russel B., Ed. New Dimensions in Popular Culture.
O'Connor, William Van. The Grotesque; An American Genre and Other Essays.
Osterweis, Rollin G. Romanticism and Nationalism in the Old South.
Papashvily, Helen Waite. All the Happy Endings.
Parks, Edd Winfield. Ante-Bellum Southern Literary Critics.
Parrington, Vernon Louis. Main Currents in American Thought.
Paterson, John. The Gospel According to James, Hardy, Conrad, Joyce, Lawrence, and Virginia Woolf.
Pattee, Fred Lewis. The First Century of American Literature; 1770-1870.
Pattee, Fred Lewis. A History of American Literature Since 1870.
Pattee, Fred Lewis. The Development of the American Short Story.
Paul, Sherman, Ed. Six Classic American Writers; An Introduction.
Pearce, Roy Harvey. Historicism Once More.
Pearson, Edmund. Dime Novels; or Following an Old Trail in Popular Literature.
Peterson, Dale L. The Clement Vision; Poetic Realism in Turgenev and James.
Petter, Henri. The Early American Novel.
Pickering, James H., Ed. The World Turned Upside Down.

GEOGRAPHICS-U.S.A.-19th CENTURY

Pizer, Donald. Realism and Naturalism;in Nineteenth-Century American Literature.
Poirier, Richard. A World Elsewhere;The Place of Style in American Literature.
Pops, Martin Leonard. The Melville Archetype.
Porte, Joel. The Romance in America;Studies in Cooper, Poe, Hawthorne, Melville and James.
Pritchard, John Paul. Criticism in America.
Rahv, Philip. Literature in America.
Rahv, Philip. Literature and the Sixth Sense.
Reed, Walter L. Meditations on the Hero.
Rees, Robert A., and Earl N. Harbert, Eds. Fifteen American Authors Before 1900.
Rickels, Milton. George Washington Harris.
Rickels, Milton. Thomas Bangs Thorpe;Humorist of the Old Southwest.
Ronald, Ann. Zane Grey.
Ross, Ralph Gilbert. Makers of American Thought.
Rubin, Louis D., Jr., Ed. A Bibliographical Guide to the Study of Southern Literature.
Rubin, Louis D., Jr. The Curious Death of the Novel;Essays in American Literature.
Rubin, Louis D., Jr., Ed. The Comic Imagination in American Literature.
Rubin, Louis D., Jr., and Robert D. Jacobs, Eds. Southern Renascence.
Sanderlin, George. Washington Irving As Others Saw Him.
Saul, George Brandon. In Praise of the Half-Forgotten and other Essays.
Schneider, Robert W. Five Novelists of the Progressive Era.
Scholes, Robert, and Eric Rubkin. Science Fiction;History, Science, Vision.
Schorer, Mark. The World We Imagine.
Searle, William. The Saint and the Skeptics;Joan of Arc in the Work of Mark Twain, Anatole France, and Bernard Shaw.
Seltzer, Leon F. The Vision of Melville and Conrad.
Seward, William W., Jr. Contrasts in Modern Writers.
Seyersted, Per. Kat Chopin;A Critical Biography.
Shapiro, Charles, Ed. Twelve Original Essays on Great American Novels.
Sherman, Paul, Ed. Thoreau;A Collection of Critical Essays.
Skaggs, Merrill Maguire. The Folk of Southern Fiction.
Slotkin, Richard. Regeneration Through Violence.
Smyth, Albert H. Bayard Taylor.
Snell, George. The Shapers of American Fiction;1798-1947.
Spender, Stephen. Love-Hate Relations.
Spengemann, William C. The Adventurous Muse.
Spiller, Robert E., Ed. The American Literary Revolution;1783-1837.
Spiller, Robert E. The Cycle of American Literature.
Spiller, Robert E., et al. Four Makers of the American Mind.
Spiller, Robert E., et al, Eds. Literary History of the United States.
Spiller, Robert E. The Third Dimension.
Spiller, Robert E. The Oblique Light.
Springer, Marlene. Edith Wharton and Kate Chopin;A Guide.
Staehelin-Wackernagel, Adelheid. The Cooper Monographs.
Stanzel, Franz. Narrative Situations in the Novel.
Stegner, Wallace, Ed. The American Novel from James Fenimore Cooper to William Faulkner.

Stern, Milton R., Ed. American Literature Survey.
Stevenson, Robert Louis. Edited by George Scott-Moncrieff. RLS;Selected Essays.
Stewart, George R. Bret Harte, Argonaut and Exile.
Stewart, Randall. Edited by George Core. Regionalism and Beyond.
Stone, Donald David. Novelists in a Changing World.
Stone, Edward. A Certain Morbidness A View of American Literature.
Stout, Janis P. Sodoms in Eden.
Stowe, Charles Edward. Life of Harriet Beecher Stowe.
Stowe, Harriet Beecher. The Key to Uncle Tom's Cabin.
Swigg, Richard. Lawrence, Hardy, and American Literature.
Taylor, Gordon O. The Passages of Thought.
Taylor, Walter Fuller. The Economic Novel in America.
Thompson, Gary Richard. The Gothic Imagination;Essays in Dark Romanticism.
Trilling, Diana. Claremont Essays.
Turner, Arlin. The Record of a Literary Friendship.
Tuttleton, James W. The Novel of Manners in America.
Underwood, John Curtis. Literature and Insurgency.
Van Doren, Carl. The American Novel;1789-1939.
Van Nostrand, A.D. Everyman His Own Poet.
Van Why, Joseph S. Nook Farm.
Vickery, John B., Ed. Myth and Literature;Contemporary Theory and Practice.
Vincent, Howard P., Ed. Melville and Hawthorne in the Berkshires.
Vogel, Dan. The Three Masks of American Tragedy.
Wagenknecht, Edward. Cavalcade of the American Novel.
Wagenknecht, Edward. Harriet Beecher Stowe;The Known and the Unknown.
Wager, Willis. American Literature; A World View.
Wahr, F.B. Emerson and Goethe.
Walker, Franklin. San Francisco's Literary Frontier.
Walker, Franklin Dickerson. Irreverent Pilgrims.
Walker, William E., and Robert L. Welker, Eds. Reality and Myth.
Ward, Alfred Charles. American Literature;1880-1930.
Wasserstrom, William. Heiress of all the Ages.
Weber, Carl J. Hardy and the Lady from Madison Square.
Weber, Paul C. America in Imaginative German Literature in the First Half of the 19th Century.
Wegelin, Oscar. Early American Fiction;1774-1830.
West, Thomas R. Flesh of Steel.
Whiteman, Maxwell. A Century of Fiction by American Negroes;1853-1952.
Wiley, Margaret Lenore. Studies in American Literature.
Williams, Joan, Ed. Novel and Romance, 1700-1800;A Documentary Record.
Wilson, G.F. A Bibliography of the Writings of W.H. Hudson.
Woodress, James, Ed. Eight American Authors.
Woodruff, Stuart C. Short Stories of Ambrose Bierce;A Study in Polarity.
Woolf, Virginia. Granite and Rainbow;Essays by Virginia Woolf.
Wright, Nathalia. American Novelists in Italy.
Wright, Lyle H. American Fiction; 1774-1850.
Wright, Lyle H. American Fiction; 1851-1875.
Wright, Lyle H. American Fiction; 1876-1900.

Yellin, Jean Fagan. The Intricate Knot; Black Figures in American Literature; 1776-1863.
Young, Philip. Three Bags Full.

U.S.A.-20th CENTURY

Abramowitz, Molly. Elie Wiesel; A Bibliography.
Adams, Stephen D. James Purdy.
Ahnebrink, Lars. The Beginnings of Naturalism in American Fiction.
Aichinger, Peter. The American Soldier in Fiction; 1880-1963.
Aldridge, John W., Ed. After the Lost Generation.
Aldridge, John W., Ed. Critiques and Essays on Modern Fiction; 1920-1951.
Aldridge, John W. In Search of Heresy.
Allen, Mary. The Necessary Blankness.
Allen, Walter. Contemporary Novelists.
Allen, Walter. The Modern Novel.
Altick, Richard D. The Art of Literary Research.
Anderson, David D., Ed. Sherwood Anderson; Dimensions of His Literary Art.
Andreach, Robert F. The Slain and Resurrected God.
Angoff, Allan, Ed. American Writing Today.
Angoff, Charles. The Tone of the Twenties and Other Essays.
Appel, Alfred. Nabokov's Dark Cinema.
Appel, Paul P., Ed. Homage to Sherwood Anderson.
Auchincloss, Louis. Edith Wharton; A Woman in Her Time.
Auchincloss, Louis. Pioneers and Caretakers.
Austen, Roger. Playing the Game.
Baird, Newton D. An Annotated Bibliography of California Fiction.
Baker, Houston A., Jr. Black Literature in America.
Balakian, Nona, and Charles Simmons, Eds. The Creative Present.
Barnett, James Harwood. Divorce and the American Divorce Novel; 1858-1937.
Barson, Alfred T. A Way of Seeing.
Baumann, Michael. L. B. Traven.
Baumbach, Jonathan. The Landscape of Nightmare.
Beach, Joseph Warren. American Fiction; 1920-1940.
Beja, Morris. Epiphany in the Modern Novel.
Bell, Millicent. Edith Wharton and Henry James.
Bellamy, Joe David. The New Fiction; Interviews with Innovative American Writers.
Bellman, Samuel Irving. Marjorie Kinnan Rawlings.
Bennett, Mildred R. The World of Willa Cather.
Berthoff, Warner. The Ferment of Realism; American Literature; 1884-1919.
Berthoff, Warner. Fictions and Events.
Bewley, Marius. The Eccentric Design.
Bewley, Marius. Masks and Mirrors.
Bigsby, C.W.E., Ed. The Black American Writer; Volume I; Fiction.
Blackmur, Richard P. New Criticism in the United States.
Blackmur, Richard P. A Primer of Ignorance.
Blake, Fay M. The Strike in the American Novel.
Blake, Nelson Manfred. Novelists America; Fiction as History; 1910-1940.
Blanck, Jacob, Comp. Bibliography of American Literature; Vol. 1; Henry Adams to Donn Byrne.

Blanck, Jacob, Comp. Bibliography of American Literature;Vol. 2;George W. Cable to Timothy Dwight.

Blanck, Jacob, Comp. Bibliography of American Literature;Vol. 3;Edward Eggleston to Bret Harte.

Blanck, Jacob, Comp. Bibliography of American Literature;Vol. 4;Nathaniel Hawthorne to Joseph Holt Ingraham.

Blanck, Jacob, Comp. Bibliography of American Literature;Vol. 5;Washington to Henry Wadsworth Longfellow.

Blanck, Jacob. Comp; Bibliography of American Literature;Vol. 6;Augustus Baldwin Longstreet to Thomas William Parsons.

Block, Haskell M. Naturalistic Triptych.

Bloomfield, Morton W., Ed. The Interpretation of Narrative;Theory and Practice.

Blotner, Joseph. The Modern American Political Novel;1900-1960.

Boas, George, Ed. Romanticism in America.

Bornstein, George, Ed. Romantic and Modern Revaluations of Literary Tradition.

Bourne, Randolph. History of a Literary Radical and other Essays.

Bova, Benjamin. Through Eyes of Wonder.

Bowden, Edwin T. The Dungeon of the Heart.

Bowron, Bernard R., Jr. Henry B. Fuller of Chicago.

Boyers, Robert. Excursions;Selected Literary Essays.

Branden, Nathaniel, and Barbara Branden. Who is Ayn Rand?

Bretnor, Reginald, Ed. The Craft of Science Fiction.

Bretnor, Reginald, Ed. Science Fiction, Today and Tomorrow.

Briggs, Julia. Night Visitors.

Brignano, Russell Carl. Black Americans in Autobiography.

Brinnin, John Malcolm. The Third Rose;Gertrude Stein and Her World.

Brittain, Joan T. Laurence Stallings.

Brooks, Cleanth. The Hidden God.

Brooks, Peter. The Melodramatic Imagination.

Brown, Clarence Arthur. The Achievement of American Criticism.

Brown, Deming. Soviet Attitudes Toward American Writing.

Brown, Douglas Charles. The Enduring Legacy.

Brown, John Russell. The American Novel and the Nineteen Twenties.

Browning, Preston M. Flannery O'Connor.

Bruccoli, Matthew J. John O'Hara;A Checklist.

Bruccoli, Matthew J. Kenneth Millar/Ross Macdonald;A Checklist.

Brushwood, John Stubbs. The Spanish American Novel.

Bruss, Elizabeth W. Autobiographical Acts.

Bryant, Jerry H. The Open Decision.

Bryer, Jackson R., Ed. Fifteen Modern American Authors.

Bryer, Jackson R., and Eugene Harding. Hamlin Garland and the Critics.

Buck, Pearl S., with Theodore F. Harris. For Spacious Skies.

Burbank, Rex. Sherwood Anderson.

Cady, Edwin H. The Light of Common Day.

Calhoun, Richard J., Ed. James Dickey;The Expansive Imagination.

Callow, James T. Guide to American Literature from Emily Dickinson to the Present.

Campbell, Frank D. John D. MacDonald and the Colorful World of Travis McGee.

Campbell, Harry Modean, and Ruel E. Foster. Elizabeth Madox Roberts.

Campbell, Hilbert H., and Charles E. Modlin, Eds. Sherwood Anderson.

GEOGRAPHICS-U.S.A.-20th CENTURY

Cargill, Oscar. Toward A Pluralistic Criticism.
Carr, John, Ed. Kite-Flying and Other Irrational Acts.
Carter, Everett. The American Idea.
Carter, Everett. Howells and the Age of Realism.
Chankin, Donald O. Anonymity and Death;the Fiction of B. Traven.
Charters, Ann. Kerouac;A Biography.
Chupack, Henry. James Purdy.
Churchill, Allen. The Literary Decade.
Churchill, E. Richard, and Linda R. Churchill. Fun with American Literature.
Clarke, John Henrik, Ed. William Styron's Nat Turner.
Cohen, Hennig, Ed. Landmarks of American Writing.
Coindreau, Maurice Edgar. The Time of William Faulkner.
Coles, Robert. Irony in the Mind's Life.
Cook, Richard M. Carson McCullers.
Cooke, M. G., Ed. Modern Black Novelists;A Collection of Critical Essays.
Cooley, Thomas. Educated Lives.
Cooperman, Stanley. World War I and the American Novel.
Copeland, Carolyn Faunce. Language and Time and Gertrude Stein.
Core, George, Ed. Southern Fiction Today.
Cornwell, Ethel F. The Still Point.
Cotton, Gerald B., and Hilda Mary McGill. Fiction Guides.
Cowley, Malcolm, Ed. After the Genteel Tradition;American Writers; 1910-1930.
Cowley, Malcolm. Exile's Return;A Literary Odyssey of the 1920s.
Cowley, Malcolm. The Literary Situation.
Cowley, Malcolm. Think Back on Us.
Cox, Martha Heasley, and Wayne Chatterton. Nelson Algren.
Cox, C. B. The Free Spirit.
Coxe, Louis Osborne. Enabling Acts; Essays in Criticism.
Crothers, George D., Ed. Invitation to Learning;English and American Novels.
Cullen, John B. Old Times in the Faulkner Country.
Culp, D. W., Ed. Twentieth Century Negro Literature.
Curley, Dorothy Nyren, et al., Eds. Modern American Literature;Vol. 4;Supplement to the Fourth Edition.
Davis, Arthur Paul. From the Dark Tower.
Davis, Arthur P. The New Negro Renaissance;An Anthology.
Davis, Robert H., and Arthur B. Maurice. The Caliph of Bagdad.
DeCamp, Lyon Sprague. Lovecraft; A Biography.
DeMille, George E. Literary Criticism in America;A Preliminary Survey.
Deodene, Frank, and William P. French. Black American Fiction Since 1952.
Derleth, August, and Donald Wandrei, Eds. H. P. Lovecraft;Selected Letters;1929-1931.
Derleth, August William. Some Notes on H. P. Lovecraft.
Detweiler, Robert. Four Spiritual Crises in Mid-Century American Fiction.
Dick, Bernard F. The Apostate Angel;A Critical Study of Gore Vidal.
Doig, Ivan, Comp. The Streets We Have Come Down.
Dolan, Paul J. Of War and War's Alarms.
Donaldson, Norman. In Search of Dr. Thorndyke.
Duffey, Bernard. The Chicago Renaissance in American Letters.
Eakin, Paul John. The New England Girl.

Eastman, Max. The Literary Mind; Its Place in An Age of Science.
Eckley, Wilton. Harriette Arnow.
Edel, Leon. The Modern Psychological Novel.
Edmiston, Susan, and Linda D. Cirino. Literary New York;A History and Guide.
Edwards, Clifford D. Conrad Richter's Ohio Trilogy.
Eichelberger, Clayton L. Published Comment on William Dean Howells through 1920.
Elkins, A. C., Jr., and L. J. Forstner. The Romantic Movement Bibliography;1936-1970.
Ellmann, Mary. Thinking About Women.
Ellmann, Richard. Golden Codgers.
Engel, Monroe, Ed. Uses of Literature.
Fabre, Michel. The Unfinished Quest of Richard Wright.
Falk, Robert, and Hayden Clark, Eds. Literature and Ideas in America.
Fanning, Michael. France and Sherwood Anderson;Paris Notebook, 1921.
Farr, Finis. Margaret Mitchell of Atlanta.
Feied, Frederick. No Pie in the Sky.
Fennimore, Keith J. Booth Tarkington.
Fetherling, Doug. The Five Lives of Ben Hecht.
Fiedler, Leslie. The Collected Essays of Leslie Fiedler.
Fiedler, Leslie. Love and Death in the American Novel.
Fiedler, Leslie, A. The Return of the Vanishing American.
Fiedler, Leslie, A. Waiting for the End.
Field, Andrew. Nabokov;A Bibliography.
Field, Louise Maunsell. Ellen Glasgow;Novelist of the Old and the New South.

Fiske, Marjorie. Book Selection and Censorship.
Foerster, Norman. Image of America.
Fogle, Richard H., Comp. Romantic Poets and Prose Writers.
Ford, Hugh. Published in Paris;American and British Writers;Printers, and Publishers in Paris;1920-1939.
Ford, Nick Aaron. The Contemporary Negro Novel.
Foster, Richard. The New Romantics.
Fowler, Douglas. Reading Nabokov.
Fraiberg, Louis. Psychoanalysis and American Literary Criticism.
Franklin, Benjamin. Anais Nin;A Bibliography.
French, Warren G., and Walter E. Kidd, Eds. American Winners of the Nobel Literary Prize.
French, Warren. The Social Novel at the End of an Era.
French, Warren, Ed. The Forties;Fiction, Poetry, Drama.
French, Warren, Ed. The Fifties;Fiction, Poetry, Drama.
French, Warren G. The Twenties;Fiction, Poetry, Drama.
Friedman, Lenemaja. Shirley Jackson.
Friedman, Melvin J. William Styron.
Frohock, W. M. The Novel of Violence in America.
Frohock, W. M. Strangers to this Ground;Cultural Diversity in Contemporary American Writing.
Frye, Northrop. The Well-Tempered Critic.
Fuller, Edmund. Man in Modern Fiction.
Gaston, Edwin W., Jr. Conrad Richter.
Gayle, Addison, Jr. The Way of the New World.
Geismar, Maxwell. The Last of the Provincials.
Geismar, Maxwell. Rebels and Ancestors.

GEOGRAPHICS-U.S.A.-20th CENTURY

Geismar, Maxwell. Writers in Crisis.
Gelfant, Blanche Housman. The American City Novel.
Gerber, Philip L. Willa Cather.
Gerstenberger, Donna, and George Hendrick. The American Novel; 1789-1959.
Gilman, Richard. The Confusion of Realms.
Gindin, James. Harvest of a Quiet Eye.
Glicksberg, Charles Irving. The Literature of Nihilism.
Glicksberg, Charles Irving. Tragic Vision in Twentieth Century Literature.
Gloster, Hugh M. Negro Voices in American Fiction.
Goble, Neil. Asimov Analyzed.
Godshalk, William Leigh. In Quest of Cabell.
Goldman, Sherli Evens. Mary McCarthy;A Bibliography.
Goldsmith, David H. Kurt Vonnegut; Fantasist of Fire and Ice.
Goodman, Paul. The Structure of Literature.
Gordon, Michael. Juvenile Delinquency in the American Novel;1905-1965.
Gossett, Louise Y. Violence in Recent Southern Fiction.
Gottesman, Ronald. The Literary Manuscripts of Upton Sinclair.
Gottesman, Ronald. Upton Sinclair; An Annotated Checklist.
Gray, Richard J. The Literature of Memory;Modern Writers of the American South.
Green, Dorothy. Ulysses Bound.
Green, Elizabeth Lay. The Negro in Contemporary American Literature.
Green, Martin. Re-Appraisals;Some Commonsense Readings in American Literature.
Green, Martin. Transatlantic Patterns.
Green, Rose Basile. The Italian-American Novel.
Greiner, Donald J. Comic Terror; The Novels of John Hawkes.
Gross, Seymour L., and John Edward Hardy, Eds. Images of the Negro in American Literature.
Grover, Dorys C. Vardis Fisher;The Novelist as Poet.
Gruber, Frank. Zane Grey;A Biography.
Guerard, Albert Joseph. The Triumph of the Novel.
Guetti, James. The Limits of Metaphor.
Gunn, Drewey Wayne. American and British Writers in Mexico;1556-1973.
Gurian, Jay. Western American Writing;Tradition and Promise.
Guth, Dorothy Lobrano. Letters of E. B. White.
Guttenberg, Barnett. Web of Being.
Hackett, Alice Payne, and James Henry Burke. 80 Years of Best Sellers;1895-1975.
Hackett, Francis. On American Books.
Hall, James. The Lunatic Giant in the Drawing Room.
Handy, William J. Modern Fiction;A Formalist Approach.
Harap, Louis. The Image of the Jew in American Literature.
Hardy, Barbara. The Appropriate Form;An Essay on the Novel.
Hardy, John Edward. Katherine Anne Porter.
Hardy, John Edward. Man in the Modern Novel.
Harper, Howard M., Jr. Desperate Faith.
Harris, Charles B. Contemporary American Novelists of the Absurd.
Harris, Janet. A Century of American History in Fiction.
Hartley, L. P. The Novelist's Responsibility.

GEOGRAPHICS-U.S.A.-20th CENTURY

Harwell, Richard, Ed. Margaret Mitchell's Gone with the Wind Letters;1936-1949.

Hassan, Ihab. Radical Innocence.

Hassan, Ihab. Contemporary American Literature;1945-1972.

Hassan, Ihab. The Literature of Silence;Henry Miller and Samuel Beckett.

Hauck, Richard Boyd. A Cheerful Nihilism.

Hayashi, Tetsumaro. John Steinbeck; A Concise Bibliography.

Heiney, Donald. Recent American Literature To 1930.

Heiney, Donald. Recent American Literature.

Heiney, Donald. Recent American Literature After 1930.

Herman, Linda. Corpus Delicti of Mystery Fiction.

Hersey, John Richard. Ralph Ellison; A Collection of Critical Essays.

Hicks, Granville, and Jack Alan Robbins. Literary Horizons.

Hilfer, Anthony Channell. The Revolt from the Village;1915-1930.

Hillegas, Mark R. The Future as Nightmare.

Hipkiss, Robert A. Jack Kerouac, Prophet of the New Romanticism.

Hobson, Fred C. Serpent in Eden.

Hocks, Richard A. Henry James and Pragmatistic Thought.

Hoffman, Michael J. Gertrude Stein.

Hoffman, Frederick J. The Twenties.

Hollowell, John. Fact and Fiction;The New Journalism and the Nonfiction Novel.

Holman, C. Hugh. The Roots of Southern Writing.

Holman, C. Hugh. Three Modes of Modern Southern Fiction.

Hopkins, Lee Bennett. More Books by More People.

Hosillos, Lucila V. Philippine-American Literary Relations;1898-1941.

Howard, David, et al., Eds. Tradition and Tolerance in Nineteenth-Century Fiction.

Howe, Irving, Ed. Edith Wharton;A Collection of Critical Essays.

Hoyt, Charles Alva, Ed. Minor American Novelists.

Hubbell, Jay B. The South in American Literature;1607-1900.

Hubbell, Jay B. Southern Life in Fiction.

Hudgens, Betty Lenhardt, Comp. Kurt Vonnegut, Jr.;A Checklist.

Hudson, Theodore R. From LeRoi Jones to Amiri Baraka;The Literary Works.

Huff, Mary Nance, Comp. Robert Penn Warren;A Bibliography.

Humphrey, Robert. Stream of Consciousness in the Modern Novel.

Hunter, James. B. F. Skinner and Contemporary Literature.

Inge, M. Thomas, Ed. Ellen Glasgow; Centennial Essays.

Jackson, Thomas H., Ed. Twentieth Century Interpretations of Miss Lonelyhearts.

Janssens, G. A. M. The American Literary Review.

Jessup, Josephine Lurie. Faith of Our Feminists.

Johnson, R. L. The American Heritage of James Norman Hall.

Johnston, Alva. The Case of Erle Stanley Gardner.

Jones, Howard Mumford. Guide to American Literature and Its Backgrounds Since 1890.

Jones, Peter G. War and the Novelist;Appraising the American War Novel.

Kallsen, Loren J., Ed. Kentucky Tragedy;A Problem in Romantic Attitudes.

Karanikas, Alexander. Tillers of a Myth.

Karolides, Nicholas J. The Pioneer in the American Novel;1900-1950.

GEOGRAPHICS-U.S.A.-20th CENTURY

Kartiganer, Donald M., and Malcolm A. Griffith. Theories of American Literature.
Kazin, Alfred. Bright Book of Life.
Kazin, Alfred. On Native Grounds.
Kazin, Alfred, Ed. The Open Form; Essays for Our Time.
Kazin, Alfred. On Native Grounds.
Kegan, Robert. The Sweeter Welcome.
Kellogg, Grace. The Two Lives of Edith Wharton; The Woman and Her Work.
Kellogg, Jean Defrees. Dark Prophets of Hope.
Kennard, Jean E. Number and Nightmare; Forms of Fantasy in Contemporary Fiction.
Kenner, Hugh. A Homemade World; The American Modernist Writer.
Kiernan, Brian. Images of Society and Nature.
Kiernan, Robert F. Katherine Anne Porter and Carson McCullers; A Reference Guide.
Kirk, Clara Marburg. W. D. Howells; Traveler From Altruria; 1889-1894.
Klinkowitz, Jerome. Literary Disruptions; the Making of a Post-Contemporary American Fiction.
Klotman, Phyllis R. Another Man Gone.
Knight, Damon. In Search of Wonder.
Knight, Grant C. The Strenuous Age in American Literature.
Kolb, Harold H., Jr. Illusion of Life; American Realism As a Literary Form.
Kostelanetz, Richard, Ed. Younger Critics of North America.
Kramer, Victor A. James Agee.
Krawitz, Henry. A Post-Symbolist Bibliography.
Kuehl, John, and Jackson R. Bryer, Eds. Dear Scott/Dear Max; The Fitzgerald-Perkins Correspondence.
Kuehl, John Richard. John Hawkes and the Craft of Conflict.
LaFrance, Marston, Ed. Patterns of Commitment in American Literature.
Langer, Lawrence L. The Holocaust and the Literary Imagination.
Langford, Richard E., et al, Eds. Essays in Modern American Literature.
Larsen, Erling. James Agee.
Lawall, Sarah N. Critics of Consciousness; The Existential Structures of Literature.
Leary, Lewis, Ed. American Literary Essays.
Leavis, F. R. Anna Karenina and other Essays.
Lee, Alfred Pyle. A Bibliography of Christopher Morley.
Lee, Lawrence L. Vladimir Nabokov.
Lee, Robert Edson. From West to East.
Lehan, Richard. A Dangerous Crossing.
Leisy, Ernest E. The American Historical Novel.
LeRoy, Gaylord C., Ed. Preserve and Create.
Leverence, John. Irving Wallace; A Writer's Profile.
Levine, George and David Leverenz, Eds. Mindful Pleasures; Essays on Thomas Pynchon.
Lewis, Gerald E. Up Here in Maine.
Lewis, R. W. B. Trials of the Word.
Lewis, Wyndham. Men Without Art.
Lindberg, Gary H. Edith Wharton and the Novel of Manners.
Litz, A. Walton, Ed. Modern American Fiction; Essays in Criticism.
Long, E. Hudson. O. Henry; The Man and His Work.
Long, Frank Belknap. Howard Phillips Lovecraft; Dreamer on the Nightside.
Lowenthal, Leo. Literature, Popular Culture, and Society.
Lundquist, James. Chester Himes.
Lutwack, Leonard. Heroic Fiction.

Lyon, Thomas J. Frank Waters.
Lyons, John O. The College Novel in America.
MacLeod, Anne. A Moral Tale.
MacMillan, Dougald. Transition;The Story of a Literary Era;1927-1938.
MacShane, Frank. Raymond Chandler.
McCarthy, Harold T. The Expatriate Perspective.
McCarthy, Mary. On the Contrary; Articles of Belief.
McCarthy, Mary. The Writing on the Wall and Other Literary Essays.
McCormack, Thomas, Ed. Afterwords; Novelists on Their Novels.
McCormick, John. The Middle Distance.
McCormick, John. Catastrophe and Imagination.
McDaniel, John N. The Fiction of Philip Roth.
McDowell, Frederick P. W. Elizabeth Madox Roberts.
McFarland, Dorothy Tuck. Flannery O'Connor.
McNeir, Waldo and Leo B. Levy, Eds. Studies in American Literature.
Macy, John Albert. American Writers on American Literature by 37 Contemporary Writers.
Madden, David, Ed. Tough Guy Writers of the Thirties.
Madden, David, Ed. Remembering James Agee.
Magny, Edmonde. Translated by Eleanor Hochman. The Age of the American Novel.
Major, Mabel, and T. M. Pearce. Southwest Heritage;A Literary History with Bibliographies.
Margolies, Edward. Native Sons.
Malin, Irving, Ed. Contemporary American-Jewish Literature.
Martin, Jay. Harvests of Change.
Mason, Bobbie Ann. The Girl Sleuth.
Mason, Bobbie Ann. Nabokov's Garden;A Study of Ada.
Maurice, Arthur Bartlett. New York in Fiction.
May, John R. The Pruning Word.
May, John R. Toward a New Earth; Apocalypse in the American Novel.
Mellow, James R. Charmed Circle; Gertrude Stein and Company.
Mencken, H. L. Edited by William H. Nolte. H. L. Mencken's Smart Set Criticism.
Merry, Bruce. Anatomy of the Spy Thriller.
Mersand, Joseph. Traditions in American Literature.
Meyer, Roy W. The Middle Western Farm Novel in the Twentieth Century.
Michaud, Regis. The American Novel To-day;A Social and Psychological Study.
Miles, Rosalind. The Fiction of Sex; Themes and Functions of Sex Difference in the Modern Novel.
Miller, James E., Jr. Quests Surd and Absurd.
Miller, Wayne Charles. An Armed America;Its Face in Fiction.
Millett, Fred B. Contemporary American Authors.
Millett, Kate. Sexual Politics.
Millgate, Michael. American Social Fiction;James to Cozzens.
Milne, Gordon. The Sense of Society; A History of the American Novel of Manners.
Milton, John R., Comp. The Literature of South Dakota.
Miron, Dan. A Traveler Disguised; A Study in the Rise of Modern Yiddish Fiction in the Nineteenth Century.
Mizener, Arthur. Twelve Great American Novels.
Mizener, Arthur. The Sense of Life in the Modern Novel.
Mizener, Sharon Fusselman. Manhattan Transients;A Critical Essay.
Mooney, Harry J., Jr. The Fiction and Criticism of Katherine Anne Porter.

GEOGRAPHICS-U.S.A.-20th CENTURY

Morgan, H. Wayne. American Writers in Rebellion.

Morrell, David. John Barth; An Introduction.

Morris, Robert K., and Irving Malin, Eds. The Achievement of William Styron.

Morris, Wright. Edited by Robert E. Knoll. Conversations with Wright Morris; Critical Views and Responses.

Morris, Wright. The Territory Ahead.

Morton, Donald E. Vladimir Nabokov.

Munson, Gorham Bert. Waldo Frank; A Study.

Murphy, John J., Ed. Five Essays on Willa Cather; the Merrimack Symposium.

Myers, Carol Fairbanks. Women in Literature; Criticism of the Seventies.

Nabokov, Vladimir. Strong Opinions.

Nagel, James, Comp. Critical Essays on Catch-22.

Nance, William L. Katherine Anne Porter and the Art of Rejection.

Nelson, Gerald B. Ten Versions of America.

Neumann, Alfred R., and David V. Erdman, Eds. Modern Language Association of America; Literature and the Other Arts; A Select Bibliograph; 1952-1958.

Nevins, Francis M. Royal Bloodline; Ellery Queen, Author and Detective.

Nevius, Blake, Comp. The American Novel; Sinclair Lewis to the Present.

Nevius, Blake. Edith Wharton; A Study of her Fiction.

Nevius, Blake. Robert Herrick; The Development of a Novelist.

New York City Public Library. No Crystal Stair; A Bibliography of Black Literature.

Nist, John, Ed. Style in English.

Noble, David W. The Eternal Adam and the New World Garden.

Norton, Charles A. Melville Davisson Post; Man of Many Mysteries.

Nye, Russel B., Ed. New Dimensions in Popular Culture.

O'Brien, John. Interviews with Black Writers.

O'Connor, Flannery. Mystery and Ma-Manners.

O'Connor, William Van. The Grotesque; An American Genre and Other Essays.

O'Connor, William Van. Seven Modern American Novelists.

O'Faolain, Sean. The Vanishing Hero.

Ohlin, Peter. Agee.

Olander, Joseph D., and Martin Harry Greenberg, Eds. Arthur C. Clarke.

Olander, Joseph D., and Martin Harry Greenberg, Eds. Isaac Asimov.

Olderman, Raymond M. Beyond the Waste Land; A Study of the American Novel in the Nineteen-Sixties.

Oliver, Grace A. A Study of Maria Edgeworth.

Owings, Mark. The Revised H. P. Lovecraft Bibliography.

Panichas, George Andrew. The Politics of Twentieth-Century Novelists.

Parker, Dorothy. The Portable Dorothy Parker.

Parrington, Vernon Louis. Main Currents in American Thought.

Patrouch, Joseph F. The Science Fiction of Isaac Asimov.

Pattee, Fred Lewis. A History of American Literature Since 1870.

Pattee, Fred Lewis. The Development of the American Short Story.

Paul, Sherman, Ed. Six Classic American Writers.

Pearce, Roy Harvey. Historicism Once More.

Peden, William Harwood. The American Short Story; Continuity and Change.

Pendo, Stephen. Raymond Chandler on Screen; His Novels into Film.
Perry, Dick. Reflections of Jesse Smith on a Land of Many Moods.
Perry, Margaret. Silence to the Drums; A Survey of the Literature of the Harlem Renaissance.
Petit, Arthur G. Mark Twain and the South.
Pieratt, Asa B. Kurt Vonnegut, Jr.; A Descriptive Bibliography and Annotated Secondary Checklist.
Pinsker, Sanford. The Comedy that "hoits"; An Essay on the Fiction of Philip Roth.
Pizer, Donald, Ed. The Literary Criticism of Frank Norris.
Podhoretz, Norman. Doings and Undoings.
Poets and Writers, Inc. A Directory of American Fiction Writers.
Poirier, Richard. A World Elsewhere; The Place of Style in American Literature.
Porges, Irwin. Edgar Rice Burroughs; The Man and His Works.
Porter, Katherine Anne. The Collected Essays and Occasional Writings of Katherine Anne Porter.
Pritchard, John Paul. Criticism in America.
Proffer, Carl R., Ed. Soviet Criticism of American Literature in the Sixties.
Pullar, Philippa. Frank Harris; A Biography.
Rahv, Philip. Literature in America.
Rahv, Philip. Literature and the Sixth Sense.
Raleigh, John Henry. Time, Place, and Idea; Essays on the Novel.
Rand, Ayn. The Romantic Manifesto.
Ratner, Marc L. William Styron.
Reginald, R. Contemporary Science Fiction Authors.
Reid, Randall. The Fiction of Nathanael West; No Redeemer, No Promised Land.
Rice, Howard Crosby. Rudyard Kipling in New England.
Richardson, Robert. Literature and Film.
Rideout, Walter B. The Radical Novel in the United States; 1900-1954.
Rideout, Walter B., Ed. Sherwood Anderson; A Collection of Critical Essays.
Robbins, Jack Alan, Ed. Granville Hicks in the New Masses.
Robbins, Jack Alan, Ed. Literary Essays; 1954-1974.
Rodgers, Bernard F., Jr. Philip Roth; A Bibliography.
Ronald, Ann. Zane Grey.
Rose, Ellen Cronan. The Tree Outside the Window; Doris Lessing's Children of Violence.
Roselle, Daniel. Transformations.
Ross, Ralph Gilbert. Makers of American Thought; An introduction to Seven American Writers.
Ross, T. J. Film and the Liberal Arts.
Routh, H. V. Money, Morals and Manners As Revealed in Modern Literature.
Rubin, Louis D., Jr. The Faraway Country; Writers of the Modern South.
Rubin, Louis D., Jr. A Bibliographical Guide to the Study of Southern Literature.
Rubin, Louis D., Jr. Death of the Novel; Essays in American Literature.
Rubin, Louis D., Jr. The Comic Imagination in American Literature.
Rubin, Louis D., Jr., and Robert D. Jacobs. South; Modern Southern Literature in its Cultural Setting.
Rubin, Louis D., Jr., and Robert D. Jacobs. Southern Renascence; The Literature of the Modern South.
Ruland, Richard, Ed. The Spirit of Place.
Ruland, Richard. The Rediscovery of American Literature.

GEOGRAPHICS-U.S.A.-20th CENTURY

Ruotolo, Lucio. Six Existential Heroes;The Politics of Faith.
Russell, Francis. Three Studies in Twentieth Century Obscurity.
Saito, George, and Philip Williams. Soseki and Salinger;American Students on Japanese Fiction.
Sampson, Edward C. E. B. White.
Saul, George Brandon. In Praise of the Half-Forgotten and Other Essays.
Schatt, Stanley. Kurt Vonnegut, Jr.
Schneider, Daniel J. Symbolism;the Manichean Vision.
Schneider, Robert W. Five Novelists of the Progressive Era.
Scholes, Robert. Structural Fabulation;An Essay on the Fiction of the Future.
Schorer, Mark. The World We Imagine;Selected Essays by Mark Schorer.
Schulberg, Budd. The Four Seasons of Success.
Schulz, Max F. Black Humor Fiction of the Sixties.
Schulz, Max F. Bruce Jay Friedman.
Schulz, Max F. Radical Sophistication.
Schwarzschild, Bettina. Not-Right House;Essays on James Purdy.
Scott, James B. Djuna Barnes.
Scott, Nathan A., Jr. Ed. Adversity and Grace.
Scotto, Robert M. Three Contemporary American Novelists;An Annotated Bibliography of Works by and about John Hawkes, Joseph Heller and Thomas Pynchon.
Seib, Kenneth. James Agee;Promise and Fulfillment.
Seward, William W., Jr. Contrasts in Modern Writers.
Shapiro, Charles, Ed. Twelve Original Essays on Great American Novels.
Shaughnessy, Mary Rose. Women and Success in American Society in the works of Edna Ferber.
Shockley, Ann Allen. Living Black American Authors;A Biographical Directory.
Simon, Linda. The Biography of Alice B. Toklas.
Skaggs, Merrill Maguire. The Folk of Southern Fiction.
Slade, Joseph W. Thomas Pynchon.
Slote, Bernice, and Virginia Faulkner, Eds. The Art of Willa Cather.
Slusser, George Edgar. The Bradbury Chronicles.
Slusser, George Edgar. The Farthest Shores of Ursula K. Le Guin.
Slusser, George Edgar. Harlan Ellison;Unrepentant Harlequin.
Smith, Myron J. Cloak-and-Dagger Bibliography;An Annotated Guide to Spy Fiction;1937-1975.
Snell, George. The Shapers of American Fiction;1798-1947.
Solotaroff, Theodore. The Red Hot Vacuum.
Spacks, Patricia Meyer. Contemporary Women Novelists;A Collection of Critical Essays.
Spatz, Jonas. Hollywood in Fiction.
Spender, Stephen. Love-Hate Relations;English and American Sensibilities.
Spiegel, Alan. Fiction and the Camera Eye.
Spiller, Robert E. The Cycle of American Literature;An Essay in Historical Criticism.
Spiller, Robert E., et al., Eds. Literary History of the United States.
Spiller, Robert E. The Oblique Light.
Spiller, Robert E. The Third Dimension.
Stallman, Robert Wooster, Ed. Critiques and Essays in Criticism;1920-1948.
Stark, John O. The Literature of Exhaustion;Borges, Nabokov and Barth.
Starrett, Vincent. Born in a Bookshop;Chapters from the Chicago Renascence.

Stegner, Wallace, Ed. The American Novel from James Fenimore Cooper to William Faulkner.
Stein, Gertrude. Lectures in America.
Stephens, Martha. The Question of Flannery O'Connor.
Stevens, Michael. V. Sackville-West; A Critical Biography.
Stewart, John L. The Burden of Time.
Stewart, Lawrence Delbert. Paul Bowles; The Illumination of North Africa.
Stewart, Randall. Edited by George Core. Regionalism and Beyond; Essays of Randall Stewart.
Stone, Edward. A Certain Morbidness; A View of American Literature.
Stouck, David. Willa Cather's Imagination.
Straumann, Heinrich. American Literature in the Twentieth Century.
Stroud, Parry. Stephen Vincent Benet.
Stuckey, W. J. The Pulitzer Prize Novels; A Critical Backward Look.
Sullivan, Walter. A Requiem for the Renascence; The State of Fiction in the Modern South.
Sullivan, Walter. Death by Melancholy; Essays on Modern Southern Fiction.
Sutton, William Alfred. Black Like It Is/Was; Erskine Caldwell's Treatment of Racial Themes.
Sutton, William A. The Road to Winesburg.
Tanner, Tony. City of Words; American Fiction; 1950-1970.
Tarrant, Desmond. James Branch Cabell; The Dream and the Reality.
Taylor, Lloyd C. Margaret Ayer Barnes.
Tennenhouse, Leonard, Ed. The Practice of Psychoanalytic Criticism.
Thomas, Alfred K. The Epic of Evolution; Its Etiology and Art.
Thorp, Willard. American Writing in the Twentieth Century.
Tischler, Nancy M. Black Masks; Negro Characters in Modern Southern Fiction.
Tobin, Richard L., Comp. The Golden Age.
Tominaga, Thomas T. Iris Murdoch and Muriel Spark; A Bibliography.
Tomkins, Mary E. Ida M. Tarbell.
Tooker, Dan. Fiction! Interviews with Northern California Novelists.
Treat, Lawrence, Ed. The Mystery Writer's Handbook.
Trilling, Diana. Claremont Essays.
Turner, Darwin T. In A Minor Chord.
Tuttleton, James W. The Novel of Manners in America.
Tytell, John. Naked Angels; The Lives and Literature of the Beat Generation.
Umphlett, Wiley Lee. The Sporting Myth and the American Experience.
Underwood, John Curtis. Literature and Insurgency; Ten Studies in Racial Evolution.
Updike, John. Assorted Prose.
Van Doren, Carl. The American Novel; 1789-1939.
Van Nostrand, A. D. Everyman His Own Poet.
Vannatta, Dennis P. Nathanael West; An Annotated Bibliography of the Scholarship and Works.
Vickery, John B., Ed. Myth and Literature; Contemporary Theory and Practice.
Vidal, Gore. Matters of Fact and Fiction; Essays 1973-1976.
Vinson, James. Contemporary Novelists.
Vitelli, James R. Van Wyck Brooks; A Reference Guide.
Vogel, Dan. The Three Masks of American Tragedy.
Wagenknecht, Edward. Cavalcade of the American Novel.
Wager, Willis. American Literature; A World View.

Wagner, Linda Welshimer. Hemingway and Faulkner;Inventors/Masters.

Walcutt, Charles Child. American Literary Naturalism;A Divided Stream.

Walcutt, Charles Child. Seven Novelists in the American Naturalist Tradition;An Introduction.

Waldmeir, Joseph J. American Novels of the Second World War.

Waldmeir, Joseph J., Ed. Recent American Fiction;Some Critical Views.

Waldrip, Louise, and Shirley Ann Bauer. A Bibliography of the Works of Katherine Anne Porter and A Bibliography of the Criticism of the Works of Katherine Anne Porter.

Walker, Dorothea. Alice Brown.

Walker, Franklin. San Francisco's Literary Frontier.

Walker, William E., and Robert L. Welker, Eds. Reality and Myth.

Wallach, Mark I. Christopher Morley.

Walpole, Hugh, Sir. The Art of James Branch Cabell.

Ward, Alfred Charles. American Literature;1880-1930.

Wasserstrom, William. Heiress of all the Ages.

Watkins, Floyd C. The Flesh and the Word;Eliot, Hemingway, Faulkner.

Weatherby, William J. Squaring Off.

Webb, Constance. Richard Wright.

Weinberg, Helen. The New Novel in America.

Wells, Geoffrey Harry. Deucalion;Or, The Future of Literary Criticism.

Wells, Walter. Tycoons and Locusts.

West, Thomas R. Flesh of Steel;Literature and the Machine in American Culture.

Westbrook, Max, Ed. The Modern American Novel;Essays in Criticism.

Weston, Harold. Form in Literature; A Theory of Technique and Construction.

Wharton, Edith. The Writing of Fiction.

Whitbread, Thomas B., Ed. Seven Contemporary Authors.

White, Ray L., Ed. Achievement of Sherwood Anderson;Essays in Criticism.

Whiteman, Maxwell. A Century of Fiction by American Negroes;1853-1952.

Wicker, Brian. The Story-Shaped World;Fiction and Metaphysics; Some Variations on a Theme.

Widmer, Eleanor, and Kingsley Widmer, Eds. Freedom and Culture.

Wilson, Edmund. The Bit Between My Teeth.

Wilson, Edmund. Classics and Commercials.

Wilson, Edmund. The Shock of Recognition.

Wilson, Edmund. Letters on Literature and Politics;1912-1972.

Wilson, Edmund. The Triple Thinkers;Twelve Essays on Literary Subjects.

Wilson, Edmund. The Wound and the Bow;Seven Studies in Literature.

Wilson, Robert A. Gertrude Stein;A Bibliography.

Wintle, Justin. The Pied Pipers;Interviews with the Influential Creators of Children's Literature.

Witham, W. Tasker. The Adolescent in the American Novel;1920-1960.

Woodress, James Leslie. Willa Cather;Her Life and Art.

Woodress, James Leslie. American Fiction;1900-1950.

Wright, Nathalia. American Novelists in Italy.

Yates, Norris W. The American Humorist.

Young, James O. Black Writers of the Thirties.

Young, Philip. Three Bags Full.

Zavarzadeh, Mas'ud. The Mythopoeic Reality.

GEOGRAPHICS-U.S.A.

For complete citations of critical works on the following authors associated with this Country, please consult the Author Criticism and Main Listing Sections.

U.S.A.-18th CENTURY

Bierce, Ambrose
Franklin, Benjamin
Hopkinson, Francis

U.S.A.-19th CENTURY (1800-1918)

Alcott, Louisa May
Billings, Josh
Brown, Charles Brockden
Calvert, George Henry
Chesnutt
Conrad, Joseph
Cooper, James Fenimore
Crane, Stephen
Curtis, George William
DeForest, John William
Dunbar, Paul Lawrence
Emerson, Ralph Waldo
Fuller, Margaret
Gladden, Washington
Harris, George Washington
Harte, Bret
Hawthorne, Nathaniel
Henry, O
Howells, William S.
Irving, Washington
Jewett, Sarah
King, Grace
London, Jack
Melville, Herman
Norris, Frank
Philips, David Graham
Poe, Edgar Allen
Robinson, Roland E.
Rowson, Susanna
Simms, William Gilmore
Stockton, Frank
Stowe, Harriet Beecher
Thoreau, Henry David
Thorpe, Thomas Bangs
Twain, Mark
Webster, Noah

POST WW I 1919-1939

Babbitt, Irving
Barnes, Djuna
Benet, Stephen Vincent
Brooks, Van Wick
Brown, Alice
Buck, Pearl
Burroughs, Edgar Rice
Cabell, James Branch
Caldwell, Erskine
Cather, Willa
Dos Passos, John
Dreiser, Theodore
Eliot, T.S.
Farrel, James T.
Faulkner, William
Ferber, Edna
Fisher, Vardis
Fitzgerald, F. Scott
Frank, Waldo
Garland, Hamlin
Glasgow, Ellen
Gregory, Horace
Grey, Zane
Hall, James Norman
Hecht, Ben
Hemingway, Ernest
Herrick, Robert
Huneker, James
Lewis, Sinclair
McCarthy, Mary
Marquand, John
Mencken, H.L.
Mitchell, Margaret
Morley, Christopher
Parker, Dorothy
Porter, Katherine Anne

GEOGRAPHICS-U.S.A.

Pound, Ezra
Ransom, John Crowe
Rawlings, Marjorie Kinnan
Roberts, Elizabeth Madox
Roberts, Kenneth
Rolfe, Frederick William
Sedgwick, Catharine Maria
Sinclair, Upton
Stallings, Laurence
Stein, Gertrude
Steinbeck, John
Stuart, Jesse
Tarbell, Ida M.
Tarkington, Booth
Tate, Allen
Wallace, Irving
West, Nathaniel
Wharton, Edith
White, E. B.
Wolfe, Thomas

POST WW II
1946-Present

Agee, James
Algren, Nelson
Arnow, Harriette
Asinov, Isaac
Atherton, Gertrude
Baldwin, James
Barth
Bellow, Saul
Berger, Thomas
Bradbury, Ray
Burroughs, William S.
Carr
Chandler, Raymond
Chopin, Kate
Coover
Cozzens, James Gould
Donleavy, J. P.
Ellison, Harlan
Ellison, Ralph
Friedman, Bruce Jay
Hawkes, John
Heggen, Thomas

Heller, Joseph
Hicks, Granville
Himes, Chester
Jackson, Shirley
Kerouac, Jack
Lovecraft, H. P.
MacDonald, Ross
Mailer, Norman
Miller, Henry
Morris, Wright
Nin, Anais
Oates, Joyce Carol
O'Connor, Flannery
O'Hara, John
Pynchon, Thomas
Rand, Ayn
Richter, Conrad
Roth, Philip
Salinger, J. D.
Stafford, Jean
Stegner, Wallace
Styron, William
Thurber, James
Toomer, Jean
Traven, B.
Trilling, Lionel
Updike, John
Vidal, Gore
Vonnegut, Kurt
Wallace, Irving
Wallant
Warren, Robert Penn
Waters, Frank
Welty, Eudora
White, Stewart Edward
Wiesel, Elie
Wilson, Edmund
Wright, Richard

GEOGRAPHICS-CANADA

Anthony, Geraldine. John Coulter.
Armitage, A. D., and Nancy Tudor. Canadian Essay and Literature Index.
Baker, R. P. A. History of English-Canadian Literature.
Baker, Ray P. History of English-Canadian Literature to the Confederation;Its Relation to the Literature of Great Britain and the U. S.
Ballstadt, Carl, Ed. The Search for English-Canadian Literature.
Beasley, David. The Canadian Don Quixote.
Bourinot, J. G., et al. Our Intellectual Strength and Weakness.
Bowker, Alan, Ed. The Social Criticism of Stephen Leacock.
Chambers, Robert D. Sinclair Ross and Ernest Buckler.
Coan, Otis W., and Richard G. Lillard. America in Fiction.
Cotnam, Jacques. Contemporary Quebec.
Djwa, Sandra. E. J. Pratt;The Evolutionary Vision.
Egoff, Sheila A. The Republic of Childhood;A Critical Guide to Canadian Children's Literature in English.
Frye, Northrop. Anatomy of Criticism;Four Essays.
Frye, Northrop. The Critical Path.
Frye, Northrop.The Stubborn Structure.
Gnarowski, Michael.Leonard Cohen; the Artist and His Critics.
Grove, Frederick P. The Letters of Frederick Philip Grove.
Hambleton, Ronald. Mazo de La Roche of Jalna.
Harrison, Dick. Unnamed Country.
Jones, D. G. Butterfly on Rock.
Klinck. Carl F., Ed.Literary History of Canada.
McArthur, Peter. Stephen Leacock.
MacCullich, Clare. The Neglected Genre.
McDonough, Irma, Ed. Canadian Books for Children.
Mandel, Eli. Another Time.
Mandel, Eli. Contexts of Canadian Criticism.
Morely, Patricia A. The Comedians.
Moyles, R. G. English-Canadian Literature to 1900.
Northey, Margot.The Haunted Wilderness.
Pacey, Desmond. Creative Writing in Canada.
Phelps, Arthur L., Ed. Canadian Writers.
Ricoeur, Paul.The Rule of Metaphor.
Staines, David, Ed. The Canadian Imagination.
Stevens, Peter. Modern Canadian Prose;A Guide to Information Sources.
Stevenson, Lionel. Appraisals of Canadian Literature.
Story, Norah. Oxford Companion to Canadian History and Literature.
Thomas, Clara. Canadian Novelists.
Thwaite, Mary F. From Primer to Pleasure in Reading.
Toye, William, Ed. Supplement to the Oxford Companion to Canadian History and Literature.
Tremaine, Marie. Bibliography of Canadian Imprints;1751-1800.
Tucker, Ferris. Modern Commonwealth Literature.
Waelti-Walter, Jennifer. Michel Butor.
Wallace, William S. Dictionary of North American Authors Deceased Before 1950.
Watters, Reginald E., and Inglis F. Bell. On Canadian Literature; 1806-1960.
Wilson, Edmund. O Canada;An American's Notes on Canadian Culture.
Woodcock, George, Ed. A Choice of Critics.

GEOGRAPHICS-CANADA

Young, Al. Ernest Buckler.

Included in this Section are names of Canadian authors who are discussed at great length along with others about whom critical mentions are too brief to constitute a separate entry in the Author Section of this book, although they will readily be found in the general books on Canadian intellectual history.

For complete citations of critical works on the starred authors pertaining to this country, please consult the Author Section.

Andersons, Clara Rothwell
Archibald, Edith J.   1854-1934
Atkin, Grace Murray
Atwood, Margaret*   1939-
Baird, Irene
Barnard, Leslie Gordon   1890-1961
Barry, Robertine   1866-1910
Beck, Lily Adams   0000-1931
Birney, Earle   1904-
Blair, Marie-Claire   1939-
Brooke, Frances   1724-1789
Bouveing, George   1935-
Buckler, Ernest*   1908-
Buies, Arthur   1840-1891
Butor, Michael*   1926-
Callaghan, Morley   1903-
Cape, Judith   1916-
Caurier, Roch   1937-
Chapman, Ethel
Chauvequ, P. J. O.   1820-1890
Chisholm, A. M.   1872-1960
Cohen, Leonard*   1934-
Connor, Ralph   1860-1937
Cornell, Beaumont S.   1892-1958
Day, Frank Parker   1881-1950
Davies, Robertson   1913-
DeMille, James   1836-1880
Dix, Maurice B.

Duncan, Sara Jeannette   1862-1922
Dunn, Oscar   1845-1885
Durkin, Douglas Leader   1884-
Engel, Marian   1933-
Fabre, Hector   1834-1910
Faucher de St. Maurice   1844-1897
Foley, Pearl B.   (d. 1953)
Footner, Hulburt
Frechette, Louis Honore   1831-1904
Gagnon, Ernest   1834-1915
Gainer, Hugh   1913-
Gaspe, Philipe Aubert de   1814-
Gibbon, John Murray   1875-1952
Gleason-Huguenin, Mrs.
Goldsmith, Olver   1794-1861
Gomery, Percy   1881-1960
Grainger, Martin Allerdale
                               1874-1941
Gregory, Claudius   1889-1944
Grignon, Claude-Henri   1894-
Grove, Fred*   1913-
Grove, Frederick Phillip   1871-1948
Haig-Brown, Roderick   1908-
Haliburton, Thomas C.   1796-1865
Herben, J. F.   1860-1923
Hibert, Anne   1916-
Hood, Robin Allison
Jacob, Fred   1882-1926
Jones, H. J. O. Bedford   1887-1949
Kingsley, Harold
Klein, Abraham Moses   1909-1972
Kreisel, Henry   1922-
Kroetch, Robert   1927-
Lacombe, Patrice
Larue, Hubert   1833-1881
Laurence, Margaret   1926-
Layton, Irving   1912-
Leacock, Stephen*   1869-1944
Legendre, Napoleon   1841-1907
Lemay, Pamphile   1837-1918
Lemelin, Roger   1919-
Levine, Norman   1924-
Lusignan, Alphonse   1843-1892
McCulloch, John Herries
McCulloch, Thomas   1776-1843
Macemen, Gwendolyn   1941-
MacLennan, Hugh   1907-
Maclieth, Madge

McDowell, Franklin Davey	1888-1965	Roy, Gabrielle	1909-
MacPherson, Jay	1931	Salverson, Laura Goodman	1890-
Mitchell, W. O.	1914-	Seine, Jessie G.	
Montgomery, Lucy Maude	1876?-1942	Seton, Ernest Thompson	1860-1946
		Sheard, Virna	1865?-1943
Moorhouse, Hopkins	1882-	Slater, Patrick	1882-1951
Morton, Guy E.	1884-1948	Smith, A. J. M.	1902-
Mowat, Farley	1921-	Souster, Raymond	1921-
Myrand, Ernest	1854-1921	Sprigge, Elizabeth	1900-
Nevers, Edmond de	1862-1906	Stead, Robert J. C.	1880-1959
Niven, Frederick	1874-1944	Stephen, Alexander Maitland	1882-1942
Ostenso, Martha	1900-1963	Stewart, James Livingstone	
Packard, Frank L.	1877-1942	Sullivan, Alan	1868-1947
Panneton, Philippe	1895-1960	Tache, Joseph Charles	1821-1894
Paquet, Louis-Adolphe	1859-1942	Wallace, W. F.	1886-1958
Pratt, E. J.	1882-1964	Watson, Robert	1882-1948
Raddall, Thomas	1903-	Watson, Sheila	1919-
Ray, Camille		Wiebe, Rudy	1934-
Richler, Mordecai	1931-	Wilkinson, Anne	1910-1961
Roberts, Sir Charles G. D.	1860-1945	Wilson, Ethel	1890-
Ross, Sinclair*	1908-	Wiseman, Adele	
Routhier, Sir Adolphe-Basil	1839-1920		

Subject Index

ABSURDISM

See COMEDY/HUMOR.

ADULTERY

See SEXUALITY.

ALLEGORY

Becker, John E. Hawthorne's Historical Allegory.
Clifford, Gay. The Transformations of Allegory.
Gold, Joseph. William Faulkner;A Study in Humanism from Metaphor to Discourse.
Nnolim, Charles E. Melville's "Benito Cereno".
Stone, Edward. A Certain Morbidness;A View of American Literature.
Wiesenfarth, Joseph. Henry James and the Dramatic Analogy.

ANTHROPOLOGY

See CULTURE.

ARCHETYPES

Fiedler, Leslie A. Love and Death in the American Novel.
Mersand, Joseph. Traditions in American Literature.
Morse, J. Mitchell. Prejudice and Literature.
Pops, Martin Leonard. The Melville Archetype.

Slotkin, Richard. Regeneration through Violence.
Tischler, Nancy M. Black Masks;Negro Characters in Modern Southern Fiction.

ARMED FORCES

See WAR.

AUTHORS IN EXILE

Berthoff, Warner. Fictions and Events.
Cowley, Malcolm. Exile's Return.
Fiedler, Leslie A. Waiting for the End.
Ford, Hugh. Published in Paris.
Hoffman, Frederick J. The Twenties.
McCarthy, Harold T. The Expatriate Perspective.
MacMilan, Dougald. Transition;The Story of a Literary Era 1927-1938.
O'Faolain, Sean. The Vanishing Hero.
Simon, Linda. The Biography of Alice B. Toklas.
Stone, Edward. A Certain Morbidness.
Toklas, Alice B. Staying on Alone.

AUTOBIOGRAPHY AND BIOGRAPHY

Adams, Maurianne, Ed. Autobiography.
Allibone, Samuel Austin. A Critical Dictionary of English Literature and British and American Authors Living and Deceased.
Bewley, Marius. Masks and Mirrors.
Blasing, Mutlu Konuk. The Art of Life.
Bruss, Elizabeth W. Autobiographical Acts.

Cockshut, A.O.J. Truth to Life.
Cooley, Thomas. Educated Lives.
Ellmann, Richard. Golden Codgers.
Gohdes, Clarence. Bibliographical Guide to the Study of the Literature of the U.S.A.
Havlice, Patricia Pate. Index to Literary Biography.
Solotaroff, Theodore. The Red Hot Vacuum.
Spiller, Robert E. The Oblique Light.
Trachtenberg, Alan, Ed. Memoirs of Waldo Frank.
Weintraub, Stanley, Ed. Biography and Truth.

BEHAVIORISM

See PSYCHOLOGY.

BIBLE

See RELIGION.

BIOGRAPHY
(As Subject)

See AUTOBIOGRAPHY AND BIOGRAPHY - as subject.

BIOLOGY

See SCIENCE.

BLACK AUTHORS

Baker, Houston A., Jr. Black Literature in America.
Baker, Houston A. Singer of Daybreak.
Balakian, Nona, and Charles Simmons, Eds. The Creative Present.
Baumbach, Jonathan. The Landscape of Nightmare.
Bigsby, C.W.E., Ed. The Black American Writer; Vol. I; Fiction.
Bluestein, Gene. The Voice of the Folk.
Brignano, Russell Carl. Black Americans in Autobiography.
Chesnutt, Helen M. Charles Waddell Chesnutt; Pioneer of the Color Line.
Clack, Doris H. Black Literature Resources; Analysis and Organization.
Clarke, John Henrik, Ed. William Styron's Nat Turner.
Cooke, M.G., Ed. Modern Black Novelists; A Collection of Critical Essays.
Covo, Jacqueline. The Blinking Eye; Ralph Waldo Ellison.
Culp, D.W., Ed. Twentieth Century Negro Literature.
Davis, Arthur Paul. From the Dark Tower.
Davis, Arthur Paul, Comp. The New Negro Renaissance.
Deodene, Frank, and William P. French. Black American Fiction Since 1952.
Dickinson, Donald C. A Bio-Bibliography of Langston Hughes; 1902-1967.
Eckman, Fern Marja. The Furious Passage of James Baldwin.
Emanual, James A. Langston Hughes.
Fabre, Michel. The Unfinished Quest of Richard Wright.
Fiedler, Leslie A. The Collected Essays of Leslie Fiedler, Vol. II.
Ford, Nick Aaron. The Contemporary Negro Novel.
French, Warren, Ed. The Fifties; Fiction, Poetry, Drama.

BLACKS IN LITERATURE

Gayle, Addison, Jr. The Way of the New World.
Gilbertson, Catherine. Harriet Beecher Stowe.
Gilman, Richard. The Confusion of Realms.
Gloster, Hugh M. Negro Voices in American Fiction.
Gossett, Louise Y. Violence in Recent Southern Fiction.
Green, Elizabeth Lay. The Negro in Contemporary American Literature.
Gross, Seymour L., and John Edward Hardy, Eds. Images of the Negro in American Literature.
Holloway, Jean. Hamlin Garland; A Biography.
Hudson, Theodore R. From LeRoi Jones to Amiri Baraka; the Literary Works.
Jackson, Blyden. The Waiting Years; Essays on American Negro Literature.
Kartiganer, Donald M., and Malcolm A Griffith. Theories of American Literature.
Klotman, Phyllis R. Another Man Gone.
Littlejohn, David. Black on White; A Critical Survey of Writing by American Negroes.
Lundquist, James. Chester Himes.
McCarthy, Harold T. The Expatriate Perspective.
Mailer, Norman. Existential Errands.
Major, Clarence. The Dark and Feeling.
Margolies, Edward. Native Sons; A Critical Study of Twentieth-Century Negro American Authors.
May, John R. Toward A New Earth.
Mencken, H. L. Edited by William H. Nolte. H. L. Mencken's Smart Set Criticism.
New York City Public Library. No Crystal Stair; A Bibliography of Black Literature.
O'Brien, John. Interviews with Black Writers.
O'Daniel, Therman B. James Baldwin; A Critical Evaluation.
O'Daniel, Therman B., Ed. Langston Hughes; Black Genius.
Perry, Margaret. Silence to the Drums.
Podhoretz, Norman. Doings and Undoings.
Rose, Alan Henry. Demonic Vision.
Rosenblatt, Roger. Black Fiction.
Ruotolo, Lucio P. Six Existential Heroes; The Politics of Faith.
Shockley, Ann Allen. Living Black American Authors.
Straumann, Heinrich. American Literature in the Twentieth Century.
Turner, Darwin T. In a Minor Chord.
Waldmeir, Joseph J., Ed. Recent American Fiction.
Weatherby, William J. Squaring Off; Mailer versus Baldwin.
Whiteman, Maxwell. A Century of Fiction by American Negroes; 1853-1952.
Whitlow, Roger. Black American Literature; A Critical History.
Wright, Richard. A Biography by Constance Webb.
Young, James O. Black Writers of the Thirties.

BLACKS IN LITERATURE

Baker, Houston A., Jr. Black Literature in America.
Baker, Houston A. Singers of Daybreak.
Bone, Robert. The Negro Novel in America.
Broderick, Dorothy M. Image of the Black in Children's Fiction.
Clarke, John Henrik, Ed. William Styron's Nat Turner.
Culp, D. W. Ed. Twentieth Century Negro Literature.

Davis, Arthur P., Comp. The New Negro Renaissance;An Anthology.
Early, James. The Making of Go Down, Moses.
Gayle, Addison. The Way of the New World;The Black Novel in America.
Geismar, Maxwell, Ed. Mark Twain and the three R's;Race,Religion, Revolution.
Green, Elizabeth Lay. The Negro in Contemporary American Literature.
Grejda, Edward S. Equality in the Writings of Herman Melville.
Gross,Seymour L., and John Edward Hardy, Eds.Images of the Negro in American Literature.
Jackson, Blyden. The Waiting Years; Essays on American Negro Literature.
Klotman, Phyllis R. Another Man Gone.
Margolies, Edward. Native Sons.
Mays, Benjamin E. The Negro's God; as Reflected in His Literature.
Nilon, Charles H. Faulkner and the Negro.
Petit, Arthur G. Mark Twain and the South.
Rose, Alan Henry. Demonic Vision; Racial Fantasy and Southern Fiction.
Rosenblatt, Roger. Black Fiction.
Rubin, Louis D., Jr., Ed. A Bibliographical Guide to the Study of Southern Literature.
Stowe, Harriet Beecher. The Key to Uncle Tom's Cabin.
Sutton, William Alfred. Black Like It Is/Was.
Takaki, Ronald T. Violence in the Black Imagination.
Tischler, Nancy M. Black Masks;Negro Characters in Modern Southern Fiction.
Wagenknecht, Edward. Cavalcade of the American Novel.
Whitlow, Roger. Black American Literature;A Critical History.
Yellin, Jean Fagan. The Intricate Knot.
Young, James O. Black Writers of the Thirties.

CENSORSHIP

Alpert, Hollis, et al. Censorship;For and Against.
American Library Association. Freedom of Inquiry;Supporting the Library Bill of Rights.
Blackmur, R.P. Dirty Hands or the True-Born Censor.
Clot, Harry M. Censorship and Freedom of Expression.
Clot, Harry M. Obscenity and Public Morality.
Craig, Alec. Above All Liberties.
Daily, Jay E. The Anatomy of Censorship.
DeGrazia, Edward. Censorship Landmarks.
Downs, Robert B., Ed. First Freedom;Liberty and Justice in the World of Books and Reading.
Ernst, M.L., and W.Seagle. To the Pure.
Ernst, M.L., and A.Lindey. The Censor Marches On.
Ernst, Morris L., and Alan U.Schwartz. Censorship.
Fiske, Majorie. Book Selection and Censorship.
Ford, Hugh. Published in Paris.
Hoyt, Olga G., and Edwin P.Hoyt. Censorship in America.
Lewis, Felice F. Literature, Obscenity and Law.
Lewis, Wyndham. The Writer and the Absolute.
McClellan, Grant S. Censorship in the United States.
McLachlan, Bruce. Censorship.

Moon, Eric, Ed. Book Selection and Censorship in the Sixties.
Oboler, Eli. The Fear of the Word; Censorship and Sex.
Phelan, John, Ed. Communications Control.
Rist, Ray C., Ed. Pornography Controversy.
Schroeder, Theodore A. Free Speech.
Snyder, Gerald S. The Right to be Informed; Censorship in the United States.
Widmer, Eleanor, and Kingsley Widmer, Eds. Freedom and Culture.
Witham, W. Tasker. The Adolescent in the American Novel; 1920-1960.

CHILDREN

Blount, Margaret. Animal Land; The Creatures of Children's Fiction.
Broderick, Dorothy M. Image of the Black in Children's Fiction.
Churchill, E. Richard, and Linda R. Churchill, and Edward H. and Kay Reynolds Blair. Fun with American Literature.
DeJovine, F. Anthony. The Young Hero in American Fiction.
Dunning, Stephen. Teaching Literature to Adolescents; Short Stories.
Egoff, Sheila A. The Republic of Childhood.
Field, Elinor Whitney, Ed. Horn Book Reflections on Children's Books and Reading.
Fisher, Margery Turner. Who's Who in Children's Books.
Gordon, Michael. Juvenile Delinquency in the American Novel; 1905-1965.
Gurko, Leo. Thomas Wolfe; Beyond the Romantic Ego.
Haviland, Virginia. Children and Literature; Views and Reviews.
Hopkins, Lee Bennett. More Books by More People.
Hotchkiss, Jeanette. American Historical Fiction and Biography for Children and Young People.
Jacobs, William Jay. Edgar Allan Poe; Genius in Torment.
James, Philip Brutton. Children's Books of Yesterday.
Jan, Isabelle. On Children's Literature.
Jones, Howard Mumford, and Richard M. Ludwig. Guide to American Literature and Its Backgrounds Since 1890.
Jordan, Alice Mabel. From Rollo to Tom Sawyer and other Papers.
Kingston, Carolyn T. The Tragic Mode in Children's Literature.
LaBeau, Dennis, Ed. Children's Authrs and Illustrators.
Larrick, Nancy. A Parent's Guide to Children's Reading.
Lewis, Claudia. Writing for Young Children.
Lonsdale, Bernard J., and Helen K. Mackintosh. Children Experience Literature.
Lukens, Rebecca J. A Critical Handbook of Children's Literature.
MacCann, Donnarae, and Olga Richard. The Child's First Books; A Critical Study of Pictures and Tests.
MacLeod, Anne. A Moral Tale.
McDonough, Irma, Ed. Canadian Books for Children.
Madden, David, Ed. Tough Guy Writers of the Thirties.
Maksym, Tom, Ed. Short World Biographies.
Mason, Bobbie Ann. The Girl Sleuth.
Parker, Dorothy. The Portable Dorothy Parker.
Prager, Arthur. Rascals at Large, or The Clue in the Old Nostaglia.
Rudman, Masha Kabakow. Children's Literature; An Issues Approach.
Smaridge, Norah. Famous Literary Teams for Young People.

Southall, Ivan. A Journey of Discovery;On Writing for Children.
Sutherland, Zena. Children and Books.
Thwaite, Mary F. From Primer to Pleasure in Reading.
Turner, Ernest Sackville. Boys will be Boys;The Story of Sweeney Todd.
White, Mary Lou. Children's Literature;Criticism and Response.
Wintle, Justin. The Pied Pipers.

CHRISTIANITY

See RELIGION.

COMEDY/HUMOR

Beach, Joseph Warren. American Fiction;1920-1940.
Brashear, Minnie M., and Robert M. Rodney, Eds. The Art, Humor and Humanity of Mark Twain.
Cohen, Hennig, Ed. Humor of the Old Southwest.
Cooper, L. Aristotelian Theory of Comedy.
Covici, Pascal, Jr. Mark Twain's Humor;The Image of a World.
Cox, James M. Mark Twain;The Fate of Humor.
Flibbert, Joseph. Melville and the Art of Burlesque.
Goldstein, Jeffrey H. The Psychology of Humor;Theoretical Perspectives and Empirical Issues.
Gurewitch, Morton L. Comedy;The Irrational Vision.
Hall, Ernest Jackson. The Satirical Element in the American Novel.
Halperin, John, Ed. The Theory of the Novel;New Essays.
Harris, Charles B. Contemporary American Novelists of the Absurd.
Hauck, Richard Boyd. A Cheerful Nihilism.
Inge, M. Thomas, Ed. The Frontier Humorists;Critical Views.
Jones, Howard Mumford, and Richard M. Ludwig. Guide to American Literature and Its Backgrounds Since 1890.
Leyburn, Ellen Douglass. Strange Alloy.
Lynn, Kenneth S. Mark Twain and Southwestern Humor.
Masinton, Charles G. J. P. Donleavy; the Style of his Sadness and Humor.
Meeker, Joseph W. The Comedy of Survival.
Morley, Patricia A. Hugh Hood and Rudy Wiebe;The Comedians.
Parks, Edd Winfield. Ante-Bellum; Southern Literary Critics.
Pattee, Fred Lewis. The First Century of American Literature;1770-1870.
Pollard, Richard N., and Hazel M. Pollard. From Human Sentience to Drama;Principles of Critical Analysis, Tragic and Comedic.
Rickels, Milton. Thomas Bangs Thorpe;Humorist of the Old Southwest.
Rogers, Franklin R. Mark Twain's Burlesque Patterns.
Rubin, Louis D., Jr., Ed. A Bibliographical Guide to the Study of Southern Literature.
Rubin, Louis D., Jr., Ed. The Comic Imagination in American Literature.
Schulz, Max F. Black Humor Fiction of the Sixties.
Sorell, Walter. Facets of Comedy.
Tuttleton, James W. The Novel of Manners in America.
Waldmeir, Joseph J., Ed. Recent American Fiction;Some Critical Views.

CRITICAL THEORY

Wallace, Ronald. Henry James and the Comic Form.
Yates, Norris W. The American Humorist.

See also Individual Authors

Aleichem, Shalom
Barth, John
Bierce, Ambrose
Cervantes, Miguel de
Flaubert, Gustave
Franklin, Benjamin
Irving, Washington
Thorpe, Thomas Bangs
Thurber, James
Twain, Mark
Voltaire

CONDEMNED BOOKS

See CENSORSHIP.

CRITICAL THEORY

Berthoff, Warner. Fictions and Events.
Blackmur, R.P. The Lion and the Honeycomb.
Brown, Clarence Arthur. The Achievement of American Criticism.
Brownell, W.C. Criticism; An Essay on Function, Form and Method.
Cargill, Oscar. Toward a Pluralistic Criticism.
Cazamian, Louis Francois. Criticism in the Making.
Charvat, William. The Origins of American Critical Thought; 1810-1835.
Cowley, Malcolm. The Literary Situation.
DeMille, George E. Literary Criticism in America.
Erskine, John. The Literary Discipline.
Falk, Robert, Ed. Literature and Ideas in America.
Fischer, John, and Robert B. Silvers, Ed. Writing in America.
Foster, Richard. The New Romantics; A Reappraisal of the New Criticism.
Frye, Northrop. Anatomy of Criticism; Four Essays.
Frye, Northrop. The Critical Path.
Frye, Northrop. The Educated Imagination.
Frye, Northrop. The Stubborn Structure; Essays on Criticism and Society.
Frye, Northrop. The Well-Tempered Critic.
Gilman, Richard. The Confusion of Realms.
Goodman, Paul. The Structure of Literature.
Holman, C. Hugh, Comp. The American Novel Through Henry James.
Irmscher, William F. The Nature of Literature; Writing on Literary Topics.
Jones, Howard Mumford. The Theory of American Literature.
Kaplan, Morton, and Robert Kloss. The Unspoken Motive.
Karanikas, Alexander. Tillers of a Myth; Southern Agrarians as Social and Literary Critics.
Leavis, Frank Raymond, Ed. Towards Standards of Criticism.
Lindauer, Martin S. The Psychological Study of Literature.
Maier, Norman R.F. A Psychological Approach to Literary Criticism.
Marks, Lester Jay. Thematic Design in the Novels of John Steinbeck.
May, Charles E., Ed. Short Story Theories.
Pearce, Roy Harvey. Historicism Once More.

Pollard, Richard N., and Hazel M. Pollard. From Human Sentience to Drama.
Pritchard, John Paul. Return to the Fountains.
Pritchard, John Paul. Criticism in America.
Ruland, Richard. The Rediscovery of American Literature.
Ruland, Richard, Ed. The Native Muse; Theories of American Literature.
Slatoff, Walter J. With Respect to Readers; Dimensions of Literary Response.
Smith, David Nichol. The Functions of Criticism.
Smith, Samuel Stephenson. The Craft of the Critic.
Spiller, Robert E. The Third Dimension; Studies in Literary History.
Stallman, Robert Wooser, Ed. The Critic's Notebook.
Stallman, Robert Wooster. Critiques and Essays in Criticism; 1920-1948.
Stein, Gertrude. Lectures in America.
Stovall, Floyd, Ed. The Development of American Literary Criticism.
Straumann, Heinrich. American Literature in the Twentieth Century.
Van Nostrand, Albert D., Ed. Literary Criticism in America.
Wells, Geoffrey Harry. Deucalion; or, The Future of Literary Criticism.
Weston, Harold. Form in Literature.
Woolf, Virginia. Granite and Rainbow.

Eakin, Paul John. The New England Girl.
Earnest, Ernest. The Single Vision.
Green, Rose Basile. The Italian-American Novel.
Holman, C. Hugh, Comp. The American Novel Through Henry James.
Howe, Irving. The Critical Point on Literature and Culture.
Jones, W. T. Romantic Syndrome; Toward a New Method in Cultural Anthropology and History of Ideas.
Jones, Howard Mumford, and Richard M. Ludwig. Guide to American Literature and Its Backgrounds Since 1890.
Leavis, Frank Raymond. Mass Civilisation and Minority Culture.
Lowenthal, Leo. Literature, Popular Culture, and Society.
McCarthy, Mary. On the Contrary; Articles of Belief.
MacLeod, Anne. A Moral Tale.
Mudrick, Marvin. On Culture and Literature.
Mumford, Lewis. The Golden Day; A Study in American Literature and Culture.
Rubin, Louis D., Jr., and Robert D. Jacobs, Eds. Southern Renascence.
Rubin, Louis D., Jr., and Robert D. Jacobs, Eds. South; Modern Southern Literature in its Cultural Setting.
Trilling, Lionel. Beyond Culture.
Truzzi, Marcello. The Humanities As Sociology.
West, Thomas R. Flesh of Steel.

CULTURE

Albrecht, Milton C., et al., Eds. Sociology of Art and Literature.
Detweiler, Robert. Four Spiritual Crises in Mid-Century American Fiction.

CUSTOMS

See CULTURE.

DARWINISM

See SCIENCE.

DETECTIVE STORIES

See MYSTERY AND SUSPENSE.

DIALECTICAL MATERIALISM

See MARXISM.

EROTICISM

See SEXUALITY.

ETHNIC

Abramowitz, Molly. Elie Wiesel;A Bibliography.
Barnett, Louise K. The Ignoble Savage;American Literary Racism.
Bolger, Stephen Garrett. The Irish Character in American Fiction; 1830-1860.
Brushwood, John S. The Spanish American Novel.
Butwin, Joseph, and Frances Butwin. Sholom Aleichem.
Chapman, Abraham, Ed. Literature of the American Indians.
Chapman, Abraham, Ed. Jewish-American Literature.
Dabney, Lewis M. The Indians of Yoknapatawpha.
Early, James. The Making of Go Down, Moses.
Fiedler, Leslie A. The Collected Essays of Leslie Fiedler, Vol. II.
Fiedler, Leslie A. The Return of the Vanishing American.
Fiedler, Leslie A. Waiting for the End.
Green, Rose Basile. The Italian-American Novel.
Grismer, Raymond Leonard. A Reference Index to Twelve Thousand Spanish American Authors.
Harap, Louis. The Image of the Jew in American Literature.
Hirschfelder, Arlene B. American Indian and Eskimo Authors.
Hsu, Kai-yu. Asian-American Authors.
Ifkovic, Edward, Ed. American Letter;Immigrant and Ethnic Writing.
Kamman, William Frederic. Socialism in German American Literature.
Major, Mabel, and T.M. Pearce. Southwest Heritage.
Malin, Irving, Ed. Contemporary American-Jewish Literature.
Mersand, Joseph. Traditions in American Literature.
Miron, Dan. Sholem Aleykhem;Person, Persons, Presence.
Mumford, Lewis. The Golden Day;A Study in American Literature and Culture.
Richman, Sidney. Bernard Malamud.
Rubin, Louis D., Jr., Ed. The Comic Imagination in American Literature.
Rubin, Louis D., Jr. Death of the Novel;Essays in American Literature.
Ruotolo, Lucio P. Six Existential Heroes.
Samuel, Maurice. The World of Sholom Aleichem.
Schulz, Max F. Radical Sophistication;Studies in Contemporary Jewish-American Novelists.
Slotkin, Richard. Regeneration through Violence.
Solotaroff, Theodore. The Red Hot Vacuum;and Other Pieces on the Writing of the Sixties.
Walden, Daniel, Ed. On Being Jewish; American Jewish Writers from Cahan to Bellow.

EUROPEAN WAR

See WAR.

EVOLUTION

See SCIENCE.

EXISTENTIALISM

Ingarden, Roman. The Cognition of the Literary Work of Art.
Kennard, Jean E. Number and Nightmare; Forms of Fantasy in Contemporary Fiction.
Killinger, John. Hemingway and the Dead Gods.
Lawall, Sarah N. Critics of Consciousness.
Lehan, Richard. A Dangerous Crossing.
Reed, Peter J. Kurt Vonnegut, Jr.
Ruotolo, Lucio P. Six Existential Heroes.
Straumann, Heinrich. American Literature in the Twentieth Century.
Sullivan, Walter. Death by Melancholy.
Waldmeir, Joseph J., Ed. Recent American Fiction.

EXPATRIATE

See AUTHORS IN EXILE.

FANTASY

See SCIENCE FICTION AND FANTASY.

FILM

Appel, Alfred. Nabokov's Dark Cinema.
Bryan, Margaret B. Writing about Literature and Film.
Fischer, John, and Robert B. Silvers, Eds. Writing in America.
McLachlan, Bruce. Censorship; A Study of the Censorship of Books, Films and Plays in New Zealand.
Magny, Claude-Edmonde. Translated by Eleanor Hochman. The Age of the American Novel.
Pendo, Stephen. Raymond Chandler on Screen.
Richardson, Robert. Literature and Film.
Ross, T. J. Film and the Liberal Arts.
Seward, William W., Jr. Contrasts in Modern Writers.
Spatz, Jonas. Hollywood in Fiction.
Spiegel, Alan. Fiction and the Camera Eye.
Wagner, Geoffrey Atheling. The Novel and the Cinema.

FOREIGN COUNTRY

Anderson, Carl L. Poe in Northlight; The Scandinavian Response to His Life and Work.
Asselineau, Roger, Ed. The Literary Reputation of Hemingway in Europe.
Baetzhold, Howard G. Mark Twain and John Bull.
Brinnin, John Malcolm. Dylan Thomas in America.
Coindreau, Maurice Edgar. Translated by George McMillan Reeves. The Time of William Faulkner; A French View of Modern American Fiction.

Covo, Jacqueline. The Blinking Eye; Ralph Waldo Ellison and his American, French, German & Italian Critics, 1952-1971.
Denny, Margaret, and William H. Gilman, Eds. The American Writer and the European Tradition.
Fanning, Michael. France and Sherwood Anderson.
Faust, Bertha. Hawthorne's Contemporaneous Reputation.
Ferguson, John DeLancey. American Literature in Spain.
Gohdes, Clarence. American Literature in Nineteenth Century England.
Gohdes, Clarence. Bibliographical Guide to the Study of the Literature of the U.S.A.
Grover, Philip. Henry James and the French Novel.
Gunn, Drewey Wayne. American and British Writers in Mexico;1556-1973.
Hemminghaus, Edgar H. Mark Twain in Germany.
Hetherington, Hugh W. Melville's Reviewers; British and American; 1846-1891.
Hosillos, Lucila V. Philippine-American Literary Relations;1898-1941.
Jones, Joseph Jay. Radical Cousins.
Kennell, Ruth Epperson. Theodore Dreiser and the Soviet Union;1927-1945.
Kvam, Wayne E. Hemingway in Germany.
Leary, Lewis, Ed. American Literary Essays.
Lehan, Richard. A Dangerous Crossing.
Lundblad, Jane. Nathaniel Hawthorne and European Literary Tradition.
Mantz, Harold Elmer. French Criticism of American Literature Before 1850.
Margolies, Edward. Native Sons.
Maves, Carl. Sensuous Pessimism.
Miner, Earl Roy. The Japanese Tradition in British and American literature.
Nettels, Elsa. James and Conrad.
Piper, Henry Dan, Ed. Think Back on Us.
Proffer, Carl R., Ed. and Translated By. Soviet Criticism of American Literature in the Sixties.
Rice, Howard Crosby. Rudyard Kipling in New England.
Ruland, Richard. America in Modern European Literature.
Sevigg, Richard. Lawrence, Hardy, and American Literature.
Solomon, Eric. Stephen Crane in England.
Stone, Edward. A Certain Morbidness; A View of American Literature.
Straumann, Heinrich. American Literature in the Twentieth Century.
Strout, Cushing, Ed. Hawthorne in England.
Swigg, Richard. Lawrence, Hardy, and American Literature.
Weber, Carl. Hardy in America; A Study of Thomas Hardy and His American Readers.
Weber, Paul C. America in Imaginative German Literature in the First Half of the 19th Century.
Wegelin, Christof. The Image of Europe in Henry James.
Weinberg, Helen. The New Novel in America.
Wright, Nathalia. American Novelists in Italy.

GAY

See HOMOSEXUALITY.

GOTHIC AND HORROR

Birkhead, Edith. The Tale of Terror.

Briggs, Julia. Night Visitors.
Gregory, Horace. Spirit of Time and Place.
Hoyt, Charles Alva, Ed. Minor American Novelists.
LaFrance, Marston, Ed. Patterns of Commitment in American Literature.
Lewis, Wyndham. Men Without Art.
Loshe, Lillie Deming. The Early American Novel;1789-1830.
Lundblad, Jane. Nathaniel Hawthorne and the Tradition of Gothic Romance.
Moers, Ellen. Literary Women.
Northey, Margot. The Haunted Wilderness.
O'Connor, William Van. The Grotesque;An American Genre and Other Essays.
Pattee, Fred Lewis. The Development of the American Short Story.
Penzoldt, Peter, Ph.D. The Supernatural in Fiction.
Summers, Montague. Gothic Quest;A History of the Gothic Novel.
Thompson, G.R. Poe's Fiction;Romantic Irony in the Gothic Tales.
Thompson, Gary Richard. The Gothic Imagination.
Warfel, Harry Redcay. Charles Brockden Brown, American Gothic Novelist.
Watt, William W. Shilling Shockers of the Gothic School.
Westbrook, Max, Ed. The Modern American Novel.
Woolf, Virginia. Granite and Rainbow.

GREAT WAR

See WAR.

HERO

Amis, Kingsley. New Maps of Hell.

Cornillon, Susan Koppelman, Ed. Images of Women in Fiction Feminist Perspectives.
DeFalco, Joseph. The Hero in Hemingway's Short Stories.
DeJovine, F. Anthony. The Young Hero in American Fiction;A Motif for Teaching Literature.
Feied, Frederick. No Pie in the Sky.
Geist, Stanley. Herman Melville.
LaFrance, Marston, Ed. Pattersn of Commitment in American Literature.
Lebowitz, Alan. Progress into Silence;A Study of Melville's Heroes.
Levins, Lynn Gartrell. Faulkner's Heroic Design.
Lieber, Todd M. Endless Experiments.
Longley, John Lewis, Jr. The Tragic Mask.
Madden, David, Ed. Tough Guy Writers of the Thirties.
Mizener, Arthur. The Sense of Life in the Modern Novel.
Reed, Walter L. Mediations on the Hero.
Seward, William W., Jr. Contrasts in Modern Writers.
Slotkin, Richard. Regeneration through Violence.
Wells, Walter. Tycoons and Locusts.
Weinberg, Helen. The New Novel in America.

HISTORY

Aichinger, Peter. The American Soldier in Fiction;1880-1963.
Beasley, David. The Canadian Don Quixote.
Beck, Warren A., and Myles L. Clowers, Eds. Understanding American History through Fiction.
Becker, John E. Hawthorne's Historical Allegory.

HISTORY

Bell, Michael Davitt. Hawthorne and the Historical Romance of New England.

Berthoff, Warner. Fictions and Events.

Blake, Nelson Manfred. Novelists' America.

Bremmer, Robert H., Ed. Essays on History and Literature.

Brown, Clarence Arthur. The Achievement of American Criticism.

Callahan, John F. The Illusions of a Nation.

Cowley, Malcolm. The Literary Situation.

Culp, D.W., Ed. Twentieth Century Negro Literature.

Dickinson, A.T., Jr. American Historical Fiction.

Emerson, Everett, Ed. American Literature;1764-1789.

Etulain, Richard W., Ed. The Popular Western;Essays Toward a Definition.

Etulain, Richard W. Western American Literature;A Bibliography of Interpretive Books and Articles.

Foerster, Norman, Ed. The Reinterpretation of American Literature.

Gayle, Addison, Jr. The Way of the New World.

Gohdes, Clarence. Bibliographical Guide to the Study of the Literature of the U.S.A.

Gross, Harvey. Contrived Corridor; History and Fatality in Modern Literature.

Gross, Seymour L., and John Edward Hardy, Eds. Images of the Negro in American Literature.

Harris, Janet. A Century of American History in Fiction.

Hassan, Ihab. Radical Innocence.

Heiney, Donald. Recent American Literature.

Heiney, Donald. Recent American Literature to 1930.

Henderson, Harry B. Versions of the Past.

Hoffman, Frederick J. The Twenties.

Hollowell, John. Fact and Fiction.

Hotchkiss, Jeanette. American Historical Fiction and Biography for Children and Young People.

Hubbell, Jay B. The South in American Literature;1607-1900.

Inge, M. Thomas, Ed. The Frontier Humorists;Critical Views.

Irwin, Leonard Bertram. A Guide to Historical Fiction for the Use of Schools, Libraries and the General Reader.

Jones, Howard Mumford, and Richard M. Ludwig. Guide to American Literature and Its Backgrounds Since 1890.

Karolides, Nicholas J. The Pioneer in the American Novel;1900-1950.

Kolodny, Annette. The Lay of the Land.

Leary, Lewis Gaston. Soundings;Some Early American Writers.

Leisy, Ernest E. The American Historical Novel.

Levin, David. In Defense of Historical Literature.

Lively, Robert A. Fiction Fights the Civil War.

Loshe, Lillie Deming. The Early American Novel;1789-1830.

Lukas, Georg. The Historical Novel.

Lynn, Kenneth S. Visions of America.

McGarry, Daniel D. World Historical Fiction Guide.

Martin, Jay. Harvests of Change;American Literature;1865-1914.

Miller, Wayne Charles. An Armed America;Its Face in Fiction.

Milne, Gorden. The American Political Novel.

Morris, Wesley. Toward a New Historicism.

Nield, Jonathan. A Guide to Best Historical Novels and Tales.

Nye, Russel B., Ed. New Dimensions in Popular Culture.

Pearce, Roy Harvey. Historicism Once More.

Peyre, Henri. Historical and Critical Essays.
Pickering, James H., Ed. The World Turned Upside Down.
Roselle, Daniel. Transformations, 2; Understanding American History through Science Fiction.
Simpson, Lewis P. The Dispossessed Garden; Pastoral and History in Southern Literature.
Staehelen-Wackernagel, Adelheid. The Copper Monographs.
Thwaite, Mary F. From Primer to Pleasure in Reading.
Wagenknecht, Edward. Cavalcade of the American Novel.

HOMOSEXUALITY

Austen, Roger. Playing the Game.
Foster, Jeannette H. Sex Variant Women in Literature.
Norton, Rictor. The Homosexual Literary Tradition.
Rule, Jane. Lesbian Images.
Seward, William W., Jr. Contrasts in Modern Writers.
Simon, Linda. The Biography of Alice B. Toklas.

HORROR

See GOTHIC AND HORROR.

HUMANISM

Blackmur, R. P. The Lion and the Honeycomb.
Browne, Ray B. Melville's Drive to Humanism.
Cox, C. B. The Free Spirit.
Gold, Joseph. William Faulkner.

Hoffman, Frederick J. The Twenties.
Parks, Edd Winfield. Ante-Bellum Southern Literary Critics.
Straumann, Heinrich. American Literature in the Twentieth Century.

HUMOR

See COMEDY/HUMOR.

IMAGERY

Frohock, W. M. Strangers to this Ground.
Gale, Robert L. The Caught Image.
Holder-Barell, Alexander. The Development of Imagery and its Functional Significance in Henry James's Novels.
Jones, D. G. Butterfly on Rock.
LaFrance, Marston. Patterns of Commitment in American Literature.
Martin, Jay. Harvests of Change.
Raban, Jonathan. The Technique of Modern Fiction.
Richardson, Robert. Literature and Film.
Sears, Sallie. The Negative Imagination.
Stone, Edward. Voices of Despair.
Temple, Ruth Z. The Critic's Alchemy.
Weinstein, Philip M. Henry James and the Requirements of the Imagination.
Ziolkowski, Theodore. Disenchanted Images.

IMPERIALISM

See POLITICS.

JOURNALISM

See PUBLICATIONS.

LESBIANISM

See HOMOSEXUALITY.

LOST GENERATION

See WAR.

LOVE

Balakian, Nona, and Charles Simmons, Eds. The Creative Present.
Black, Michael H. The Literature of Fidelity.
Fiedler, Leslie. Love and Death in the American Novel.
Fowlie, Wallace. Love in Literature; Studies in Symbolic Expression.
Gould, James A., and John J. Iorio. Love, Sex and Identity.
Holbrook, David. Quest for Love.
Kartiganer, Donald M., and Malcolm A Griffith. Theories of American Literature.
Lewis, Robert W., Jr. Hemingway on Love.
McCarthy, Harold T. The Expatriate Perspective.
Markle, Joyce B. Fighters and Lovers; Theme in the Novels of John Updike.
Mencken, H. L. Edited by William H. Nolte. H. L. Mencken's Smart Set Criticism.
Petter, Henri. The Early American Novel.
Spender, Stephen. Love-Hate Relations.

Waldmeir, Joseph J., Ed. Recent American Fiction.
Wasserstrom, William. Heiress of all the Ages.
Witham, W. Tasker. The Adolescent in the American Novel;1920-1960.
Woolf, Virginia. Granite and Rainbow.

MAGAZINES

See PUBLICATIONS.

MARXISM

Aaron, Daniel. Writers on the Left.
Craig, David, Ed. Marxists on Literature;An Anthology.
Eagleton, Terence. Criticism and Ideology.
Hawthorn, Jeremy. Identity and Relationship.
Jameson, Fredric. Marxism and Form.
LeRoy, Gaylord C., and Ursula Beitz, Eds. Preserve and Create.
Prawer, Siegbert Salomon. Karl Marx and World Literature.
Robbins, Jack Alan, Ed. Granville Hicks in the New Masses.
Rudich, Norman, Ed. Weapons of Criticism;Marxism in America and the Literary Tradition.
Wilson, Edmund. The Triple Thinkers.
Zirkle, Conway. Evolution, Marxian Biology and the Social Scene.

MELODRAMA

See SENTIMENTALISM.

METAPHYSICS

See PHILOSOPHY

MILITARISM

See WAR.

MORALITY/ETHICS

Beach, Joseph Warren. American Fiction;1920-1940.
Bryant, Jerry H. The Open Decision.
Clor, Harry M. Obscenity and Public Morality.
Craig, Alec. Above All Liberties.
Crews, Frederick C. The Tragedy of Manners.
Drakeford, John W., and Jack Hamm. Pornography;The Sexual Mirage.
Goldstein, Michael J., et al. Pornography and Sexual Deviance.
Gregor, Ian and Brian Nicholas. The Moral and the Story.
Klinkowitz, Jerome, and John Somer, Eds. The Vonnegut Statement.
Lewis, Felice F. Literature, Obscenity and Law.
Lewis, Wyndham. Time and Western Man.
MacLeod, Anne. A Moral Tale.
Raleigh, John Henry. Time, Place, and Idea;Essays on the Novel.
Rist, Ray C., Ed. Pornography Controversy.
Trilling, Lionel. A Gathering of Fugitives.
West, Thomas Reed. Nature, Community and Will.

MOVIES

See FILM.

MYSTERY/SUSPENSE

Allen, Richard Stanley, Comp. Detective Fiction;Crime and Compromise.
Ball, John. The Mystery Story;an Appreciation.
Barnes, Melvin P. The Best Detective Fiction;A Guide from Godwin to the Present.
Borrowitz, Albert. Innocence and Arsenic;Studies in Crime and Literature.
Briggs, Julia. Night Visitors.
Bruccoli, Matthew Joseph. Kenneth Millar/Ross Macdonald;A Checklist.
Burack, A.S., Ed. Writing Detective and Mystery Fiction.
Davis, David Brion. Homicide in American Fiction;1798-1860.
Donaldson, Norman. In Search of Dr. Thorndyke.
Gribben, Lenore S. Who's Whodunit.
Harper, Ralph. The World of the Thriller.
Herman, Linda. Corpus Delicti of Mystery Fiction.
Highsmith, Patricia. Plotting and Writing Suspense Fiction.
Johnston, Alva. The Case of Erle Stanley Gardner.
MacShane, Frank, Ed. Raymond Chandler.
Madden, David, Ed. Tough Guy Writers of the Thirties.
Mason, Bobbie Ann. The Girl Sleuth.
Merry, Bruce. Anatomy of the Spy Thriller.
Nevins, Francis M., Jr., Ed. The Mystery Writer's Art.
Nevins, Francis M. Royal Bloodline; Ellery Queen, Author and Detective.
Norton, Charles A. Melville Davisson Post;Man of Many Mysteries.

Petter, Henri. The Early American Novel.
Smith, Myron J. Cloak-and-Dagger Bibliography; An Annotated Guide to Spy Fiction;1937-1975.
Steunbrunner, Chris, and Otto Penzler, Eds. Encyclopedia of Mystery and Detection.
Symons, Julian. Mortal Consequence.
Treat, Lawrence, Ed. The Mystery Writer's Handbook.

MYSTICISM

Banta, Martha. Henry James and the Occult.
Parks, Edd Winfield. Ante-Bellum Southern Literary Critics.
Senior, John. Way Down and Out;The Occult Symbolist Literature.
Strelka, Joseph P., Ed. Anagogic Qualities of Literature.
Wagenknecht, Edward. Cavalcade of the American Novel.
Wolf, William J. Thoreau;Mystic, Prophet, Ecologist.
Ziolkowski, Theodore. Disenchanted Images;A Literary Iconology.

MYTHOLOGY

Adams, Richard P. Faulkner;Myth and Motion.
Armstrong, John. Paradise Myth.
Baker, Ronald L. Folklore in the Writings of Rowland B. Robinson.
Berthoff, Warner. Fictions and Events.
Bluestein, Gene. The Voice of the Folk;Folklore and American Literary Theory.
Brylowski, Walter. Faulkner's Olympian Laugh.
Burrows, David J., et al. Myths and Motifs in Literature.
Callahan, John F. The Illusions of a Nation.
Chapman, Abraham, Ed. Literature of the American Indians.
Chiari, Joseph. Symbolisme from Poe to Mallarme.
DeCamp, Lyon Sprague. Literary Swordsmen and Sorcerers.
Donoghue, Denis. Thieves of Fire.
Franklin, H. Bruce. The Wake of the Gods.
Frohock, W. M. Strangers to this Ground.
Frye, Northrop. Myth and Symbol; Critical Approaches and Applications.
Gohdes, Clarence. Bibliographical Guide to the Study of the Literature of the U.S.A.
Green, Elizabeth Lay. The Negro in Contemporary American Literature.
Hauck, Richard Boyd. A Cheerful Nihilism.
Hoffman, Daniel. Form and Fable in American Fiction.
Karanikas, Alexander. Tillers of a Myth.
Karolides, Nicholas J. The Pioneer in the American Novel;1900-1950.
Kostelanetz, Richard, and Tom Montag, Eds. Younger Critics of North America.
McPherson, Hugo. Hawthorne as Myth-Maker.
May, John R. The Pruning Word.
Mayerson, Philip. Classical Mythology in Literature.
Morris, Wright. The Territory Ahead.
Noble, David W. The Eternal Adam and the New World Garden.
Noel, Thomas. Theories of the Fable in the Eighteenth Century.
Rahv, Philip. Literature and the Sixth Sense.
Reaver, J. Russell. Emerson as Mythmaker.

NATURALISM

Righter, William. Myth and Literature.

Rubin, Louis D., Jr., Ed. A Bibliographical Guide to the Study of Southern Literature.

Sachs, Viola. The Myth of America; Essays in the Structures of Literary Imagination.

Sharpless, F. Parvin. Symbol and Myth in Modern Literature.

Slotkin, Richard. Regeneration through Violence.

Snell, Edwin Marion. The Modern Fables of Henry James.

Spatz, Jonas. Hollywood in Fiction.

Sweeney, Gerard M. Melville's Use of Classical Mythology.

Umphlett, Wiley Lee. The Sporting Myth and the American Experience.

Vickery, John B. The Literary Impact of the Golden Bough.

Walker, William E., Ed. Reality and Myth.

West, Victor Royce. Folklore in the Works of Mark Twain.

Westbrook, Max, Ed. The Modern American Novel.

White, John J. Mythology in the Modern Novel.

Williams, David. Faulkner's Women; the Myth and the Muse.

Zavarzadeh, Mas'ud. The Mythopeic Reality;The Postwar American Nonfiction Novel.

NATIONALISM

See POLITICS.

NATURALISM

Ahnebrink, Lars. The Beginnings of Naturalism in American Fiction.

Block, Haskell M. Naturalistic Triptych.

Cowley, Malcolm. The Literary Situation.

Elias, Robert H. Theodore Dreiser; Apostle of Nature.

Heiney, Donald. Recent American Literature.

Hoffman, Michael J. The Subversive Vision.

Howe, Irving. The Critical Point on Literature and Culture.

Jones, Howard Mumford, and Richard M. Ludwig. Guide to American Literature and Its Backgrounds Since 1890.

Kartiganer, Donald M., and Malcolm A. Griffith.

Kazin, Alfred. On Native Grounds.

Kolodny, Annette. The Lay of the Land.

McIntosh, James. Thoreau as Romantic Naturalist.

Martin, Jay. Harvests of Change.

Mizener, Arthur. The Sense of Life in the Modern Novel.

Morgan, H. Wayne. American Writers in Rebellion.

Noble, David W. The Eternal Adam and the New World Garden.

Norris, Frank. The Responsibilities of the Novelist and Other Literary Essays.

Pattee, Fred Lewis. A History of American Literature Since 1870.

Pizer, Donald, Ed. The Literary Criticism of Frank Norris.

Pizer, Donald. Realism and Naturalism in Nineteenth-Century American Literature.

Powers, Lyall H. Henry James and the Naturalist Movement.

Rahv, Philip. Literature and the Sixthe Sense.

Snell, George. The Shapers of American Fiction;1798-1947.

Sherman, Paul, Ed. Thoreau;A Collection of Critical Essays.

Wagenknecht, Edward. Cavalcade of the American Novel.
Walcutt, Charles C. American Literary Naturalism.
Willey, Basil. Eighteenth Century Background;Studies on the Idea of Nature in the Thought of the Period.

NEWSPAPERS

See PUBLICATIONS.

NOVEL

Ames, Van Meter. Aesthetics of the Novel.
Baumbach, Jonathan. The Landscape of Nightmare.
Beja, Morris. Epiphany in the Modern Novel.
Bewley, Marius. The Eccentric Design.
Blake, Nelson Manfred. Novelists' America.
Blotner, Joseph. The Modern American Political Novel;1900-1960.
Bryant, Jerry H. The Open Decision.
Burgess, Anthony. The Novel Now.
Cowie, Alexander. The Rise of the American Novel.
Fischer, John, and Robert B. Silvers, Eds. Writing in America.
Frohock, W. M. The Novel of Violence in America.
Gayle, Addison. The Way of the New World;the Black Novel in America.
Hall, James. The Lunatic Giant in the Drawing Room.
Halperin, John, Ed. The Theory of the Novel;New Essays.
Harris, Charles B. Contemporary American Novelists of the Absurd.
Heilman, Robert Bechtold. America in English Fiction;1760-1800.
Hollowell, John. Fact and Fiction.
Jones, Howard Mumford. Jeffersonianism and the American Novel.
Leary, Lewis, Ed. American Literary Essays.
Loshe, Lillie Deming. The Early American Novel;1789-1830.
McCarthy, Mary. On the Contrary; Articles of Belief.
Magny, Claude-Edmonde. The Age of the American Novel.
Nolte, William H., Ed. H. L. Mencken's Smart Set Criticism.
Shapiro, Charles, Ed. Twelve Original Essays on Great American Novels.
Spiegel, Alan. Fiction and the Camera Eye.
Taylor, Gordon O. The Passages of Thought.
Tuttleton, James W. The Novel of Manners in America.
Van Doren, Carl. The American Novel.
Wagner, Geoffrey Atheling. The Novel and the Cinema.
Wolfe, Thomas. The Story of a Novel.

OBSCENITY

Clor, Harry M. Obscenity and Public Morality.
Drakeford, John W., and Jack Hamm. Pornography;The Sexual Mirage.
Ernst, M. L., and W. Seagle. To the Pure;A Study of Obscenity and the Censor.
Goldstein, Michael J., et al. Pornography and Sexual Deviance.
Gregor, Ian, and Brian Nicholas. The Moral and the Story.
Hewitt, Cecil R., Ed. Does Pornography Matter?
Holbrook, David, Ed. The Case Against Pornography.
Lewis, Felice F. Literature, Obscenity and Law.

Rist, Ray C., Ed. Pornography Controversy; Changing Moral Standards in American Life.

PARODY

See SATIRE.

PERIODICALS

See PUBLICATIONS.

PHILOSOPHY

Auerbach, Erich. Mimesis; the Representation of Reality in Western Literature.
Bernstein, John. Pacifism and Rebellion in the Writings of Herman Melville.
Boyd, John D. The Function of Mimesis and Its Decline.
Branden, Barbara. Who is Ayn Rand?
Burke, Kenneth. The Philosophy of Literary Form.
Cary, Joyce. Art and Reality; Ways of the Creative Process.
Currie, Robert. Genius; An Ideology in Literature.
Engel, Monroe. Uses of Literature.
French, Warren, Ed. The Forties; Fiction, Poetry, Drama.
Friedman, Norman. Form and Meaning in Fiction.
Glicksberg, Charles Irving. The Literature of Nihilism.
Gohdes, Clarence. Bibliographical Guide to the Study of Literature of the U.S.A.
Hocks, Richard A. Henry James and Pragmatistic Thought.
Ingarden, Roman. The Cognition of the Literary Work of Art.
Irmscher, William F. The Nature of Literature.
Jones, Granville M. Henry James's Psychology of Experience.
Jones, Howard Mumford, and Richard M. Ludwig. Guide to American Literature and Its Backgrounds since 1890.
Jones, Howard Mumford. Jeffersonianism and the American Novel.
Jones, W. T. Romantic Syndrome; Toward a New Method in Cultural Anthropology and History of Ideas.
Karanikas, Alexander. Tillers of a Myth.
Kegan, Robert. The Sweeter Welcome; Voices for a Vision of Affirmation.
Kellogg, Jean Defrees. Dark Prophets of Hope.
Killinger, John. Hemingway and the Dead Gods.
Kolodny, Annette. The Lay of the Land; Metaphor as Experience and History in American Life and Letters.
Lawall. Critics of Consciousness.
Lewis, Wyndham. Time and Western Man.
Lubbock, Percy. The Craft of Fiction.
Luccock, Halford E. American Mirror; Social, Ethical and Religious Aspects of American Literature.
Martin, Jay. Harvests of Change; American Literature; 1865-1914.
Michaud, Regis. The American Novel To-Day.
Mizener, Arthur. The Sense of Life in the Modern Novel.
Mueller, Gustav E. Philosophy of Literature.
Nolte, William H., Ed. H. L. Mencken's Smart Set Criticism.
Olson, Elder, Ed. Aristotle's Poetics and English Literature.
Patrides, C. A., Ed. Aspects of Time.
Pollock, Thomas Clark. The Nature of Literature.

Rand, Ayn. The Romantic Manifesto.
Richards, Ivor Armstrong. Beyond.
Schwartz, Elias. The Forms of Feeling.
Scott, Nathan A., Jr., Ed. Adversity and Grace.
Spencer, Sharon. Space, Time and Structure in the Modern Novel.
Swigg, Richard. Lawrence, Hardy, and American Literature.
West, Thomas Reed. Nature, Community and Will.

PICARESQUE

See HERO.

POLITICS

Aaron, Daniel. Writers on the Left.
American Library Association. Freedom of Inquiry; Supporting the Library Bill of Rights.
Amis, Kingsley. New Maps of Hell.
Angoff, Charles. The Tone of the Twenties and Other Essays.
Auster, Paul, Trans. Essays Written and Spoken; Jean-Paul Satre.
Blotner, Joseph. The Modern American Political Novel; 1900-1960.
Craig, David, Ed. Marxists on Literature; An Anthology.
Dickinson, H. T., Ed. Politics and Literature in the Eighteenth Century.
Dolan, Paul J. Of War and War's Alarms.
Enzensberger, Hans Magnus. The Consciousness Industry; On Literature, Politics and the Media.
Glicksberg, Charles I. The Literature of Commitment.
Hall, Ernest Jackson. The Satirical Element in the American Novel.
Hubbell, Jay B. The South in American Literature; 1607-1900.
Kamman, William Frederic. Socialism in German American Literature.
Korshin, Paul J., Ed. Studies in Change and Revolution.
Kostelanetz, Richard. The End of Intelligent Writing; Literary Politics in America.
LeRoy, Gaylord C., and Ursula Beitz, Eds. Preserve and Creat.
Lukacs, Georg. Realism in Our Time; Literature and the Class Struggle.
Lukacs, Georg. Writer and Critic; and Other
McCarthy, Mary. On the Contrary; Articles of Belief.
McWilliams, John P., Jr. Political Justice in a Republic.
Mencken, H. L. Edited by William H. Nolte. H. L. Mencken's Smart Set Criticism.
Millett, Kate. Sexual Politics.
Milne, Gordon. The American Political Novel.
Moravia, Alberto. Man as an End; A Defense of Humanism.
Panichas, George Andrew. The Politics of Twentieth-Century Novelists.
Petit, Arthur G. Mark Twain and the South.
Phelan, John, Ed. Communications Control; Readings in the Motives and Structures of Censorship.
Piper, Henry Dan, Ed. Think Back on Us; A Contemporary Chronical of the 1930's by Malcolm Crowley.
Rideout, Walter. The Radical Novel in the United States 1900-1954.
Robbins, Jack Alan. Granville Hicks in the New Masses.
Swingewood, Alan. The Novel and Revolution.
Underwood, John C. Literature and Insurgency.
Waldman, M. The Propaganda Novel.
Widmer, Eleanor and Kingsley Widmer, Eds. Freedom and Culture.

Wilson, Elena, Ed. Letters on Literature and Politics;1912-1972.
Winegarten, Renee. Writers and Revolution.

POPULAR FICTION

Etulain, Richard W., Ed. The Popular Western;Essays Toward a Definition.
Gnarowski, Michael. The Artist and His Critics.
Goldsmith, David H. Kurt Vonnegut; Fantasist of Fire and Ice.
Hackett, Alice Payne, and James Henry Burke. 80 Years of Best Sellers;1895-1975.
Hart, James David. The Popular Book;A History of America's Literary Taste.
Johnston, Alva. The Case of Erle Stanley Gardner.
Koontz, Dean R. Writing Popular Fiction.
McCormack, Thomas, Ed. Afterwords;Novelists on Their Novels.
Madden, David, Ed. Tough Guy Writers of the Thirties.
Merry, Bruce. Anatomy of the Spy Thriller.
Nye, Russel B., Ed. New Dimensions in Popular Culture.
Papashvily, Helen Waite. All the Happy Endings.
Pearson, Edmund. Dime Novels;or, Following an Old Trail in Popular Literature.
Reed, Peter J. Kurt Vonnegut, Jr.
Schatt, Stanley. Kurt Vonnegut, Jr.
Tominaga, Thomas T. Iris Murdoch and Muriel Spark;A Bibliography.
Wadlington, Warwick. The Confidence Game in American Literature.

PORNOGRAPHY

See OBSCENITY.

PROPAGANDA

See POLITICS.

PSYCHOANALYSIS

See PSYCHOLOGY.

PSYCHOLOGY

Basler, Roy P. Sex, Symbolism and Psychology in Literature.
Beach, Joseph Warren. American Fiction;1920-1940.
Bewley, Marius. The Eccentric Design.
Bonapart, Marie. Life and Works of Edgar Allan Poe.
Buck, Gertrude. The Metaphor;A Study in the Psychology or Rhetoric.
Crews, Frederick C. Out of my System.
Crews, Frederick, Ed. Psychoanalysis and Literary Process.
Crews, Frederick. The Sins of the Fathers.
Edel, Leon. The Modern Psychological Novel.
Fraiberg, Louis Benjamin. Psychoanalysis and American Literary Criticism.
Gohdes, Clarence. Bibliographical Guide to the Study of the Literature of the U.S.A.
Goldstein, Jeffrey H. The Psychology of Humor.
Gordon, David J. Literary Art and the Unconscious.
Heilbrun, Carolyn G. Toward a Recognition of Androgyny.
Heiney, Donald. Recent American Literature.
Heiney, Donald. Recent American Literature to 1930.

PSYCHOLOGY

Heintz, Ann Christine. Persuasion.
Holland, Norman Norwood. The Dynamics of Literary Response.
Humphrey, Robert. Stream of Consciousness in the Modern Novel.
Hunter, James. B.F. Skinner and Contemporary Literature.
Jones, Granville M. Henry James's Psychology of Experience.
Kaplan, Morton, and Robert Kloss. The Unspoken Motive.
Kiell, Norman. Varieties of Sexual Experience; Psychosexuality in Literature.
Krook, Dorothea. The Ordeal of Consciousness in Henry James.
Lee, Vernon. The Handling of Words.
Lindauer, Martin S. The Psychological Study of Literature.
Maier, Norman R.F., and H. Willard Reninger. A Psychological Approach to Literary Criticism.
Michaud, Regis. The American Novel To-Day; A Social and Psychological Study.
Millett, Kate. Sexual Politics.
Morrison, Claudia C. Freud and the Critic.
Nolte, William H., Ed. H.L. Mencken's Smart Set Criticism.
Nin, Anais. The Novel of the Future.
Paris, Bernard J. A Psychological Approach to Fiction.
Pearce, Roy Harvey. Historicism Once More.
Pollock, Thomas Clark. The Nature of Literature.
Pollard, Richard N., and Hazel M. Pollard. From Human Sentience to Drama; Principles of Critical Analysis, Tragic and Comedic.
Rose, Ellen Cronan. The Tree Outside the Window; Doris Lessing's Children of Violence.
Steele, Richard Lowell. Thomas Wolfe; A Study in Psychoanalytic Literary Criticism.
Stone, Edward. A Certain Morbidness; A View of American Literature.
Straumann, Heinrich. American Literature in the Twentieth Century.
Takaki, Ronald T. Violence in the Black Imagination.
Taylor, Gordon O. The Passages of Thought.
Tennenhouse, Leonard, Ed. The Practice of Psychoanalytic Criticism.
Tharpe, Jac. Nathaniel Hawthorne; Identity and Knowledge.
Trilling, Lionel. Beyond Culture; Essays on Literature and Learning.
Trilling, Lionel. A Gathering of Fugitives.
Trilling, Lionel. The Liberal Imagination; Essays on Literature and Society.
Vernon, John. The Garden and the Map.
Witham, W. Tasker. The Adolescent in the American Novel; 1920-1960.

See also individual authors:

Bombal, Maria Luisa
Carpentier, Alejo
Faulkner, William
Gogol, Nikolai
Hesse, Herman
James, Henry
Kafka, Franz
Onetti, Juan Carlos

See also:

SYMBOLISM
SEXUALITY
REALISM

See also general Critical and Literary Theory under Country Listings, e.g. France-Critical Theory, History and Criticism, etc.

PSYCHOSEXUALITY

See SEXUALITY.

PUBLICATIONS

Amis, Kingsley. New Maps of Hell; A Survey of Science Fiction.
Gohdes, Clarence. Bibliographical Guide to the Study of the Literature of the U.S.A.
Hubbell, Jay B. The South in American Literature; 1607-1900.
Janssens, G.A.M. The American Literary Review; A Critical History; 1920-1950.
MacMillan, Dougald. Transition; The Story of a Literary Era; 1927-1938.
Pattee, Fred Lewis. The First Century of American Literature; 1770-1870.
Tobin, Richard L., Comp. The Golden Age; The Saturday Review 50th Anniversary Reader.

PULP MAGAZINES

See PUBLICATIONS.

RACE RELATIONS

Barnett, Louise K. The Ignoble Savage.
Grejda, Edward S. The Common Continent of Men.
Pettit, Arthur G. Mark Twain and the South.
Scholes, Robert, and Eric Rubin. Science Fiction; History, Science, Vision.
Sutton, William Alfred. Black Life It Is/Was; Erskine Caldwell's Treatment of Racial Themes.

REALISM

Auerbach, Erich. Mimesis; The Representation of Reality in Western Literature.
Berthoff, Warner. The Ferment of Realism.
Bryant, Jerry H. The Open Decision.
Cady, Edwin H. The Light of Common Day; Realism in American Fiction.
Carter, Everett. Howells and the Age of Realism.
Carter, Everett. The American Idea; The Literary Reaction to American Optimism.
Cary, Joyce. Art and Reality; Ways of the Creative Process.
Falk, Robert. The Victorian Mode in American Fiction; 1865-1885.
Foerster, Norman, Ed. The Reinterpretation of American Literature.
Grant, Damian. Realism.
Halperin, John, Ed. The Theory of the Novel; New Essays.
Heiney, Donald. Recent American Liturature to 1930.
Hemmings, Frederick. The Age of Realism.
Kartiganer, Donald M., and Malcolm A. Griffith. Theories of American Literature.
Kazin, Alfred. On Native Grounds.
Kolb, Harold H., Jr. Illusion of Life.
Leary, Lewis, Ed. American Literary Essays.
Luccock, Halford E. American Mirror; Social, Ethical and Religious Aspects of American Literature.
Lukacs, Georg. Realism in Our Time.
Mizener, Arthur. The Sense of Life in the Modern Novel.
Morgan, H. Wayne. American Writers in Rebellion.

REFERENCE WORKS

Noble, David W. The Eternal Adam and the New World Garden.
Parks, Edd Winfield. Ante-Bellum Southern Literary Critics.
Parrington, Vernon Louis. Main Currents in American Thought.
Peterson, Dale E. The Clement Vision; Poetic Realism in Turgenev and James.
Pizer, Donald. Realism and Naturalism in Nineteenth-Century American Literature.
Proffer, Carl R., Tranlated and Edited by. Soviet Criticism of American Literature in the Sixties; An Anthology.
Rahv, Philip. Literature in America.
Snell, George. The Shapers of American Fiction; 1798-1947.
Solomon, Eric. Stephen Crane; From Parody to Realism.
Spender, Stephen. New Realism; A Discussion.
Stern, J.P. On Realism.

REFERENCE WORKS

Concordances

Crosland, Andrew T. A Concordance to The Great Gatsby.
Runyan, Harry. A Faulkner Glossary.
Smart, George K. Religious Elements in Faulkner's Early Novels; A Selective Concordance.

Dictionaries

Allibone, Samuel Austin. A Critical Dictionary of English Literature and British and American Authors Living and Deceased; From the Earliest Accounts to the Latter Half of the Nineteenth Century.
Encyclopedia of World Literature in the 20th Century.
Johnson, Rossiter. A Dictionary of Famous Names in Fiction, Drama, Poetry, History and Art.
Kirk, John Foster. A Supplement to Alibone's Critical Dictionary of English Literature and British and American Authors.
Ramsay, Robert L., and Frances G. Emberson. A Mark Twain Lexicon.
Shaw, Harry. Concise Dictionary of Literary Terms.
Wallace, William S. Dictionary of North American Authors Deceased Before 1950.

Handbooks and Guides

Bateson, Frederick Wilse, and Harrison T. Meserole. A Guide to English and American Literature.
Carpenter, Frederic Ives. Emerson Handbook.
Day, Martin Steele. A Handbook of American Literature.
Gross, Seymour L., Ed. A Scarlet Letter Handbook.
Irwin, Leonard Bertram. A Guide to Historical Fiction for the Use of Schools, Libraries, and the General Reader.
Jones, Howard Mumford. Guide to American Literature and Its Backgrounds Since 1890.
Kiernan, Robert F. Katherine Anne Porter and Carson McCullers; A Reference Guide.
Larrick, Nancy. A Parent's Guide to Children's Reading.
Long, E. Hudson. Mark Twain Handbook.
Reader's Adviser; A Layman's Guide to Literature.
Smith, Martin Seymout. Funk & Wagnalls Guide to Modern World Literature.
Stevens, Peter. Modern Canadian Prose; A Guide to Information Sources.

REFERENCE WORKS

Tenney, Thomas. Mark Twain; A Reference Guide.
Tuck, Dorothy. Crowell's Handbook of Faulkner.
Vinson, James, and Kirkpatrick, D.L. Eds. Contemporary Writers Series.
Wagner, Linda W. Ernest Hemingway; A Reference Guide.
Waldhorn, Arthur. A Reader's Guide to Ernest Hemingway.
Ward, Alfred Charles. Longman Companion to Twentieth Century Literature.
Whitcomb, Selden L. Chronological Outlines of American Literature.
White, Glenn. Connecticut Handbook.

Indexes

Allen, Walter. Contemporary Novelists.
Armitage, A.D., and Nancy Tudor. Canadian Essay and Literature Index.
Havlice, Patricia Pate. Index to Literary Biography.
Kehler, Dorothea. Problems in Literary Research; A Guide to Selected Reference Works.
LaBeau, Dennis, Ed. Children's Authors and Illustrators; An Index to Biographical Dictionaries.
New England Science Fiction Association. Index to the Science Fiction Magazines; 1966-1970.
O'Connor, Evangeline Maria. An Analytical Index to the Works of Nathaniel Hawthorne.
Poets and Writers, Inc. A Directory of American Fiction Writers.

Plots and Characters

Blount, Margaret. Animal Land; The Creatures of Children's Fiction.
Brodtkorb, Paul, Jr. Ishmael's White World.
Campbell, Frank D. John D. MacDonald and the Colorful World of Travis McGee.
Dabney, Lewis M. The Indians of Yoknapatawpha.
Edel, Leon. The Modern Psychological Novel.
Fisher, Margery Turner. Who's who in Children's Books.
Ford, Margaret Patricia, and Suzanne Kincaid. Who's who in Faulkner.
Gale, Robert L. Plots and Characters in the Fiction and Sketches of Nathaniel Hawthorne.
Gale, Robert L. Plots and Characters in the Fiction of Henry James.
Halperin, John, Ed. The Theory of the Novel; New Essays.
Hauck, Richard Boyd. A Cheerful Nihilism.
Hayashi, Tetsumaro, Ed. John Steinbeck; A Dictionary of his Fictional Characters.
Hayashi, Tetsumaro. A New Steinbeck Bibliography; 1929-1971.
Hayashi, Tetsumaro, Ed. A Study Guide to Steinbeck; A Handbook to his Major Works.
Johnson, Rossiter. A Dictionary of Biographies of Authors Represented in the Authors Digest Series.
Jordan, Alice Mabel. From Rollo to Tom Sawyer, and other Papers.
Lebowitz, Alan. Progress into Silence; A Study of Melville's Heroes.
Leeming, Glenda. Who's who in Henry James.
Longley, John Lewis, Jr. The Tragic Mask.
McCarthy, Mary. On the Contrary; Articles of Belief.
McNeir, Waldo, and Leo B. Levy, Eds. Studies in American Literature.
Miller, James E., Jr. A Reader's Guide to Herman Melville.
Nelson, Gerald B. Ten Versions of America.

Nnolim, Charles E. Melville's "Benito Cereno"; A Study in Meaning of Name Symbolism.
Page, Sally R. Faulkner's Women; Characterization and Meaning.
Putt, S. Gorley. Henry James; A Reader's Guide.
Stone, Edward. A Certain Morbidness; A View of American Literature.
Swan, H. Who's Who in Fiction?
Vincent, Howard P., Ed. Bartleby the Scrivener.

REGIONALISM

General

Allen, Walter. The Modern Novel in Britain and the United States.
Auchincloss, Louis. Pioneers and Caretakers; A Study of 9 American Women Novelists.
Beach, Joseph Warren. American Fiction; 1920-1940.
Bewley, Marius. Masks and Mirrors.
Bourne, Randolph. History of A Literary Radical and Other Essays.
Cowie, Alexander. The Rise of the American Novel.
Doig, Ivan, Comp. The Streets We Have Come Down.
Dunlap, George Arthur. The City in the American Novel; 1789-1900.
Fiske, Marjorie. Book Selection and Censorship.
Gelfant, Blanche Housman. The American City Novel.
Gohdes, Clarence. Literature and Theater of the States and Regions of the U.S.A.; An Historical Bibliography.
Gohdes, Clarence. Bibliographical Guide to the Study of the Literature of the U.S.A.
Gregory, Horace. Spirit of Time and Place.
Heiney, Donald. Recent American Literature to 1930.
Hoffman, Frederick J. The Twenties.
Howe, Irving. The Critical Point on Literature and Culture.
Jones, Howard Mumford and Richard M. Ludwig. Guide to American Literature and Its Backgrounds Since 1890.
LaFrance, Marston, Ed. Patterns of Commitment in American Literature.
Lee, Robert Edson. From West to East.
Leisy, Ernest E. The American Historical Novel.
Martin, Jay. Harvests of Change; American Literature; 1865-1914.
Paterson, John. The Gospel According to James, Hardy, Conrad, Joyce, Lawrence and Virginia Woolf.
Pattee, Fred Lewis. A History of American Literature Since 1870.
Rahu, Philip. Literature and the Sixth Sense.
Rahu, Philip. Literature in America.
Rubin, Louis D., Jr. Death of the Novel; Essays in American Literature.
Rutland, Richard, Ed. The Spirit of Place.
Seward, William W., Jr. Contrasts in Modern Writers.
Stewart, Randall. Edited by George Core. Regionalism and Beyond.
Stout, Janis P. Sodoms in Eden; The City in American Fiction Before 1860.
Wagenknecht, Edward. Cavalcade of the American Novel.
Waldemeir, Joseph J., Ed. Recent Am American Fiction; Some Critical Reviews.

East

Berbrich, Joan D. Three Voices from Paumanok.

REGIONALISM

Buell, Lawrence. Literary Transcendentalism;Style and Vision in the American Renaissance.
Eakin, Paul John. The New England Girl.
Edmiston, Susan and Linda D. Cirino. Literary New York;A History and Guide.
Lewis, Gerald E. Up Here in Maine.
Maurice, Arthur Bartlett. New York in Fiction.
Mizener, Sharon Fusselman. Manhattan Transients;A Critical Essay.
Rice, Howard Crossby. Rudyard Kipling in New England.
Shepherd, Henry Eliot. The Representative Authors of Maryland.
Van Why, Joseph S. Nook Farm.
White, Glenn. Connecticut Handbook.

West

Baird, Newton D. An Annotated Bibliography of California Fiction; 1664-1970.
Bennett, Mildred R. The World of Willa Cather.
Brown, L.K., Completed by Leon Edel. Willa Cather;A Critical Biography.
Cohen, Hennig, Ed. Humor of the Old Southwest.
Etulain, Richard W., Ed. The Popular Western;Essays Toward A Definition.
Etulain, Richard W. Western American Literature;A Bibliography of Interpretative Books and Articles.
Fiedler, Leslie A. The Return of the Vanishing American.
Folsom, James K. The American Western Novel.
Gaston, Edwin W., Jr. The Early Novel of the Southwest.
Gruber, Frank. Zane Grey.
Gurian, Jay. Western American Writing.
Haslam, Gerald W. Jack Schaefer.
Haslam, Gerald W., Ed. Western Writing.
Inge, M. Thomas. The Frontier Humorists;Critical Views.
Knoll, Robert E., Ed. Conversations with Wright Morris;Critical Views and Responses.
Lynn, Kenneth S. Mark Twain and Southwestern Humor.
Major, Mabel and T.M. Pearce. Southwest Heritage:A Literary History with Bibliographies.
Milton, John R. The Literature of South Dakota.
Pilkington, William T. My Blood's Country;Studies in Southwestern Literature.
Powell, Lawrence Clark. Southwest Classics;The Creative Literature of the Arid Lands.
Powell, Lawrence Clark. Books;West, Southwest;Essays on Writers, Their Books, and their Land.
Rickels, Milton. Thomas Bangs Thorpe;Humorist of the Old Southwest.
Ronald, Ann. Zane Grey.
Schmitter, Dean Morgan, Ed. Mark Twain;A Collection of Criticism.
Spatz, Jonas. Hollywood in Fiction; Some Versions of the American Myth.
Tooker, Dan. Fiction! Interviews with Northern California Novelists.
Verland, Orm. James Fenimore Cooper's The Prairie.
Walker, Franklin. San Francisco's Literary Frontier.
Wells, Walter. Tycoons and Locusts; A Regional Look at Hollywood Fiction of the 1930's.
West, Victor Royce. Folklore in the Works of Mark Twain.

North

Duffey, Bernard. The Chicago Renaissance in American Letters;A

Critical History.
Edwards, Clifford D. Conrad Richter's Ohio Trilogy.
Marple, Alice. Iowa Authors and Their Works;A Contribution Toward A Bibliography.
Meyer, Roy Willard. The Middle Western Farm Novel in the Twentieth Century.
Reigelman, Milton M. The Midland; A Venture in Literary Regionalism.
Starrett, Vincent. Born in a Bookshop;Chapters from the Chicago Renascence.
Titus, William A. Wisconsin Writers; Sketches and Studies.

South

Barner, Florence Elberta. Texas Writers of Today.
Carr, John, Ed. Kite-Flying and Other Irrational Acts.
Cook, Sylvia Jenkins. From Tobacco Road to Route 66;the Southern Poor White in Fiction.
Core, George, Ed. Southern Fiction Today;Renascence and Beyond.
Field, Louise Maunsell. Ellen Glasgow;Novelist of the Old and the New South;An Appreciation.
Going, William Thornbury. Essays on Alabama Literature.
Gray, Richard J. The Literature of Memory;Modern Writers of the American South.
Hobson, Fred C. The Serpent in Eden;H. L. Mencken and the South.
Holliday, Carl. A History of Southern Literature.
Holman, C. Hugh. The Roots of Southern Writing.
Hubbell, Jay B. Literary Essays and Reminiscences.
Jehlen, Myra. Class and Character in Faulkner's South.
Johnson, James Gibson. Southern Fiction Prior to 1860;An Attempt at a First-Hand Bibliography.
Kallsen, Loren J., Ed. Kentucky Tragedy;A Problem in Romantic Attitudes.
Karanikas, Alexander. Tillers of a Myth;Southern Agrarians as Social and Literary Critics.
Leary, Lewis Gaston. William Faulkner of Yoknapatawpha County.
O'Connor, Flannery. Sally and Robert Fitzgerald, Eds. Mystery and Manners.
Osterweis, Rollin. Romanticism and Naturalism in the Old South.
Parks, Edd Winfield. Ante-Bellum Southern Literary Critics.
Rose, Alan Henry. Demonic Vision; Racial Fantasy and Southern Fiction.
Rubin, Louis D., Jr., Ed. A Bibliographical Guide to the Study of Southern Literature.
Rubin, Louis D., Jr. The Faraway Country;Writers of the Modern South.
Rubin, Louis D., Jr., Ed. South;Modern Southern Literature in Its Cultural Setting.
Rubin, Louis D., Jr., Ed. Southern Literary Study;Problems and Possibilities.
Rubin, Louis D., Jr., and Robert D. Jacobs. Southern Renascence;The Literature of the Modern South.
Skaggs, Merrill Maguire. The Folk of Southern Fiction.
Sullivan, Walter. A Requiem for the Renascence;The State of Fiction in the Modern South.
Tischler, Nancy M. Black Masks;Negro Characters in Modern Southern Fiction.

RELIGION

Andreach, Robert F. The Slain and Resurrected God.
Barth, J. Robert, Ed. Religious Perspectives in Faulkner's Fiction.
Beatson, Peter. The Eye in the Mandala;Patrick White;A Vision of Man and God.
Bretnor, Reginald, Ed. Science Fiction, Today and Tomorrow.
Brooks, Cleanth. The Hidden God;Studies in Hemingway, Faulkner, Yeats, Eliot, and Warren.
Braswell, William. Melville's Religious Thought;An Essay in Interpretation.
Brown, Douglas Charles. The Enduring Legacy;Biblical Dimensions in Modern Literature.
Cary, Norman Reed. Christian Criticism in the Twentieth Century.
Detweiler, Robert. Four Spiritual Crises in Mid-Century American Fiction.
Douglas, Ann. The Feminization of American Culture.
Ensor, Allison. Mark Twain and The Bible.
Ericson, Edward E., Ed. Religion and Modern Literature;An Anthology.
Fick, Leonard J. The Light Beyond; A Study of Hawthorne's Theology.
Fogle, Richard Harter. Hawthorne's Fiction;The Light and the Dark.
Folsom, James K. Man's Accidents and God's Purposes.
Franklin, H. Bruce. The Wake of the Gods;Melville's Mythology.
French, Warren, Ed. The Fifties;Fiction, Poetry, Drama.
Geismar, Maxwell, Ed. Mark Twain and the three R's:Race, Religion, Revolution-and Related Matters.
Gohdes, Clarence. Bibliographical Guide to the Study of the Literature of the U.S.A.
Gros, Louis, Kenneth. Literary Interpretations of Biblical Narratives.
Gross, Theodore L., and Stanley Wertheim. Hawthorne, Melville, Stephen Crane;A Critical Bibliography.
Hall, Ernest Jackson. The Satirical Element in the American Novel.
Herbert, Thomas Walter. Moby Dick and Calvinism;A World Dismantled.
Hunt, John Wesley. William Faulkner;Art in Theological Tension.
Jessup, Josephine Lurie. Faith of Feminists.
Jones, Howard Mumford, and Richard M. Ludwig. Guide to American Literature and Its Backgrounds Since 1890.
Jones, Granville M. Henry James's Psychology of Experience.
Kegan, Robert. The Sweeter Welcome;Voices for a Vision of Affirmation.
Killinger, John. Hemingway and the Dead Gods.
Kort, Wesley A. Narrative Elements and Religious Meanings.
Kunkel, Francis Leo. Passion and the Passion:Sex and Religion in Modern Literature.
Leisy, Ernest E. The American Historical Novel.
Luccock, Halford E. American Mirror;Social, Ethical and Religious Aspects of American Literature.
Lynch, William F. Christ and Apollo; The Dimensions of the Literary Imagination.
McHaney, Thomas L. William Faulkner's The Wild Palms;A Study.

Magny, Claude-Edmonde. Translated by Eleanor Hochman. The Age of the American Novel.
Margolies, Edward. Native Sons;A Critical Study of Twentieth-Century Negro American Authors.
Martin, Jay. Harvests of Change;American Literature;1865-1914.
May, Rollo, Ed. Symbolism in Religion and Literature.
May, John R. Toward a New Earth; Apocalypse in the American Novel.
Mays, Benjamin E. The Negro's God as Reflected in His Literature.
Michaud, Regis. The American Novel To-Day;A Social and Psychological Study.
Moseley, James G. A Complex Inheritance;The Idea of Self-Transcendence in the Theology of Henry James, Sr., and the Novels of Henry James.
Oates, Joyce Carol. New Heaven, New Earth;The Visionary Experience in Literature.
O'Brien, John, and Richard Finholt, Eds. No Signs from Heaven.
O'Connor, Flannery. Mystery and Manners. Edited by Sally and Robert Fitzgerald.
Phelen, John, Ed. Communications Control;Readings in the Motives and Structures of Censorship.
Prickwett, S. Romanticism and Relition.
Rahv, Philip. Literature and the Sixth Sense.
Richardson, Kenneth E. Force and Faith in the Novels of William Faulkner.
Rubin, Louis D., Jr., and Robert D. Jacobs. Southern Renascence.
Ruland, Vernon. Horizons of Criticism;An Assessment of Religious-Literary Options.
Schmerling, Hilda L. Finger of God.
Scott, Nathan A., Jr., Ed. Adversity and Grace.
Sharp, Sister M. Corona. The Confidante in Henry James.
Simpson, Lewis P. The Dispossessed Garden;Pastoral and History in Southern Literature.
Smart, George K. Religious Elements in Faulkner's Early Novels.
Strelka, Joseph P., Ed. Anagogic Qualities of Literature.
Thompson, Lawrance. Melville's Quarrel with God.
Tuttleton, James W. The Novel of Manners in America.
Waldmeir, Joseph J., Ed. Recent American Fiction;Some Critical Views.
Walker, Franklin Dickerson. Irreverent Pilgrims;Melville, Browne and Mark Twain in the Holy Land.
Webb, Eugene. The Dark Dove;the Sacred and Secular in Modern Literature.
Wiggins, James B., Ed. Religion as Story.
Wirt, Sherwood Eliot. You Can Tell the World.

RELIGIOUS HUMANISM

See RELIGION.

REVOLUTION

See POLITICS, MARXISM.

ROMANTICISM

Abrams, Meyer H. Mirror and the Lamp.
Abrams, Meyer H. Natural Supernaturalism.
Babbitt, Irving. Spanish Character and Other Essays.

ROMANTICISM

Bank, Stanley, Ed. American Romanticism;A Shape for Fiction.
Barfield, O. Romanticism Comes of Age.
Bell, Michael Davitt. Hawthorne;and the Historical Romance of New England.
Benoit, Raymond. Single Nature's Double Name.
Bloom, Harold. Ringers in the Tower.
Boas, George, Ed. Romanticism in America.
Bornstein, George, Ed. Romantic and Modern;Revaluations of Literary Tradition.
Chandler, Elizabeth Lathrop. A Study of the Sources of the Tales and Romances Written by Nathaniel Hawthorne Before 1853.
Dekker, George, and John P. McWilliams, Eds. Fenimore Cooper;The Critical Heritage.
Dermott, Robert J., and Sanford E. Marovitz, Eds. Artful Thunder.
Dudley, Edward and Maxmillian E. Novak, Eds. The Wild Man Within.
Elkins, A. C., and L. J. Forstner, Eds. The Romantic Movement Bibliography;1936-1970.
Fass, Barbara. La Belle Dame Sans Merci and The Acsthetics of Romanticism.
Foerster, Norman, Ed. The Reinterpretation of American Literature.
Fogle, Richard Harter. The Permanent Pleasure;Essays on Classics of Romanticism.
Fogle, Richard Harter, Comp. Romantic Poets and Prose Writers.
Forst, Lilian R. Romanticism in Perspective.
Foster, Edward H. The Civilized Wilderness;Backgrounds to American Literature.
Foster, Richard. The New Romantics;A Reappraisal of the New Criticism.
Frye, Northrop. The Secular Scripture.
Furst, Lilian R. Romanticism.
Furst, Lilian R. Romanticism in Perspective.
Glickner, Robert, and Gerald Enscoe, Eds. Romanticism;Points of View.
Hayter, Alethea. Opium and the Romantic Imagination.
Heiney, Donald. Recent American Literature.
Heiney, Donald. Recent American Literature to 1930.
Hepworth, Brian. The Rise of Romanticism.
Hoffman, Michael J. The Subversive Vision.
Jones, W. T. Romantic Syndrome;Toward a New Method in Cultural Anthropology and History of Ideas.
Kallsen, Loren J., Ed. Kentucky Tragedy;A Problem in Romantic Attitudes.
Leary, Lewis, Ed. American Literary Essays.
Lewis, Gerald E. Up Here in Maine.
Lewis, Wyndham. Men Without Art.
Lewis, Wyndham. Time and Western Man.
Lieber, Todd M. Endless Experiments;Essays on the Heroic Experience in American Romanticism.
Lieberman, Elias. The American Short Story.
Liljegren, Stan R. Revolt Against Romanticism in American Literature.
Lundblad, Jane. Nathaniel Hawthorne and the Tradition of Gothic Romance.
McCarthy, Harold T. The Expatriate Perspective.
McIntosh, James. Thoreau as Romantic Naturalist.
Massey, Irving J. Uncreating Word;Romanticism and the Object.
Osterweis, Rollin G. The Myth of the Lost Cause;1865-1900.
Osterweis, Rollin G. Romanticism and Nationalism in the Old South.

Parks, Edd Winfield. Ante-Bellum Southern Literary Critics.
Parrington, Vernon Louis. Main Currents in American Thought.
Pattee, Fred Lewis. The Development of the American Short Story.
Pattee, Fred Lewis. The First Century of American Literature;1770-1870.
Pattee, Fred Lewis. A History of American Literature Since 1870.
Paul, Sherman, Ed. Thoreau;A Collection of Critical Essays.
Peck, H. Daniel. A World by Itself.
Peckham, Morse, Ed. Romanticism; The Culture of the Nineteenth Century.
Peyre, Henri. What is Romanticism?
Pizer, Donald, Ed. The Literary Criticism of Frank Norris.
Porte, Joel. The Romance in America.
Prickwett, S. Romanticism and Religion.
Rand, Ayn. The Romantic Manifesto.
Reed, Walter L. Meditations on the Hero;A Study of the Romantic Hero in Nineteenth-Century Fiction.
Reilly, R. J. Romantic Religion;A Study of Barfield, Lewis, Williams and Tolkien.
Reilly, R. J. Romanticism.
Rubin, Louis D., Jr., Ed. The Comic Imagination in American Literature.
Slotkin, Richard. Regeneration through Violence.
Snell, George. The Shapers of American Fiction;1798-1947.
Spiller, Robert E. The Cycle of American Literature.
Spiller, Robert E. The Third Dimension;Studies in Literary History.
Stern, Milton R., Ed. American Literature Survey.
Stubbs, John Caldwell. The Pursuit of Form;A Study of Hawthorne and the Romance.
Thompson, Gary Richard. The Gothic Imagination;Essays in Dark Romanticism.
Thompson, Gary Richard. Poe's Fiction;Romantic Irony in the Gothic Tales.
Thorburn, David, and Geoffrey Hartman, Eds. Romanticism;Vistas, Instances, Continuities.
Tuttleton, James W. The Novel of Manners in America.
Van Nostrand, A. D. Everyman His Own Poet.
Wagenknecht, Edward. Cavalcade of the American Novel.
Williams, Joan, Ed. Novel and Romance;1700-1800;A Documentary Record.
Wilson, Phillip. William Satchell.

SATIRE

Clark, John R., and Anna L. Motto, Eds. Satire;That Blasted Art.
Elliott, Robert C. Power of Satire; Magic, Ritual, Art.
Feinberg, Leonard. Introduction to Satire.
Feinberg, Leonard. The Satirist;His Temperament, Motivation, and Influence.
FitzGerald, Gregory. Modern Satiric Stories.
Hall, Ernest J. Satirical Element in the American Novel.
Heilman, Robert Bechtold. America in English Fiction;1760-1800.
Highet, Gilbert. Anatomy of Satire.
Hodgart, Matthew. Satire.
Hopkins, Kenneth. Portraits in Satire.
Kazin, Alfred. On Native Grounds.
Kernan, Alvin B. Plot of Satire.
Knox, Ronald A. Essays in Satire.
Lewis, Wyndham. Men Without Art.
Miller, Wayne Charles. An Armed America;Its Face in Fiction.

SCIENCE

Petter, Henri. The Early American Novel.
Pollard, Arthur. Satire.
Sanders, Charles. The Scope of Satire.
Solomon, Eric. Stephen Crane; From Parody to Realism.

SCIENCE

Bova, Benjamin. Through Eyes of Wonder; Science Fiction and Science.
Bretnor, Reginald, Ed. Science Fiction; Today and Tomorrow.
Dingle, Herbert. Science and Literary Criticism.
Eastman, Max. Literary Mind; Its Place in an Age of Science.
Gode Von Aesch, Alexander. Natural Science in German Romanticism.
Huxley, Aldous. Literature and Science.
Lintot, Bernard. Literature and Science.
Pollock, Thomas Clark. The Nature of Literature.

SCIENCE FICTION-FANTASY

Aldiss, Brian Wilson. Billion Year Spree; The True History of Science Fiction.
Allen, L. David. Science Fiction; An Introduction.
Amis, Kingsley. New Maps of Hell.
Aquino, John. Science Fiction as Literature.
Ash, Brian. Faces of the Future; The Lessons of Science Fiction.
Barnes, Myra Edwards. Linguistics and Languages in Science Fiction-Fantasy.
Blish, James, Ed. The Issue at Hand.
Blish, James, Ed. More Issues at Hand.
Bova, Benjamin. Notes to a Science Fiction Writer.
Bova, Benjamin. Through Eyes of Wonder; Science Fiction and Science.
Bretnor, Reginald, Ed. The Craft of Science Fiction.
Bretnor, Reginald, Ed. Science Fiction; Today and Tomorrow; A Discursive Symposium.
Clareson, Thomas D. Science Fiction Criticism; An Annotated Checklist.
Cockcroft, Thomas G. L. Index to the Weird Fiction Magazines.
Cole, Walter R., Ed. A Checklist of Science-Fiction Anthologies.
Davenport, Basil. Inquiry into Science Fiction.
DeCamp, Lyon Sprague. Literary Swordsmen and Sorcerers; The Makers of Heroic Fantasy.
DeCamp, Lyon Sprague. Lovecraft; A Biography.
Franklin, H. Bruce. Future Perfect.
Goble, Neil. Asimov Analyzed.
Gove, Philip Babcock. The Imaginary Voyage in Prose Fiction.
Green, Roger Lancelyn. Into Other Worlds; Space-Flight in Fiction, from Lucien to Lewis.
Gunn, James E. Alternate Worlds.
Hersey, John Richard, Ed. Ralph Ellison; A Collection of Critical Essays.
Hillegas, Mark R. The Future as Nightmare; H. G. Wells and the Anti-Utopians.
Kennard, Jean E. Number and Nightmare; Forms of Fantasy in Contemporary Fiction.
Ketterer, David. New Worlds for Old.
Knight, Damon. In Search of Wonder.
Lonsdale, Bernard J., and Helen K. Mackintosh. Children Experience Literature.
Lundwall, Sam J. Science Fiction; What It's All About.
Miller, Marjorie M. Isaac Asimov; A Checklist of Works Published in the United States.

Moskowitz, Samuel. Explorers of the Infinite;Shapers of Science Fiction.
Moskowitz, Samuel. The Immortal Storm;A History of Science Fiction Fandom.
Moskowitz, Samuel. Seekers of Tomorrow;Masters of Modern Science Fiction.
New England Science Fiction Association. Index to the Science Fiction Magazines;1966-1970.
O'Faolain, Sean. The Vanishing Hero.
Olander, Joseph D., and Martin Harry Greenberg, Eds. Arthur C. Clarke.
Olander, Joseph D., and Martin Harry Greenberg, Eds. Isaac Asimov.
Panshin, Alexei, and Cory Panshin. SF in Dimension;A Book of Explorations.
Patrouch, Joseph F. The Science Fiction of Isaac Asimov.
Penzoldt, Peter. The Supernatural in Fiction.
Pfeiffer, John R. Fantasy and Science Fiction;A Critical Guide.
Pohl, Frederik, Ed. The Science Fiction Roll of Honor.
Rabkin, Eric S. The Fantastic in Literature.
Reed, Peter J. Kurt Vonnegut, Jr.
Reginald, R. Contemporary Science Fiction Authors.
Rose, M. Science Fiction;A Collection of Critical Essays.
Roselle, Daniel, Ed. Transformations; Understanding World History Through Science Fiction.
Roselle, Daniel. Transformations 2; Understanding World History Through Science Fiction.
Rottensteiner, Franz. The Science Fiction Book;An Illustrated History.
Scholes, Robert. Structural Fabulation;An Essay on the Fiction of the Future.
Scholes, Robert. Science Fiction;History, Science, Vision.
Slusser, George Edgar. The Bradbury Chronicles.
Slusser, George Edgar. The Farthest Shores of Ursula K. LeGuin.
Slusser, George Edgar. Harlan Ellison;Unrepentant Harlequin.
Straumann, Heinrich. American Literature in the Twentieth Century.
Warner, Harry, Jr. All Our Yesterdays.
Wolfe, Charles K., Ed. Planets and Dimensions;Collected Essays of Clark Ashton Smith.
Woolf, Virginia. Granite and Rainbow.

SENTIMENTALISM

Brissenden, R. F. Virtue in Distress.
Brown, Herbert Ross. The Sentimental Novel in America;1789-1860.
Cowie, Alexander. The Rise of the American Novel.
Fiedler, Leslie A. Love and Death in the American Novel.
Loshe, Lillie Deming. The Early American Novel;1789-1830.

SEXUALITY

Amis, Kingsley. New Maps of Hell.
Armstrong, Judith. The Novel of Adultery.
Drakeford, John W., and Jack Hamm. Pornography;The Sexual Mirage.
Ellmann, Mary. Thinking About Women.
Goldstein, Michael J., et al. Pornography and Sexual Deviance.
Gould, James A., and John J. Iorio. Love, Sex and Identity.
Heilbrun, Carolyn G. Toward A Recognition of Androgyny.
Howe, Irving. The Critical Point on Literature and Culture.

SHORT STORY

Irwin, John T. Doubling and Incest/Repetition and Revenge;A Speculative Reading of Faulkner.
Kiell, Norman. Varieties of Sexual Experience.
Kunkel, Francis Leo. Passion and the Passion;Sex and Religion in Modern Literature.
McCarthy, Mary. On the Contrary; Articles of Belief.
Miles, Rosalind. The Fiction of Sex; Themes and Functions of Sex Difference in the Modern Novel.
Miller, Henry. Sunday After the War.
Millett, Kate. Sexual Politics.
Norton, Rictor. The Homosexual Literary Tradition.
Oboler, Eli. The Fear of the Word; Censorship and Sex.
Perkins, Michael. The Secret Record; Modern Erotic Literature.
Phelan, John, Ed. Communications Control;Readings in the Motives and Structures of Censorship.
Scholes, Robert, and Eric Rabkin.
Spender, Stephen. Love-Hate Relations;English and American Sensibilities.
Tuttleton, James W. The Novel of Manners in America.
Wasserstrom, William. Heiress of all the Ages.
Witham, W. Tasker. The Adolescent in the American Novel;1920-1960.

See also:

LOVE
HOMOSEXUALITY

SHORT STORY
(As Subject)

Bewley, Marius. The Eccentric Design.

Dunning, Stephen. Teaching Literature to Adolescents;Short Stories.
Kenner, Hugh. Studies in Change;A Book of the Short Story.
Lieberman, Elias. The American Short Story.
May, Charles E., Ed. Short Story Theories.
O'Brien, Edward Joseph, Ed. The Advance of the American Short Story.
O'Faolain, Sean. The Short Story.
Pattee, Fred Lewis. The Development of the American Short Story.
Peden, William. The American Short Story;Front Line in the National Defense of Literature.
Peden, William. The American Short Story;Continuity and Change.
Savage, Arthur W., and Norman W. Wilson. How to Analyze the Short Story.
Walker, Warren S. Twentieth-Century Short Story Explication.
Wilcox, Earl J. Fundamentals of Fiction.
Williams, Blanche Colton. Our Short Story Writers.

SOCIALISM

See MARXISM.

SOCIETY

Albrecht, Milton C., Et al., Eds. Sociology of Art and Literature;A Reader.
Aldridge, John W. In Search of Heresy.
Angoff, Charles. The Tone of the Twenties and Other Essays.
Baker, Houston A., Jr. Black Literature in America.
Barnett, James Harwood. Divorce

SOCIETY

and the American Divorce Novel; 1858-1937.

Berger, Morroe. Real and Imagined Worlds;The Novel and Social Science.

Bewley, Marius. Masks and Mirrors.

Black, Michael H. The Literature of Fidelity.

Blake, Fay M. The Strike in the American Novel.

Blotner, Joseph. The Modern American Political Novel;1900-1960.

Blues, Thomas. Mark Twain and the Community.

Bowden, Edwin T. Dungeon of the Heart.

Brown, John Russell. The American Novel and the Nineteen Twenties.

Bryant, Jerry H. The Open Decision.

Cornillon, Susan Koppelman, Ed. Images of Women in Fiction Feminist Perspectives.

Craig, David. The Real Foundation; Literature and Social Change.

Daiches, David. Literature and Society.

Davis, David Brion. Homicide in American Fiction;1798-1860;A Study in Social Values.

Deegan, Dorothy Yost. The Stereotype of The Single Women in American Novels.

Douglas, Ann. The Feminization of American Culture.

Duncan, Hugh Dalziel. Language and Literature in Society.

Earnest, Ernest. The Single Vision; The Alienation of American Intellectuals.

Eastman, Max. The Literary Mind; Its Place in an Age of Science.

Emrich, Wilhelm. Literary Revolution and Modern Society and Other Essays.

Falk, Robert. The Victorian Mode in American Fiction;1865-1885.

Feied, Frederick. No Pie in the Sky.

Fiedler, Leslie A. Waiting for the End.

Flory, Claude Reherd. Economic Criticism in American Fiction;1792 to 1900.

French, Warren, Ed. The Fifties;Fiction, Poetry, Drama.

French, Warren. The Social Novel at the End of an Era.

French, Warren, Ed. The Twenties; Fiction, Poetry, Drama.

Frohock, W. M. Strangers to this Ground;Cultural Diversity in Contemporary American Writing.

Frye, Northrop. The Critical Path; An Essay on the Social Context of Literary Criticism.

Gallagher, Edward Joseph. Early Puritan Writers;A Reference Guide.

Gayle, Addison. The Way of the New World;The Black Novel in America.

Geismar, Maxwell, Ed. Mark Twain and the Three R's;Race, Religion, Revolution-and Related Matters.

Glicksberg, Charles Irving. The Literature of Commitment.

Gloster, Hugh M. Negro Voices in American Fiction.

Gordon, Michael. Juvenile Delinquency in the American Novel;1905-1965.

Green, Elizabeth Lay. The Negro in Contemporary American Literature.

Grejda, Edward S. Equality in the Writings of Herman Melville.

Gross, Seymour L., and John Edward Hardy, Eds. Images of the Negro in American Literature.

Hall, Ernest Jackson. The Satirical Element in the American Novel.

Hardwick, Elizabeth. A View of My Own;Essays in Literature and Society.

Hassan, Ihab. Radical Innocence;Studies in the Contemporary American Novel.

Heilman, Robert Bechtold. America in English Fiction;1760-1800.

SOCIETY

Heiney, Donald. Recent American Literature.
Holman, C. Hugh, Comp. The American Novel Through Henry James.
Hough, Robert L. The Quiet Rebel; William Dean Howells as Social Commentator.
Howe, Irving. The Critical Point on Literature and Culture.
Hubbell, Jay B. The South in American Literature;1607-1900.
Jones, Howard Mumford, and Richard M. Ludwig. Guide to American Literature and Its Backgrounds since 1890.
Kaplan, Justin. Mark Twain and His World.
Karanikas, Alexander. Tillers of a Myth.
Klinkowitz, Jerome, and John Somer, Eds. The Vonnegut Statement.
Kolb, Harold H., Jr. Illusion of Life.
LaFrance, Marston, Ed. Patterns of Commitment in American Literature.
Laurenson, Diana T., and Alan Swingewood. The Sociology of Literature.
Leary, Lewis, Ed. American Literary Essays.
Lieberman, Elias. The American Short Story;A Study of the Influence of Locality in its Development.
Lowenthal, Leo. Literature, Popular Culture, and Society.
Luccock, Halford E. American Mirror;Social, Ethical and Religious Aspects of American Literature; 1930-1940.
Lukacs, Georg. Realism in Our Time.
MacLeod, Anne Scott. A Moral Tale; Children's Fiction and American Culture;1820-1860.
Marcus, Steven. Representations;Essays on Literature and Society.
Margolies, Edward. Native Sons;A Critical Study of Twentieth-Century Negro American Authors.

Meeker, Joseph W. The Comedy of Survival;Studies in Literary Ecology.
Michaud, Regis. The American Novel To-Day;A Social and Psychological Study.
Millgate, Michael. American Social Fiction;James to Cozzens.
Mills, Gordon. Hamlet's Castle;The Study of Literature as a Social Experience.
Milne, Gordon. The Sense of Society; A History of the American Novel of Manners.
Moore, T. Inglis. Social Patterns in Australian Literature.
Moravia, Alberto. Man as an End;A Defense of Humanism.
Morse, J. Mitchell. Prejudice and Literature.
Nelson, Gerald B. Ten Versions of America.
Osterweis, Rollin G. Romanticism and Nationalism in the Old South.
Pearce, Roy Harvey. Historicism Once More.
Pearson, Bill. Fretful Sleepers and Other Essays.
Petit, Arthur G. Mark Twain and the South.
Phelan, John, Ed. Communications Control;Readings in the Motives and Structures of Censorship.
Pizer, Donald, Ed. The Literary Criticism of Frank Norris.
Podhoretz, Norman. Doings and Undoings.
Proffer, Carl R., Ed. and Translator. Soviet Criticism of American Literature in the Sixties.
Rahv, Philip. Literature in America.
Rideout, Walter B. The Radical Novel in the United States;1900-1954.
Rist, Ray C., Ed. Pornography Controversy.
Rose, Alan Henry. Demonic Vision; Racial Fantasy and Southern Fiction.

Scott, Nathan A., Jr., Ed. Adversity and Grace;Studies in Recent American Literature.

Seward, William W., Jr. Contrasts in Modern Writers.

Slotkin, Richard. Regeneration Through Violence;The Mythology of the American Frontier;1600-1860.

Solotaroff, Theodore. The Red Hot Vacuum;and Other Pieces on the Writing of the Sixties.

Spender, Stephen. Love-Hate Relations;English and American Sensibilities.

Spradley, James P., and George E. McDonough. Anthropology Through Literature.

Spiller, Robert E. The Third Dimension;Studies in Literary History.

Staehelin-Wackernagel, Adelheid. The Cooper Monographs.

Steiner, George. Language and Silence.

Stineback, David C. Shifting World; Social Change and Nostalgia in the American Novel.

Stone, Edward. Voices of Despair.

Stowe, Harriet Beecher. The Key to Uncle Tom's Cabin.

Straumann, Heinrich. American Literature in the Twentieth Century.

Strelka, Joseph P., Ed. Literary Criticism and Sociology.

Sullivan, Walter. Death by Melancholy;Essays on Modern Southern Fiction.

Swingewood, Alan. The Novel and Revolution.

Takaki, Ronald T. Violence in the Black Imagination;Essays and Documents.

Tavuchis, Nicholas. The Family through Literature.

Taylor, Walter Fuller. The Economic Novel in America.

Tischler, Nancy M. Black Masks;Negro Characters in Modern Southern Fiction.

Trilling, Lionel. Liberal Imagination;Essays on Literature and Society.

Truzzi, Marcello. The Humanities As Sociology.

Tuttleton, James W. The Novel of Manners in America.

Umphlett, Wiley Lee. The Sporting Myth and the American Experience.

Violette, Augusta Genevieve. Economic Feminism in American Literature Prior to 1848.

Wagenknecht, Edward. Cavalcade of the American Novel.

West, Thomas Reed. Nature, Community and Will.

Widmer, Eleanor, and Kingsley Widmer, Eds. Freedom and Culture; Literary Censorship in the Seventies.

Wilson, Edmund. Classics and Commercials.

Winegarten, Renee. Writers and Revolution;the Fatal Lure of Action.

SOCIOLOGY

See CULTURE.

STREAM OF CONSCIOUSNESS

See PSYCHOLOGY.

STRUCTURALISM

Boon, James A. From Symbolism to Structuralism.

Calloud, Jean. Structural Analysis of the Narrative.

Culler, Jonathan D. Structuralist Poetics.

Ingarden, Roman. The Cognition of the Literary Work of Art.
Scholes, Robert. Structuralism in Literature; An Introduction.

SUSPENSE

See MYSTERY AND SUSPENSE.

SYMBOLISM

Armstrong, John. Paradise Myth.
Basler, Roy P. Sex, Symbolism and Psychology in Literature.
Beach, Joseph W. Obsessive Images.
Bewley, Marius. The Eccentric Design.
Blackmur, R. P. The Lion and the Honeycomb.
Boon, James A. From Symbolism to Structuralism.
Bowra, Cecil M. Heritage of Symbolism.
Burke, Kenneth. The Philosophy of Literary Form.
Butler, Christopher. Number Symbolism.
Chadwick, Charles. Symbolism.
Chapman, Abraham, Ed. Literature of the American Indians.
Chiari, Joseph. Symbolisme from Poe to Mallarme.
Cornell, Kenneth. Symbolist Movement.
Elder, Marjorie J. Nathaniel Hawthorne; Transcendental Symbolist.
Feidelson, Charles, Jr. Symbolism and American Literature.
Fogle, Richard Harter. Hawthorne's Fiction; The Light and the Dark.
Fowlie, Wallace. Love in Literature; Studies in Symbolic Expression.
Frye, Northrop. Myth and Symbol; Critical Approaches and Applications.

Howe, Irving, Ed. The Idea of the Modern in Literature and the Arts.
Knight, Damon. In Search of Wonder.
Krawitz, Henry. A Post-Symbolist Bibliography.
May, Rollo, Ed. Symbolism in Religion and Literature.
Nnolim, Charles E. Melville's "Benito Cereno"; A Study in Meaning of Name Symbolism.
Senior, John. Way Down and Out.
Sharpless, F. Parvin. Symbol and Myth in Modern Literature.
Stone, Edward. A Certain Morbidness; A View of American Literature.
Strelka, Joseph P., Ed. Perspectives in Literary Symbolism.
Symons, Arthur. Symbolist Movement in Literature.
Temple, Ruth Z. The Critic's Alchemy.
Tindall, William Y. Literary Symbol.
Vargo, Edward P. Rainstorms and Fire; Ritual in the Novels of John Updike.
Webb, Eugene. The Dark Dove; The Sacred and Secular in Modern Literature.
Wilson, Edmund. Axel's Castle.
Ziolkowski, Theodore. Disenchanted Images; A Literary Iconology.

TECHNIQUE

General

Abbe, George, Ed. Stephen Vincent Benet on Writing.
Anderson, Sherwood. The "Writer's Book".
Bader, A. L., Ed. To the Young Writer.
Barnet, Sylvan. Barnet and Stubb's Practical Guide to Writing.
Barzun, Jacques. Simple and Direct; A Rhetoric for Writers.

TECHNIQUE

Beach, Joseph Warren. The Twentieth Century Novel;Studies in Technique.

Blackmur, R.P. A Primer of Ignorance.

Bloomfield, Morton W., Ed. The Interpretation of Narrative;Theory and Practice.

Bradbury, Ray. Zen and the Art of Writing;and, The Joy of Writing; Two Essays.

Buck, Gertrude. The Metaphor;A Study in the Psychology of Rhetoric.

Caldwell, Erskine. Call It Experience;The Years of Learning How to Write.

Calloud, Jean. Structural Analysis of the Narrative.

Cameron, Eleanor. The Green and Burning Tree.

Cohn, Jill Wilson. Writing;The Personal Voice.

Curry, Martha Mulroy, Ed. The "Writer's Book" by Sherwood Anderson;A Critical Edition.

Elgin, Suzette Haden. Pouring Down Words.

Field, Elinor Whitney, Ed. Horn Book Reflections on Children's Books and Reading.

Fletcher, Richard M. The Stylistic Development of Edgar Allan Poe.

Foster-Harris. The Basic Formulas of Fiction.

Friedman, Norman. Form and Meaning in Fiction.

Hall, Lawrence Sargent. How Thinking is Written.

Hardy, Barbara Nathan. Tellers and Listeners;The Narrative Imagination.

Highet, Gilbert. Explorations.

Horgan, Paul. Approaches to Writing.

Hulme, T.E. Notes on Language and Style.

Kinsella, Paul. The Techniques of Writing.

Kort, Wesley A. Narrative Elements and Religious Meanings.

Lewis, Claudia. Writing for Young Children.

Lubbock, Percy. The Craft of Fiction.

Margulis, Joel B. An Awareness of Language.

Moore, Thomas H., Comp. Henry Miller on Writing;From the Published and Unpublished Works of Henry Miller.

O'Connor, Flannery. Mystery and Manners.

Pichaske, David R. Writing Sense;A Handbook of Composition.

Schaefer, Martha. The Writing Process;Step by Step.

Shaw, Harry. 20 Steps to Better Writing.

Southall, Ivan. A Journey of Discovery;On Writing for Children.

Stein, Gertrude. How to Write.

Troyka, Lynn Quitman. Guide to Writing.

Weston, Harold. Form in Literature; A Theory of Technique.

Whitten, Mary E. Creative Pattern Practice.

Wittig, Susan. Steps to Structure.

Criticism

Barnett, Sylvan. A Short Guide to Writing About Literature.

Bryan, Margaret B. Writing About Literature and Film.

Kytle, Ray, Comp. The Wrought Response;Reading and Writing About Literature.

Roberts, Edgar V. Writing Themes About Literature.

Fiction

Boulton, Marjorie. The Anatomy of the Novel.

Braine, John. Writing a Novel.

Bretnor, Reginald, Ed. The Craft of Science Fiction.

TECHNIQUE

Burack, A. S., Ed. Techniques of Novel Writing.
Burack, A. S., Ed. Writing Detective and Mystery Fiction.
Burnett, Hallie S., and Whit Burnett. Fiction Writer's Handbook.
Cameron, Eleanor. The Green and Burning Tree.
Cassill, R. V. Writing Fiction.
Curry, Peggy Simpson. Creating Fiction from Experience.
Derleth, August. Writing Fiction.
Derrick, C. The Writing of Novels.
Egri, Lajos. The Art of Creative Writing.
Graham, Kenneth. English Criticism of the Novel; 1865-1900.
Highsmith, Patricia. Plotting and Writing Suspense Fiction.
Hildick, Wallace. Word for Word.
Kabler, Erich. The Inward Turn of Narrative.
Knott, William C. The Craft of Fiction.
Koontz, Dean R. Writing Popular Fiction.
MacAuley, R. Technique in Fiction.
McCleary, Dorothy. Creative Fiction Writing.
McCormack, Thomas, Ed. Afterwords; Novelists on Their Novels.
McHugh, V. Primer of the Novel.
Meredith, Robert C. The Professional Story Writer and His Art.
Mirrielees, Edith Ronald. Story Writing.
Mystery Writers of America. The Mystery Writer's Handbook.
Nahal, Chaman. The Narrative Pattern in Ernest Hemingway's Fiction.
Nist, John, Ed. Style in English.
Owen, Jean Z. Professional Fiction Writing.
Palmer, Florence K. The Confession Writer's Handbook.
Raban, Jonathan. The Technique of Modern Fiction.
Reed, Joseph W., Jr. Faulkner's Narrative.
Richardson, R. Literature and Film.
Rockwell, F. A. How to Write Plots That Sell.
Rockwell, F. A. Modern Fiction Techniques.
Smith, Helen Reagan. Basic Story Techniques.
Somerlott, Robert. The Writing of Modern Fiction.
Spencer, Sharon. Space, Time, and Structure in the Modern Novel.
Stevick. P. The Chapter in Fiction.
Sturmelian, Leon. Techniques of Fiction Writing.
Thomas, P. E. A Guide for Authors.
Treat, Lawrence, Ed. The Mystery Writer's Handbook.
Ullyette, Jean M. Guidelines for Creative Writing.
Vaid, Krishna Baldev. Technique in the Tales of Henry James.
Wharton, Edith. The Writing of Fiction.
White, John J. Mythology in the Modern Novel; A Study of Pre-figurative Techniques.
Wicker, B. The Story-Shaped World.
Williams, Nan Schram. Confess for Profit; Writing and Selling the Personal Story.
Wolfe, Thomas. The Story of a Novel.

Mystery and Suspense:

Burack, A. S., Ed. Writing Detective and Mystery Fiction.
Highsmith, Patricia. Plotting and Writing Suspense Fiction.
Nevins, Francis M., Jr., Ed. The Mystery Writer's Art.
Treat, Lawrence, Ed. The Mystery Writer's Handbook.

Non-Fiction

Adams, Maurianne, Ed. Autobiography.
Cherry, Richard L., Et al. The Essay; Structure and Purpose.
Graves, Robert, and Alan Hodge. The Reader Over Your Shoulder.
Hildick, Wallace. Thirteen Types of Narrative.
Hough, George A. News Writing.
Miles, Robert. First Principles of the Essay.
Morse, Grant W. Complete Guide to Organizing and Documenting Research Papers.
Rivers, William L. Writing, Craft and Art.
Rockwell, F. A. How to Write Non-Fiction that Sells.
Stine, Jane. Investigating; Gathering Information.
Whissen, Thomas R. Components of Composition.
Williamson, Daniel Raymond. Feature Writing for Newspapers.
Zinsser, William Knowlton. On Writing Well; An Informal Guide to Writing Nonfiction.

Style (Analysis Of)

Babb, Howard S. Essays in Stylistic Analysis.
Bennett, James R. Studies in Prose Style.
Blanshard, Brand. On Philosophical Style.
Brown, Huntington. Prose Styles; Five Primary Types.
Chapman, Raymond. Linguistics and Literature.
Chatman, Seymour, Ed. Literary Style Symposium.
Cluysenaar, Anne. Aspects of Literary Stylistics.
Enkvist, Nils E., Et al. Linguistics and Style.
Fowler, Roger. Essays on Style and Language.
Fowler, Roger, Ed. Style and Structure in Literature; Essays in the New Stylistics.
Freeman, D. C. Linguistics and Literary Style.
Gray, Bennison. Style: The Problem and Its Solution.
Gray, W. B. How to Measure Readability.
Grube, G. M. Transl. Aristotle; On Poetry and Style.
Hiatt, Mary P. Artful Balance; The Parallel Structures of Style.
Hulme, T. E. Notes on Language and Style.
Lee, Vernon. The Handling of Words and Other Studies in Literary Psychology.
Nist, John, Ed. Style in English.
Poirier, Richard. A World Elsewhere; The Place of Style in American Literature.
Porter, Katherine Anne. The Selected Essays of Katherine Anne Porter.
Spencer, Herbert. Literary Style and Music.
Trimble, John R. Writing with Style; Conversations on the Art of Writing.
Turner, George. Stylistics.
Weintraub, Stanley, Ed. Biography and Truth.
Williams, C. B. Style and Vocabulary; Numerical Studies.

Reference

Burns, Shannon. An Annotated Bibliography of Texts on Writing Skills.

TECHNOLOGY

See SCIENCE.

TRADITION

See CULTURE.

TRANSCENDENTALISM

Buell, Lawrence. Literary Transcendentalism;Style and Vision in the American Renaissance.
Christy, M.E. The Orient in American Transcendentalism;A Study of Emerson, Thoreau and Alcott.
Elder, Marjorie J. Nathaniel Hawthorne;Transcendental Symbolist.
Gohdes, Clarence. Bibliographical Guide to the Study of the Literature of the U.S.A.
Hoffman, Michael J. The Subversive Vision;American Romanticism in Literature.
Jones, Joseph Jay. Radical Cousins; Nineteenth Century American and Australian Writers.
Metzger, Charles R. Emerson and Greenough;Transcendental Pioneers of an American Esthetic.
Tanner, Tony. The Reign of Wonder.
Woodbury, Charles J. Talks with Emerson.

VIOLENCE

See SOCIETY.

WAR

Aichinger, Peter. The American Soldier in Fiction;1880-1963.
Aldridge, John W., Ed. After the Lost Generation.
Allen, Walter. The Modern Novel in Britain and the United States.
Benson, Frederick R. Writers in Arms;The Literary Impact of the Spanish Civil War.
Bryant, Jerry H. The Open Decision.
Cooperman, Stanley. World War I and the American Novel.
Cowley, Malcolm. Edited by Henry Dan Piper. Think Back On Us;A Contemporary Chronical of the 1930's by Malcolm Cowley.
Dolan, Paul J. Of War and War's Alarms.
Fiedler, Leslie A. Waiting for the End.
Gayle, Addison, Jr. The Way of the New World.
Howe, Irving. The Critical Point on Literature and Culture.
Hubbell, Jay B. The South in American Literature;1607-1900.
Jones, Peter G. War and the Novelist;Appraising the American War Novel.
Klein, Holger, Ed. The First World War in Fiction;A Collection of Critical Essays.
Korshin, Paul J., Ed. Studies in Change and Revolution.
Lively, Robert A. Fiction Fights the Civil War.
Mersand, Joseph. Traditions in American Literature;A Study of Jewish Characters and Authors.
Miller, Wayne Charles. An Armed America;Its Face in Fiction.
Nagel, James, Comp. Critical Essays on Catch-22.
Nelson, Gerald B. Ten Versions of America.
Pattee, Fred Lewis. The First Century of American Literature;1770-1870.
Pickering, James H., Ed. The World Turned Upside Down.
Rubin, Louis D., Jr., and Robert D. Jacobs, Eds. Southern Renascence.
Stewart, Randall. Edited by George

Core. Regionalism and Beyond; Essays of Randall Stewart.
Swingewood, Alan. The Novel and Revolution.
Waldmeir, Joseph J. American Novels of the Second World War.

WOMEN

Abramowitz, Molly. Elie Wiesel; A Bibliography.
Allen, Mary. The Necessary Blankness; Women in Major American Fiction of the Sixties.
Auchincloss, Louis. Edith Wharton; A Woman in Her Time.
Auchincloss, Louis. Pioneers and Caretakers; A Study of 9 American Women Novelists.
Balakian, Nona, and Charles Simmons, Eds. The Creative Present.
Beauvoir, Simone de. The Second Sex.
Bewley, Marius. Masks and Mirrors.
Blake, Nelson Manfred. Novelists' America; Fiction as History; 1910-1940.
Brinnin, John Malcolm. The Third Rose; Gertrude Stein and Her World.
Bryer, Jackson R., Ed. Fifteen Modern American Authors.
Cassady, Carolyn. Heart Beat; My Life with Jack and Neal.
Christy, A. E. The Orient in American Transcendentalism.
Cook, Richard M. Carson McCullers.
Cooperman, Stanley. World War I and the American Novel.
Copeland, Carolyn Faunce. Language and Time and Gertrude Stein.
Cornillon, Susan Koppelman, Ed. Images of Women in Fiction Feminist Perspective.
Cowie, Alexander. The Rise of the American Novel.
Cox, C. B. The Free Spirit; A Study of Liberal Humanism.
Diamond, Arlyn, and Lee R. Edwards, Eds. The Authority of Experience in Feminist Criticism.
Donovan, Josephine, Ed. Feminist Literary Criticism; Explorations in Theory.
Douglas, Ann. The Feminization of American Culture.
Eakin, Paul John. The New England Girl.
Eckley, Wilton. Harriette Arnow.
Ellmann, Mary. Thinking About Women.
Field, Louise Maunsell. Ellen Glasgow; Novelist of the Old and the New South.
Foster, Edward Halsey. Catharine Maria Sedgwick.
Foster, Jeannette H. Sex Variant Women in Literature.
French, Warren, Ed. The Fifties; Fiction, Poetry, Drama.
French, Warren G., and Walter E. Kidd, Eds. American Winners of the Nobel Literary Prize.
Frohock, W. M. The Novel of Violence in America.
Geismar, Maxwell. The Last of the Provincials; The American Novel; 1915-1925.
Geismar, Maxwell. Rebels and Ancestors; The American Novel; 1890-1915.
Gelfant, Blanche Housman. The American City Novel.
Gerber, Philip L. Willa Cather.
Gilbertson, Catherine. Harriet Beecher Stowe.
Goldman, Sherli Evens. Mary McCarthy; A Bibliography.
Gossett, Louise Y. Violence in Recent Southern Fiction.
Green, Dorothy. Ulysses Bound; Henry Handel Richardson and Her Fiction.
Grumbach, Doris. The Company She Kept.

Gulliver, Lucile. Louisa May Alcott; A Bibliography.
Haas, Robert Bartlett, Comp. A Catalogue of the Published and Unpublished Writings of Gertrude Stein.
Hambleton, Ronald. Mazo de LaRoche of Jalna.
Hardwick, Elizabeth. Seduction and Betrayal;Women and Literature.
Hardy, John Edward. Katherine Anne Porter.
Hardy, John Edward. Man in the Modern Novel.
Harris, Theodore F. Pearl S. Buck;A Biography.
Hendrick, George. Katherine Anne Porter.
Higginson, Thomas Wentworth. Margaret Fuller Ossoli.
Hoffman, Frederick J. The Twenties.
Holman, C. Hugh. Three Modes of Modern Southern Fiction.
Howe, Irving, Ed. Edith Wharton;A Collection of Critical Essays.
Howe, Julia Ward. Margaret Fuller; (Marchesa Ossoli).
Hubbell, Jay B. The South in American Literature;1607-1900.
Inge, M. Thomas, Ed. Ellen Glasgow; Centennial Essays.
Jessup, Josephine Lurie. Faith of Our Feminists.
Kazin, Alfred. On Native Grounds.
Kellogg, Grace. The Two Lives of Edith Wharton;The Woman and Her Work.
Kelly, William W. Ellen Glasgow;A Bibliography.
Kiernan, Brian. Images of Society and Nature;Seven Essays on Australian Novels.
Kiernan, Robert F. Katherine Anne Porter and Carson McCullers;A Reference Guide.
Lee, Robert Edson. From West to East;Studies in the Literature of the American West.

Lewis, Edith. Willa Cather Living; A Personal Record.
McCarthy, Mary. On the Contrary; Articles of Belief.
McDowell, Frederick P. W. Elizabeth Madox Roberts.
McMaster, Helen Neill. Margaret Fuller as a Literary Critic.
Mason, Bobbie Ann. The Girl Sleuth.
Matthiessen, Francis Otto. Sarah Orne Jewett.
Mellow, James R. Charmed Circle; Gertrude Stein and Company.
Michaud, Regis. The American Novel To-Day;A Social and Psychological Study.
Miller, James E., Jr. Quests Surd and Absurd;Essays in American Literature.
Moers, Ellen. Literary Women.
Mooney, Harry J., Jr. The Fiction and Criticism of Katherine Anne Porter.
Murphy, John J. Five Essays on Willa Cather;The Merrimack Symposium.
Myers, Carol Fairbanks. Women in Literature;Criticism of the Seventies.
Nance, William L. Katherine Anne Porter and the Art of Rejection.
Nevius, Blake. Edith Wharton;A Study of Her Fiction.
O'Connor, William Van, Ed. Seven Modern American Novelists;An Introduction.
Page, Sally R. Faulkner's Women; Characterization and Meaning.
Parker, Dorothy. The Portable Dorothy Parker.
Pearson, Carol, and Katherine Pope. Who Am I This Time?
Petter, Henri. The Early American Novel.
Pizer, Donald, Ed. The Literary Criticism of Frank Norris.
Podhoretz, Norman. Doings and Undoings.

WOMEN IN LITERATURE

Rand, Ayn. The Romantic Manifesto.
Rogers, Katherine. The Troublesome Helpmate.
Rosenfelt, Deborah Silverton. Strong Women;An Annotated Bibliography of Literature for the High School Classroom.
Rule, Jane. Lesbian Images.
Ruotolo, Lucio P. Six Existential Heroes;The Politics of Faith.
Russell, Francis. Three Studies in Twentieth Century Obscurity.
Scott, James B. Djuna Barnes.
Seyersted, Per   Chopin;A Critical Biography.
Shapiro, Charles, Ed. Twelve Original Essays on Great American Novels.
Shaughnessy, Mary Rose. Women and Success in American Society in the Works of Edna Ferber.
Simon, Linda. The Biography of Alice B. Toklas.
Slote, Bernice, Ed. The Art of Willa Cather.
Slusser, George Edgar. The Farthest Shores of Ursula K. LeGuin.
Spacks, Patricia Meyer, Ed. Contemporary Women Novelists;A Collection of Critical Essays.
Spacks, Patricia Ann Meyer. The Female Imagination.
Springer, Marlene. Edith Wharton and Kate Chopin;A Guide.
Stein, Gertrude. Lectures in America.
Stein, Gertrude. How to Write.
Stouck, David. Willa Cather's Imagination.
Stowe, Harriet Beecher. The Key to Uncle Tom's Cabin.
Straumann, Heinrich. American Literature in the Twentieth Century.
Tanner, Tony. The Reign of Wonder.
Taylor, Lloyd C. Margaret Ayer Barnes.
Tominaga, Thomas T. Iris Murdoch and Muriel Spark;A Bibliography.
Tuttleton, James W. The Novel of Manners in America.
Violette, Augusta Genevieve. Economic Feminism in American Literature Prior to 1848.
Wagenknecht, Edward. Cavalcade of the American Novel.
Wagenknecht, Edward. Harriet Beecher Stowe;The Known and the Unknown.
Waldmeir, Joseph J., Ed. Recent American Fiction;Some Critical Views.
Waldrip, Louise, and Shirley Ann Bauer. A Bibliography of the Works of Katherine Anne Porter.
Walker, Dorothea. Alice Brown.
Walker, William E., and Robert L. Welker, Eds. Reality and Myth.
Warren, Barbara. Feminine Image in Literature.
Wharton, Edith. The Writing of Fiction.
Wilson, Robert A. Gertrude Stein;A Bibliography.
Wise, Winifred E. Harriet Beecher Stowe;Woman with a Cause.
Woodress, James Leslie. Willa Cather;Her Life and Art.

WOMEN IN LITERATURE

Bell, Millicent. Edith Wharton and Henry James;The Story of their Friendship.
Bennett, Mildred R. The World of Willa Cather.
Brown, L. K. Willa Cather;A Critical Biography.
Cassady, Carolyn. Heart Beat;My Life with Jack and Neal.
Deegan, Dorothy Yost. The Stereotype of The Single Woman in American Novels.
Erskine, John. Leading American Novelists.

Fuller, Edmund. Man in Modern Fiction;Some Minority Opinions on Contemporary American Writing.
Hardwick, Elizabeth. Seduction and Betrayal;Women and Literature.
Kellogg, Grace. The Two Lives of Edith Wharton;The Woman and Her Work.
Kostelanetz, Richard, Ed. Younger Critics of North America.
McCarthy, Mary. On the Contrary; Articles of Belief.
McCracken, Elizabeth. The Feminine in Fiction.
Mencken, H. L. Edited by William H. Nolte. H. L. Mencken's Smart Set Criticism.
Miles, Rosalind. The Fiction of Sex; Themes and Functions of Sex Difference in the Modern Novel.
Moers, Ellen. Literary Women.
Morse, J. Mitchell. Prejudice and Literature.
Papashvily, Helen Waite. All the Happy Endings.
Pattee, Fred Lewis. The Development of the American Short Story.
Pearson, Carol, and Katherine Pope. Who Am I This Time?
Porter, Katherine Anne. The Collected Essays;and Occasional Writings of Katherine Anne Porter.
Shaughnessy, Mary Rose. Women and Success in American Society in the Works of Edna Ferber.
Spender, Stephen. Love-Hate Relations.
Stowe, Charles Edward. Life of Harriet Beecher Stowe.
Tomkins, Mary E. Ida M. Tarbell.
Wasserstrom, William. Heiress of all the Ages.
Weil, Dorothy. In Defense of Women; Susanna Rowson.
Williams, David. Faulkner's Women; The Myth and the Muse.

WORLD WAR

See WAR.

REFERENCE - BIBLIOGRAPHIES

Abramowitz, Molly. Elie Wiesel.
Altick, Richard D., and Andrew Wright. Selective Bibliography for the Study of English and American Literature.
Baird, Newton D. An Annotated Bibliography of California Fiction.
Bassett, J. William Faulkner;An Annotated Checklist of Criticism.
Blanck, Jacob, Comp. Bibliography of American Literature;Vol. 1; Henry Adams to Donn Byrne.
Blanck, Jacob, Comp. Bibliography of American Literature;Vol. 2; George W. Cable to Timothy Dwight.
Blanck, Jacob, Comp. Bibliography of American Literature;Vol. 3; Edward Eggleston to Bret Harte.
Blanck, Jacob, Comp. Bibliography of American Literature;Vol. 4; Nathaniel Hawthorne to Joseph Holt Ingraham.
Blanck, Jacob, Comp. Bibliography of American Literature;Vol. 5; Washington Irving to Henry Wadsworth Longfellow.
Blanck, Jacob, Comp. Bibliography of American Literature;Vol. 4; Augustus Baldwin Longstreet to Thomas William Parsons.
Bowden, Edwin T. James Thurber;A Bibliography.
Branch, Edgar. A Bibliography of James T. Farrell's Writings;1920-1957.
Brasch, Ila Wales. A Comprehensive Annotated Bibliography of American Black English.

REFERENCE - BIBLIOGRAPHIES

Brenni, Vito J., Comp. William Dean Howells.

Brignano, Russell Carl. Black Americans in Autobiography.

Browne, Nina E., Comp. A Bibliography of Nathaniel Hawthorne.

Bruccoli, Matthew J., and C. E. Frazer Clark, Jr., Eds. First Printings of American Authors.

Bruccoli, Matthew J. F. Scott Fitzgerald; A Descriptive Bibliography.

Bruccoli, Matthew J. John O'Hara; A Checklist.

Bruccoli, Matthew J. Kenneth Millar/Ross Macdonald; A Checklist.

Bruccoli, Matthew J., and C. E. Frazer Clark, Jr., Comp. Hemingway at Auction; 1930-1973.

Bryer, Jackson R. The Critical Reputation of F. Scott Fitzgerald.

Burns, Shannon. An Annotated Bibliography of Texts on Writing Skills.

Clack, Doris H. Black Literature Resources; Analysis and Organization.

Clareson, Thomas D. Science Fiction Criticism.

Clark, C. E. Frazer, Comp. Hawthorne at Auction; 1894-1971.

Coan, Otis W., and Richard G. Lillard. America in Fiction.

Cohn, Louis Henry. A Bibliography of the Works of Ernest Hemingway.

Cole, Walter R., Ed. A Checklist of Science-Fiction Anthologies.

Cotton, Gerald B., and Hilda Mary McGill. Fiction Guides.

Crisler, Jesse E., and Joseph R. McElrath, Jr. Frank Norris; A Reference Guide.

Deodene Frank, and William P. French. Black American Fiction Since 1952.

Doyle, Paul A. Guide to Basic Information Sources in Enclish Literature.

Elkins, A. C., Jr., and L. J. Forstner. The Romantic Movement Bibliography; 1936-1970.

Etulain, Richard W. Western American Literature.

Field, Andrew. Nabokov; A Bibliography.

Field, Leslie A., Comp. Bernard Malamud; A Collection of Critical Essays.

Fogle, Richard H., Comp. Romantic Poets and Prose Writers.

Franklin, Benjamin. Anais Nin; A Bibliography.

Gaer, Joseph, Ed. Bret Harte; Bibliography and Biographical Data.

Gaer, Joseph. Upton Sinclair; Bibliography and Biographical Data.

Gallagher, Edward Joseph. Early Puritan Writers; A Reference Guide.

Gerstenberger, Donna, and George Hendrick. The American Novel.

Gohdes, Clarence. Literature and Theater of the States and Regions of the U.S.A.

Gohdes, Clarence. Bibliographical Guide to the Study of the Literature of the U.S.A.

Goldman, Sherli Evens. Mary McCarthy.

Goldstone, Adrian H., and John R. Payne. John Steinbeck.

Gottesman, Ronald. Upton Sinclair; An Annotated Checklist.

Gottesman, Ronald. The Literary Manuscripts of Upton Sinclair.

Grismer, Raymond Leonard. A Reference Index to Twelve Thousand Spanish American Authors.

Gross, Theodore L., and Stanley Wertheim. Hawthorne, Melville, Stephen Crane; A Critical Bibliography.

Gulliver, Lucile. Louisa May Alcott.

Haas, Robert Bartlett, Comp. A Catalogue of the Published and Unpublished Writings of Gertrude Stein.

REFERENCE - BIBLIOGRAPHIES

Hackett, Alice Payne, and James Henry Burke. Years of Best Sellers; 1895-1975.

Hanneman, Audre. Ernest Hemingway.

Hatzfeld, Helmut A. Critical Bibliography of New Stylistics Applied to the Romance Literature;1953-1965.

Hayashi, Tetsumaro. John Steinbeck.

Heartman, Charles Frederick;A Bibliography of First Printings of the Writings of Edgar Allan Poe.

Hildreth, Margaret. Harriet Beecher Stowe;A Bibliography.

Holt, Guy. A Bibliography of the Writings of James Branch Cabell.

Hotchkiss, Jeanette. American Historical Fiction and Biography for Children and Young People.

Hudgens, Betty Lenhardt. Kurt Vonnegut, Jr.;A Checklist.

Huff, Mary Nance, Comp. Robert Penn Warren.

Hyneman, Esther F. Edgar Allan Poe.

James, Philip Brutton. Children's Books of Yesterday.

Johnson, James Gibson. Southern Fiction Priot to 1860;An Attempt at a First-Hand Bibliography.

Johnson, Merle DeVore. A Bibliography of the Works of Mark Twain, Samuel Longhorne Clemens.

Kelly, William W. Ellen Glasgow;A Bibliography.

Kennedy, Arthur G., and Donald B. Sands. Revised by William E. Colburn. A Concise Bibliography for Students of English.

Kerr, Elizabeth Margaret. Bibliography of the Sequence Novel.

Kesselring, Marion Louise. Hawthorne's Reading;1828-1850.

Kirby, David K. American Fiction to 1900;A Guide to Information Sources.

Kirk, John Foster. A Supplement to Allibone's Critical Dictionary of English Literature and British and American Authors.

Krawitz, Henry. A Post-Symbolist Bibliography.

Langfield, William R., and Philip C. Blackburn.Washington Irving.

Lee, Alfred Pyle. A Bibliography of Christopher Morley.

McDonald, Edward David. A Bibliography of the Writings of Theodore Dreiser.

McGarry, Daniel D. World Historical Fiction Guide.

McHaney, Thomas L. William Faulkner;A Reference Guide.

McNamee, Lawrence F. Dissertations in English and American Literature.

McNamee, Lawrence F. Dissertations in English and American Literature;Supplement One.

Marple, Alice. Iowa Authors and Their Works;A Contribution Toward A Bibliography.

Mason, Bobbie Ann. The Girl Sleuth.

Massey, Linton R., Comp. "Man Working,";1919-1962;William Faulkner.

Meriwether, James B. The Literary Career of William Faulkner;A Bibliographical Study.

Michel, Pierre. James Gould Cozzens.

Miller, Marjorie M. Isaac Asimov; A Checklist.

Minnigerode, Meade. Some Personal Letters of Herman Melville and a Bibliography.

Myers, Carol Fairbanks. Women in Literature;Criticism of the Seventies.

Myerson, Joel, and Arthur H. Miller, Jr. Melville Dissertations;An Annotated Directory.

Neumann, Alfred R., and David V. Erdman, Eds. Literature and the Other Arts;A Select Bibliography; 1952-1958.

Nield, Jonathan. A Guide to Best Historical Novels and Tales.

REFERENCE - BIBLIOGRAPHIES

Orton, Vrest. Dreiserana;A Book About His Books.
Owings, Mark. The Revised H.P. Lovecraft Bibliography.
Patterson, Margaret C. Literary Research Guide.
Peet, Louis Harman. Handy Book of American Authors.
Pfeiffer, John R. Fantasy and Science Fiction;A Critical Guide.
Phillips, LeRoy. A Bibliography of the Writings of Henry James.
Pieratt, Asa B. Kurt Vonnegut, Jr.; A Descriptive Bibliography and Annotated Secondary Checklist.
Pownall, David E. Articles on Twentieth Century Literature;An Annotated Bibliography;1954 to 1970.
Reginald,R., Ed. Contemporary Science Fiction Authors.
Ricks, Beatrice. Herman Melville;A Reference Bibliography;1900-1972.
Rodgers, Bernard F., Jr. Philip Roth;A Bibliography.
Rogers, Douglas G. Sherwood Anderson;A Selective, Annotated Bibliography.
Rosa, Alfred F. Contemporary Fiction in America and England;1950-1970.
Rosenfelt, Deborah Silverton. Strong Women.
Rubin, Louis D., Jr., Ed. A Bibliographical Guide to the Study of Southern Literature.
Samuels, Lee. A Hemingway Checklist.
Schroeder, Theodore A. Free Speech Bibliography.
Scotto, Robert M. Three Contemporary American Novelists.
Sealts, Merton M., Jr. Melville's Reading;A Checklist of Books Owned and Borrowed.
Sheehy, Eugene P., and Kenneth A. Lohf, Comp. Sherwood Anderson.
Smith, Myron J. Sea Fiction Guide.
Sokoloff, B.A. John Updike;A Comprehensive Bibliography.

Sokoloff, B.A., and Mark E. Posner. Saul Bellow;A Comprehensive Bibliography.
Sonnenschein, William Swan. The Best Books;A Reader's Guide and Literary Reference Book.
Spiller, Robert E., and Philip C. Blackburn. A Descriptive Bibliography of the Writings of James Fenimore Cooper.
Springer, Haskell S. Washington Irving;A Reference Guide.
Springer, Marlene. Edith Wharton and Kate Chopin.
Stafford, William T. A Name, Title, and Place Index to the Critical Writings of Henry James.
Stieg, Lewis F., Comp. Irving Stone; A Bibliography.
Story, Norah. Oxford Companion to Canadian History and Literature.
Swigart, Leslie Kay, Comp. Harlan Ellison;A Bibliographical Checklist.
Taylor, C. Clarke. John Updike;A Bibliography.
Tremaine, Marie. Bibliography of Canadian Imprints.
Vannatta, Dennis P. Nathanael West; An Annotated Bibliography of the Scholarship and Works.
Vitelli, James R. Van Wyck Brooks; A Reference Guide.
Waldrip, Louise, and Shirley Ann Bauer. A Bibliography of the Works of Katherine Anne Porter.
Walker, Dale L., Comp. The Fiction of Jack London;A Chronological Bibliography.
Watters, Reginald E. Checklist of Canadian Literature and Background Materials.
Watters, Reginald E., and Inglis F. Bell. On Canadian Literature;1860-1960.
Wegelin, Oscar. Early American Fiction;1774-1830.
Weixlmann, Joseph. John Barth.

REFERENCE - BIBLIOGRAPHIES

Whiteman, Maxwell. A Century of Fiction by American Negroes;1853-1952.

Williams, Ames W., and Vincent Starrett. Stephen Crane;A Bibliography.

Williams, Stanley T., and Mary Ellen Edge, Comp. A Bibliography of the Writings of Washington Irving; A Check List.

Wilson, Robert A., Comp. Gertrude Stein;A Bibliography.

Wright, Lyle H. American Fiction; 1851-1875;A Contribution Toward A Bibliography.

Wright, Lyle H. American Fiction; 1876-1900;A Contribution Toward A Bibliography.

Young, Philip, and Charles W. Mann. The Hemingway Manuscripts;An Inventory.

List of Authors with Dates

LIST OF AUTHORS

ADAMS, Henry, 1838-1918.

AGAPIDA, Antonio, See Washington Irving.

AGEE, James, 1909-1955.

AIKEN, Conrad Potter, 1889-1973.

ALCOTT, Louisa May, 1832-1888.

ALDRICH, Thomas Bailey, 1836-1907.

ALGREN, Nelson, 1909-

ALLEN, James Lane, 1849-1925.

ALLSTON, Washington, 1779-1843.

ANDERSON, Sherwood, 1876-1941.

ARNOW, Harriette, 1908-

ARTHUR, Timothy Shay, 1809-1885.

ASIMOV, Isaac, 1920-

ATHERTON, Gertrude, 1857-1948.

ATWOOD, Margaret, 1939-

AUCHINCLOSS, Louis Stanton, 1917-

AUSTIN, Mary, 1868-1934.

BALDWIN, James, 1924-

BARAKA, Amiri, 1934- See also LeRoi Jones

BARLOW, R.H., 1920- (Leckie, Robert Hugh)

BARNES, Djuna, 1892-

BARNES, Margaret Ayer, 1886-1967.

BARTH, John, 1930-

BEAGLE, Peter S., 1939-

BEATTY, Richmond Croom,

BEER, Thomas, 1889-1940.

BELLAMY, Edward, 1850-1898.

BELLOW, Saul, 1915-

BENCHLY, Robert, 1889-1945.

BENET, Stephen Vincent, 1898-1943.

BERGER, Thomas, 1924-

BIERCE, Ambrose, 1842-1914.

BILLINGS, Josh, See Henry Wheeler Shaw.

BISHOP, Leonard, 1922-

BLOCH, Robert, 1917-

BOLDREWOOD, Rolf, 1826-1915, (Thomas Alexander Browne).

BOWLES, Paul, 1911-

BOYD, James, 188-1944.

BOYLE, Kay, 1903-

BRADBURY, Ray, 1920-

BRADFORD, William, 1590-1657.

BRITTON, Nan, 1896- ?

BROMFIELD, Louis, 1896-1956.

BROOKS, Van Wyck, 1886-1963.

BROWN, Alice, 1857-1948.

BROWN, Charles Brockden, 1771-1810.

LIST OF AUTHORS

BROWNE, John Ross, 1821-1875.

BUCK, Pearl S., 1892-1973.

BUCKLER, Ernest, 1908-

BURGESS, Anthony, 1917-

BURKE, Kenneth Duva, 1897-

BURROUGHS, Edgar Rice, 1875-1950.

BURROUGHS, William S., 1857-1898.

BUTOR, Michael, 1926-

CABELL, James Branch, 1879-1958.

CABLE, George Washington, 1844-1925.

CAHAN, Abraham, 1860-1951.

CAIN, James M., 1892-

CALDWELL, Erskine, 1903-

CALVERT, George Henry, 1803-1889.

CAPOTE, Truman, 1924-

CARPENTER, Don, 1931-

CARR, John Dickson, 1905?-

CATHER, Willa, 1873-1947.

CHANDLER, Raymond, 1888-1959.

CHEEVER, John, 1912-

CHESNUTT, Charles Waddell, 1858-1932.

CHOPIN, Kate, 1851-1904.

CLARKE, Arthur C., 1917-

CLARKE, Marcus, 1846-1888.

CLEMENS, Samuel Langhorne, 1835-1910.

COHEN, Leonard, 1934-

CONNELL, Evan S., 1924-

COOK, W. Paul,

COOKE, John Esten, 1830-1886.

COOPEL, Alfred, See A. Coppel.

COOPER, James Fenimore, 1789-1851.

COOVER, Robert, 1932-

COPPEL, Alfred, 1921-

COTTON, John, 1584-1652.

COULTER, John, 1851-1928.

COWLEY, Malcom, 1898-

COZZENS, James Gould, 1903-

CRANE, Stephen, 1871-1911.

CRAWFORD, Mary Caroline, 1874-1932.

CRAYON, Geoffrey, See Washington Irving.

CREVECOEUR, J. Hector St. John de, 1735-1813.

CRICHTON, Robert, 1925-

CULLEN, Countee, 1903-1946.

CUMMINS, Maria Susanne, 1827-1866.

LIST OF AUTHORS

CURTIS, George William, 1824-1892.

DANA, Richard Henry, 1815-1882.

DARK, Eleanor, 1901-

DAVIDSON, Donald Grady, 1893-1968.

DE FOREST, John W., 1826-1906.

DE VOTO, Bernard, 1897-1955.

DEWEY, John, 1859-1952.

DICKEY, James, 1923-

DONLEAVY, James Patrick, 1926-

DOS PASSOS, John, 1896-1970.

DREISER, Theodore, 1871-1945.

DUNCAN, Isadora, 1878-1927.

DURRELL, Lawrence, 1912-

EDE, H. S.

E. D. E. N., Mrs.

EDGEWORTH, Maria, 1767-1849.

EDWARDS, Jonathan, 1703-1758.

EGGLESTON, Edward, 1837-1902.

ELLISON, Harlan, 1934-

ELLISON, Ralph W., 1914-

EMERSON, Ralph Waldo, 1803-1882.

FARRELL, James T., 1904-

FAUCET, Jessie

FAULKNER, William, 1897-1962.

FAY, Theodore Sedgwick, 1807-1898.

FERBER, Edna, 1887-1968.

FISHER, Dorothy Canfield, 1879-1958.

FISHER, Vardio, 1895-1968.

FITZGERALD, F. Scott, 1896-1940.

FLEMING, Sarah Lee

FLINT, Timothy, 1780-1840.

FORD, Ford Madox, 1873-1939.

FRANK, Waldo D., 1889-1967.

FRANKLIN, Benjamin, 1706-1790.

FREEMAN, Austin, 1862-1943.

FRENEAU, Phillip, 1752-1832.

FRIEDMAN, Bruce J., 1930-

FULLER, Margaret, 1810-1850.

FURPHY, Joseph, 1843-1912.

GAINES, Ernest J., 1933-

GALE, Zona, 1874-1938.

GARDNER, Erle Stanley, 1889-1970.

GARDNER, Leonard

GARLAND, Hamlin, 1860-1940.

GLADDEN, WASHINGTON, 1836-1918.

GLASGOW, Ellen, 1874-1945.

GOLD, Herbert, 1924-

LIST OF AUTHORS

GOLDING, William, 1911-

GOODWIN, H. B., 1896- ?

GORDON, Caroline, 1895-

GRUS, Dorothy

GREY, Zane, 1875-1939.

GRIMKE, Sarah, 1792-1873.

GROVE, Fred, 1913-

HALL, James Norman, 1887-1951.

HAMMETT, Dashiell, 1894-1961.

HANDEL, Henry

HARDING, Rebecca

HARLAND, Marion, 1830-1922, (Mrs. A. Payson Terhune).

HARPER, Frances E. Watkins, 1825-1911.

HARRIS, Frank, 1854-1931.

HARRIS, George Washington, 1814-1869.

HARRIS, Joel Chanler, 1848-1908.

HARTE, Bret, 1836-1902.

HAWKES, John, 1925-

HAWTHORNE, Nathaniel, 1804-1864.

HAY, William, 1700?-1755.

HECHT, Ben, 1894-1964.

HEGGEN, Thomas, 1919-1949.

HELLER, Joseph, 1923-

HEMINGWAY, Ernest, 1899-1961.

HENLY, Caroline Lee

HENRY, O., 1862-1910, (William Sydney Porter)

HERBERT, XAVIER, 1911-

HERGESHEIMER, Joseph, 1880-1954.

HERRICK, Robert, 1868-1938.

HICKS, Granville, 1901-

HIGGINSON, Thomas Wentworth, 1823-1911.

HIMES, Chester, 1909-

HOLLAND, Josia Gilbert, 1819-1881.

HOLMES, Oliver Wendell, 1809-1894.

HOOD, Hugh, 1928-

HOOKER, Thomas, 1586-1647.

HOPKINS, Pauline E., 1859-1930.

HOPKINSON, Francis, 1737-1791.

HOWE, E. W., 1853-1937.

HOWE, L., 1905- ?

HOWELLS, W. D., 1837-1920.

HUGHES, Langston, 1902-1961.

HURSTON, Zora Neale, 1901-1960.

IRVING, Washington, 1783-1859.

ISHERWOOD, Christopher, 1904-

JACKSON, Shirley, 1919-

JAMES, Henry, 1843-1916.

JEFFERS, Robinson, 1887-1962.

JEWETT, Sarah Orne, 1849-1909.

JOHNSTON, Mary, 1870-1936.

JONES, Le Roi, 1934- (see also Amiri Baraka).

KENDALL, Henry C., 1841-1882.

KEROUAC, Jack, 1922-1969.

KESEY, Ken, 1935-

KINGSLEY, Henry, 1830-1876.

KNOWLES, John, 1926-

LARDNER, Ring, 1885-1933.

LARSEN, Nella, 1893-1963.

LAWRENCE, T. E., 1888-1935.

LEACOCK, Stephen, 1869-1944.

LEIGHT, James, 1930-

LESSING, Doris M., 1919-

LEWIS, Janet, 1899-

LEWIS, Sinclair, 1885-1951.

LOCKRIDGE, Ross, 1914-1948.

LONDON, Jack, 1876-1916.

LOVECRAFT, Howard P., 1890-1937.

LOWELL, James Russell, 1819-1891.

LOWRY, Malcolm, 1909-1957.

McALMON, Robert, 1896-1956.

McCARTHY, Mary, 1912-

McCULLERS, Carson, 1917-

MacDONALD, John D., 1916-

McKAY, Claude, 1890-1948.

MAILER, Norman, 1923-

MALAMUD, Bernard, 1914-

MANDER, Jane, 1877-1949.

MARQUAND, John P., 1893-1960.

MASTERS, Edgar Lee, 1869-1950.

MATHER, Richard, 1596-1669.

MATHEWS, Brander, 1852-1929.

MELVILLE, Herman, 1819-1891.

MENCKEN, H. L., 1880-1956.

MILLER, Henry, 1891-

MITCHELL, Margaret, 1900-1949.

MORLEY, Christopher, 1890-1957.

MORRIS, Wright, 1910-

MURDOCH, Iris, 1919-

NABOKOV, Vladimir, 1899-

NIEBUHR, Reinhold, 1892-1971.

NIN, Anais, 1914-

NORRIS, Frank, 1870-1902.

OATES, Joyce Carol, 1938-

LIST OF AUTHORS

O'CONNOR, Flannery, 1925-

O'CONNOR, Frank, 1903- (Michael Odonovan)

O'HARA, John, 1905-

OLDSTYLE, Jonathan, See Washington Irving.

O'NEILL, Eugene, 1888-1953.

D'OSSOLI, Marchisa, See Sarah Margaret Fuller

PAINE, Thomas, 1737-1809.

PALMER, Nettie, 1885-1964.

PALMER, Vance, 1885-1959.

PARKER, Dorothy, 1893-1967.

PEMBERTON, Cardine H.

PERCY, Walker, 1916-

PHELPS, William Lyon, 1865-1943.

POE, Edgar Allen, 1809-1849.

PORTER, Katherine Anne, 1890-

PORTER, William Sydney, See O. Henry

POST, Melville Davisson, 1871-1930.

PURDY, James, 1923-

PYNCHON, Thomas, 1937-

QUEEN, Ellery, 1905- (Frederic Dannay & Manfred Lee).

RAND, Ayn, 1905-

RANSOM, John Crowe, 1888-1974.

RASHLEIGH, Ralph.

RAWLINGS, Marjorie K., 1896-1953.

RICHARDSON, Henry Handel, 1870-1946 (Ethel Florence Richardson).

RICHLER, Mordecai, 1931-

RICHTER, Conrad, 1890-

RICKETTS, Edward F., 1897-1948.

ROBERTS, Elizabeth Madox, 1886-1941.

ROBERTS, Kenneth, 1885-1957.

ROBINSON, Edwin Arlington, 1869-1935.

ROBINSON, Rowland E., 1912-

ROCHE, Mazo De La, 1879-1961.

ROE, E. P., 1838-1888.

ROLVAAG, Ole Edvart, 1876-1931.

ROSS, Sinclair, 1908-

ROTH, Philip, 1933-

ROWECRAFT, Charles,

RUNYON, Damon, 1880-1946.

SACKVILLE-WEST, V., 1892-1962.

SALINGER, J. D., 1919-

SAROYAN, William, 1908-

SATCHELL, William, 1860-1942.

SCHAEFER, Jack, 1907-

SCOTT, Howard

LIST OF AUTHORS

SEDGWICK, Catharine Maria, 1789-1867.

SERGEANT, Thomas, 1782-1860.

SERVINTUS, Quintus

SHAW, Henry Wheeler, 1818-1885, See Josh Billings (also Uncle Esek).

SHAW, Irwin, 1913-

SHEPARD, Thomas, 1605-1649.

SIMMS, William Gilmore, 1806-1870.

SINCLAIR, Upton, 1878-1968.

SMITH, Betty, 1904-

SMITH, C.A., 1864-1924.

SPARK, Muriel, 1918-

SPENCER, E., 1921-

STAFFORD, Jean, 1915-

STALLINGS, Laurence, 1894-1968.

STEAD, William Thomas, 1849-1912.

STEFFENS, Lincoln, 1866-1936.

STEGNER, Wallace, 1909-

STEIN, Gertrude, 1874-1946.

STEINBECK, John, 1902-1968.

STEPHENS, Ann Sophia, 1813-1886.

STEVENS, Wallace, 1879-1955.

STOCKTON, Frank R., 1834-1902.

STOWE, Harriet Beecher, 1811-1896.

STUART, Jesse, 1907-

STYRON, William, 1925-

TARKELL, Ida Minerva, 1857-1944.

TARKINGTON, Booth, 1869-1946.

TATE, Allen, 1899-

TAYLOR, Bayard, 1825-1878.

THOREAU, Henry David, 1817-1862.

THORPE, Thomas Bangs, 1815-1878.

THURBER, James, 1894-1961.

TOOMER, Jean, 1894-1967.

TRAVEN, B., 1882-1969.

TRILLING, Lionel, 1905-

TUCKER, James, 1929-

TWAIN, Mark, 1835-1910 (Samuel Langhorne Clemens).

UPDIKE, John, 1932-

VIDAL, Gore, 1925-

VONNEGUT, Kurt, 1922-

WAGSTAFFE, Launcelot, See Washington Irving.

WALLANT, Edward Lewis, 1926-1962

WARNER, Susan, 1819-1885 (Elizabeth Wetherell).

WARREN, Robert Penn, 1905-

WATERS, Frank, 1902-

LIST OF AUTHORS

WEBSTER, Noah, 1758-1843.

WEINSTEIN, Nathanael Wallenstein, See Nathanael West.

WELTY, Eudora, 1909-

WESCOTT, Glenway, 1901-

WEST, Nathanael, 1904-1940.

WHARTON, Edith, 1862-1937.

WHITE, E. B., 1899-

WHITE, Patrick, 1912-

WHITE, Stewart Edward, 1873-1946.

WHITE, William Hale, 1831-1913.

WIEBE, Rudy, 1934-

WIESEL, Elie, 1928-

WILDER, Thornton, 1897-

WILLIAMS, Mary E. Freeman, 1852-1930.

WILLIAMS, John, 1761-1818.

WILSON, Edmund, 1895-1972.

WINTHROP, Theodore, 1828-1861.

WOOLSON, Constance Fenimore, 1840-1894.

WOLFE, Thomas, 1900-1938.

WRIGHT, Richard, 1908-1960.

YOUNG, Ella, 1867-1956.

CHICOREL INDEX SERIES
ONE LOOK-UP — ONE ALPHABET

Volume 1. **Chicorel Theater Index to Plays in Anthologies, Periodicals, Discs and Tapes.** Locates plays in over 10,000 entries in books and in current periodicals. 572 p. 1970.

Volume 2. **Chicorel Theater Index to Plays in Anthologies, Periodicals, Discs and Tapes.** 11,000 additional entries in more collections & periodicals. 502 p. 1971.

Volume 3. **Chicorel Theater Index to Plays in Anthologies, Periodicals, Discs and Tapes.** Indexes plays in collections in the English language published in England. 466 p. 1972.

Volume 3A. **Chicorel Bibliography to the Performing Arts.** Locates 9,000 books and periodicals in over 300 subject categories relating to Theater and the Arts. 498 p. 1972.

Volume 4. **Chicorel Index to Poetry on Discs & Tapes: Poetry on Media.** A title, first-line, poet, director, reader & actor index. c 500 recorded media read in English;over 20,000 entires. 443 p. 1972.

Volume 5, A, B, C. **Chicorel Index to Poetry in Anthologies and Collections.** Poetry in print, over 250,000 entries by title, first line, author, editor, collection title. Lists all bibliographic elements, incl. translator and subject descriptors. c.2000 p.1974.

Volume 5, A. **Chicorel Index to Poetry in Anthologies, and Collections 1974-1977.** Companion Volume-

Volume 6, A, B, C. **Chicorel Index to Poetry** indexes and analyzes over 200,000 entries to retrospective titles.c. 2,000 p. 1975.

Volume 7, A, B. **Chicorel Index to the Spoken Arts on Discs, Tapes and Cassettes.** Locates play, poetry, story, essay, speech readings. Over 13,000 entries U.S. & foreign productions. c.500 p.ea. 1973, 1974.

Volume 8. **Chicorel Theater Index to Plays in Periodicals.** Locates plays in hundreds of periodicals up to their latest issues. Indicates dates and issues in easy to check chronological order. 502 p. 1973.

Volume 9. **Chicorel Theater Index to Plays for Young People.** Locates plays written for children and young people. Over 15,000 entries from elementary to high-school. 464 p. 1974.

Volume 10. **Chicorel Bibliography to Books on Music & Musicians.** Comprises 10,000 entries under more than 460 subject indicators such as composers, musicians, folk music for young people and more. 487 p. 1974.

Volume 11, A. **Chicorel Index to Abstracting and Indexing Services: Periodicals in Humanities and the Social Sciences. 2nd ed.** Lists the important journals and periodicals with the sources which abstract them. For use from high school through university and professional level. Contains 50,000 entires. 932 p. 1978.

Volume 12, A, B, C. **Chicorel Index to Short Stories in Anthologies and Collections.** Over 60,000 entries by author, title, translator, and anthology. Main entries contain publisher, place and year of publication, number of pages, price, LC number and subject indicators. 4 vols. 1974.

Volume 12, A/1977. **Chicorel Index to Short Stories in Anthologies and Collections 1975-1976.** Over

Volume 13, A, B, C. **Chicorel Index to Craft Books.** Vol. 13: Needlework; Crochet to Tie Dying; 13A: Glass, Enamel and Metal; 13B: Ceramics, Leather and Wood; 13C: Crafts for Education, Recreation and Therapy. c 500 p.ea. c. 30,000 entries. 1974, 1975, 1976.

Volume 14. **Chicorel Index to Reading Disabilities: An Annotated Guide.** 700 books with full bibliographic data, comprehensive evaluative annotations, up-to-date bibliography to journal articles. c.500 p. 1974.

Volume 14 A. **Chicorel Index to Reading and Learning Disabilities: Books. Annual 1976** - An up-to-date guide to diagnostic and remedial techniques in teaching reading, from K-12 and up. Indexed and selectively abstracted by subject. c. 500 p.ea. c.1500 entries ea.

Volume 15, A. **Chicorel Index to Biographies.** Contains c.21,000 entries in one alphabetical subject arrangement cross-referenced and indexed. Its scope includes all historical periods from B.C. to the present. 900 p. 1974.

Volume 16, A. **Chicorel Index to Environment and Ecology.** Including: Air and air pollution, chemicals in the environment, energy, human population and ecology, land and industrial land use, water and water pollution, wildlife and natural resources and more. 950 p. 1974.

Volume 17, A. **Chicorel Index to Urban Planning and Environmental Design.** Including: Environmental engineering, environmental health, landscape architecture, mass transportation, sewage and waste treatment systems, urban planning and more. c. 17,000 entries. c. 1,000 p. 1975.

Volume 18, A. **Chicorel Index to Learning Disorders: Books.** Abstracts and indexes approximately 3,000 books that deal with such subjects as hyperactivity, auditory agnosia, low ability students, underachievers, and others. c.500 p. ea. 1975.

Volume 19. **Chicorel Abstracts to Reading and Learning Disabilities. Annual 1976** - Selectively abstracts and indexes approximately 135 journals published in the R & LD field. Arranged by subject with author index. c. 500 p. ea.c. 1,000 entries ea.

Volume 20, A. **Chicorel Index to Poetry and Poets in Literature.** Indexes books. Subjects range from ballads to haiku, from teaching techniques to criticism. c. 20,000 entries. c. 1,000 p. 1976.

Volume 21. **Chicorel Index to Drama Literature.** Indexes current books pertaining to drama, arranged by subject, such as characterization, drama workshops, teaching techniques, American ethnic groups and many others. c. 1,000 p. 1975.

Volume 22, A. **Chicorel Index to Film Literature.** Indexes and analyzes books about films, film making, film makers and the history of commercial films. c.1,000 p. 1975.

Volume 23, A. **Chicorel Index to Literary Criticism.** Vol. 23: United States and International;Vol. 23A: England, Ireland, Scotland, Wales. Cross-referenced entries provide a comprehensive index to the literature of our time. c. 1,000 p. c. 30,000 entries, 1978.

Volume 24. **Chicorel Index to Parapsychology and Occult Books.** Over 3,000 books listed in 126 categories ranging from Astrology to Zen. 357 p. 1978.

Volume 25. **Chicorel Theater Index to Plays in Anthologies: 1970-1975.** Updates Vols. 1, 2, 3, 8 and 9 with 7,000 additional entries. c.500 p. 1976.

Volume 26. **Chicorel Index to Mental Health Book Reviews. Annual 1976** - Annotates and summarizes approximately 1,000 books reviewed in journals during the year. Over 200 source journals searched. Full bibliographic information provided for each entry, with subject index. c. 500 p.ea. c. 1500 entries ea.

Volume 27. **Chicorel Index to Videotapes and Cassettes.** The first available guide to existing videotapes and cassettes. 1978.

Ref.
Z
6514
C97
C46

JUN 11 1979